Dennis Graver's 100 Best
Scuba Quizzes

Aqua Quest Publications, Inc. ❒ New York

ISBN 1-881652-12-2

All photographs are by the author.

Printed in the United States of America
10 9 8 7 6 5 4 3 2 1

PREFACE

In 1974, Jack McKinney, editor of *Skin Diver*, conceived the idea for a national scuba quiz. At that time, I was technical director of NAUI. Jack asked me to review a ten-question quiz and I responded. Several months later, Jack sent me a letter saying that I gave him the best feedback for the quiz and asking if I would like to write the quizzes for *Skin Diver*. My first quiz appeared in the January 1975 issue. The quizzes became a popular feature of *Skin Diver*. Each year the magazine asked me for a list of quiz topics for the coming year. I have had quizzes in *Skin Diver* magazine for more than 20 years and have enjoyed using the format to educate divers.

I frequently use the quizzes to convey little-known information of importance to divers, or to correct misconceptions. As a result, some readers feel frustrated because they choose incorrect answers. At the time each quiz was published my goal was to enlighten divers about a topic. With the passage of time, I hope that divers have become better informed and able to answers questions correctly. The information that used to be on the cutting-edge is now common knowledge. I hope that my quizzes have contributed to increased common knowledge.

I have received hundreds of requests for a compilation of my *Skin Diver* quizzes. I published 80 of them in single printings of books entitled "What's Your Scuba IQ?, Volumes I and II." We are publishing this book in response to the continued interest expressed by many divers worldwide.

There have been many changes and discoveries in diving during the past 20 years. The published answers to many of my early quizzes are incorrect today. Subsequently, I had to re-write many of the old quizzes to compile this publication.

The quizzes use various formats to test knowledge. Be sure to note the instructions before you select your answers. You usually select the most correct answer, but sometimes there are several correct responses. Other approaches include completion, matching, double true-false, and listings. Read each question carefully and be sure that you understand what it asks before you select an answer. Refrain from looking at any answers until you complete an entire quiz. Frequently, an answer provides a tip that relates to a subsequent question.

You can't learn too much about diving and you should never stop learning. I hope this book helps fulfill my goal to increase diving safety through education.

Dennis K. Graver
Camano Island, WA
October 1996

Other books by Dennis Graver

Scuba Diving First Aid
Scuba Diving
Night Diving Made Simple
Navigation Made Simple
Practical Tips and Techniques for Scuba Divers
The Scuba Diver's Handy Reference
NAUI Leadership Course Instructor Guide
NAUI Diver Training Log and Recreational Dive Log
NAUI Advanced Scuba Diver Course Instructor Guide
The NAUI Openwater I Instructor Guide
The NAUI Textbook
The NAUI Textbook II
Instructor Guide for The NAUI Textbook
NAUI Student Workbook
PADI Refresher Course Workbook
PADI Advanced Diver Manual
PADI Dive Manual
PADI Course Director Guidelines
What's Your Scuba IQ?, Vol. I & II
Sport Diving A to Z

CONTENTS

❑ ❑ ❑ ❑ ❑ ❑ ❑ ❑ ❑ ❑

Section Six
□ □ □ □ □ □
Diving Activities
127

Section Seven
□ □ □ □ □ □
Diving Safety
157

Section Eight
□ □ □ □ □ □ □
Diving Skills
177

Section Nine
□ □ □ □ □ □ □ □
Diving Emergencies
199

Appendix
U.S. Navy Dive Tables
223

SECTION ONE

□

Diving Equipment

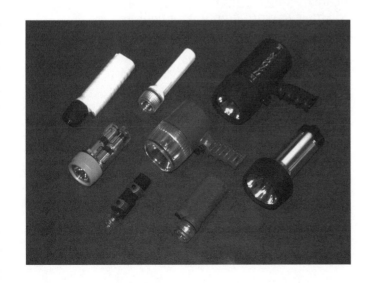

Diving Equipment

Diving is an equipment-intensive activity. Equipment enables you to survive and adapt to the alien underwater environment. The colder the water, the more encumbered you are.

Diving equipment failure is rarely the cause of diving accidents, but equipment problems (and the inability to manage the difficulties) does contribute to accidents. When you care for your equipment properly, adjust and inspect it correctly, and can manage minor problems, you minimize your risk of injury.

Perhaps the most significant aspect of equipment for divers is use. You should be familiar with your equipment and use it properly. A compass or dive computer are of little use if you do not know how to use them or use them improperly.

Less significant equipment aspects include rigging, minor repairs, maintenance, and theory of operation. Increased equipment knowledge increases your diving safety and enjoyment. Equipment problems that prevent diving are frustrating. If you attempt to dive with incomplete or malfunctioning equipment, you risk injury or death. Minimize frustration and maximize your safety with knowledge and wisdom—knowledge rightly applied.

This section tests your equipment knowledge. You can learn more on the subject by completing an Equipment Specialty course. Keep current with equipment developments by reading magazine articles. Always inspect your equipment and your buddy's equipment before every dive. You can virtually eliminate equipment problems by caring for your equipment, inspecting it frequently, adjusting it correctly, and using it properly. The less you have to worry about your equipment, the more you can concentrate on the beautiful underwater world and the activity you want to pursue while diving.

COMPASSES

In all but the clearest water, a compass is a necessary instrument for keeping track of where you are and helping you get where you want to go. All divers need to understand compass fundamentals and uses. Advanced divers should have an even higher knowledge and skill level. Find out what you know or don't know about the subject by answering the following questions.

1. Most diving compasses are the _____ type.
- ❏ A. Direct-reading card
- ❏ B. Direct-reading needle
- ❏ C. Indirect-reading card
- ❏ D. Indirect-reading needle

2. Five desirable features of a diving compass are:
- A. _____
- B. _____
- C. _____
- D. _____
- E. _____

3. The primary reason a diving compass is liquid-filled is to:
- ❏ A. Prevent pressure differential problems
- ❏ B. Dampen needle movement
- ❏ C. Prevent fogging of the cover
- ❏ D. Prevent leakage

4. What is the name of the reference line on a diving compass, and where is this line supposed to point?
- A. _____
- B. _____

5. To obtain a reciprocal heading, add _____ degrees to a compass heading.
- ❏ A. 90
- ❏ B. 120
- ❏ C. 180
- ❏ D. 360

6. The greatest factor affecting the accuracy of underwater compass navigation is:
- ❏ A. The type of compass used
- ❏ B. The length of the lubber line
- ❏ C. How the compass is held
- ❏ D. The underwater visibility

7. List four duties you have when compass navigation occupies your buddy underwater.
- A. _____
- B. _____
- C. _____
- D. _____

8. When navigating a triangular (equilateral) course, your turns must be _____ degrees if you want to return to the starting point.
- ❏ A. 60
- ❏ B. 120
- ❏ C. 180
- ❏ D. 210

9. List four actions you should take to prevent damage to a diving compass.
- A. _____
- B. _____
- C. _____
- D. _____

10. Which of the following effects is of the greatest concern to a diving navigator?
- ❏ A. Deviation
- ❏ B. Variation
- ❏ C. Declination
- ❏ D. Inclination
- ❏ E. All are of equal concern

11. To prevent compass error, you must keep all metal objects a minimum of _____ inches from the instrument.
- ❏ A. 6
- ❏ B. 12
- ❏ C. 18
- ❏ D. 36

12. List two above-water uses for a diving compass.
- A. _____
- B. _____

13. List three good sources of training for compass use:
- A. _____
- B. _____
- C. _____

COMPASSES

The best way to learn diving navigation is to complete an advanced or specialty course. Boating courses that include navigation can be beneficial. I hope this quiz provided some useful information to help keep you on course.

1. D. Indirect-reading needle. Compasses have either a magnetized disc, called a card, or a magnetized needle. Both the compass needle and the lubber line can indicate headings, depending on the type of compass. The degree bearings on a direct-reading compass ascend in a clockwise direction and the course heading aligns with the lubber line, while the degree bearings of an indirect-reading compass read 0-360 degrees in a counterclockwise direction and the course aligns with the north end of the needle or card. An indirect-reading compass has a rotary bezel with index marks that are used to indicate the course to be followed.

2. Desirable features of a diving compass include a movable bezel for determining a heading, index marks as a reminder of a heading, luminous markings for use at night and in dark water, and large and easy-to-read markings for easy viewing in dim light. The compass should also be corrosion resistant, liquid-filled, and read correctly even if tilted slightly from a level position.

3. B. Compasses could be built to withstand pressure and moisture problems, but the housings of compasses are filled with a fluid—usually oil—to dampen the oscillations, or back-and-forth movements, of the needle. The fluid makes the needle respond slowly, but increases accuracy because the needle is not as sensitive to minor movements as it would be if it were suspended in air. You are actually following an average heading when you use a liquid-filled compass.

4. The reference line on a diving compass is called a "lubber line." Point the lubber line in the direction of travel, which is called a "heading." For accurate navigation, it is extremely important that the you align the lubber line precisely with the centerline of your body. There are several "compass lock" positions for holding a compass. All the positions help ensure proper alignment of the lubber line.

5. C. A reciprocal course is one in the exact opposite direction of an original heading. Since there are 360 degrees in a circle, it is necessary to add or subtract 180 degrees to a heading to obtain a return (reciprocal) course. When your original heading is 180 degrees or less, add 180 degrees; when the original heading is greater than 180 degrees, subtract 180 degrees. If your original direction of travel was a course of 90 degrees, you would add 180 degrees to obtain your reciprocal course of 270 degrees. If your original heading were 210 degrees, you would subtract 180 degrees to obtain your reciprocal course of 30 degrees.

6. C. How the compass is held. A compass can be made to read any heading desired simply by turning the instrument. Unless a compass is properly aligned with the centerline of the body of the user, the desired destination will not be reached even though the compass indicates the proper heading. Some types of compasses are easier to use than others, and the longer the lubber line, the greater the accuracy; but these are minor factors when it comes to navigation compared to the how a compass is aligned with the body.

7. Duties you have when compass navigation occupies your buddy underwater include maintaining contact with your buddy, preventing your buddy from running into obstacles, monitoring and maintaining depth, monitoring the time and your air pressures, and visually scanning the area if searching.

8. B. 120 degrees. Many people know that the sum of the angles of a triangle total 180 degrees, so they incorrectly assume the angles of an equilateral triangle are each 60 degrees. They do not realize that the diver must make a turn that follows the outside angle of the corner of a triangle rather than the inside angle. If the leg of an equilateral triangle is extended, the new corner created is the complimentary angle of the inside angle, or 120 degrees. Triangular courses are more difficult to navigate than courses with square corners.

9. Actions you should take to prevent damage to a diving compass include keeping sand and grit out of your compass, keeping your compass from becoming hot, keeping your compass away from magnetic items and magnetic fields, and avoiding jarring or shocking the instrument.

10. A. Deviation. A compass error caused by nearby metal or magnetic fields is called deviation. A tragic accident occurred when two ice divers placed their compasses side by side to be sure that they were following the correct heading back to shore. They did not realize the two magnetized needles were attracted to each other and that neither compass was indicating a correct heading.

11. C. 18 inches. To determine what affects your diving compass and to what degree, place your compass on the floor and allow the needle to stabilize, then watch the needle to see if it moves while you pass various pieces of your diving equipment in proximity to the compass. In this manner you can find out which items of gear you need to be concerned with when navigating. Don't forget accessory items such as spearguns and cameras.

12. Above-water uses for a diving compass include taking a "fix" of a surface position for the relocation of a dive site. The bearings to several items on shore can be recorded and used for future reference. A diving compass is also useful as a back-up compass for boating. I once used my diving compass to navigate to the harbor when a dense fog arose. We were in a small boat that did not have a compass.

13. Good sources of training in the use of a compass include outdoor courses, like hiking; boating courses, such as those available from the Power Squadron or the Coast Guard Auxiliary; and intermediate and advanced diving courses. There is also excellent information available in maritime books, but knowledge does not become skill until you apply what you know. Application and practice of navigational skills are essential.

DIVE COMPUTERS

Dive computers are popular and have changed the way we dive. Computers have unique terms, limits, procedures, and rules. See how well versed you are concerning dive computers.

Q:

1. The principal advantage provided by most dive computers is:
❏ A. Extended no-decompression limits
❏ B. Digital information readout
❏ C. Multi-level time allowance
❏ D. Accurate depth readings

2. The longest battery life for currently available dive computers is:
❏ A. 500 hours
❏ B. 1,000 hours
❏ C. 8-10 years
❏ D. None of the above

3. A dive computer "ceiling" is:
❏ A. The shallowest safe depth
❏ B. The decompression stop depth
❏ C. To be prevented
❏ D. All the above

4. Dive buddies may share a dive computer provided the buddy without the dive computer is never deeper than his/her partner.
❏ A. True for some dive computers
❏ B. True for all dive computers
❏ C. False

5. The preferred on/off switch for a dive computer is:
❏ A. Manual
❏ B. Moisture activated
❏ C. Tank pressure activated
❏ D. None

6. "Scrolling" refers to a dive computer's ability to:
❏ A. Preview time/depth limits before a dive
❏ B. Review time/depth limits during a dive
❏ C. Display errors
❏ D. Alternate functions displayed

7. In the event of dive computer failure or accidental shut-off:
❏ A. Consult the dive tables prior to further diving
❏ B. Dive at depths not in excess of 27 feet
❏ C. Discontinue diving for the number of hours required by the dive computer for complete outgassing

8. A dive computer may be switched off:
❏ A. After each dive
❏ B. After the final dive of the day
❏ C. After complete outgassing has occurred
❏ D. After 12 hours

9. The majority of available dive computers may not be used above an altitude of feet.
❏ A. 1,000
❏ B. 2,000
❏ C. 8,000
❏ D. None of the above

10. You must wait at least 24 hours before flying after diving when diving with a computer.
❏ A. True
❏ B. False

11. Nearly all computers can be made to recall dive profile information from multiple previous dives.
❏ A. True
❏ B. False

12. Ascent rates for dive computers:
❏ A. Range from 20 feet per minute to 60 feet per minute
❏ B. Range from 40 feet per minute to 60 feet per minute
❏ C. Are 60 feet per minute
❏ D. All vary depending on time/depth

13. The ascent rate is a factor affecting repetitive dives when computer diving.
❏ A. True
❏ B. False

14. There are no dive computers on the market that provide a U. S. Navy repetitive group designation letter after each dive?
❏ A. True
❏ B. False

15. Decompression diving with a dive computer is:
❏ A. Prohibited
❏ B. Not recommended
❏ C. Difficult and complex
❏ D. Safe and acceptable

DIVE COMPUTERS

Dive computers have rapidly changed the way we dive. It is important to use a dive computer properly. Read, study and follow the manufacturer's recommendations. When selecting a dive computer remember they are not all the same device in different packages. They are based on different models, tables, and limits. Study the alternatives and the various features, then choose yours carefully. If you scored well on this quiz, you have a good familiarity with the available devices.

1. C. Multi-level time allowance. The maximum no-decompression limits for dive computers are actually less than U. S. Navy dive table limits. You can get a digital readout in instruments that are not dive computers. Dive computer depth readings are highly accurate, but the principal advantage of a dive computer is that nitrogen absorption is based on multi-level profiles rather than the total time at the deepest depth.

2. C. 8-10 years. Battery life for the first recreational dive computer was only about 12 hours. Technological improvements with microprocessors and other computer circuitry have greatly reduced power requirements. The battery life for most dive computers now exceeds 500 operational hours, and at least one of them claims the batteries will last 8-10 years.

3. D. All the above. A "ceiling" indicates that a diver has absorbed so much nitrogen that his or her has exceeded the no-decompression limits and must pause during ascent to decompress. Dive computers that display ceilings calculate the decompression stop depth instead of using the standard stop depths of 40, 30, 20 and 10 feet. Use a dive computer in such a way that a ceiling is never displayed.

4. C. False. Since a dive computer makes continuous calculations based on multi-level dive profiles and time underwater, each diver should have a dive computer or dive according to the standard dive table rules. If a buddy without a dive computer inadvertently dives deeper than the dive computer-equipped buddy, the buddy without a computer will be unable to determine his or her decompression status.

5. C. Tank pressure activated, or B. Moisture activated. Some type of automatic switch to activate a dive computer is far better than a manual switch. Divers may forget to activate a manual switch and may accidentally turn a manual switch off. The dive computer should be checked for operability prior to entering the water and again prior to descent.

6. A. Preview time/depth limits before a dive. "Scrolling" is a nice feature of dive computers because the time/depth limits are presented sequentially between dives to assist the user with planning. Typically, the information from the most recent dive is presented, then the display scrolls through the time/depth limits from 30 to about 130 feet.

7. C. Discontinue diving for the number of hours required by the dive computer for complete outgassing. In the event of a dive computer failure or accidental shut-off, the only way to avoid decompression problems and accurately take into account the amount of absorbed nitrogen is to terminate diving activities for the day. If dives have been well within the no-decompression limits and no diving is planned for the following day, a diver may choose to risk diving to depths of 27 feet or less, but this is not recommended.

8. C. After complete outgassing has occurred. Some dive computers switch off automatically after they have "outgassed" completely. Some take as long as 18 hours to outgas. Do not switch off your dive computer prior to complete outgassing, even if you do not plan a repetitive dive. Plans can change and the dive computer residual nitrogen information is important for safety.

9. D. None of the above. Some available dive computers function only to 1,000 feet above sea level. Others will work up to 2,000 feet. Some function up to 6,500 feet and even to 13,200 feet. Those who dive in mountain lakes will want to take the altitude feature into consideration when selecting a dive computer.

10. B. False. Several currently available Dive computers indicate when it is acceptable to fly after diving. The basis for this function may not be the same for all dive computers, however, and a conservative approach to the problem of flying after diving should be a consideration when selecting a dive computer. No matter what your computer says, it is best to wait at least 12 hours before flying after diving.

11. B. False. A nice feature of a dive computer is the ability to scroll previous dive profiles. The term for the recall feature is the log book mode, which is quite useful when it is time to fill out your log book. Not all currently-available dive computers have the feature.

12. A. Range from 20 feet per minute to 60 feet per minute. Some dive computers require an ascent rate of 33 feet per minute, some a rate of 40 to 50 feet per minute and a few allow an ascent rate of 60 feet per minute. Some computers allow a rate of 60 feet per minute at deeper depths, but limit the ascent rate to 20 feet per minute at 60 feet or less. Slow ascent rates are recommended no matter which dive computer you use.

13. B. False. An excessive ascent rate indicator is a desirable feature that is standard with many dive computers. Since decompression problems may be closely associated with ascent rates, it is helpful to have a means to know that your rate of ascent is within the operating limits of the dive computer. All computers assume that you ascend at the correct rate!

14. A. True. The obsolete Datamaster II was based on the U.S. Navy tables, but with reduced no-decompression limits. The computer calculated multi-level dives and allowed extended bottom times without decompression if you ascended to shallower water as a dive progressed. After each dive, the computer displayed a USN repetitive group designation, which allowed a diver to continue diving using the regular navy tables, if necessary.

15. B. Not recommended. Decompression diving with a dive computer is fairly easy to do but manufacturers and diver training agencies discourage the practice. When you consider that decompression is not clearly understood by anyone, it doesn't pay to gamble with such an unknown.

DIVE LIGHTS

Q:

Illumination is useful not only in wrecks and at night, but also to see in and under places during the day and view objects in their true colors. A dive light is a valuable accessory every diver should have. There is more to a light than a battery, bulb, and switch. Let's find out what you know about underwater and other types of dive lights.

1. The ideal dive light buoyancy is:
☐ A. Positive at all times
☐ B. Negative at all times
☐ C. Neutral at all times
☐ D. Positive at the surface and negative at depth

2. The beam pattern of a dive light should be:
☐ A. Wide
☐ B. Narrow
☐ C. Adjustable
☐ D. Both B and C are correct

3. The effect of a flat plexiglass port on the front of a dive light is:
☐ A. To widen the beam pattern
☐ B. To narrow the beam pattern
☐ C. Of little or no consequence
☐ D. None unless scratched

4. Which of the following battery types has a "memory" for charge and discharge patterns?
☐ A. Carbon-zinc
☐ B. Nickel-cadmium
☐ C. Lead-acid
☐ D. Mercury

5. Most rechargeable dive lights deliver nearly full intensity for:
☐ A. Less than an hour
☐ B. One to two hours
☐ C. Three to five hours
☐ D. More than five hours

6. Select the statement that is generally true:
☐ A. Dive light intensity is greater out of the water than it is in the water
☐ B. Dive light intensity is greater in the water than it is out of the water
☐ C. Dive light intensity is the same whether the light is in or out of the water

7. When you use a bulb rated at a voltage lower than the battery voltage, you:
☐ A. Increase bulb and battery life but decrease intensity
☐ B. Decrease bulb and battery life but increase intensity
☐ C. Increase battery life and intensity but decrease bulb life
☐ D. None of the above

8. Which of the following conditions indicates that you should service your dive light?
☐ A. A darkened bulb
☐ B. Swollen batteries
☐ C. Yellow-orange light color
☐ D. All the above

9. Select the incorrect statement:
☐ A. You can obtain maximum battery life with intermittent light use
☐ B. Carry a back-up dive light for night dives
☐ C. Attach the light securely to your self using a strong cord
☐ D. A quartz-halogen bulb provides more light per watt than a conventional bulb

10. Select the incorrect statement:
☐ A. Shine your light on a diver's chest to gain the person's attention at night
☐ B. Rapid up-and-down motion with a dive light is the signal that something is wrong
☐ C. It is a good idea to reserve use of an underwater light for in-water situations only
☐ D. All the above statements are true

11. Which of the following colors is acceptable for an above-water light that you might use to mark an exit location?
☐ A. Red
☐ B. Green
☐ C. Amber
☐ D. Any of the above

12. The best measure of dive light power is:
☐ A. Output wattage
☐ B. Candlepower
☐ C. Burn time
☐ D. Amperage

13. Select all correct statements concerning nickel-cadmium (Ni-cad) batteries. Ni-cad batteries:
☐ A. May be recharged hundreds of times
☐ B. Lose about 1% of their capacity per day when unused
☐ C. May be used without harm after a 50% recharge
☐ D. May be damaged when the power switch is left on after the batteries are fully discharged

14. The preferred method for chemical light attachment is:
☐ A. Tying the light to the regulator first stage
☐ B. Inserting the light beneath the mask strap in the back
☐ C. Taping the light to the regulator hose near the first stage
☐ D. Taping the light to the snorkel

15. Chemical light storage life is adversely affected by:
☐ A. Heat
☐ B. Humidity
☐ C. Physical abuse
☐ D. All the above

DIVE LIGHTS

Do you have a good dive light and a suitable back-up light? Do you know how to use and care for them properly? Have you taken a night diving specialty course? I hope this quiz has shed some light on an important diving accessory.

1. D. Positive at the surface and negative at depth. If you drop a dive light into the water accidently, the light should float. However, you should not have to chase a light to the surface if you let go of it underwater. You can achieve ideal buoyancy with some dive lights by placing a neoprene "jacket" around the light. The neoprene compresses with depth.

2. B. Narrow. The wider the beam pattern, the less intensity for any given spot. A spot-type beam has high intensity because the light is concentrated. Diffusion of light by water is sufficient to provide peripheral illumination. A few lights offer bulbs that provide both spot and flood beams simultaneously.

3. C. Of little or no consequence. A flat glass port narrows a beam pattern because the light rays refract when they pass through the glass. The refractive index of plexiglass and water are nearly identical, however, so refraction through a plexiglass port is negligible. Scratches are not a problem either because water fills them.

4. B. Nickel-cadmium. Ni-cad batteries work best when fully charged and fully discharged. When you discharge batteries partially, the batteries remember the pattern and deliver about the same amount of power during future use even when fully charged. Discharge ni-cads completely, then recharge them before storing them. Discharge and recharge ni-cads periodically when you do not use them.

5. B. One to two hours. The majority of rechargeables last about one hour, then have a rapid voltage drop. One advantage of conventional carbon-zinc batteries is that the light dims gradually when you exhaust the batteries. The light does not go out quickly as it can with rechargeable batteries. I prefer a rechargeable primary light and a conventional-battery back-up light.

6. A. Dive light intensity is greater out of the water than it is in the water. Batteries are temperature sensitive, producing less power as temperature decreases. The thermal capacity of water results in heat loss from the light, which decreases the power output. Another advantage of a neoprene jacket on a dive light is insulation. Some large dive lights generate so much heat they are unaffected by water temperature, but the heat can damage the lights if you use them out of the water.

7. B. Decrease bulb and battery life and increase intensity. The resistance of a lower voltage bulb is low, so greater current flows through the filament than the bulb is designed to manage. The higher current produces a more intense light, but at the sacrifice of decreased bulb and battery life. Higher current increases the intensity of a small dive light. If you choose the wrong bulb, however, the bulb will burn out after just a few minutes of operation. Experiment above the water before you use a higher-current bulb for diving.

8. D. All the above. Standard bulbs lose tungsten from the filament. The tungsten deposits on the inside of the bulb, causing darkening. Replace a blackened bulb before it fails. Swollen, oozing, or corroded batteries can ruin a light. A yellow-orange light color indicates weak batteries. Remove batteries before you store your lights.

9. C. Attach the light securely to yourself using a strong cord. False. A lanyard is valuable to keep the light handy, but use rubber tubing instead of line. If the light becomes caught on an obstruction, you need to be able to pull free for safety.

10. D. All the above statements are true. Shining a light into another diver's eyes at night temporarily blinds the person. The up-and-down motion of a light beam indicates a problem, while a side-to-side motion means "attention." A large "O" made with a light indicates "OK." Use a standard flashlight for above-water activities.

11. C. Amber. Red, green, and white are the navigational light colors. If you use red, green, or white lights to mark exit locations, you may confuse boaters. Amber is a popular alternate color. Amber lights are commonly available or you may place amber-colored plastic in front of a white light.

12. A. Output wattage. Candle power is a misleading rating because it specifies only the area of brightest intensity in the beam and does not accurately indicate the total amount of light generated. Battery duration for a given bulb is "burn time," which indicates how long the light will burn, but not the power of the light. Output wattage, the product of bulb current times battery voltage, is a true measure of light power.

13. All statements are correct. Ni-cad batteries last 2-4 years and may be cycled hundreds of times. Ni-cads provide nearly constant output power until about 90% discharged and are excellent for high wattage lights. The batteries completely discharge in about 90 days when you do not use them. The warmer the storage area, the more rapid the discharge. Avoid deep discharge of ni-cad batteries and mixing different brands.

14. C. Taping the light to the regulator hose near the first stage. Chemical lights tied to equipment frequently tear free. Many divers who navigate well and dive from a boat do not use snorkels. A chemical light placed beneath a mask strap may get lost. When you tape the light to your regulator hose you minimize loss possibility and provide optimum visibility both above and below water.

15. D. All the above. Heat, humidity, and physical abuse shorten chemical light storage life. Give the lights the same treatment that manufacturers recommend for all equipment—store them in a cool, dark, dry, protected area and handle them carefully.

EQUIPMENT MAINTENANCE

Proper maintenance of your dive equipment is important for safety and economy. The following questions test fundamental equipment maintenance knowledge. An active, certified diver should ace this quiz.

1. You should clean your dive equipment by_____ it in/with _____ water.
- ❏ A. Rinsing, cold
- ❏ B. Soaking, warm
- ❏ C. Rinsing, warm
- ❏ D. Soaking; hot, soapy

2. You should store your dive equipment in a storage area that is:
- ❏ A. Warm, dark and damp
- ❏ B. Cool, dark and dry
- ❏ C. Cold, sunlit and dry
- ❏ D. Hot, sunlit and humid

3. For long-term storage you should seal your dry dive equipment in plastic to prevent damage from:
- ❏ A. Ultraviolet rays
- ❏ B. Fluorocarbons
- ❏ C. Sulfur dioxide
- ❏ D. Ozone

4. Select the <u>incorrect</u> statement concerning routine buoyancy compensator (BC) maintenance:
- ❏ A. Rinse the BC internally with warm water
- ❏ B. Test the pressure relief valve every time you rinse your BC
- ❏ C. Remove the CO_2 cartridge, if any, then rinse and inspect the mechanism
- ❏ D. Drain all water from the BC, then inflate it for drying

5. When you rinse your regulator you should avoid:
- ❏ A. Allowing water into the second stage
- ❏ B. Raising the second stage higher than the first stage
- ❏ C. Soaking the regulator or using warm water
- ❏ D. Depressing the purge button on the second stage

6. Have your scuba regulator serviced:
- ❏ A. Annually
- ❏ B. Every 25 dives
- ❏ C. Every five years
- ❏ D. When the need is apparent

7. Have your scuba tank internally inspected:
- ❏ A. Annually
- ❏ B. Every five years
- ❏ C. When hydrostated
- ❏ D. Whenever emptied

8. Which of the following types of scuba tanks require internal inspection:
- ❏ A. Steel tanks
- ❏ B. Aluminum tanks
- ❏ C. Both A and B
- ❏ D. Neither A nor B

9. Have your scuba tank hydrostatically tested:
- ❏ A. Annually
- ❏ B. Every two years
- ❏ C. Every five years
- ❏ D. After a year of storage

10. Store your scuba tank:
- ❏ A. Upright and filled
- ❏ B. Upright with a few hundred psi
- ❏ C. Horizontal and filled
- ❏ D. In any position with a few hundred psi

11. Clean your tank valve after diving by:
- ❏ A. Rinsing it with cold water
- ❏ B. Soaking it in cold water
- ❏ C. Rinsing it with warm water
- ❏ D. Soaking it in warm water

12. Select the incorrect statement concerning exposure suit maintenance:
- ❏ A. Store a wet suit on a wide hanger
- ❏ B. Dry an exposure suit in the sun and store it in a dark area
- ❏ C. Store a dry suit with the zipper open
- ❏ D. Coat clean, dry latex seals with pure talc

13. Proper care for your weighting system does <u>not</u> include:
- ❏ A. Soaking or rinsing the entire system
- ❏ B. Soaking or rinsing the quick release mechanism
- ❏ C. Inspecting all functional aspects
- ❏ D. Keeping the free end of a weight belt unfrayed

14. Store a silicon dive mask in a mask box to prevent:
- ❏ A. Distortion
- ❏ B. Discoloration
- ❏ C. Breakage
- ❏ D. All the above

15. The purpose of a scuba regulator first stage dust cap is to:
- ❏ A. Keep dirt and dust out of the first stage
- ❏ B. Keep moisture out of the first stage
- ❏ C. Protect the regulator O-ring seat
- ❏ D. All the above

EQUIPMENT MAINTENANCE

How much did you spend for equipment maintenance last year? If you do not have your equipment serviced at the beginning of each dive season, it will cost you a great deal in the long run and could affect your safety. Does your equipment need professional servicing? If so, do not procrastinate any longer—have your equipment serviced before you dive again. Proper maintenance is an essential part of diving safety.

1. B. Soaking, warm. Soap causes gummy deposits on equipment. Warm water helps dissolve and loosen accumulations that cold water may not remove. Rinse your equipment after soaking it, but avoid high pressure water.

2. B. Cool, dark and dry. Temperature extremes are detrimental to equipment. Prolonged sunlight deteriorates rubber products. A humid environment can enhance fungus growth. Store your equipment inside your home instead of your garage.

3. D. Ozone. Smog contains ozone, which attacks rubber. Deterioration of car tires demonstrates the effect of ozone on rubber. Electric motors generate ozone, so keep your equipment away from freezers, refrigerators, etc. Seal your dry equipment in plastic to exclude smog and ozone.

4. B. Test the pressure relief valve every time you rinse your BC. False. Testing the pressure relief valve frequently places unnecessary stress on the BC bladder. Infrequent testing of the pressure relief valve is sufficient. Eliminating salt and mineral deposits from the manual and low pressure inflator valves is far more important than testing the relief valve.

5. D. Depressing the purge button on the second stage. If you depress the purge button with water inside the second stage, the water can flow through the intermediate pressure hose and into the first stage. Even fresh water in a regulator first stage can cause unwanted deposits.

6. A. Annually. Do not allow your regulator to go more than a year without service. When you use your regulator frequently, have it serviced every six months. Don't assume your regulator is OK because it seems to function properly. You may not be able to detect inhalation and exhalation effort levels that are unacceptable and could jeopardize your safety.

7. A. Annually. It requires a trained, qualified inspector with specialized equipment to determine what, if anything, is taking place inside a scuba cylinder. The few dollars for a professional visual cylinder inspection are a good investment in safety. If you use your scuba tank frequently, have it visually inspected every six months.

8. C. Both A and B. All scuba tanks require internal inspections. Aluminum does not rust, but water inside the tank causes corrosion in the form of aluminum oxide. Aluminum tanks are subject to electrolysis problems. Valves in aluminum tanks require periodic lubrication to prevent seizing.

9. C. Every five years. Government regulations require the testing of high pressure cylinders every five years. With proper care and regular internal inspections, a scuba tank will pass many hydrostatic tests and can last a diver for a lifetime.

10. D. In any position with a few hundred psi. Some divers believe they should store scuba tanks upright because the tank bottom is thicker than the sides. They are mistaken. Wall thickness for the bottom and sides is uniform. High pressure stresses tank metal. Stress your tank with high pressure for brief periods only. Avoid storing full tanks for long intervals.

11. D. Soaking it in warm water. Although it is not always an easy task, it is best to invert your scuba tank and soak it in warm water after diving. Soaking the valve helps eliminate deposits in critical areas, such as the burst disk relief hole. Rinse the valve after soaking it to flush away deposits.

12. B. Dry an exposure suit in the sun and store it in a dark area. The ultraviolet rays of the sun are harmful to exposure suit material. Many divers sun-dry exposure suits to speed the drying process. Minimize sunlight exposure to keep your suit soft and pliable for as long as possible. Avoid dryer heat as well.

13. A. Soaking or rinsing the entire system. Lead is a toxic substance. "Gray water" from lead rinsing can pollute the water table. Soak and rinse the quick release mechanism only. Inspect the entire system, including the compensating system and weight retainers, if any. Be sure the free end of a weight belt is neat, clean, and unfrayed.

14. D. All the above. Heavy equipment on top of an unprotected mask can crush and distort the mask. Silicon has an affinity for the colors found in neoprene. Keep your silicon mask away from all neoprene products. A mask box minimizes the risk of lens breakage. A mask box is more than just packaging. Use one.

15. D. A regulator dust cap prevents dust, water, and other foreign bodies from entering the first stage. Develop the habit of securing the dust cap in place any time your regulator is not attached to your scuba tank. If your dust cap has an O-ring groove, make sure there is an O-ring installed. It is important to protect the interior of your regulator first stage.

FIELD REPAIRS

Q:

Have you ever been in a remote area preparing to dive and had an equipment difficulty? Even if you inspect your equipment in advance, problems can still occur. What can you do to repair an item of equipment in the field? What should you do? The topic of field repairs is not commonly addressed in diving education, so this quiz should be interesting and thought-provoking. Answer all questions before looking at the answers.

Select the order of preference for each question. Assume the diver has an openwater certification and 25 logged dives. Assume all failures occur while the diver is preparing to dive in water that is 65 degrees F. If an option should not be considered at all, do not include it in your order of preference.

1. If the mask strap breaks, the diver should:
- ❑ A. Dive without a strap
- ❑ B. Replace the strap with a spare
- ❑ C. Hold the mask in place with large rubber bands
- ❑ D. Abort the dive

2. If a fin strap breaks, the diver should:
- ❑ A. Dive with one fin
- ❑ B. Replace the strap with a spare
- ❑ C. Tie the fin in place with cord or string
- ❑ D. Abort the dive

3. If the purge valve in the mask or snorkel fails, the diver should:
- ❑ A. Replace the valve with a spare
- ❑ B. Seal the valve until it can be replaced
- ❑ C. Dive with a leaky valve
- ❑ D. Abort the dive

4. If the sections of a snorkel tube separate, the diver should:
- ❑ A. Dive without a snorkel
- ❑ B. Use a spare snorkel
- ❑ C. Tape the sections together with duct tape
- ❑ D. Abort the dive

5. If the main zipper on the wet suit fails, the diver should:
- ❑ A. Dive without zipping the suit
- ❑ B. Sew the zipper closed with a sailmaker's needle
- ❑ C. Let his buddy dive, then dive with his buddy's wet suit
- ❑ D. Abort the dive

6. If the exhaust valve on the buoyancy compensator is leaking, the diver should:
- ❑ A. Dive, but not count on the BC for buoyancy control
- ❑ B. Replace the exhaust valve with a spare
- ❑ C. Disassemble, clean, and reassemble the valve
- ❑ D. Abort the dive

7. If the inflator/deflator assembly pulls off the buoyancy compensator (BC), the diver should:
- ❑ A. Dive, but not count on the BC for buoyancy control
- ❑ B. Dive without a buoyancy compensator
- ❑ C. Replace the assembly and secure it with a tie wrap
- ❑ D. Abort the dive

8. If the BC low pressure inflator sticks when depressed, the diver should:
- ❑ A. Dive, but not use the low pressure inflator
- ❑ B. Dive without a buoyancy compensator
- ❑ C. Disassemble, clean, and reassemble the valve assembly
- ❑ D. Let his buddy dive, then dive with his buddy's BC

9. If a hose on the regulator is leaking when the air is turned on, the diver should:
- ❑ A. Monitor the hose closely while diving
- ❑ B. Replace the hose with a spare
- ❑ C. Remove the hose and make the dive
- ❑ D. Abort the dive.

10. If the primary regulator second stage will not stop free flowing when the air is turned on, the diver should:
- ❑ A. Block the opening to the mouthpiece to see if the pressure build-up will stop the free flow
- ❑ B. Disassemble, inspect, adjust as necessary, and reassemble the second stage
- ❑ C. Use an extra regulator
- ❑ D. Abort the dive

11. If the extra second stage (octopus) of a regulator will not stop free flowing when the air is turned on, the diver should:
- ❑ A. Block the opening to the mouthpiece to see if the pressure build-up will stop the free flow
- ❑ B. Disassemble, inspect, adjust as necessary, and reassemble the second stage
- ❑ C. Use an extra regulator
- ❑ D. Remove the extra second stage and screw a port plug into the regulator first stage

12. If the exhaust valve of a regulator second stage is stuck in an open position, the diver should:
- ❑ A. Seal the valve until it can be replaced
- ❑ B. Disassemble, inspect, adjust as necessary, and reassemble the second stage
- ❑ C. Use an extra regulator
- ❑ D. Abort the dive

13. If the submersible pressure gauge has water inside, the diver should:
- ❑ A. Replace the gauge with a spare
- ❑ B. Dive shallowly and monitor the gauge closely while diving
- ❑ C. Dive, but have the gauge repaired or replaced at the first opportunity
- ❑ D. Use a spare regulator and gauge

14. If the O-ring is leaking on the tank, the diver should:
- ❑ A. Replace the O-ring with a spare
- ❑ B. Remove the regulator, inspect the O-ring, and test the seal again if the O-ring appears OK
- ❑ C. Remove the regulator, turn the O-ring over, and test the seal again
- ❑ D. Use a spare tank

15. If a weight belt buckle breaks or will not work, the diver should:
- ❑ A. Replace the buckle with a spare
- ❑ B. Use a spare weight belt
- ❑ C. Hold belt in place while diving
- ❑ D. Put the weights inside and on other equipment

FIELD REPAIRS

A:

How closely did your answers match those given? Many divers feel qualified to make the repairs identified in this quiz without the benefit of formal training. While it is an individual decision, the practice of self repair of equipment is discouraged. The completion of an equipment specialty course does not qualify divers to repair equipment, and it is a challenge for professional repair technicians to keep current with updates from manufacturers. Have your equipment inspected frequently by professionals. Regular servicing helps prevent failures in the field. Have repairs made professionally as needed. Have spare equipment. Have a well-stocked spare parts kit.

1. B, C, D. A good diver has a spare parts kit, which some like to call a "save-a-dive" kit. The kit has spare straps and other items that will be identified in this quiz. Al Pierce describes the rubber band technique in his book, *Scuba Lifesaving.* Diving without a mask strap is hazardous.

2. B, C, D. Extra fin straps should be part of a spare parts kit. Thin, strong cord can have many uses and should be part of the kit as well. While it is possible to swim with one fin, that skill is intended to get the diver out of the water when one fin is lost. It could be hazardous to make an entire dive with only one fin.

3. B, D. Recreational divers are not supposed to do much more than change straps on equipment needing repair. While a person may feel competent to make more complex repairs, there is a risk that the repair will not be made properly. Repairs of equipment—even the replacement of a purge valve—should be left to professionals who have been trained in the correct procedures for the repair.

4. B, D. Tape will not stick well to some snorkels, so taping is not a reliable repair. Some divers do choose to dive without a snorkel, although divers are still taught always to have a snorkel. There is a risk that you could have a long surface swim, although you could swim on your back. Whether the snorkel is essential equipment or not is your choice for this question.

5. B, D. A sailmaker's (curved) needle and thread (heavy, waxed) are great items to include in a save-a-dive kit. You can quickly sew someone into a wet suit so the person can dive. Diving one at a time some might consider an option since there is current support for solo diving. Those who support solo diving are entitled to their opinion, but many experts disagree. People are entitled to take the risk of diving alone, but they are not entitled to a correct answer for this question if they select diving alone as an option.

6. D. When it comes to the repair of a BC, we have definitely crossed the line between repairs that should be made by a recreational diver and those that should be made by trained technicians. BC's may not seem technical, but they are. Unsuccessful attempts to repair BC's have contributed to diving accidents.

7. D. What was said for question #6 applies to this question as well. If you are not qualified to repair an item of equipment, do not have replacement parts, and do not have the proper tools for the job, do not attempt the repair. Something that looks like a quick and easy fix can and has caused accidents.

8. A. Even this answer may not be acceptable if the diver is not proficient with oral BC inflation. All divers should know how to orally inflate a buoyancy compensator both above water and underwater. If you are not confident in your ability to do this and your low pressure inflator is sticking, postpone the dive until you have the BC serviced or obtain a replacement BC.

9. D. Many divers feel competent to remove or change hoses on a regulator. It seems simple and straightforward. This may be true for some, but not for all. O-rings may not be seated properly. It is not a good idea to take a chance with a life support system. If you choose to work on your regulator, you are going against the recommendations of the diving industry.

10. A, C, D. A service technician or one who has successfully completed a regulator repair course can quickly and easily remove the cover of the second stage of a regulator and make repairs in the field. Untrained divers who see this think it is simple and may try it as well. Serious problems, such as the diaphragm coming unseated, can occur. A diver—even an experienced one—should not attempt repairs to regulators, BC's, or valves.

11. A, C. It may seem very easy to remove the extra second stage and screw a port into the first stage, but many problems can result. The plug could be crossthreaded or might not be the correct one for the port. The O-ring might not be seated correctly. Avoid the unnecessary risks possible with amateur repairs.

12. C, D. You can prevent this problem. Try to exhale and inhale through your regulator when you pack it for a dive. With the dust cover in place on the first stage, you should not be able to draw air through the second stage. If you can, you have a leak in the exhaust valve, the diaphragm, or the mouthpiece. If you cannot exhale, you have a stuck exhaust valve. A problem detected at this point can be corrected before you get to the dive site.

13. D. The dive should be aborted if a spare regulator and gauge are not available. Water in the SPG is another problem that should be detected prior to arrival at the dive site. The metal in the bourdon tube mechanism of a high pressure gauge can corrode the tube quickly. The rupture of a high pressure line is a risk the diver should not take.

14. B, A, C, D. The average diver should be qualified to work with tank O-rings, although some divers do not seem to understand that sharp tools should not be used. Extra tank O-rings should be part of the diver's spare parts kit.

15. A, B. Weights should be worn correctly, or the dive should be aborted. An extra buckle is a good item to include in a spare parts kit. There are weight belt releases available that are not prone to the types of problems inherent with the standard "duck bill" type buckle. Alternate types of releases merit consideration.

SCUBA TANKS

Without a means to store compressed air, scuba diving as we know it would not exist. You know that scuba tanks store breathing air and that the tanks require maintenance to ensure safety, but do you know all that you need to know concerning high pressure cylinders? Note: Select the most correct answer to each question.

1. When filled to the pressure permitted when a plus sign follows a current hydrostatic test date, a standard 71.2 cubic foot steel tank contains _____ cubic feet of air.
- A. 64.7
- B. 71.2
- C. 78.3
- D. 80.0

2. A standard 71.2 cubic foot steel tank may be filled to a maximum working pressure of _____ psi, which provides an air volume of _____ cubic feet.
- A. 2,250, 71.2
- B. 2,250, 64.7
- C. 2,475, 64.7
- D. 2,475, 71.2

3. Avoid emptying your scuba tank completely because:
- A. You may cause metal fatigue
- B. Insects may enter the tank
- C. Moisture may enter the tank
- D. Dust may enter the tank

4. Have your scuba tank visually inspected every _____ and pressure tested every _____.
- A. Year, two years
- B. Year, five years
- C. Five years, year
- D. Year, year

5. Gross overfilling of scuba cylinders regularly may cause:
- A. Metal fatigue
- B. Moisture accumulation
- C. Valve damage
- D. A DOT citation and fine

6. A standard 71.2 cubic foot steel scuba tank, when filled to capacity, increases in pressure approximately ___ psi for each degree Fahrenheit that the tank temperature increases.
- A. One
- B. Five
- C. Six
- D. Seven

7. A standard 80 cubic foot aluminum scuba tank, when filled to capacity, increase in pressure approximately ___ psi for each degree Fahrenheit that the tank temperature increases.
- A. 1
- B. 5
- C. 6
- D. 7

8. The optimum pressure range for scuba cylinder storage is:
- A. 100 to 300 psi
- B. 500 to 1,000 psi
- C. 2,000 to 3,000 psi
- D. Empty

9. Aluminum scuba tanks, which do not rust, require no maintenance except hydrostatic pressure testing.
- A. True
- B. False

10. The weight difference between a full and an empty 80 cubic foot scuba tank is approximately:
- A. Three pounds
- B. Five pounds
- C. Six pounds
- D. Eight pounds

11. How much air does an aluminum scuba tank, which holds 80 cubic feet of air at 70 degrees F, contain at the same temperature and a pressure of 1,869 psi?
- A. 71.20 cubic feet
- B. 64.73 cubic feet
- C. 49.99 cubic feet
- D. 49.84 cubic feet

12. The rate at which you release air from a scuba tank can affect the cylinder.
- A. True
- B. False

13. When you do not use your scuba tank for a year or more, you:
- A. May breathe the air provided it has no odor
- B. Should drain and replace the air
- C. Have the air analyzed for purity
- D. May breathe the air for shallow dives only

14. It is safe to bake a paint finish onto an aluminum tank as long as the baking temperature does not exceed 375 degrees F.
- A. True
- B. False

15. Which of the following scuba tanks should be pressure tested before further use?
- A. A dented steel tank
- B. A gouged aluminum tank
- C. A tank that has been in a fire
- D. All the above

SCUBA TANKS

Scuba tanks are safe containers if used, inspected, and tested according to dive industry regulations. Scuba tanks can be extremely dangerous, however, when abused. Know what makes tanks—and the air inside them—dangerous. Handle, store, and transport scuba tanks carefully and enjoy what they allow you to do.

1. B. 71.2. A hydrostatic test date of a new 71.2 cubic foot steel tank may include a plus sign, which allows filling pressure to exceed the 2,250 psi working pressure by 10%. The tank must have the 10% overfill to contain 71.2 cubic feet. At the 2,250 working pressure, the tank holds less than 65 cubic feet. Tanks usually do not qualify for plus signs after the second and subsequent hydrostatic tests. Be aware of the difference in available air.

2. B. 2,250, 64.7. Determine the volume of air by using a ratio of tank pressures and volumes: $V1/P1 = V2/P2$. V1 is initial volume (71.2); V2 is the unknown volume (X); P1 is the initial pressure (2,475 psi); and P2 is the new tank pressure (2,250 psi). Solve for V2 (X) by cross-multiplying and dividing: $71.2/2,475 = X/2,250$. $2,475X = 160,200$. $X = 64.73$.

3. C. Moisture may enter the tank. If you empty your tank while diving, water can enter your tank through your regulator. If you store a tank with the valve open, temperature changes cause the tank to expand and contract and "breathe" moist air. Prevent tank moisture, which causes corrosion. Avoid emptying your tank completely.

4. B. Year, five years. Most air filling stations require a visual cylinder inspection annually. Some fill operators require an inspection if the tank is completely empty. Heavily-used tanks should be inspected every six months. The diving industry requires hydrostatic testing at least every five years. Also have your tank pressure tested any time you suspect it may be damaged or weakened.

5. A. Metal fatigue. Although hydrostatic testing involves pressure much higher than a tank's working pressure, regular overfilling of scuba tanks is harmful. Tank metal expands with each filling. Repeated overfilling stresses the metal and makes it brittle, gradually decreasing the life of the tank and causing it to fail hydrostatic testing prematurely. For safety and practicality, fill tanks to working pressure only.

6. B. Five. The "rule of thumb" is that pressure in a steel tank filled to 2,475 psi increases about five psi per degree F. The rule comes from the following formula: $T1/P1 = T2/P2$. T1 is the initial absolute temperature (degrees Kelvin); T2 is the new temperature (degrees Kelvin); P1 is the initial absolute pressure (2,475 + 14.7); and P2 is the unknown absolute pressure (X). Solve for P2 (X) by selecting two temperatures, then cross-multiplying and dividing. T1 = 70 degrees F; T2 = 200 degrees F; and P1 = 2,475 psi. Degrees Kelvin = Degrees F. plus 460. $(70 + 460)/(2,475 + 14.7) = (200 + 460)/X$. $530X = 1,643,202$. $X = 3,100$ psia minus 14.7 = 3,085.7 psi. The change in pressure (3,086 - 2,475 = 611 psi) divided by the change in temperature (130 degrees F) = 4.7 psi for each degree of temperature change.

7. C. Six. The rule of thumb is different for various scuba cylinders because the internal volumes and working pressures differ. T1 = 70 degrees F; T2 = 200 degrees F; P1 = 3,000. Solution: $(70 + 460)/3,000 + 14.7) = (200 + 460)/X$. $530X = 1,989,702$. $X = 3,754$ psia minus 14.7 = 3,739.5 psi. The change in pressure (3,739.5 - 3,000 = 739.5 psi) divided by the change in temperature (130 degrees F) = 5.7 psi for each degree of temperature change.

8. A. 100 to 300 psi. Do not store tanks either empty or full. The more air in your tank, the more corrosion possible when moisture is present. There is potential hazard when a stored tank contains high pressure air and a fire occurs. Heat may cause some tanks to explode before the valve burst disk ruptures. The optimum storage pressure is low, but not zero.

9. B. False. Aluminum tanks corrode, although their oxidizing process arrests itself while steel oxidizes in a way that accelerates the process. Aluminum tanks do require visual inspections and their valve threads must be lubricated periodically to prevent the valve from seizing.

10. C. Six pounds. Air at sea level weighs approximately .08 pounds per cubic foot. Eighty cubic feet of air weighs about 6.4 pounds. Your buoyancy while diving changes as you use air from your tank. Weight yourself so you are neutrally buoyant with about 300 psi so you will not have to fight to stay down at the end of a dive.

11. C. 49.99 cubic feet. For a constant temperature use the formula $P1/V1 = P2/V2$. P1 = 3,000 + 14.7; P2 = 1,869 + 14.7; V1 = 80; and V2 = unknown (X). Solve by cross-multiplying and dividing: $3,014.7X = 150,696$. $X = 49.99$ cubic feet.

12. A. True. Gas expanded under high pressure has a cooling effect. Rapid expansion of scuba tank air may cool air inside the tank so much that moisture in the air condenses inside the cylinder. The cooling causes condensation on the tank valve and may freeze the valve. Drain tanks slowly to avoid problems.

13. B. Should drain and replace the air. Oxidation inside a tank can reduce or eliminate the oxygen in air when moisture is present. Following prolonged storage, you should have a tank visually inspected before refilling it.

14. B. False. Heating aluminum cylinders reduces metal strength and could cause the tank to rupture. Any scuba tank subjected to severe heat should be hydrostatically tested before filling or use.

15. D. Scuba tanks in good condition are quite safe, but a damaged cylinder is hazardous and can cause extensive damage and severe injuries if it explodes. Don't take a chance to save a few dollars.

TANK VALVES

Q:

Divers take tank valves for granted because valves are simple and reliable. There are some important considerations that you may not have learned in your basic training. See if the following quiz helps you learn to save money and increase your diving safety.

1. All scuba tank valves are required to have:
- ❏ A. A reserve
- ❏ B. A burst disk
- ❏ C. A valve snorkel
- ❏ D. Tapered threads

2. The purpose of a valve snorkel is to:
- ❏ A. Limit the flow of air from the tank
- ❏ B. Filter the air leaving the tank
- ❏ C. Prevent material from leaving the tank
- ❏ D. Absorb small amounts of moisture

3. When your tank valve is difficult to operate, it means:
- ❏ A. The tank is full of air
- ❏ B. You should lubricate the valve
- ❏ C. The valve needs to be replaced
- ❏ D. The valve needs to be serviced

4. Open a tank valve momentarily before attaching your regulator. Do this to:
- ❏ A. Estimate the amount of air in the tank
- ❏ B. Smell the air to check quality
- ❏ C. Check the valve operability
- ❏ D. Clear dirt or moisture from the valve

5. When turning on a scuba tank valve with a scuba regulator attached, open the valve:
- ❏ A. Quickly one full turn
- ❏ B. Slowly one full turn
- ❏ C. Quickly all the way
- ❏ D. Slowly all the way

6. J-valves are so named because:
- ❏ A. They were originally listed as item "J" in an equipment catalog
- ❏ B. The interior mechanism is J-shaped
- ❏ C. The letter J represents the pull rod used to activate the reserve mechanism
- ❏ D. None of the above

7. The purpose of a reserve valve is to:
- ❏ A. Allow safe use of all available air
- ❏ B. Allow a safe, normal ascent at the end of a dive
- ❏ C. Keep water and contaminants out of the tank by preventing total air depletion
- ❏ D. Eliminate the need for dangling submersible pressure gauges

8. A J-valve operates on the principle of:
- ❏ A. Aerohydraulics
- ❏ B. A restricted orifice
- ❏ C. A spring-loaded valve
- ❏ D. A downstream valve

9. The pressure at which a J-valve operates underwater is:
- ❏ A. Gauge pressure
- ❏ B. Absolute pressure
- ❏ C. Ambient pressure
- ❏ D. Atmospheric pressure

10. When filling a tank equipped with a J-valve, the valve must be:
- ❏ A. Up, in the reserve position
- ❏ B. Down, in the non-reserve position
- ❏ C. Down for the first 500 psi, then up for the remainder of the fill
- ❏ D. Midway between the reserve and non-reserve positions

11. When twin tanks with a J-valve activate at 500 psi, the pressure in each tank after valve activation will be:
- ❏ A. 500 psi
- ❏ B. 250 psi
- ❏ C. Less than 500 psi at depth
- ❏ D. Less than 250 psi at depth

12. Some old scuba regulators have a J-valve incorporated. If you use a J-valve regulator and a J-valve tank together:
- ❏ A. The reserve pressure doubles
- ❏ B. The reserve pressure halves
- ❏ C. The reserve pressure remains constant, but you must activate both valves
- ❏ D. Neither J-valve may be used

13. Select all true statements:
- ❏ A. If you store a J-valve-equipped scuba tank with the lever down, you shorten the life of the valve
- ❏ B. A J-valve reserve mechanism is normally open when the valve lever is up, a regulator is attached, and the tank valve is open
- ❏ C. Tank valves receive about the same service frequency as tanks and regulators
- ❏ D. None of the above statements are true

14. Select the incorrect statement concerning DIN valves:
- ❏ A. A DIN valve is threaded and has a recessed O-ring
- ❏ B. A DIN valve withstands pressures in excess of 3,000 psi
- ❏ C. DIN valves require a DIN-fitted regulator
- ❏ D. Standard scuba regulators may be used with a DIN adapter

15. A scuba valve burst disk is designed to rupture at a pressure of:
- ❏ A. 140% of a scuba tank's working pressure
- ❏ B. 125% to 166% of a scuba tank's working pressure
- ❏ C. Five thirds the working pressure of a scuba tank
- ❏ D. None of the above

TANK VALVES

We often take our scuba equipment for granted because it is rugged and dependable. Knowing more about equipment is helpful. Equipment specialty courses provide the type of information contained in this quiz. Have your scuba equipment, including your tank valve, serviced annually by a professional repair facility. Even if you have good equipment knowledge, don't attempt to service scuba equipment, which requires special training, materials, and tools. When was the last time you had your tank valve serviced?

1. B. A burst disk. All valves have a disk that ruptures before the bursting pressure of a tank would be reached by overfilling or overheating. Air escaping from a ruptured disk is loud, but not dangerous. Only professionals should service tank valves. Do not attempt to replace a disk yourself.

2. C. Prevent material from leaving the tank. A tube extends from the bottom of a valve a few inches into a tank. The tube keeps loose particles and water from entering the valve and regulator if you invert the tank. Foreign material can damage your valve or regulator.

3. D. The valve needs to be serviced. Lubricating your valve could be hazardous. You may damage a valve if you continue to use it when it is difficult to operate. Valve servicing is not expensive, but replacement is.

4. D. Clear dirt or moisture from the valve. Anything in the valve opening will be forced into the regulator by high pressure. A simple, short air blast clears any foreign matter. Also use the opportunity to learn how far you need to turn the valve handle before it opens (see the next question).

5. D. Slowly all the way. Sudden, repeated valve opening damages scuba regulators. Turn the air on slowly and open the valve all the way to allow maximum air flow through the valve. A partially-opened valve can result of a loss of air flow at depth. Do turn the valve closed about one quarter turn after opening it all the way. The quarter turn helps prevent damage to the valve if you bump the valve handle while the valve is opened.

6. A. They were originally listed as item "J" in an equipment catalog. When U.S. Divers published its first catalog, they listed valves as items J and K with J identifying the reserve valve. The letter designations caught on and have become standard terms.

7. B. Allow a safe, normal ascent at the end of a dive. There are advantages to an air reserve. The most important advantage is the ability to ascend slowly and comfortably. Do not use a J-valve to extend bottom time or to replace a submersible pressure gauge.

8. C. A spring-loaded valve. A spring pushes a valve against tank pressure in J-valves. As long as the tank pressure exceeds the spring pressure, air pressure holds the valve open. When the spring pressure exceeds the tank pressure, the valve closes, keeping an air reserve until you manually open the valve by turning a lever that compresses the spring.

9. A. Gauge pressure. Tank valves do not compensate for increased pressure like a scuba regulator does. A reserve that operates at 300 psig at sea level operates at the same pressure at depth. The constant pressure poses a problem because air is available only when the tank pressure is greater than ambient pressure.

10. B. Down, in the non-reserve position. The valve is in the air flow path and held closed by a spring. High pressure air forces the valve closed, damages the reserve valve seat, and affects its operation. Be sure a J-valve tank is filled properly by presenting it for filling with the J-valve lever in the down position.

11. B. 250 psi. If you use twin tanks with a reserve on one tank, the valve maintains the full reserve pressure in one tank while you deplete the other tank. When you activate the J-valve, the pressure equalizes in the two tanks. The reserve pressure is higher for twin tanks than for a single unit.

12. C. The reserve pressure remains constant, but you must activate both valves. The valves in the configuration described are in series. Both valves function as reserves and both must be opened to obtain air at low tank pressure. Avoid a dual J-valve configuration or place one valve in the non-reserve position and leave it there.

13. D. None of the above statements are true. Lever position has no effect on valve life. Divers usually overlook valves when they have other equipment serviced. Carbon dust or rust in your valve can quickly affect your regulator performance. Tank pressure does not hold a reserve valve open continuously; the valve closes when you breathe and lowers the pressure in your regulator first stage.

14. D. Standard scuba regulators may be used with a DIN adapter. There is an adapter that allows a DIN-valve tank to be <u>filled</u> with a standard valve yoke, but do not attach a standard yoke-type regulator to the fitting. The danger is obvious. Filling valve yokes have a higher pressure rating than regulator valve yokes.

15. B. 125% to 166% of a scuba tank's working pressure. The burst pressure of the metal disk is not precise, but has a predictable range that assures pressure relief before the cylinder reaches five thirds its rated pressure.

SUBMERSIBLE PRESSURE GAUGES

Historically it took many years for a submersible pressure gauge (SPG) to become a standard item of dive equipment. Since you use an SPG for every scuba dive and since they involve high pressure air, there is important information about them that you must know. Find out if you know what you should by answering the following questions.

Q:

1. Select the correct statement concerning SPGs:

☐ A. An SPG is a device to warn you when you are low on air

☐ B. An SPG is a rugged instrument that can tolerate shock well

☐ C. The pressure reading on a modern SPG is accurate to within 25 psi

☐ D. An SPG typically is a passive device that permits monitoring of the air supply

2. An SPG reading is least accurate in the range of:

☐ A. 0 to 500 psi

☐ B. 500 to 1,000 psi

☐ C. 1,000 to 2,000 psi

☐ D. 2,000 to 3,000 psi

3. Taking your SPG to altitude or shipping it with your luggage aboard an airplane will not affect gauge accuracy.

☐ A. True

☐ B. False

4. An analog SPG is essentially a:

☐ A. Bourdon tube

☐ B. Diaphragm gauge

☐ C. Capillary tube

☐ D. Digital gauge

5. You should have a hose protector on the first stage end of your SPG high pressure hose to:

☐ A. Make the gauge hang out to the side so you can find it

☐ B. Prevent the weight of the instrument from breaking the hose fibers

☐ C. Help seal the swage fitting to the hose and prevent leakage

☐ D. All the above

6. You should not look directly at an SPG when you are out of the water because:

☐ A. Low level radiation from the luminous dial can damage your night vision

☐ B. Glare from the gauge lens makes reading the dial difficult

☐ C. The lens could injure your eyes if the gauge exploded

☐ D. You should view the gauge the way you will look at it underwater

7. Which of the following is most likely to occur if the high pressure hose of your SPG ruptures?

☐ A. The hose will flail violently until the tank is empty

☐ B. The hose will flail violently until the tank pressure reaches approximately 800 psi

☐ C. The hose will remain stationary

☐ D. The hose will remain stationary but will be split along its entire length

8. If you attach an SPG to a regulator, attach the regulator to a full tank and turn on the air, and the SPG gauge reads about 100 psi, you should suspect:

☐ A. The SPG is malfunctioning

☐ B. The tank is nearly empty

☐ C. The valve on the tank is only partially opened

☐ D. The SPG is attached to the wrong regulator port

9. If the needle on your SPG fluctuates when you inhale and exhale, the most likely problem is that:

☐ A. Your tank valve is only partially open

☐ B. Your tank is nearly empty

☐ C. Your SPG is malfunctioning

☐ D. The SPG is attached to the wrong regulator port

10. If you discover a steady stream of bubbles leaking from your SPG hose swivel fitting, you should:

☐ A. Abort the dive immediately while you have air

☐ B. Continue to dive, but monitor your SPG frequently

☐ C. Take "B" action, but also have your gauge serviced as soon as possible

☐ D. Dive normally, but have the gauge serviced before you dive again

11. While diving you notice water inside your SPG. You should:

☐ A. Abort the dive immediately

☐ B. Continue diving, but don't trust the SPG accuracy

☐ C. Complete your dive, but have the gauge serviced before you use it again

☐ D. Finish the dive, then disassemble the gauge and allow it to dry

12. The tank pressure indicated by an SPG is the ____ pressure.

☐ A. Absolute

☐ B. Gauge

☐ C. Gauge pressure less ambient pressure

☐ D. Gauge pressure less intermediate pressure

13. The most significant shortcoming of an SPG is that it is:

☐ A. Expensive

☐ B. Passive

☐ C. Inaccurate

☐ D. Cumbersome

14. If a substantial leak develops in your SPG or SPG hose while diving, you should:

☐ A. Attempt to stop the leak

☐ B. Ascend normally

☐ C. Ascend using your buddy's alternate air source

☐ D. Do an emergency swimming ascent

15. You have your scuba tank filled to 3,000 psi and place it in the trunk of your car. You drive 100 miles to a dive site, assemble your equipment, and note your tank pressure is only 2,800 psi. The most likely cause of the different pressure reading is:

☐ A. The dive site altitude

☐ B. Temperature difference

☐ C. Air loss

☐ D. An inaccurate SPG

SUBMERSIBLE PRESSURE GAUGES

A:

Did you score 100 percent? If not, do not feel badly because few divers ace the quiz unless they have completed an equipment specialty course. You should see the value of learning more about your equipment. Hopefully you can make better use of your SPG now and will give yours proper care. It helps to understand diving instruments in depth.

1. D. An SPG typically is a passive device that permits monitoring of the air supply. Most SPGs will not warn you unless you look at them. One SPG has an audible warning when tank pressure reaches 500 psi. SPGs are delicate instruments that you should protect from shock. Consider your SPG a passive, relative indicator of tank pressure.

2. A. 0 to 500 psi. Frequently there are no psi increments for the last 500 psi on the dial of SPGs. The zero point can vary from day to day and gauge to gauge. A halfway reading in the red zone of an SPG does not necessarily mean the tank pressure is 250 psi. The rule about ending a dive with 500 psi is sound advice.

3. B. False. Reduced atmospheric pressure at altitude does affect SPGs, especially if the gauge has a needle stop. Analog SPG gauges should be part of your carry-on baggage when you fly to a dive destination.

4. A. Bourdon tube. A Bourdon tube is a curved tube that pressure tries to straighten. Analog SPGs have spiral-wound Bourdon tubes. American gauges have maximum pressure readings of 3,000 to 4,000 psi. The maximum pressure readings for European gauges is 4,500 psi (300 bar).

5. B. Prevent the weight of the instrument from breaking the hose fibers. An SPG, which usually is in a console with other instruments, places a strain on the high pressure hose, which breaks hose fibers at the metal fitting near the regulator first stage. A hose protector helps prevent the fiber breakage. Check for corrosion under the hose protector from time to time because trapped salt deposits attack the metal.

6. C. The lens could injure your eyes if the gauge exploded. SPGs have a rubber blowout plug in the back of the case. The plug is supposed to relieve pressure if the gauge explodes. If something covers the plug, the gauge lens would blow out if the gauge exploded. To be safe, view the gauge from an angle when out of the water.

7. C. The hose will remain stationary. Low pressure hoses flail when they rupture, but not high pressure hoses. Why? Because high pressure hoses have a restricted orifice (.005 inches). The volume of air passing through the restricted opening is small, so the effect is not as devastating as it would be without a restriction.

8. D. The SPG is attached to the wrong regulator port. The high pressure port on a regulator usually has the marking "HP." If you attach the SPG to a low pressure port, the gauge reads intermediate pressure. A worse mistake is to attach a low pressure hose to a high pressure port. Modern regulators have different sized ports for low and high pressure hoses.

9. A. Your tank valve is only partially open. If the SPG needle drops sharply when you inhale, then recovers while you exhale, you are not receiving sufficient air. You deplete the air from the first stage faster than the tank can supply it through the valve restriction and the SPG gauge reacts. Avoid opening your tank valve only slightly to check tank pressure. Either open tank valves all the way or close them completely.

10. C. Take "B" action, but also have your gauge serviced as soon as possible. The restricted orifice prevents a rapid depletion of your air supply, but your air will be gone sooner than normal owing to the leakage. A leak is not an emergency, but you should not ignore it. Monitor your gauge frequently, then have the gauge repaired as soon as you can.

11. C. Complete your dive, but have the gauge serviced before you use it again. Water inside the casing means water is in contact with the thin metal high pressure Bourdon tube inside the casing. Corrosion can weaken the tube wall and lead to a rupture and explosion. Do not procrastinate. Have your leaky SPG serviced at the first opportunity if you notice moisture inside it.

12. B. Gauge Pressure. The SPG reads tank pressure directly with an instrument calibrated to indicate zero pressure at sea level. Gauge pressure does not include atmospheric pressure, which is a component of absolute pressure. Gauge pressure plus atmospheric pressure equals absolute pressure.

13. B. Passive. An SPG is of no value if you do not monitor it. You must develop the habit of checking your gauge and your buddy's gauge frequently while diving. The deeper you dive, the more frequently you should monitor the gauges.

14. B. Ascend normally. A common SPG misconception is that a leak rapidly depletes the air supply. If the gauge came completely off the hose of an SPG underwater, you still would be able to ascend normally.

15. B. Temperature difference. The pressure of a fixed volume of gas varies directly with the absolute temperature of the gas. A tank is warmer after filling than it is hours later. Cool air temperatures also cause a lower tank pressure. Tank pressure varies about 5 psi per degree F in 71.2 cubic foot steel tanks and about 6 psi per degree in aluminum 80's.

VISUAL CYLINDER INSPECTIONS

You probably are aware that periodic visual inspections of scuba cylinders are required, but do you know who requires them, how frequently they are required, what should comprise a proper inspection, and who is qualified to perform the inspections? Test your knowledge in all these areas and more with the following quiz.

1. Federal law requires the pressure testing of scuba cylinders every five years.
❏ A. True
❏ B. False

2. Federal and diving industry regulations require the visual inspection of compressed gas cylinders annually.
❏ A. True
❏ B. False

3. Scuba cylinders receiving heavy use should be visually inspected:
❏ A. Monthly
❏ B. Every three months
❏ C. Every six months
❏ D. Annually

4. Aluminum scuba cylinders require visual inspections:
❏ A. Less frequently than steel tanks
❏ B. More frequently than steel tanks
❏ C. As often as steel tanks

5. Corrosion occurs in steel tanks, but not in aluminum scuba cylinders.
❏ A. True
❏ B. False

6. Visual cylinder inspections should be performed only by:
❏ A. Certified inspectors
❏ B. Dive store personnel
❏ C. Diving retailers who have internal inspection lights
❏ D. DOT-licensed inspectors

7. The minimum number of distinct steps for a proper visual inspection of a scuba cylinder is:
❏ A. 3
❏ B. 5
❏ C. 8
❏ D. 10

8. The primary reason for special lubrication of the valve threads for an aluminum scuba tank is to:
❏ A. Ensure a high pressure seal
❏ B. Prevent seizing of the valve
❏ C. Lubricate joining threads
❏ D. Prevent cylinder odor

9. Aluminum tanks must be condemned if they are exposed to temperatures in excess of ____ degrees F and steel tanks must be condemned if exposed to temperatures in excess of ____ degrees F:
❏ A. 250, 500
❏ B. 350, 600
❏ C. 500, 900
❏ D. 725, 975

10. Select any and all of the items that must be removed from a scuba cylinder prior to a visual inspection:
❏ A. Protective netting
❏ B. Tank boot
❏ C. Tank valve
❏ D. Back pack
❏ E. Stickers

11. The minimum number of specialized tools (not counting common hand tools) required to conduct a proper visual cylinder inspection is:
❏ A. 3
❏ B. 5
❏ C. 8
❏ D. 11

12. Select all correct answers: A visual cylinder inspection is recommended:
❏ A. For all new cylinders
❏ B. For new steel cylinders
❏ C. If a cylinder has been exposed to rough treatment
❏ D. If a tank is completely emptied of air.
❏ E. After tumbling and cleaning

13. Select all correct answers. Maintenance problems unique to steel tanks include:
❏ A. Corrosion beneath the tank boot
❏ B. Corrosion beneath exterior plastic coatings
❏ C. Depleting oxygen content of air in the tank
❏ D. Tank valve seizing

14. The most likely cause of premature condemnation of an aluminum scuba cylinder is:
❏ A. Cracks in upper neck of tank
❏ B. Cracks where bottom joins side of tank
❏ C. Wall thickness reduction due to salt water corrosion
❏ D. All the above equally

15. Any cylinder that does not pass a formal visual cylinder inspection must:
❏ A. Pass a hydrostatic test before it may be returned to service
❏ B. Be permanently removed from service
❏ C. Be re-inspected by a senior inspector prior to removal from service
❏ D. Not be filled to more than 75% of the rated pressure

16. The minimum number of undamaged cylinder neck threads for proper mating to a scuba tank valve is:
❏ A. 5
❏ B. 7
❏ C. 9
❏ D. 13

VISUAL CYLINDER INSPECTIONS

A correct visual inspection is not a simple procedure when done properly. Insist that your tank be inspected by trained and certified inspectors. Ask to see their certification before the inspection and afterwards request a copy of the evaluation form completed during the inspection. A sample copy of an excellent cylinder inspection evaluation form may be obtained by sending a self-addressed, stamped envelope to Professional Scuba Inspectors, 6531 N.E. 198th St., Seattle, Washington 98155.

1. B. False. Federal regulations concerning the pressure testing of compressed gas cylinders do not pertain to personal scuba cylinders, however, universally-accepted unwritten regulations within the diving industry do require the hydrostatic testing of cylinders at least every five years. Self-regulation is needed and valuable.

2. B. False. Again, there are no federal regulations concerning annual visual cylinder inspections, but there is an industry-wide standard of practice to require them for the protection of both the owner and air station employees. A formal visual inspection is required as part of hydrostatic testing procedures.

3. B. Every three months. Cylinders used in rental programs and for training purposes require more frequent inspections than privately-owned tanks. Any cylinder should also be visually inspected whenever the owner suspects the tank may have been damaged in some way.

4. C. As often as steel tanks. Some divers think that since aluminum does not rust that visual inspections are not required as frequently, but they are incorrect. Several problems unique to alu- minum tanks, including their own form of corrosion, require them to be inspected annually as well.

5. B. False. Corrosion does occur in aluminum tanks. The words corrosion and rust mean essentially the same thing— both are the oxidation of metal. Traditionally, the word rust has been assigned to Ferric oxide (oxidation of iron). The word corrosion is commonly associated with non-ferris metals. Ferric oxidation (rust) is an accelerating process—once started, it tends to progress at an increasing rate. The oxidation of aluminum tends to be a decelerating process. As aluminum oxide corrosion develops, it creates a partial barrier to further corrosion and can provide some protection to the corroded surface. Serious corrosion of aluminum can and does occur under special circumstances, however.

6. A. Certified inspectors. Visual inspections should be performed only by inspectors who have been trained and certified to a nationally-recognized standard equivalent to that issued by Professional Scuba Inspectors (PSI).

7. B. 5. The main steps of a proper visual cylinder inspection include preparing the cylinder for evaluation, tank exterior inspection, tank interior inspection, tank threads and tank valve inspections. An evaluation form must be completed and a sticker affixed to the cylinder. All steps, including sub-steps, involved in a proper inspection total 18!

8. B. Prevent valve seizing. Galvanic action between the brass of a valve and the aluminum of a tank can result in seizure of the valve threads. A special dielectric compound applied to the valve threads helps prevent such seizures.

9. B. 350, 600. Aluminum scuba cylinders lose their tensile strength when overheated. Several explosions have occurred after finishes were baked onto aluminum tanks by uninformed owners. Don't risk using a cylinder if you suspect it has been exposed to intense heat, such as a fire.

10. A, B, C, D and perhaps E. All items must be removed from a cylinder for it to receive a proper inspection. Items to remove include the backpack, any protective netting, tank boot, tank valve, and stickers (only when they obscure tank damage).

11. C. 8. Specialized tools required to perform a proper cylinder inspection include a cylinder restraining device, a multi-bulb inspection light, a tumbler, a tank dryer, a magnifying mirror and light, probes, a pit reference gauge, and a torque wrench. Merely peering into a tank illuminated by light from a single bulb does not constitute a proper inspection.

12. A, B, C, D and E. New cylinders should be visually inspected. Items ranging from metal shavings to dead rodents have been discovered inside new tanks. An empty tank may contain moisture or water. Any tank subjected to unusual abuse should

also be inspected for dents, gouges, etc. by a certified technician. Tumbling and cleaning a tank may reveal pitting that was obscured by corrosion or contaminates.

13. A, B and C. Corrosion can take place between plastic protective coatings and the exterior of a tank, and may be difficult to detect. Boots on steel tanks also provide an area in which corrosion can thrive. Rusting inside a steel tank can definitely lower the percentage of oxygen of air in the cylinder. Valve seizing is not a problem with steel tanks.

14. A. Cracks in upper neck of tank. Aluminum tanks of a commonly-used alloy are subject to cracks in the neck and valve thread area. Special tools and knowledge are needed to detect these cracks, which are not uncommon. Be safe by allowing only by a trained and certified visual inspector to inspect your cylinder.

15. B. Be permanently removed from service. Be aware that if your cylinder does not meet the established standards for a visual inspection the tank must be removed from service. Removal is usually achieved by stamping out the codings on the neck of the tank and by rendering useless the valve threads in the neck of the tank.

16. C. 9. A new tank is required to have 13 undamaged threads for valve mating. If more than four of those 13 threads become damaged, the inspector is required to remove the cylinder from service.

WEIGHTING SYSTEMS

There are more types of weights and more weighting systems on the market today than ever before. What are the advantages and disadvantages of various configurations? How are you supposed to care for your weighting system? What are the important features of a weighting system? There may be more to weighting systems than you think.

1. The two basic types of weighting systems are:
   A. _____
   B. _____

2. The most desirable shape for weights is:
   ❏ A. Curved (hip weights)
   ❏ B. Rectangular
   ❏ C. Cylindrical (bullet-shaped)
   ❏ D. Round (shot)

3. The single most important feature of a weighting system is the _____ _____ (two words).

4. The second most important feature of a weight belt is _____ _____ (several words).

5. The amount of strap protruding from a buckled weight belt should not exceed:
   ❏ A. Three inches (7.6 cm)
   ❏ B. Six inches (15 cm)
   ❏ C. One foot (30 cm)
   ❏ D. 18 inches (46 cm)

6. Don a weight belt so it releases:
   ❏ A. With the wearer's right hand.
   ❏ B. With the wearer's left hand.
   ❏ C. With the wearer's dominant hand.
   ❏ D. Any of the above are correct.

7. The ideal positioning of weights on a weight belt is to have:
   ❏ A. The weights evenly distributed all the way around the belt.
   ❏ B. Two sections of weights with each section positioned directly on the side of the hip.
   ❏ C. Two sections of weights with each section positioned slightly behind each hip.
   ❏ D. Two sections of weights with each section positioned slightly forward of each hip.

8. Four items to inspect on a weight belt are:
   A. _____
   B. _____
   C. _____
   D. _____

9. Three advantages of integrated weighting systems are:
   A. _____
   B. _____
   C. _____

10. Two disadvantages of an integrated weighting system are:
   A. _____
   B. _____

11. It makes little or no difference what type or size of lead shot you use for a weighting system.
   ❏ A. True
   ❏ B. False

12. Correct weighting for a dive is the amount that allows you to:
   ❏ A. Float at the surface with a full breath and sink when you exhale
   ❏ B. Remain at depth with no air in your BC
   ❏ C. Hover at a depth of 10 feet with 300 psi of air in your scuba tank
   ❏ D. Barely sink with a full breath

13. It is a good idea to rinse your weights with clean, fresh water when you return home after diving.
   ❏ A. True
   ❏ B. False

14. Select the most correct statement.
   ❏ A. If "grey water" seeps from a weighting system, you should replace the weights in the system
   ❏ B. If you find weights underwater, you should remove them from the environment
   ❏ C. The personal pouring of weights is discouraged because lead is a hazardous material
   ❏ D. All the above statements are true

15. Three factors affecting the selection of a weighting system are:
   A. _____
   B. _____
   C. _____

WEIGHTING SYSTEMS

A:

Did the quiz increase your awareness about weight systems and the seriousness of lead in our environment? Did you have twelve or more correct answers? If so, congratulate yourself. You know your weighting systems and you have environmental awareness concerning lead. Do you have experience with both types of weighting systems? If not, you might consider trying both the unfamiliar type and a combination of both types. Your objectives are to achieve comfort and a perfect horizontal position when swimming underwater.

1. The two basic types of weighting systems are weight belts and integrated weighting systems. There are several versions of each type. Weights may be threaded onto, wrapped around, or placed inside a weight belt. Lead shot or packets of lead shot may be contained inside a hollow backpack or a weight belt or attached to a buoyancy compensator in an integrated system.

2. D. Round (shot). There is no direct physical contact with lead shot, which requires some type of container. When the shot is contained in pouches or inside a fabric belt, the weight is less likely to cause damage than hard weights when dropped. Shot-filled weight belts are more comfortable than belts with hard weights.

3. The single most important feature of a weighting system is the <u>quick</u> release. There is no weighting system feature more important than the means to release the weights in an emergency. The release may be a buckle, a pull cable, or a pin. The release must function easily and instantly.

4. The second most important feature of a weight belt is a <u>means</u> of <u>compensating</u> for suit compression. A wet suit compresses during descent. Without a means of compensation, a weight belt becomes loose at depth. The thicker the wet suit, the greater the problem. There are a variety of clever designs for compensation. The feature is more important than the design.

5. B. Six inches. Too much excess strap can make a weight belt difficult to release in an emergency. Allow two inches per weight for rectangular weights being threaded onto a belt. Rethread the buckle end of the belt to take up any excess webbing. The free end of the belt should not extend beyond the buckle more than six inches when the belt is in place and buckled.

6. A. With the wearer's right hand. A right-hand release is recommended as a standard configuration so a rescuer can quickly discard a weight belt in an emer-

gency. It can be easy to remove a belt when you know the way it releases, but when you don't know what to expect, delays can result.

7. D. Two sections of weights with each section positioned slightly forward of each hip. Keep the center section of a weight belt clear to avoid interference with the back pack or scuba tank. Wear equal amounts of weight on each side. The most stable swimming position is achieved with the weights just forward of the hips. Secure the weights with weight retainers.

8. Four items to inspect on a weight belt are (1) the quick release function, (2) the compensating function, (3) the free end (to be sure it is not frayed), and (4) the weight retainers (to make sure they are correctly positioned and are not broken).

9. Advantages of integrated weighting systems are improved trim (swimming angle), distribution of weight over a wider area, less strain on the lower back while swimming, and the elimination of the weight belt.

10. Disadvantages of an integrated weighting system are a heavier scuba unit and a higher center of gravity when wearing the unit out of water. With some systems, it can be difficult to change the amount of weight used.

11. False. It does make a difference what type or size of lead shot is used in a weighting system. Smaller shot (#6 or #8) allows more weight per volume than larger shot (#2 or #4). Hardened and/or coated weight causes less pollution than soft, uncoated weight.

12. C. Hover at a depth of 10 feet with 300 psi of air in your scuba tank. You can estimate buoyancy at the surface, but optimum weighting requires fine tuning to determine exactly how much weight you need for a safety decompression stop without a line to hold. Remember that buoyancy changes as you use air from your tank and that tanks of different sizes also affect your buoyancy.

13. B. False. It probably is <u>not</u> a good idea to rinse your weights with clean, fresh water when you return home after diving. Any lead residue rinsed away will contaminate the environment. Lead will not rust. Rinse the quick release, but avoid rinsing the lead. Pocket-type weight belts are good because you can remove the weights and rinse the belt.

14. D. All the statements are true. "Grey water" is a health hazard. If your weights are oxidizing, replace them with new, coated weights or hardened lead shot. Lead left in the underwater enviroment is a pollutant. Remove old weights and fishing sinkers and recycle the lead. Automobile battery service centers will accept the old lead. Handling lead or breathing the fumes from molten lead are hazardous activities. Lead is a hazardous material. Avoid handling raw lead. Wash your hands thoroughly as soon as possible if you do handle lead. Keep lead away from children because lead poisoning can retard their development.

15. Factors affecting the selection of a weighting system are your physical characteristics (short-waisted, waist size, back problems, etc.), the amount of weight you require, and the frequency of changes of weights. Two large weights locked securely to a weight belt may not be desirable if you have lower back problems, dive in both fresh and salt water, and use different types of exposure suits frequently. Other factors to consider are special features, fashion, and budget.

Bonus tips: All your weight does not need to be in one system. A weight belt combined with an integrated system can provide the advantages of both systems. Two weight belts—one with 30% of the weight worn above another one with 70% of the weight—can provide several advantages over a single belt.

SECTION TWO

□ □

Diving Environment

Diving Environment

Surroundings is the synonym for environment—the aggregate of all the external conditions and influences affecting the life and development of an organism. All the external conditions and influences we encounter while diving comprise the diving environment.

The diving environment varies. We dive in oceans, lakes, rivers, springs, and quarries; in calm, still waters and in rough, moving waters; in clean and turbid waters; in cold and warm waters; during different seasons of the year; at varying altitudes; around various underwater plants, animals, and formations; in different parts of the world; and at different times of day and night.

Our aquatic environment is a vast, wonderful playground for recreational diving. Because the diving environment varies greatly from place to place, we need area orientations. We need to know how local conditions affect our diving and how to deal with the environmental effects.

The general public does not see the underwater environment like divers see it. Divers have an obligation to help conserve natural resources and preserve them for future generations. We need to learn about the environment, care for it, and respect it. We need to help protect our underwater surroundings and encourage others to assist us in the effort.

The aquatic environment is too strong to fight. It helps to literally "go with the flow." When water moves, we need to know how to use the movement to our advantage and how to avoid the adverse effects of water movement.

The animals we encounter while diving rate high as attractions. A few animals are dangerous and can cause serious injury. There are keys to avoiding aquatic life injuries. We need to know the keys and then use them whenever and wherever we dive.

Section Two is a series of quizzes that test your understanding of conservation, terminology, fresh water diving, water movement, and area orientations. Learn more about the subject by taking an underwater environment specialty course. It is more fun to dive when you understand the physical and biological aspects of the aquatic environment.

AREA ORIENTATIONS

It is common for divers to travel to pursue their interests in the underwater world. What should you do to become acquainted with new areas. How can you obtain an orientation to diving in a different environment? Are orientations essential? Compare your thoughts and feelings with the information contained in the following quiz.

1. The primary objective of an area orientation is to:
❑ A. Make diving safer
❑ B. Make diving more enjoyable
❑ C. Learn where the best diving is
❑ D. Become familiar with dive hazards

2. A certification for diving qualifies a person to dive:
❑ A. In the same type water in which trained, e.g, fresh water
❑ B. In the type of conditions in which trained
❑ C. Anywhere under favorable conditions
❑ D. Only in the area in which training occurred

3. Benefits of area orientations include:
❑ A. Learning about good dive sites
❑ B. Learning to avoid potential problems
❑ C. Meeting potential dive buddies
❑ D. All the above

4. Additional area orientation benefits include:
❑ A. Familiarization with laws and regulations
❑ B. Getting answers to questions
❑ C. Learning about aquatic life
❑ D. All the above and more

5. Area orientations deal with environmental diving conditions, not diving techniques.
❑ A. True
❑ B. False

6. Which of the following activities is not a requirement for an area orientation dive?
❑ A. A check of fundamental diving skills
❑ B. Aquatic life identification
❑ C. Water movement familiarization
❑ D. Entry and exit procedures

7. An area orientation should consist of:
❑ A. A slide show, a briefing, a dive, and a debriefing
❑ B. A briefing, at least two dives, and a debriefing
❑ C. Two briefings, at least two dives, and two debriefings
❑ D. None of the above

8. Which of the following may be included as part of an area orientation dive?
❑ A. A basic diving skills review
❑ B. A buoyancy check
❑ C. Credit toward a diving environment specialty rating
❑ D. Any or all the above

9. Area orientation dives usually are:
❑ A. Provided as a community service by dive clubs
❑ B. Provided at no cost by local divers
❑ C. A professional service
❑ D. Combined with local training dives

10. It is best to arrange area orientation dives in advance, with or through:
❑ A. Diver training organizations
❑ B. Dive clubs
❑ C. Dive stores or resorts
❑ D. Dive instructors

11. Arrange in order of preference from most desirable to least desirable the following orientation means:
❑ A. Local divers
❑ B. A dive instructor
❑ C. A professional dive guide
❑ D. Books

12. Which of the following is of greatest importance during an area orientation?
❑ A. Exposure factors (sun, cold, etc.)
❑ B. Hazardous life
❑ C. Area hazards
❑ D. Water movement

13. You need area orientations until achieving the rating of:
❑ A. Advanced scuba diver
❑ B. Divemaster
❑ C. Instructor
❑ D. None of the above

14. Complete: When I travel to an area I have not dived previously, I _____ get a formal orientation to diving in that area.
❑ A. Always
❑ B. Usually
❑ C. Seldom
❑ D. Never

15. The more experience a diver has, the less value the area orientation dives have.
❑ A. True
❑ B. False

AREA ORIENTATIONS

Orientation dives are not widely advertised nor highly promoted, but they are available upon request. If you scored well, congratulations. If you didn't do well, I hope you are impressed with the value of orientations. Do yourself and your dive buddy a favor on your next trip by making advance reservations for a professional orientation. Your trip will be more rewarding and enjoyable.

1. A. Make diving safer. All the answers are correct, but A is the most correct. When you minimize risk, you increase enjoyment because you feel more confident and at ease. Enjoyment is the goal. Safety is a means to achieve your goal.

2. D. Only in the area in which training occurred. B is not a good choice because conditions may appear similar from area to area, but there can be significant differences. While you may be able to dive in many areas, you are not necessarily qualified to dive in them.

3. D. All the above. There are positive reasons for getting orientations as well as the serious ones such as safety. You can frequently meet others who are visiting an area and learn the best locations for diving.

4. D. All the above plus more. It should be obvious that orientations are not only needed, but valuable. You could have an unpleasant experience if you do not have an orientation. You are likely to have fun and avoid problems if you do have one.

5. B. False. Area orientations deal with diving techniques needed in an area owing to environmental conditions. Good examples are entry and exit techniques, which vary greatly from one place to another.

6. A. A check of fundamental diving skills. While a skills check may be included in an orientation dive, a check is not required and often not included. Request refresher training if it has been awhile since your last dive.

7. D. None of the above. You can give yourself credit if you chose C, however. The idea is that one dive is not enough. You need time to digest the experience, get answers to questions, and apply what you learned from the first supervised dive. The more supervised dives you make, the better.

8. D. Any or all the above. You can arrange to include refresher training as part of your dive, but the guide needs to be an instructor. A buoyancy check should be included if there is any change in the equipment you use or in the water density. Since you are learning about the environment, you can get credit toward and underwater environment specialty rating.

9. C. A professional service. A proper orientation dive requires the time of a professional, who should be compensated for services. Use a professional to get the best possible service. Budget for area orientations when you plan a trip. The cost usually is quite reasonable.

10. C. Dive stores or resorts. Dive businesses are the best option because they offer professional services on a regular basis. Training organizations can refer you to facilities.

11. C, B, A, D. A professional dive guide is better for orientations than in a instructor because the guide usually has more experience diving the local sites. Area instructors are an excellent alternative. Any orientation is better than none at all, but seek professional services first.

12. D. Water movement. Divers are often concerned with hazards such as dangerous life forms and underwater obstacles, but currents and surf conditions pose more serious problems. Ask questions concerning water movement when you dive in a new area.

13. D. None of the above. There is no level of training at which an orientation is no longer required. After diving the world over, an instructor still needs to know what to look out for in a new area.

14. A, B. Give yourself two points if you answered A, one if you answered B, and none if you answered C or D. Orientation dives are not just a good idea, they are highly desirable.

15. B. False. The more experienced you become the more apparent the value of orientations. Seasoned divers develop respect for varying environments and are not bashful about asking questions concerning local procedures.

CONSERVATION

Conservation is everyone's business. Divers are particularly involved with conservation because they see what happens when it isn't practiced. What should be done? See if you are aware of our problems and what to do about them. Select the best choice for each question.

1. Fish and game officials define conservation as:
- A. Abstaining from use of the resources
- B. Obtaining the maximum yield from the resources
- C. Wise use of the resources
- D. None of the above

2. The pollution most detrimental to the diving environment is:
- A. Oil
- B. Litter
- C. Sewage
- D. Thermal

3. The litter that has the worst effect in the dive environment is/are:
- A. Plastic bags
- B. Cans and bottles
- C. Food
- D. Paper

4. Fish with DDT usually have the substance in their:
- A. Fat
- B. Liver
- C. Meat only
- D. Entire body

5. Phosphates from non-biodegradable detergents can cause which of the following effects in the diving environment?
- A. Algae blooms
- B. Area oxygen depletion
- C. Large fish kills
- D. All the above

6. Which of the following items has the greatest effect on fish populations?
- A. Spearfishing
- B. Commercial fishing
- C. Sewage and industrial wastes
- D. Thermal pollution

7. Which of the following actions has the greatest positive effect on aquatic resources?
- A. Cessation of sewage and industrial waste dumping
- B. Banning game taking by recreational and commercial interests
- C. Ceasing use of non-biodegradable detergents and DDT
- D. Preventing offshore oil development and hydroelectric thermal pollution

8. Fish and game laws usually are based on a ____% natural resource yield percentage.
- A. 15
- B. 10
- C. 5
- D. 3

9. Which of the following practices is most detrimental to aquatic resource management?
- A. Taking undersized game
- B. Taking game out of season
- C. Taking more than the legal limit
- D. All are equally detrimental

10. Which of the following diver practices is <u>not</u> harmful to the aquatic environment?
- A. Removal of living creatures
- B. Physical contact with reefs
- C. Handling and feeding animals
- D. All the practices are harmful

11. Responsible underwater hunters take what type game?
- A. Only the largest animals
- B. Mature animals of moderate size
- C. The smallest legal-size animals
- D. Any and all of the above

12. Which of the following diver practices does <u>not</u> help conserve aquatic life?
- A. Anchoring boats away from reefs
- B. Retrieving bottles and cans found while diving
- C. Retrieving monofilament, lead, and stainless steel leaders
- D. Reporting lost or discarded fishing nets and traps

13. Which of the following groups helps preserve the aquatic environment?
- A. Center for Marine Conservation
- B. Project Reefkeeper
- C. Oceanic Society
- D. All the above

14. The single, most significant conservation action a diver can take is to:
- A. Abstain from taking any living organism
- B. Report polluters
- C. Educate non-divers about the effects of pollution
- D. Support stricter fish and game regulations

CONSERVATION

A:

Yes, conservation is everyone's business, but aquatic conservation is divers' business because we can see what the vast majority of people can't. We must be responsible divers. We must do all we can to educate others. We must support aquatic conservation organizations. We must avoid all possible personal pollution and exhort others to do likewise. Divers are a small percentage of the population, but collectively we can have a positive effect on our environment. Please do your part.

1. C. Wise use of the resources. Fish and game commissions and the Department of Fisheries define conservation as, "The protection, management, and wise use of natural resources." The objective of conservation is to determine the sustained yield our resources will bear and protect the resources so sustained yield will be possible. The issue of the day should be the protection of our resources from pollution, not the methods used to take the yield.

2. C. Sewage. A single, major city dumps nearly a million gallons of sewage into our waters daily. The process of bacterial action to break down the sewage consumes vast quantities of oxygen. The oxygen depletion kills fish and aquatic life. Heavy metals and industrial effluents in sewage poison animals and inhibit reproductive ability. Improved sewage treatment should be our major concern.

3. A. Plastic bags. While unsightly and hazardous, cans and bottles provide homes for many creatures. Tossing bottles and cans into the water is not encouraged, but their effect is not as harmful as many people believe it is. Food and paper are unsightly, but are biodegradable. Litter is not condonable. Non-biodegradable materials, including plastic bags and foam cups, are bad for the aquatic environment. Animals mistake the objects for food, eat them, and die. Plastic items also entangle and trap or choke animals. Keep the diving environment free from plastic and Styrofoam.

4. A. Fat. The food chain passes DDT from animal to animal. Since people are at the top of the chain, we ingest residual chemicals. Avoid DDT in fish by trimming the fat, which contains most of the pesticide. Trim the fatty sections along the belly and beneath the dorsal fin. Predatory fish usually contain larger amounts of DDT than fish with less voracious appetites.

5. D. All the above. Phosphates stimulate algae growth, which would seem to create oxygen. As the algae dies, decomposition uses oxygen and produces hydrogen sulfide, which, in turn, causes a reaction that uses more oxygen. The overall effect is the suffocation of life from a lack of oxygen. Phosphates can cause rapid plant growth, which can seriously clog waterways. Always use low-phosphate detergents.

6. C. Sewage and industrial wastes. Contrary to what many believe, our greatest problem is not what people take or how it is taken. Using our waters as dump sites and septic tanks destroys many times more life than commercial fishing and recreational diving. The resource yield will increase when we stop sewage and industrial waste pollution.

7. A. Cessation of sewage and industrial waste dumping. I want to further emphasize our most serious problem. Oil pollution, which receives a great deal of publicity, is not nearly as detrimental to life as invisible, silent poisons from commercial dumping. Phosphates and thermal pollution are harmful, but their effect is a small fraction of the damage caused by sewage, municipal wastes, and industrial effluents.

8. B. 10. If protected, a given resource should permit a sustained 10% yield. Indiscriminate violation of regulations designed to manage and protect the resources combined with pollution seriously deteriorates the base that is supposed to sustain the yield. We must control pollution and stop fish and game regulation violations.

9. D. All are equally detrimental. States conduct expensive studies to determine resource extent, then base resource management on the existing base. If greed practices alter the base—the breeding stock and the juveniles of a species—resource management becomes invalid. Game laws and regulations are supposed to permit the continued taking of game for food, not the prevention of taking. Fish and game violations reduce future resources.

10. D. All the practices are harmful. You can't conserve aquatic life by killing it. Taking living organisms must be done responsibly. Take only what you need and from areas that have the resource to sustain a yield. Control buoyancy and avoid contact with the bottom and with reefs and structures that contain living creatures. Coral is delicate and grows slowly. Handling and feeding animals can cause their death.

11. B. Mature animals of moderate size. Trophy hunters take the fittest and strongest of the breed. Quantity hunters often take animals that have not had the opportunity to reproduce. Responsible hunters go to remote areas where game is plentiful, take only what they can eat, and take mature animals. Remember the objective of conservation is to sustain a yield.

12. B. Retrieving bottles and cans found while diving. Unless you encounter a broken bottle in shallow water, leave bottles and cans alone. The containers are homes for many small animals. Do not add to unsightly litter by using our waters as disposal sites for bottles and cans, however.

13. D. All the above. Do you belong to or contribute to any conservation organizations? You can make a difference by organizing fund-raising events. "Clean-up" dives to help the environment can be harmful if you do not know what you are doing. Seek assistance from an environmental organization, then coordinate with the organization to help them raise funds so they can increase public awareness.

14. C. Educate non-divers about the effects of pollution, or B. Report polluters. We can't all be environmental inspectors, but we can help everyone we know understand the horrific problems pollution poses. If you become aware of a pollution source, do all you can to stop it. More importantly, however, do all you can to convince your friends that we must stop polluting our waters before it is too late for the life that remains to recover.

ENVIRONMENTAL TERMINOLOGY

Q:

Divers need underwater environment knowledge. Much of what you need to know about the diving environment is within the terms used to describe various effects and conditions. See how much you know about the freshwater and saltwater environments by matching the 39 terms and definitions of this quiz. Use each term only once.

Terms:

A. Algae
B. Backrush
C. Bloom
D. Ciguatera
E. Coriolis
F. Crest
G. Drift
H. Ebb
I. Epilimnion
J. Fetch
K. Flood
L. Halocline
M. Hypolimnion
N. Isotherm
O. Longshore
P. Neap
Q. Overturn
R. Period
S. Phytoplankton
T. Plunging
U. Rip
V. Seiche
W. Set
X. Sets
Y. Slack water
Z. Spilling
AA. Spring
BB. Surf
CC. Surge
DD. Swash
EE. Swells
FF. Tetrodotoxin
GG. Thermocline
HH. Trough
II. Tsunami
JJ. Turbidity
KK. Upwelling
LL. Wavelength
MM. Zooplankton

Definitions:

1. The highest point of a wave:_____
2. The speed of a current:_____
3. The movement of water away from land caused by a falling tide:_____
4. The distance over which the wind blows at sea:_____
5. The movement of water toward land during a rising tide:_____
6. An abrupt transition between waters of differing salinities:_____
7. Lower than normal tides:_____
8. The length of time for two crests to pass a fixed point:_____
9. A strong current moving away from shore through a narrow opening:_____
10. The oscillating movement of a closed body of water:_____
11. The direction of a current:_____
12. Higher than normal tides:_____
13. The periodic combining of two wave trains:_____
14. The back-and-forth motion underwater caused by passing waves:_____
15. The term for the regular action of waves in deep water as they move away from generating winds:_____
16. The term for breaking waves releasing energy in shallow water:_____
17. An abrupt transition between waters of differing temperatures:_____
18. The low point between two waves:_____
19. Giant waves caused by underwater earthquakes:_____
20. The upward movement of water caused by wind:_____
21. The horizontal distance between adjacent crests or troughs of a wave:_____
22. Non-flowering aquatic plants:_____
23. The most common type of fish poisoning:_____
24. Waters of equal temperature:_____
25. The deflecting effect of winds and currents caused by the rotation of the earth:_____
26. The layer of water above the thermocline:_____
27. The uprush of water on the face of a beach:_____
28. The wind-caused circulation of a closed body of water:_____
29. Reduced visibility caused by suspended sediment:_____
30. Poor visibility caused by overpopulation of algae or plankton:_____
31. Algae that use sunlight to produce carbohydrates:_____
32. The type of breaker that peaks quickly and breaks suddenly:_____
33. The brief period at high tide and low tide during which there is no water movement:_____
34. Animal plankton that generally feed on phytoplankton:_____
35. The type of breaker that forms far from shore and continues to break to the beach:_____
36. A current flowing parallel to shore in the surf zone:_____
37. The return flow of water from the face of a beach:_____
38. The most dangerous of all fish poisonings and found in pufferfish:_____
39. The layer of water below the thermocline:_____

ENVIRONMENTAL TERMINOLOGY

A:

Diving environment knowledge is good, but the wise application of knowledge is better. Apply what you know to minimize environmental risks. If you are unfamiliar with many of the quiz terms, consider taking an advanced scuba course. You will learn about the environment and much more. I believe all scuba divers should complete an advanced scuba diving course.

1. The highest point of a wave is its crest (F).

2. The speed of a current is its drift (G).

3. The movement of water away from land caused by a falling tide is an ebb (H).

4. The distance over which the wind blows at sea is the fetch (J).

5. The movement of water toward land during a rising tide is a flood (K).

6. An abrupt transition between waters of differing salinities is a halocline (L).

7. Lower than normal tides are neap (P) tides.

8. The length of time for two crests to pass a fixed point is the period (R) of a wave.

9. A strong current moving away from shore through a narrow opening is a rip (U) current.

10. The oscillating movement of a closed body of water is a seiche (V).

11. The direction of a current is its set (W).

12. Higher than normal tides are spring (AA) tides.

13. The periodic combining to two wave trains forms sets (X) of waves.

14. The back-and-forth motion under water caused by passing waves is surge (CC).

15. The term for the regular action of waves in deep water as they move away from generating winds is swells (EE).

16. The term for breaking waves releasing energy in shallow water is surf (BB).

17. An abrupt transition between waters of differing temperatures is a thermocline (GG).

18. The low point between two waves is a trough (HH).

19. Giant waves caused by underwater earthquakes are Tsunami (II).

20. The upward movement of water caused by wind is upwelling (KK).

21. The horizontal distance between adjacent crests or troughs of a wave is a wavelength (LL).

22. Non-flowering aquatic plants are algae (A).

23. The most common type of fish poisoning is ciguatera (D).

24. Waters of equal temperature are an isotherm (N).

25. The deflecting of winds and currents caused by the rotation of the earth is the Coriolis (E) effect.

26. The layer of water above the thermocline is the epilimnion (I).

27. The uprush of water on the face of a beach is swash (DD).

28. The wind-caused circulation of a closed body of water is an overturn (Q).

29. Reduced visibility caused by suspended sediment is turbidity (JJ).

30. Poor visibility caused by overpopulation of algae or plankton is a bloom (C).

31. Algae that use sunlight to produce carbohydrates are phytoplankton (S).

32. The type of breaker that peaks quickly and breaks suddenly is a plunging (T) breaker.

33. The brief period at high tide and low tide during which there is no water movement is slack water (Y).

34. Animal plankton that generally feed on phytoplankton are zooplankton (MM).

35. The type of breaker that breaks far from shore and continues to break to the beach is a spilling (Z) breaker.

36. A current flowing parallel to shore in the surf zone is a longshore (O) current.

37. The return flow of water from the face of a beach is backrush (B).

38. The most dangerous of all fish poisonings and found in pufferfish is tetrodotoxin (FF).

39. The layer of water below the thermocline is the hypolimnion (M).

Scoring:
  28-31 = Diver level
  32-35 = Advanced level
  36-39 = Instructor level

FRESHWATER DIVING

Q:

There is good diving in lakes, rivers, quarries, and springs. There is much more written about ocean diving than freshwater diving. The following questions test your freshwater diving knowledge.

1. During an initial freshwater dive an ocean diver should:
- ❏ A. Easily handle the dive conditions
- ❏ B. Receive an orientation to the local environment
- ❏ C. Dive only with a local dive instructor
- ❏ D. Limit depth to 30 feet (10 m) or less

2. Freshwater dive activities are limited to:
- ❏ A. Wreck and ice diving
- ❏ B. Spearfishing and ice diving
- ❏ C. All general underwater activities
- ❏ D. None of the above

3. Typical freshwater dive conditions in temperate zones are:
- ❏ A. Cold, clear water
- ❏ B. Warm, turbid water
- ❏ C. Cold, turbid water
- ❏ D. Warm, clear water

4. The principal factors affecting freshwater visibility are:
- ❏ A. Pollution and plankton
- ❏ B. Silt and plankton
- ❏ C. Algae and silt
- ❏ D. Pollution and algae

5. Using the same equipment, which of the following weighting adjustments must an ocean diver make for neutral buoyancy in freshwater?
- ❏ A. Add weight equal to 2.5% of the total weight of the diver and equipment
- ❏ B. Subtract weight equal to 2.5% of the total weight of the diver and equipment
- ❏ C. Make no weighing changes
- ❏ D. Subtract weight equal to 2.5% of the total weight of the diver, excluding the equipment

6. To use the U. S. Navy Dive Tables for freshwater diving:
- ❏ A. Add 3% of the depth to the apparent depth
- ❏ B. Subtract 3% of the depth from the apparent depth
- ❏ C. Use the apparent depth for dive planning
- ❏ D. Decrease time limits by 3%

7. An abrupt change in water temperature with depth in freshwater lakes is:
- ❏ A. Generally predictable
- ❏ B. Completely predictable
- ❏ C. Seldom encountered
- ❏ D. Always encountered

8. You would normally encounter fish in freshwater lakes:
- ❏ A. In deep water during the summer and in shallower water in the spring and fall
- ❏ B. In shallow water during the summer and in deeper water in the spring and fall
- ❏ C. At all levels during all seasons
- ❏ D. Below the thermocline

9. When excessive nutrients enter a body of freshwater and cause increased plant growth, the animal life in the area usually:
- ❏ A. Dies
- ❏ B. Thrives
- ❏ C. Hibernates
- ❏ D. Is unaffected

10. Wood and metal objects submerged in freshwater deteriorate at:
- ❏ A. The same rate as those submerged in saltwater
- ❏ B. A faster rate than those submerged in saltwater
- ❏ C. A slower rate than those submerged in saltwater
- ❏ D. A rate dependent upon the specific gravity of the material

11. The most troublesome freshwater diving hazard during entries is:
- ❏ A. Waves and drop-offs
- ❏ B. Mud and debris
- ❏ C. Aquatic animals
- ❏ D. Boat traffic

12. When diving in temperate freshwater lakes, divers should be most concerned about:
- ❏ A. Sediment and silt
- ❏ B. Hydrogen sulfide
- ❏ C. Boat traffic
- ❏ D. Cold

13. Cold surface water in a lake during summer months is most likely the result of:
- ❏ A. Strong offshore winds
- ❏ B. Strong onshore winds
- ❏ C. Cold water flowing into the lake
- ❏ D. An extended period of overcast days

14. Annual changes in lakes can best be summarized as:
- ❏ A. Heating and stratifying plus cooling and mixing
- ❏ B. Cooling and stratifying plus heating and mixing
- ❏ C. Minimal owing to thermal stratification
- ❏ D. Unpredictable

15. Select the incorrect statement concerning freshwater dives at altitudes above 1,000 feet (300 m):
- ❏ A. You must convert the apparent depth to an equivalent sea level depth
- ❏ B. You must increase the rate of ascent as altitude increases
- ❏ C. Decompression stop depths are deeper at altitude than at sea level
- ❏ D. An out-of-breath diver who surfaces could lose consciousness

FRESHWATER DIVING

A:

Did you encounter a few surprises in the quiz? Do you have a new freshwater diving perspective? Inland divers should score well and ocean divers should realize there is much more to freshwater diving than a lack of salt. There is more to diving in freshwater than many divers believe. Give it a try, but get an orientation first.

1. B. Receive an orientation to the local environment. There are many physical and biological differences between freshwater and saltwater sites. When diving in any new environment, maximize safety with a formal orientation. A local dive guide, instructor, or experienced diver can provide the orientation.

2. C. All general underwater activities. Freshwater divers, in addition to diving under ice and on excellent wrecks, engage in underwater photography, spearfishing, treasure hunting, collecting, and nearly all underwater activities. Contrary to what many divers think, there are numerous things to interest freshwater divers.

3. C. Cold, turbid water. When you dive in fresh water you usually have to contend with limited visibility and cold water. In addition, you may encounter swift currents in rivers. Altitude poses special problems. Freshwater diving can demand complex skills, procedures, and knowledge.

4. C. Algae and silt. Algae blooms reduce visibility, especially in shallow water. Fine silt on the bottom can instantly diminish visibility when disturbed. Pollution can cause or contribute to reduced visibility, but divers usually avoid polluted dive sites.

5. B. Subtract weight equal to 2.5% of the total weight of the diver and equipment. Freshwater weighs about 1.6 pounds per cubic foot less than saltwater. The density difference between salt and freshwater is about 2.5% (64.0 - 62.4 = 1.6. 1.6/64 = .025). The diver displaces the same amount of freshwater as saltwater, so the diver needs less weight. The amount to remove is a percentage of the total weight—diver and equipment.

6. C. Use the apparent depth for dive planning. Although the Navy tables are based on saltwater and freshwater is 3% less dense than saltwater, the difference amounts to only 3 feet for a 100 foot dive. Most depth gauges have a error factor equal to or greater than the density difference. Don't risk DCS by altering your dive schedule for freshwater.

7. A. Generally predictable. An abrupt change in temperature with increasing depth—a thermocline—varies with the season of the year. Strong winds can cause a lake to overturn, but seasonal thermoclines are predictable. Expect thermoclines in freshwater lakes.

8. A. In deep water during the summer and in shallower water in the spring and fall. Fish remain within narrow temperature ranges that change with depth according to the time of year. Fish prefer the colder, deeper waters of lakes in the summer and approach the surface only when the surface temperature lowers.

9. A. Dies. Chemicals and fertilizers finding their way into lakes and ponds cause eutrophication, a process that stimulates plant growth. The plants die, decay, and produce a lethal gas. Do all you can to discourage water pollution. Don't be a polluter. Avoid detergents containing phosphates.

10. C. A slower rate than those submerged in saltwater. Freshwater preserves objects much better than saltwater. Hunting for artifacts is an exciting and rewarding freshwater diving activity. Items hundreds of years old have been recovered in nearly their original condition.

11. B. Mud and debris. Be careful about contact with the bottom. If you sink into mud, you may lose your fin when trying to pull your foot out. You might sink onto an object that could cut you or give you a puncture wound. Other concerns are slippery areas, fishing line and lures, and insects. An orientation to freshwater diving is important.

12. D. Cold. In some lakes boating activity is so great divers are afraid to surface. Cottonmouth snakes, snapping turtles, alligators, catfish, and muskrats are potentially dangerous freshwater animals. No hazard is as great as silent, insidious cold, which is the number one stressor in diving. Guard against heat loss beneath the thermoclines.

13. A. Strong offshore winds. A wind of sufficient velocity and duration blowing offshore causes surface water to flow away from shore. Colder water flows up from the bottom to replace the water blown away from shore. When a wind persists, the entire water column can reach a cold isothermic condition, even during summer months.

14. A. Heating and stratifying plus cooling and mixing. Spring and early summer temperatures warm surface water until it warms faster than it can mix. The water stratifies and forms a thermocline until fall, which cools the surface water. Mixing occurs until the surface water is colder than the water at the bottom. Following another stratification and a winter reverse thermocline, the cycle repeats itself in the spring.

15. B. You must increase the rate of ascent as altitude increases. False. The rate of ascent decreases approximately two feet for each 1,000 feet of altitude. Altitude diving, like ice diving, is a specialty that requires training to minimize the risk of injury.

RIVER DIVING

Diving in rivers can be exciting and fun. The best freshwater dives I have made have been in rivers. Moving water can pose special problems, however. You need to be aware of the hazards of and the established practices for river diving if you intend to dive in them. See how familiar you are with river diving.

1. It is best to dive against the current in a river.
❏ A. True
❏ B. False

2. Always have a buddy within touching distance when river diving.
❏ A. True
❏ B. False

3. River currents are strongest at the surface and on the outside of a bend.
❏ A. True
❏ B. False

4. Currents in rivers tend to flow straight down the river bed.
❏ A. True
❏ B. False

5. There are special dive equipment requirements for river diving.
❏ A. True
❏ B. False

6. Add extra weight to your weighting system when you dive in a river.
❏ A. True
❏ B. False

7. If you are carried toward a potential hazard while river diving, swim at a right angle to the object so you can avoid it.
❏ A. True
❏ B. False

8. If you are pulled downward by a current while river diving, your only option is to ride it out.
❏ A. True
❏ B. False

9. Searches in rivers are successful more frequently than searches in other bodies of water.
❏ A. True
❏ B. False

10. Diving conditions in rivers remain fairly constant compared to other bodies of water.
❏ A. True
❏ B. False

11. If you are carried toward a large, round boulder in a river, you are in danger of hitting the boulder.
❏ A. True
❏ B. False

12. The right and left banks of a river are relative to the downstream course of the river.
❏ A. True
❏ B. False

13. If you drift down a river in a strong current, it is OK to grab something to stop as long as your buddy does likewise.
❏ A. True
❏ B. False

14. List ten potential hazards you might encounter while river diving:
    A. _____
    B. _____
    C. _____
    D. _____
    E. _____
    F. _____
    G. _____
    H. _____
    I. _____
    J. _____

15. There is no formal, sanctioned training available for river diving.
❏ A. True
❏ B. False

RIVER DIVING

I hope you realize that river diving definitely requires special training. The activity can be exciting and rewarding. Dive in rivers only under the right circumstances. If you have not dived the lower Colorado or another clear, interesting river, give it a try after you complete the training. With proper training, preparation, equipment, orientation, and support, river diving is pure fun.

1. B. False. Working against the current can lead to exhaustion. Although you are supposed to begin dives against the current generally, the rule does not apply when the current is strong. Strong river currents orient obstructions so they point downstream. You will run directly into obstructions by going upstream.

2. B. False. A diver should be tended on a line when the water is turbid, which is the case in most rivers. In addition to a tender, a standby diver should be present and ready to enter the water to lend assistance. River diving requires special training.

3. A. True. Water in rivers flows in layers, which move at different velocities at different depths. The closer to the bottom, the slower the flow. The term for layered water movement is laminar flow. Water accelerates around the outside of river bends. The current on bends causes undercutting of the bank. River diving requires specialized knowledge as well as skills.

4. B. False. The banks of the river, the river bed, and objects within the river set up counter currents and eddies, which change frequently. While the overall trend is for water to move downstream, the water moves in a zig-zag fashion. Divers need to know that water can flow across a river and even opposite to the main flow.

5. A. True. A river diver should be tended and wear a special harness for line attachement. A helmet and knee and elbow pads are recommended. A redundant scuba unit is a good idea.

6. B. False. Extra weight is helpful when diving in currents, but do not add it to your weighting system. Use a weighted line or hand-hold the extra weights.

7. B. False. If you swim at right angles, you increase your cross-sectional area and will be carried toward the object faster. You have a better chance of avoiding an object if you swim away at a 45 degree angle.

8. B. False. Often it is best to ride out a down-running river current, but if the current is not too strong and you can use a leverage point, you may be able to push off at an angle, catch an outside current, and avoid being pulled down.

9. B. False. Although your search is in a confined area, currents, obstructions, and poor visibility cause river searches to have poor success rates when compared to other bodies of water.

10. B. False. Rivers are especially prone to seasonal changes and extremely unpredictable. Knowledge from local, experienced divers is essential for safety when diving in rivers.

11. B. False. When the water flows against an object, such as a boulder, the water generates a back pressure that diverts oncoming water around the object. Water will carry you around a round boulder. The cushioning effect does not occur with pointed rocks or large, flat surfaces.

12. A. True. The right bank of a river is the bank on the right side when you face downstream.

13. B. False. If you grab an object in a strong current, there is a good chance that your mask will be swept away. It is best to just "go with the flow."

14. Potential river hazards include trees, tree limbs, wire, fishing line, fishing hooks, fishing lures, fishing nets, log jams, debris, cars, rapids, sucking holes, whirlpools, counter currents, strong currents, and poor visibility.

15. B. False. More than one diver training organization allows instructors to obtain sanctioning for specialties such as river diving or swift water diving. Limited visibility training also is available and is helpful for those who need or want to dive in rivers.

SURF PASSAGES

Q:

Surf surprises many divers the first time they pass through it to go diving. Divers with surf experience often are surprised at the difference in technique required at new dive sites. Test your knowledge of the special skill of surf passage.

1. The surf zone is the area:
- ❑ A. Where the waves are breaking
- ❑ B. From where waves begin to break to the shore
- ❑ C. Extending from a depth of two feet to a depth of ten feet
- ❑ D. From where waves begin to break and the backrush ends

2. During surf passages your buoyancy compensator should be:
- ❑ A. Deflated
- ❑ B. Partially inflated
- ❑ C. Half inflated
- ❑ D. Removed

3. Immediately after a wave breaks, your buoyancy in surf is _____ it was before the wave broke.
- ❑ A. Greater than
- ❑ B. Less than
- ❑ C. The same as
- ❑ D. Any of the above

4. During surf passages you should have your scuba regulator:
- ❑ A. In your mouth
- ❑ B. In your right hand
- ❑ C. Lying on your right shoulder
- ❑ D. Inside your BC pocket

5. You should hold your mask firmly on your face:
- ❑ A. With your fingers spread to permit vision
- ❑ B. At all times while in the surf zone
- ❑ C. Until clear of the water when exiting
- ❑ D. All the above

6. During surf entries a surface float should be:
- ❑ A. Beneath you
- ❑ B. Towed
- ❑ C. Pushed
- ❑ D. Held aloft

7. During surf exits a surface float should be:
- ❑ A. Beneath you
- ❑ B. Towed
- ❑ C. Pushed
- ❑ D. Held aloft

8. You usually should lie down and begin swimming during surf exits when the water is:
- ❑ A. Knee deep
- ❑ B. Thigh deep
- ❑ C. Waist deep
- ❑ D. Chest deep

9. The optimum standing position for a diver entering surf is:
- ❑ A. Facing the surf
- ❑ B. Facing away from the surf
- ❑ C. Sideways to the surf
- ❑ D. None of the above

10. During surf entries and exits you should:
- ❑ A. Touch the bottom as little as possible
- ❑ B. Shuffle your feet along the bottom
- ❑ C. Keep you feet about shoulder width when standing
- ❑ D. All the above

11. Select the most difficult surf passage:
- ❑ A. An entry through rolling breakers
- ❑ B. An exit through rolling breakers
- ❑ C. An exit through plunging breakers
- ❑ D. An entry through plunging breakers

12. Crawling is recommended:
- ❑ A. For all surf exits
- ❑ B. For steep surf exits
- ❑ C. For those inexperienced in surf exits
- ❑ D. Whenever standing exits are difficult

13. Select the false statement:
- ❑ A. Surf exits can be more difficult than entries
- ❑ B. Divers should not stop in the surf zone
- ❑ C. Don fins before all surf entries
- ❑ D. Hold spearguns parallel to shore during surf exits

14. There are no special equipment considerations for diving in surf.
- ❑ A. True
- ❑ B. False

15. Select the true statement:
- ❑ A. Duck beneath incoming waves when exiting from surf
- ❑ B. Measure the time between waves before you attempt a surf entry
- ❑ C. Watch incoming waves during entries, but not during exits
- ❑ D. All the above statements are false

SURF PASSAGES

A:

Is there more to surf passages than you expected? Surf diving is a specialty that definitely requires training. If you have never dived through surf, do not attempt it without training. If you have surf experience, be sure to get an orientation to any new condition. Do not dive when the surf is large. The dive will be poor and the hazards posed by the large surf are great.

1. B. From where waves begin to break to the shore. The surf zone, also called the surf line, can be narrow on steep beaches or wide on shallow, sloping beaches. It is important to be familiar with surf terminology. You need to know what it means when instructed not to stop in the surf zone.

2. A. or B. Deflated or partially inflated. During entries you should swim beneath waves. During exits you must avoid riding the tops of breaking waves or you could go "over the falls." If properly weighted for diving (neutral), you should not need to inflate your BC for a surf passage.

3. B. Less than. A breaking wave aerates water, making the water less dense. Buoyancy is related to the weight of the water displaced, so buoyancy decreases when the water you displace weighs less. The buoyancy reduction duration is only a few seconds, but it can be alarming to the unsuspecting.

4. A. In your mouth. There are good reasons for keeping your regulator in your mouth, not the least of which is to keep sand out of the device. Surf suspends a great deal of sand in the water. It is easier to breathe from your regulator than your snorkel and you are less likely to choke. The surf zone is no place to have a choking fit.

5. D. All the above. A lost mask in surf is extremely difficult to locate. Develop the habit of holding your mask at all times while in the surf zone. Lines to prevent loss can be dangerous. I discourage mask attachment. Wear your mask strap lower than normal on the back of your head so your mask will fall around your neck instead of slipping off your head.

6. B. Towed. You should duck beneath incoming waves during entries, so you should tow your float. Be prepared for a strong tug after a wave passes you and strikes your float. Do not tie the line to yourself. Do keep the line fairly short. Have your dive flag well secured to the float or the surf will strip it from its staff.

7. C. Pushed. When you approach shore in surf, hold the float by its tow line and push it ahead. When a wave catches the float, hold the line, but not the float. If necessary, you can release the float and allow it to surf to shore. Avoid the temptation to ride the float. Do not attempt surfing exits.

8. A. Knee deep. The less time you are upright in the surf zone, the better. Start swimming as soon as possible. If you are lying down, you can't fall down. Pull yourself along with your hands whenever possible. Use short kick strokes until you reach deeper water. You will need buoyancy for shallow, rocky areas. Surf passages over rocks requires special training.

9. C. Sideways to the surf. In some areas and under certain conditions, it is appropriate to wade some distance in the surf zone. When it is OK to wade, you will be most stable if you "put a shoulder" into a wave than when you present your entire back to the wave. Avoid facing oncoming waves while standing in the surf zone.

10. D. All the above. If you must wade, shuffle your feet to avoid stepping on rays, urchins, etc. and to detect holes and rocks. As waves approach, stop moving and position your feet about shoulder width for stability. Keep your knees bent. Remember that swimming through surf usually is better than wading.

11. C. An exit through plunging breakers. My experience has proven that the steepness of the beach, the strength of the backrush, the suddenness of the break, and other factors make exits through plunging breakers the most difficult surf passage. Don't be fooled by an easy entry.

12. D. Whenever standing exits are difficult. If there is a chance you will fall or get knocked down, stay down. Crawling provides four-point stability. Crawl on steep beaches when exiting. Crawl when in doubt. Don't allow your regulator to drag when you crawl.

13. C. Don fins before all surf entries. Techniques vary from area to area. Wading without fins may be essential at some dive sites. At other sites it may be necessary to run and jump into the water after a wave breaks, slip on a fin, and kick out before the next wave breaks. Learn the technique for each area and surf condition.

14. B. False. You can lose fins in surf. Divers in some areas wear special straps to secure their fins. Secure your console. Arrange equipment to minimize sand retention. Wear durable boots. Use a weight belt release that a wave is not likely to open.

15. B. Measure the time between waves before you attempt a surf entry. If you count the seconds between waves while you prepare to dive and time the interval between wave sets, you can negotiate the surf zone with increased safety and ease. Enter between wave sets. When a wave passes, count to yourself so you know when to expect the next wave.

Bonus information:
1. Do not leave equipment lying near the water's edge in a surf area.
2. Do not adjust equipment in the surf zone. Exit the water, make any needed adjustments, and re-enter.
3. Do not swim parallel to incoming waves.
4. Physical contact with a buddy is OK when surf height is three feet or less.

TIDES

Changing tides affect nearly all divers at some time. There is more to the subject than just the rising and falling of water. Knowledge of the tides can increase your diving safety and enjoyment. The following questions test your knowledge of the subject to an advanced level. Compare your answers with those on the next page.

1. The number of tides occurring on the earth at any one time is:
❑ A. 1
❑ B. 2
❑ C. 4
❑ D. 8

2. Tides are produced by the gravitational attraction between the earth and:
❑ A. Sun
❑ B. Moon
❑ C. Other planets and stars
❑ D. All of the above

3. Tides may be considered long period waves with a wavelength equal to:
❑ A. 26 miles
❑ B. 144 miles
❑ C. One fourth of the earth's circumference
❑ D. A hemisphere of the earth

4. The effect of the ____ on tides is about twice that of the ____.
❑ A. Sun, moon
❑ B. Moon, sun
❑ C. Sun, planets and stars
❑ D. Moon, planets and stars

5. Unequal tides for different areas result from:
❑ A. Interference of water movement by land masses
❑ B. The position of the moon relative to the earth
❑ C. The tilt of the earth on its axis
❑ D. All of the above

6. The alignment of the tide-producing celestial bodies produces:
❑ A. Spring tides
❑ B. Neap tides
❑ C. Low tids
❑ D. Rip tides

7. Spring tides and neap tides occur at intervals of approximately:
❑ A. One week
❑ B. Two weeks
❑ C. Four weeks
❑ D. None of the above

8. The highest tides may be expected:
❑ A. During a full or new moon when the moon is at perigee
❑ B. During a first or last quarter moon when the moon is at perigee
❑ C. During a full or new moon when the moon is at apogee
❑ D. During a first or last quarter when the moon is at apogee

9. Tidal changes on an open coast maybe expected to occur.
❑ A. Every six hours
❑ B. Every six hours, 12 minutes and 30 seconds
❑ C. Every twelve hours
❑ D. Every twelve hours and 25 minutes

10. An incoming tide is termed a(an) ____ and an outgoing tide is called a(an) ____.
❑ A. Rush, flow
❑ B. Flow rush
❑ C. Ebb, flood
❑ D. Flood, ebb

11. The strongest tidal current may be expected:
❑ A. Just before high tide
❑ B. Just before low tide
❑ C. Midway between tidal changes
❑ D. A and B, but not C

12. Mixed tides are:
❑ A. A combination of diurnal and semi-diurnal tides
❑ B. Tides with unequal heights
❑ C. The result of freshwater bodies connected to the sea
❑ D. A and B, but not C

13. Which of the following factors has the greatest effect on the height of a tide?
❑ A. Natural period of oscillation of a body of water
❑ B. Time of month
❑ C. Time of year
❑ D. Weather and atmospheric pressure

14. List at least three ways in which tidal changes affect diving:
A. _____
B. _____
C. _____

15. List three actions divers affected by the tides should take:
A. _____
B. _____
C. _____

TIDES

Tides affect diving operations for a great many. Tidal changes are not constant. The heights of tides may vary more than 30 feet for locations only a few hundred miles apart. Fortunately, tides are predictable and forecasts are readily available for most areas. Obtain tide tables for your area and consult them as part of the planning you do in advance of a dive. Whenever possible, plan your dive for slack water. As usual, this quiz could not cover everything you should know about the subject, but it should whet your appetite for more knowledge. You can learn a great deal more about the environment, including tides, in an advanced diver course. Why don't you plan a flood tide of knowledge soon?

1. C. 4. The moon and sun pulling on the earth cause water to bulge on one side, while the centrifugal force of rotation produces a similar bulge on the opposite side of the earth. These two bulges represent high tides where they occur, and water drawn from the areas in between the bulges causes low tides there. These four tides are present continuously, but several factors affect their amplitude.

2. D. All of the above. The moon's gravitational pull on the earth is the primary force creating the tides. The sun's influence is about half that of the moon's and the influence of other heavenly bodies is much less, but still a factor. The distance and relationship between the various celestial bodies as they revolve around each other greatly affect the tides.

3. D. A hemisphere of the earth. Refer to answer number one. The length of a wave is the distance between two successive crests or troughs. Tides are essentially extremely long waves. According to answer number one, four evenly divided tides around the earth would result in a wavelength equal to one-half of the earth's circumference, or one complete hemisphere.

4. B. Moon, sun. The moon is tiny compared to the sun, but it is much closer to the earth. In such relative proximity to our planet, our small moon exerts about twice the influence on the tides as the sun.

5. D. All of the above. The moon passes nearer the earth at some times than at others and is at an angle relative to the earth, not directly in the line with the equator. The earth also tilts on its axis as it rotates and this changes its position relative to the moon. Friction, as water passes over land masses, slows the flow of water. Land masses also interfere with tidal flow, which must pass around and through restrictions. All of these factors result in unequal tides in various locations.

6. A. Spring tides. When the sun and the moon are aligned with the earth during full and new moons, the highest tides of the period result. These tides are termed "spring tides" and are higher than the usual high tides for an area. Such drastic tidal changes often reduce underwater visibility because the tides reach very high on shore and move larger than normal amounts of water.

7. B. Two weeks. Spring tides and neap tides (lower than normal tides) coincide with phases of the moon. Spring tides occur every two weeks during the full and new moons. Neap tides are produced when the sun and moon are at right angles to the earth and occur during the first and last quarters of the lunar phase, which are also on a two week schedule.

8. A. During a full or new moon when the moon is at perigee. When the moon is in its nearest orbit to the earth (at perigee), the lunar tidal range is increased and "perigean tides" occur; when the moon is farthest from the earth (at apogee), the smaller apogean tides occur. The greatest tides of the year occur when perigean tides occur during spring tide conditions.

9. B. Every six hours, 12 minutes and 30 seconds. A "lunar day" is 50 minutes longer than a regular day. Thus, a complete tidal cycle (two high tides and two low tides) takes 24 hours and 50 minutes. A tidal change on an open coast occurs about every six hours.

10. D. Flood, ebb. The periodic horizontal flow of water associated with the rise and fall of the tide is tidal current. Water movement toward shore or upstream resulting from a tidal change is a flood, while movement away from shore or downstream is an ebb. At each reversal of current a short period of little or no current, called slack water, exists. Usually the best diving conditons exist during slack water at high tide.

11. C. Midway between tidal changes. During the flow of water from tidal change to tidal change, the velocity of the tidal current varies from zero at slack water to a maximum, called strength of flood or strength of ebb, about midway between the periods of slack water. The velocity then begins decreasing and returns to zero during the next slack water period.

12. D. A and B but not C. Mixed tides are common along the Pacific Coast of the United States. These tides are characterized by unequal high tide heights and are a combination of diurnal (daily) and semi-diurnal (twice daily) tides. Diurnal tides are indigenous to the northern shore of the Gulf of Mexico, while semi-diurnal tides, consisting of two high and two low water situations daily with relatively equal high and low water heights, are common to the Atlantic Coast of the United States.

13. A. Natural period of oscillation of a body of water. The tendency of a body of water is to rock back and forth within its basin, just as water set into motion in a bowl does. The frequency of the oscillations depends upon the dimension of the bowl. Earthly bodies of water are set into motion by the tides and have natural periods of oscillation, which determine to a great extent the type of tides an area has and their heights. The other factors listed in the possible answers also affect the height of tides, but not as much as the oscillating effect.

14. Ways in which tidal changes affect diving: Visibility is affected. Tidal currents may be produced. In some areas, these currents can be very strong. The depth of the water is changed. This affects boat ramps, entry and exit areas, surge, waves, etc.

15. Actions divers affected by the tides should take: Consult tide tables and plan to dive at high tide. Evaluate the tidal current and tidally produced conditons prior to entering the water for a dive. Plan to use tidal currents to assist movement while diving.

CURRENTS

Q:

Currents in water are like wind in air—fluid in motion. The most significant difference is that water is 800 times more dense than air, so even a slight water current is extremely strong. A fully-equipped scuba diver can sustain a swimming speed of slightly more than one knot only briefly. If you fight water movement, you lose. You must understand currents and use them to your advantage. Test your current knowledge.

1. The terms for the direction and speed of a current are:
- ❏ A. Heading and velocity
- ❏ B. Bearing and velocity
- ❏ C. Drift and set
- ❏ D. Set and drift

2. When a 20-knot wind blows across water in the same direction for 12 hours, the surface current generated by the wind is approximately:
- ❏ A. 2.0 knots
- ❏ B. 1.2 knot
- ❏ C. 0.6 knot
- ❏ D. 0.4 knot

3. A strong current moving away from shore through a narrow opening is a:
- ❏ A. Rip tide
- ❏ B. Rip current
- ❏ C. Longshore current
- ❏ D. Transitory current

4. Tidal currents are strongest during:
- ❏ A. The first one third of the duration of a tide
- ❏ B. The second one third of the duration of a tide
- ❏ C. The final one third of the duration of a tide
- ❏ D. High tide or low tide

5. Waves breaking on a shore create a current that flows parallel to the shore.
- ❏ A. True
- ❏ B. False

6. A current may flow one direction at the surface and in the opposite direction a few feet beneath the surface.
- ❏ A. True
- ❏ B. False

7. Select the one true statement:
- ❏ A. Currents flow within the Great Lakes because there are different water levels in the lakes
- ❏ B. There is a significant reduction in current flow below a thermocline
- ❏ C. You usually encounter spiraling currents along river banks
- ❏ D. All of the above are true

- ❏ E. None of the above are true

8. You are in an anchored, 33-foot boat. It takes a floating object 20 seconds to drift the length of the boat. The surface current is approximately:
- ❏ A. One knot
- ❏ B. 2/3 knot
- ❏ C. 1/3 knot
- ❏ D. 1/4 knot

9. Improved visibility and colder water generally follow a strong wind that blows:
- ❏ A. Offshore
- ❏ B. Onshore
- ❏ C. Along the shore
- ❏ D. None of the above

10. To escape from a whirlpool current in a river you should:
- ❏ A. Ditch your weights and inflate your buoyancy compensator
- ❏ B. Always go with the flow
- ❏ C. Swim toward the middle of the river
- ❏ D. Ascend in the center of the whirlpool

11. To escape from a downwelling current on a drop-off you should:
- ❏ A. Ditch your weights and inflate your buoyancy compensator
- ❏ B. Swim upward and inflate your buoyancy compensator
- ❏ C. Swim away from the drop-off and inflate your buoyancy compensator
- ❏ D. Swim away from the drop-off and ditch your weights

12. List four accessory items a diver should have when diving in a current:
- A. _____
- B. _____
- C. _____
- D. _____

13. You are diving from your boat and there is no one aboard. You and your buddy surface with 500 psi from a depth of 30 feet and discover you are

50 yards downstream from your boat in a one knot current. You should:
- ❏ A. Establish buoyancy, signal for help, and wait for assistance
- ❏ B. Have your buddy hold your scuba unit while you swim hard to reach the boat, then pick up your buddy
- ❏ C. Descend, swim upcurrent beyond the boat, and surface
- ❏ D. Swim across the current until clear of it, swim upstream beyond the boat, then swim back to your boat

14. Sketch a current-indicating buoy that you can use to signal slack water in areas with strong tidal currents.

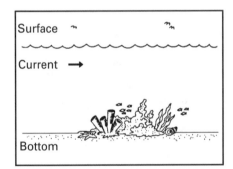

Surface

Current →

Bottom

CURRENTS

A:

Did you learn anything about currents? I hope you learned to respect water movement. Whenever you dive in moving water, you need to know what to expect and the correct procedures. With nearly 30 years of diving experience I'm still learning about currents. I approach any new situation cautiously. Before diving in any moving water, be trained to recognize and manage water movement, ask questions, and follow the example of skilled local divers. Drift diving in currents is a specialty. To dive safely in currents, be trained and qualified, then acquire experience gradually. That's sound advice for any aspect of diving.

1. D. Set and drift. The following information is paraphrased from Chapman's: The SET of a current is the direction toward which it is flowing. A current that flows from north to south is a southerly current. (Note that wind direction is opposite, i.e., a wind from north to south is a northerly wind.) The DRIFT of a current is its speed, normally in knots, except for river currents, which are in miles per hour. State current drift to the nearest tenth of a knot.

2. D. 0.4 knot. Surface currents from winds develop at a rate of two percent of the wind speed every twelve hours, provided the wind blows continuously in the same direction. Two percent of 20 knots is 0.4 knot.

3. B. Rip current. When waves pass over a formation and break, water rushes onto the face of a beach. When the formation restricts the return flow of the uprush and has a narrow gap to funnel the elevated water, a rip current results. The formation may be a sand bar, a reef, or human-made structures.

4. B. The second one third of duration. A tide rises or falls approximately 1/12th of its range during the first hour of duration, 2/12ths of its range during the second hour of duration, 3/12ths of its range during the third and fourth hours of duration, 2/12ths of its range during the fifth hour of duration, and 1/12th of its range during the final hour of duration. The horizontal movement of water (tidal current), corresponds to the height of the tide.

5. A. True. When waves approach a shore at an angle, contact with the bottom slows the leading edge and bends the wave so they break nearly parallel to shore. Because the waves do not break exactly parallel to shore, they move water in the direction they break—along the shore. The term for the resulting water movement is a longshore current.

6. A. True. Water flows in layers. The term for this phenomena is laminar flow. A strong, wind-generated current can reverse the surface flow of water so a layer of water near the surface moves in a dif- ferent direction than the water beneath the surface. Note both surface and underwater currents when diving and use the surface current to assist you to your exit point.

7. D. All of the above are true. The purpose of this question is to point out that you may not know what to expect when you dive in new areas. Ocean divers who believe they understand currents may be alarmed by freshwater currents. Freshwater divers may be surprised by rip currents and downwellings in the ocean. Always obtain an orientation for any unfamiliar diving locations, especially when there are currents.

8. A. One knot. The speed of a current is approximately one knot when the water moves 100 feet in one minute. Since the floating object moves 33 feet in 20 seconds, it will move 99 feet in 60 seconds. Measuring the time it takes a floating object to travel a known distance is a good way to estimate current drift.

9. C. Along the shore. The spin of the earth causes water to move at an angle to the wind. When the wind blows from the north along the west coast of the U.S., an offshore current moves surface water away from shore. Cold water from the depths replaces the surface water. The term for the upward-flowing current is an upwelling.

10. D. Ascend in the center of the whirlpool. I was taken from a depth of 20 feet to 60 feet in a river whirlpool, which deposited me in its eye on the river bottom. When I tried to escape the whirlpool horizontally, it caught me and put me back in the eye on the bottom. I finally escaped by ascending in the center of the whirlpool. At the surface I fully inflated my buoyancy compensator and swam across the swirling water. I discussed my experience with other river divers, who told me that what I was fortunate enough to discover was the correct technique.

11. C. Swim away from the drop-off and inflate your buoyancy compensator. A combination of tidal change, winds, and a drop-off can create a strong downward flowing current. Find out where such currents occur and avoid them. Many divers have had terrifying experiences in downwellings. If caught unexpectedly, move away from the face of the drop-off to escape the downward flow and use buoyancy to resist the current. Be prepared to vent your BC when you escape from the current.

12. Accessory items a diver should have when diving in a current are: **(1) a whistle; (2) an inflatable signal tube, e.g., scuba tuba; (3) a signal mirror; (4) a small waterproof strobe light for signaling at night.** When you prepare for current diving, ask yourself the following question: If you were swept away by a current, how would you signal for assistance?

13. C. Descend, swim upcurrent beyond the boat, and surface. You might become exhausted trying to swim 50 yards against a one knot current. You should not leave your buddy alone. If close to land, you could swim to shore, walk well upcurrent of your boat, and swim back out. The best option, however, is to use your reserve air to swim along the bottom where the current is minimal. Avoid such situations. Have someone remain in the boat. Attach a long trail line to the stern of the vessel. Surface upcurrent from your boat.

14. The diagram illustrates a current-indicating buoy that will signal slack water. The small buoy will float to the surface when the current subsides.

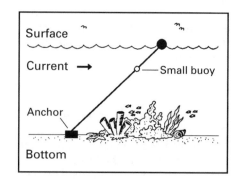

VENOMOUS AQUATIC LIFE

Fortunately there are only a few aquatic animals that are potentially hazardous to divers; and, even more fortunately, injuries from these animals are few in number. You must, however, understand how you can be injured and be able to avoid injury. Testing that knowledge is the purpose of this quiz.

Match the following terms to their definitions: (Use one answer twice)

___ 1. Toxin
___ 2. Phytotoxin
___ 3. Zootoxin
___ 4. Parenteral Toxin
___ 5. Venom
___ 6. Poison
___ 7. Pedicellaria
___ 8. Nematocyst
___ 9. Ciguatera
___10. Scomboid

A. Poisonous matter secreted by certain animals
B. Any agent that chemically injures an organism
C. Poison formed by the metabolism of a plant or animal
D. Animal poison
E. Venom apparatus of a sea urchin
F. A type of fish poisoning
G. Plant poison
H. Toxin delivered by a venom apparatus
J. The stinging cell of coelenterates

11. People differ in sensitivity to a given venom.
❏ A. True
❏ B. False

12. Corals, anemones and jellyfishes have similar stinging cells.
❏ A. True
❏ B. False

13. Marine venoms can usually be detoxified by heat.
❏ A. True
❏ B. False

14. Respiratory arrest may result from several oral toxins.
❏ A. True
❏ B. False

15. The blue ring octopus has the same type of toxin as a pufferfish.
❏ A. True
❏ B. False

16. All aquatic envenomation wounds should be rinsed with the freshest water available.
❏ A. True
❏ B. False

17. Select all correct answers. Soaking the wound in non-scalding hot water for 30-90 minutes is a correct first aid procedure for:
❏ A. Stingray envenomations
❏ B. Scorpionfish envenomations
❏ C. Catfish stings
❏ D. Starfish punctures
❏ E. Sea urchin punctures

18. Select all correct answers. Soaking the wound with vinegar is a correct first aid procedure for:
❏ A. Sea sponge irritation
❏ B. Jellyfish stings
❏ C. Fire coral stings
❏ D. Sea cucumber irritation
❏ E. Bristleworm stings

19. The most serious type of fish poisoning results from eating:
❏ A. Barracuda or amberjack
❏ B. Fish not kept chilled
❏ C. Blowfish or pufferfish
❏ D. All of the above produce similar poisoning

20. Select all correct answers. To avoid injury from venomous aquatic life, a diver should:
❏ A. Always wear protective clothing while diving
❏ B. Always wear gloves while diving
❏ C. Avoid touching unknown plants and animals
❏ D. Move slowly and carefully
❏ E. Watch where hands and feet are placed while diving

VENOMOUS AQUATIC LIFE

Entire books have been written on the subject of venomous aquatic life and several excellent ones are available. You owe it to yourself to know more about this subject than could be covered in this simple quiz. Consider reading a good book about hazardous aquatic life and also learning more by continuing your education in diving. Information on the subject of this quiz is part of a comprehensive Advanced Diver course, a course that every diver should complete. And, since many of the venomous injuries can produce respiratory arrest, you should be trained in artificial respiration. Every diver should be able to perform cardio-pulmonary resuscitation.

1. - C	6. - B
2. - G	7. - E
3. - D	8. - J
4. - H	9. - F
5. - A	10. - F

Any agent that chemically harms you is a poison. A toxin is a poison produced within a plant or animal. Toxin may be ingested (an oral toxin), or it may be delivered by means of a sting or bite. When an animal secretes a poisonous matter, the substance is called venom. When an animal delivers venom by a venom apparatus (bite, sting, puncture), it is called a Parenteral toxin. Poisons produced by plants are phytotoxins, while those produced by animals are zootoxins.

There are several types of fish poisoning, which is generally termed "ichthyosarcotoxism." Common types of fish poisoning include ciguatera, scomboid, and tetrodotoxin poisoning. Ciguatera poisoning results from eating fish—usually large fish—which eat a certain species of algae. Scomboid poisoning results from eating fish which have not been kept chilled. Tetrodotoxin poisoning—the most serious—can result from eating exotic fish such as pufferfish or blowfish.

11. A. True. The reactions of people to aquatic toxins range from no noticeable reaction, to mild irritation, to rapid death. A venomous injury should not be taken lightly based on personal experience. Be prepared to render proper first aid and to obtain prompt medical treatment for injuries.

12. A. True. All Coelenterates—corals, anemones and jellyfishes—have "nematocysts," which are microscopic stinging cells consisting of a venom sac; a "trigger" hair; and a hollow, coiled spine that thrusts outward when triggered and injects venom into a victim. Fortunately the nematocysts of many animals are too small to inflict an injury on a human; but a few of them can sting people, and some of them are capable of causing death. Know your Coelenterates!

13. A. True. Most aquatic venoms are a protein-type toxin that can be neutralized by literally "cooking" it. It is fortunate that cooking can be accomplished at a temperature that does not burn humans. Soaking wounds in water that is 110-113 degrees F for 30 to 90 minutes detoxifies many venoms. Instant "hot packs" or some means to prepare hot water should be part of diving first aid preparation.

14. A. True. Various aquatic poisons, including fish poisoning, shellfish poisoning, and some parenteral toxins, can cause death by paralysis of the respiratory system. Artificial respiration may be effective for those patients with respiratory arrest. All divers should be capable of performing artificial respiration. If you are not currently qualified to administer first aid and cardio-pulmonary resuscitation, take courses or refresher courses. Although serious injuries in diving are rare, you never know when you may be called upon to save your buddy's life.

15. A. True. The tiny blue ring octopus has tetrodotoxin in its salivary glands and probably acquires the poison through the food it eats. While tetrodotoxin is ingested by eating pufferfish or "fugu," the venom is injected by a bite from the octopus. This is a potent neurotoxin, so the colorful little octopus of the South Pacific should be left alone.

16. B. False. This is almost true, because it literally applies to every type of envenomation except that of a jellyfish. Stings from a jellyfish should first be rinsed with seawater. It is important for all other wounds to be cleansed thoroughly to reduce the chances of infection. Medical attention should be sought for all serious wounds, which should not be tightly closed until properly treated.

17. All answers are correct. Literally any puncture wound involving marine envenomation will respond to first aid which includes the application of heat. Soaking is best, but hot compresses may be used and changed frequently. "Hot packs", which produce heat chemically, may also be used.

18. All answers are correct. Plain, white vinegar that may be obtained in a grocery store is an excellent item to include in a diving first aid kit. For many years divers have believed that alcohol is effective for treating jellyfish stings, but studies have shown that it makes stings worse. Vinegar should be the first choice for most irritations, isopropyl alcohol second (except for jellyfish stings), and one quarter strength ammonia as the third choice. All these solutions should be part of your diving first aid kit in addition to a good quantity of pure water.

19. C. Blowfish or pufferfish. Scomboid poisoning, caused by eating fish that has not been kept cold, produces nausea and vomiting within an hour. Ciguatera poisoning, resulting from eating some reef fish, usually produces symptoms within six to twelve hours and generally produces gastrointestinal problems. Tetrodotoxin poisoning—the most dangerous of all food poisonings—is a potent chemical found in pufferfish. It can cause death within minutes. Prompt medical attention is needed for all types of fish poisoning.

20. All answers are correct. Protect yourself by covering up while diving. If you don't know what something is, leave it alone; and if you know an animal to be venomous, don't mess with it. Be especially careful when turning over rocks or pieces of coral and when diving at night. Dive neutrally buoyant and look where you place your hands and feet. Be especially wary of animals that are especially colorful or beautiful. Many are able to get away with such displays because they are extremely venomous. Always check with local divers to learn about the hazardous life in an area. Keep your risks to a minimum.

SECTION THREE

□ □ □

Decompression & Recompression

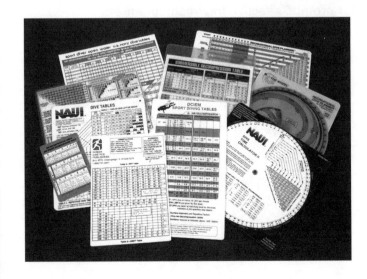

Decompression & Recompression

Decompression illness remains a mystery in spite of more than 150 years of scientific research. The only certainty is that there is a statistical probability that you will experience symptoms if you absorb more nitrogen than normal and ascend too rapidly. Certain precautions will reduce the likelihood that you will experience symptoms.

The statistical probability of decompression sickness is the basis for various dive tables, dive computer algorithms, and dive procedures. You should be able to calculate repetitive dives using dive tables. Dive computer owners should be familiar with computer terminology and recommended procedures for computer-aided diving.

Precautionary decompression is a recommended risk-reducing procedure. Medical personnel use hyperbaric chambers to treat decompression illness casualties. The quizzes in this section test your knowledge of the two foregoing topics as well as your ability to calculate dive table problems and your dive computer knowledge.

By the time you complete the Section Three quizzes, you should be impressed with the value of diving conservatively. Always give yourself a margin of safety so you can minimize the probability that you will experience decompression sickness.

An unpublished and frequent sign and symptom of decompression illness is denial. If you do not feel well after diving, suspect the affliction and seek medical evaluation. Permanent residual neurological symptoms can result from treatment delays. Diving safety is no accident (or prompt, effective treatment for an accident).

To answer quizzes refer to the U.S. Navy Dive Tables on page 223.

DECOMPRESSION

Q:

Probably no aspect of diving has been studied as much as decompression, but it is still not completely understood. Decompression sickness is the number one serious ailment for recreational scuba divers. See how well you understand the modern concepts of this important topic. If you miss a few of the following questions, you won't get bent; but if you don't understand the concepts, you might experience decompression sickness.

1. A dive is a decompression dive only if you exceed the no-decompression limits.
❐ A. True
❐ B. False

2. Spending 20 minutes at 100 feet is more likely to result in decompression sickness than three trips to 100 feet for five minutes each with two minutes between the descents.
❐ A. True
❐ B. False

3. In-water treatment for decompression sickness is appropriate for "pain only" symptoms.
❐ A. True
❐ B. False

4. Bubbles in body tissues and blood increase in size owing to gas diffusion as well as from Boyle's Law.
❐ A. True
❐ B. False

5. The bubbles of decompression sickness always form in the veins.
❐ A. True
❐ B. False

6. The presence of bubbles that do not produce symptoms of bends was first theorized in:
❐ A. 1670
❐ B. 1845
❐ C. 1945
❐ D. 1972

7. A short "bounce dive" to free an anchor after a series of repetitive dives with no bends symptoms can cause decompression sickness.
❐ A. True
❐ B. False

8. The primary value of recompression is the shrinking of the bubbles in the body.
❐ A. True
❐ B. False

9. You are more likely to get bent the first day of a diving vacation than you are on your fourth or fifth day of diving.
❐ A. True
❐ B. False

10. Select all correct answers. For which of the following symptoms following a dive to 90 feet would you seek immediate recompression?
❐ A. Numbness in the legs
❐ B. "Pins and needles" feeling in the legs
❐ C. Weakness and fatigue
❐ D. Coughing and respiratory distress

11. Select all correct answers. First aid for decompression sickness includes:
❐ A. Having the casualty lie down
❐ B. Inclining the casualty with head down and feet up
❐ C. Breathing the highest possible oxygen concentration
❐ D. Aspirin
❐ E. Artificial respiration

12. Select all correct answers. Which of the following after-dive activities can trigger decompression sickness?
❐ A. Exercise
❐ B. A hot water shower or bath
❐ C. Flying
❐ D. Drinking alcohol

13. Complete each of the following procedures that reduce the likelihood of decompression sickness.
❐ A. Remain well within the no decompression _____.
❐ B. Ascend _____.
❐ C. Make a _____ for a few minutes at the end of each dive.
  D. Repetitive dives should be progressively _____.

14. The correct depth for a decompression stop is from the:
❐ A. Top of the diver's head to the surface
❐ B. Diver's regulator mouthpiece to the surface
❐ C. Diver's chest to the surface
❐ D. Diver's feet to the surface

15. A diver stops at 40 feet for 1/4 the time required at the 10-foot stop, at 30 feet for 1/3 the 10-foot stop tims, at 20 feet for 1/2 the 10-foot stop time, and 10 feet for 1 1/2 times the 10-foot stop time because:
❐ A. The diver omitted required decompression
❐ B. Stopping provides a safety factor
❐ C. The 10-foot stop was crowded with divers
❐ D. The diver is not up-to-date

DECOMPRESSION

What you don't know about bends can hurt you. If you didn't score well on this quiz, enroll in a comprehensive advanced scuba course soon, or at least read a good book about decompression. Keep your dives well within the no-decompression limits. Ascend slowly—slower than the 60 feet per minute standard limit. Make a stop between 10 and 30 feet at the end of every dive. Avoid "bounce" dives. Beware of after-dive activities that can lead to decompression sickness. You can avoid the bends by following the recommended procedures.

1. B. False. You literally decompress as you surface from every dive because you absorb excess nitrogen while exposed to increased pressure. Just because staged decompression is not required does not mean you do not decompress. The outgassing is why your ascent rate is critical, especially near the surface.

2. B. False. Each time you surface from 100 feet, bubbles may form within you, even if you are not close to the no-decompression limits. These bubbles may not produce symptoms following one or two ascents, but may collect and cause bends during repeated ascents. Don't bounce up and down while diving, especially when diving deeper than 60 feet.

3. B. False. In-water treatment is not recommended for any form of decompression sickness. You compound an already complex problem. Obtain medical treatment, even if the treatment will be delayed. Decompression sickness requires medical attention you cannot receive in the water.

4. A. True. As ambient pressure decreases, bubbles enlarge, but not greatly because a sphere is the most efficient shape for volume. The internal pressure decreases when the bubble size increases. The internal pressure reduction is significant because it allows gas to diffuse into the bubbles, expand them more, and exacerbate the problem.

5. B. False. For a long time it was believed that bubbles always formed in the venous system of the body. Researchers now believe bubbles can and do form in the tissues, veins, arteries or all these areas.

6. C. 1945. Dr. Albert R. Behnke first theorized the presence of "silent bubbles"—those present that did not produce symptoms of decompression sickness—in 1945. Ultrasonic bubble detection equipment used since the 1970's confirms the presence of asymptomatic bubbles in divers. These studies form the basis for the "no bubble" no-decompression limits used in several modern diving computers.

7. A. True. Small, asymptomatic bubbles in the blood after diving become trapped in the capillary beds of the lungs, where they eventually break down without causing problems. A bounce dive, however, can push the bubbles through the circulatory system where they coalesce and produce symptoms of decompression sickness. Avoid bounce dives following repetitive dives.

8. B. False. As mentioned previously, the diameter of a bubble (sphere) changes little with a significant change in pressure. What actually happens during recompression is that the internal pressure of the bubbles is increased so that gas migrates out of them. Slow decompression prevents them from growing again. Breathing a high oxygen concentration reduces bubble size by diffusion—the movement of molecules from an area of higher concentration to an area of less concentration.

9. B. False. Contrary to what you may have learned, you have not completely outgassed after a 12 hour surface interval. Slow tissues in your body still contain residual nitrogen, which is carried over from day to day and which can build to the point where decompression sickness occurs. It is now recommended that you refrain from diving for one day following three consecutive days of diving.

10. A, B, C and D. All the symptoms are signs of serious decompression sickness. If you experience any of the signs, discontinue diving and seek recompression treatment at once. You should suspect the bends if you have any unusual symptoms up to two days after diving, especially when you experience problems with vision, balance or sense of feeling.

11. A and C. A decompression sickness casualty should lie down, remain still, and breathe oxygen. The classic modified Trendelenberg (head-down) position was for arterial gas embolism. Experts now discouage use of the Trendelenberg position for any diving injury. Aspirin may mask symptoms without providing corrective action. Artificial respiration should not be necessary for bends cases. Stable bends casualties should drink water because dehydration aggravates decompression sickness.

12. A, B, C, and D. Anything that stimulates circulation to the extremities can lead to DCS symptoms. Avoid pulling the anchor, alcohol, etc. Flying contributes to the problem by further lowering the ambient pressure and fostering bubble growth. Limit elevation above sea level as much as possible for 12 hours following no-decompression dives and for at least 24 hours following dives with required decompression.

13. A. Remain well within the no-decompression limits. A five minute safety factor is suggested. **B.** Ascend slowly. Rates slower than 60 feet per minute are now the trend. **C.** Make a stop for a few minutes at the end of each dive. Two to three minutes between 10 and 30 feet is an excellent safety margin. **D.** Repetitive dives should be progressively shallower.

14. B. Diver's regulator mouthpiece to the surface. Years ago divers were encouraged to maintain chest level at the stop depth and not to vary the depth more than one foot. Exact depth is not as critical today. It is acceptable to maintain your decompression stop depth within a few feet of the target depth, especially if you use a dive computer.

15. D. The diver is not up-to-date. The procedure described is an out-dated technique for omitted decompression. The diver exited the water, obtained a new tank, and re-entered the water within five minutes if asymptomatic. The modern procedure is to remain out of the water, rest, breathe oxygen, and drink water. If symptoms develop, seek medical treatment.

DIVE TABLES

Q:

Use the U.S. Navy dive tables and the following maximum time limits: 40 feet-130 min., 50 feet-80 min., 60 feet-50 min., 70 feet-40 min., 80 feet-35 min., 90 feet-25 min., 100 feet-20 min. Include a two-minute safety stop for all repetitive dives. Bottom time includes descent, ascent and safety stop times. A _required_ stop means bottom time exceeds the _reduced_ time limit. When bottom time exceeds the _reduced_ time limit, but not the U.S. Navy nodecompression limit, the required decompression time is five minutes. Assume a maximum ascent rate of one foot /min.

1. A. The letter group for a dive to 60 feet for 25 minutes is ___.
   B. After a one-hour surface interval the letter group is ___.
   C. The maximum repetitive dive time for 60 feet without required decompression is ____ minutes.
   D. The letter group following the second dive with maximum bottom time is ___.

2. A. The letter group for a dive to 51 feet for 21 minutes is ___.
   B. After a one hour and 57 minute surface interval the letter group is ___.
   C. The maximum repetitive dive time for 51 feet without required decompression is ___ minutes.
   D. The total ascent time for the second dive is approximately ___ minutes and the ending letter group is ____.

3. A. The letter group for a dive to 73 feet for 27 minutes is ___.
   B. After a one hour and 45 minute surface interval the letter group is ___.
   C. The maximum depth for a 20 minute repetitive dive that does not exceed the reduced time limit is ___ feet.
   D. The letter group following the second dive is ___.

4. A. The letter group for a dive to 80 feet for 30 minutes is ___.
   B. The minimum surface interval for a 25-minute repetitive dive to 60 feet without required decompression is _____.
   C. The minimum total ascent time for the second dive is ___ minutes.
   D. The letter group following the second dive is ___.

5. A. The letter group for a dive to 90 feet for 20 minutes is ___.
   B. After a one-hour surface interval the letter group is ___.
   C. Circle correct response: A second dive to 41 feet for 40 minutes _requires_ a/an ___ minute decompression stop/does not require a stop.
   D. The letter group following the second dive is ___.

6. A. The letter group for a dive to 41 feet for 40 minutes is ____.
   B. After a one-hour surface interval the letter group is ___.
   C. Circle correct response: A second dive to 90 feet for 20 minutes _requires_ a/an ___ minute decompression stop/does not require a stop.
   D. The letter group following the second dive is ___.

7. The rule of repetitive diving that questions five and six illustrate is:
   _____

8. A. The letter group for a Group C diver who dives to 70 feet for 25 minutes is ___.
   B. After a two hour and five minute surface interval the letter group is ___.
   C. Circle correct response: Another dive to 60 feet for 23 minutes _requires_ a/an ___ minute decompression stop/does not require a stop.
   D. The letter group following the last dive is ___.

9. A. The letter group for a dive to 60 feet for 25 minutes is ___.
   B. After an eight minute surface interval the letter group is ___.
   C. Circle correct response: A second dive to 55 feet for 25 minutes _requires_ a/an ___ minute decompression stop/does not require a stop.
   D. The letter group following the second dive is ___.

10. A. The letter group for a freshwater dive to 102 feet for 18 minutes is ___.
    B. After a one-hour surface interval the letter group is ___.
    C. Circle correct response: A second dive to 68 feet for 14 minutes _requires_ a/an ___ minute decompression stop/does not _require_ a stop.
    D. The letter group following the second dive is ___.

11. A. The letter group for a cold dive to 90 feet for 25 minutes is ___.
    B. The minimum surface interval for a 30-minute second dive to a depth of 70 feet without required decompression is ___ hours and ___ minutes.
    C. The letter group following the second dive is ___.
    D. The minimum time before flying following the second dive is ___ hours and ____ minutes.

12. After a dive that _requires_ decompression, you should refrain from diving again for at least ___ hours.

13. After a dive that _requires_ decompression, you should refrain from flying for at least ___ hours.

14. If you ascend from a depth of 80 feet to a depth of 20 feet in 30 seconds, you should: _____
_____.

15. You need to use special tables for equivalent sea level depths when diving at elevations above _____ feet.

DIVE TABLES

In spite of studies and books about decompression, one hard fact merits every diver's awareness: Decompression remains a mystery. It is important to adhere to the practices emphasized in this quiz: Don't push table limits, make safety decompression stops, and be conservative. If you had difficulty with the table computations, take a refresher scuba course.

1. A. Group E
   B. Group D
   C. 26 minutes
   D. Group H

2. A. Group E
   B. Group D
   C. 26 minutes
   D. 3 minutes, Group H
Question two is exactly the same as question one except that the numbers make it appear different. When you exceed a dive table number, use the next greater number: 51 feet is a 60-foot schedule. Although the surface interval in question #2 is nearly an hour longer than in question #1, the ending letter group is the same. Ascent time includes a two-minute safety stop.

3. A. Group G
   B. Group E
   C. 60 feet
   D. Group H

4. A. Group G
   B. 2:00
   C. 3 minutes
   D. Group H
The Residual Nitrogen Time (RNT) for the repetitive 25-minute dive cannot exceed 25 minutes (25 + 25 = 50, which is the max. reduced limit). The first 60-foot letter group with an RNT less than 25 minutes is D. The minimum time for a group G diver to attain group D is two hours. Total bottom time following the second dive is 25 minutes plus 24 minutes RNT = 49 minutes.

5. A. Group F
   B. Group E
   C. Does not require a stop
   D. Group J

6. A. Group F
   B. Group E
   C. Requires a seven-minute decompression stop
   D. Group J

7. Make the deepest dive first. For a series of dives, proceed from deepest to shallowest depths. Note the dive schedules for questions five and six are identical. The only difference is the order of the dives. The profiles in question six are within the no-decompression limits, but the combined profiles in question seven can bend a diver. Follow all dive table rules.

8. A. Group H
   B. Group E
   C. Requires a five-minute decompression stop
   D. Group J
Total bottom time for the second dive is 23 minutes dive time plus 30 minutes RNT = 53 minutes. Since total bottom time exceeds the reduced time limit (50 minutes), the required decompression time is five minutes.

9. A. Group E
   B. Group E
   C. Does not require a stop
   D. Group H
When the surface interval between dives is less than ten minutes and the dives are to the same or next greater depth, ignore the surface interval, add the bottom times, and use the deepest depth for table calculations. The total dive profile for question nine is 60 feet for 50 minutes. Avoid "yo-yo" dives, however. The minimum recommended surface interval is one hour.

10. A. Group F
    B. Group E
    C. Does not require a stop
    D. Group H
The U.S. Navy tables are based on saltwater, which is 2.5% denser than freshwater. Theoretically 102 feet of freshwater equals 99 feet of seawater and 68 feet of freshwater equals 66 feet of seawater. Most depth gauges are not accurate enough for such fine distinctions, however. Avoid splitting hairs when planning dives. It is better to be conservative than technically correct.

11. A. Group H
    B. 24 hours (not 4:50)
    C. Group F
    D. 12 hours
Use the next greater time for cold dive calculations. Since the 90/30 profile requires decompression, you should not dive again for 24 hours (see next answer).

When making a cold dive, it is best to reduce bottom time by one letter group because adding time can push you past the maximum time limits. The minimum recommended delay before flying after diving is 12 hours.

12. 24 hours. While the U.S. Navy does not prohibit repetitive dives that require decompression, recreational diving opposes the practice. When you exceed the no-decompression limits during a dive, refrain from further diving for at least 24 hours.

13. 24 hours. The minimum delay before flying after diving is 12 hours, but you should wait at least 24 hours following dives with required decompression. Several dive organizations recommend that whenever possible you wait at least 48 hours after a decompression dive.

14. Increase your stop time (safety or required) by the difference in time between the actual ascent time and the time it would have taken to ascend at the rate of one foot per second. For the example in the question, increase your stop time by 30 seconds. Safety decompression stops can compensate for several common diving errors.

15. 1,000 feet (300 meters). Dives at elevations above 1,000 feet are altitude dives, which require special tables, procedures, and training.

MULTI-LEVEL DIVING

Q:

Interest in multi-level (ML) diving has been keen for many years. The procedure allows a diver to spend time at multiple depths during a dive and not have to use the deepest depth and the total time for decompression status. Where did the procedure originate? What are the current recommendations concerning its use? Are you diving at multiple levels correctly?

1. Multi-level diving was first developed by and is currently used by:
❏ A. The U.S. Navy
❏ B. Commercial diving companies
❏ C. Technical divers
❏ D. None of the above

2. A dive table procedure for multi-level diving was first introduced to the recreational diving community in:
❏ A. 1957
❏ B. 1972
❏ C. 1976
❏ D. 1979

3. The procedure to determine bottom time for multi-level dives involves:
❏ A. Calculating depth changes as repetitive dives
❏ B. Determining an equivalent bottom time
❏ C. The use of the average depth of a dive
❏ D. A or B, but not C

4. The procedures for ML diving are part of the educational curriculum of:
❏ A. The U. S. Navy
❏ B. Diver training organizations
❏ C. Commercial diving schools
❏ D. Both B and C

5. Which of the following rules do not apply to ML diving?
❏ A. Keep at least one group back from the no-decompression limit for any depth
❏ B. Make a safety decompression stop at the end of an ML dive
❏ C. Ascend at least 30 feet when changing depths
❏ D. The time spent at one depth should not include the time required to ascend to a shallower depth

6. ML diving should be done only by:
❏ A. Divemasters and instructors
❏ B. Resort dive guides for set locations
❏ C. Commercial divers
❏ D. Trained, qualified divers

7. If you do ML diving, you should use the procedure for:
❏ A. Single dives only
❏ B. Repetitive dives only
❏ C. Single or repetitive dives
❏ D. Single dives shallower than 130 feet

8. The ideal profile for ML diving is:
❏ A. Square
❏ B. Sawtooth
❏ C. Step (deep to shallow)
❏ D. Step (shallow to deep)

9. With the exception of complex dive table calculations, there is/are no means available to permit divers to do ML dives.
❏ A. True
❏ B. False

10. ML diving is appropriate for the _____ certification level.
❏ A. Advanced scuba diver
❏ B. Deep diving specialty
❏ C. Divemaster
❏ D. None of the above

11. ML diving procedures have been published primarily to:
❏ A. Encourage its use by recreational divers
❏ B. Discourage its use by recreational divers
❏ C. Obtain information concerning the procedure
❏ D. Educate divers concerning correct technique

12. There is no evidence that repetitive ML diving is any more hazardous than repetitive constant-depth dives.
❏ A. True
❏ B. False

13. There is little risk of decompression sickness following ML dives with deep excursions because you literally decompress during the latter stages of ML dives.
❏ A. True
❏ B. False

14. There are no official dive tables for multi-level diving.
❏ A. True
❏ B. False

15. If you and your buddy do a ML dive and remain within a few feet of each other throughout the dive, you may safely use your buddy's decompression status for dive planning.
❏ A. True
❏ B. False

MULTI-LEVEL DIVING

I hope this quiz sheds light on a topic that is somewhat misunderstood. Divers often lack dive table calculation proficiency. Based on the deficiency, I discourage table-calculated ML dives except when controlled by dive guides at resorts. Dive computers support ML dives and can increase bottom time when used properly. Abide by the rules for ML diving when you dive with a computer and remember to use common sense. Be conservative for safety's sake.

1. B. Commercial diving companies. Several commercial diver companies have developed and use dive tables and procedures. The companies employ experts to develop and test special procedures to meet working diver needs. Multi-level diving is an example of a special commercial diving procedure.

2. C. 1976. I first introduced ML diving at the Eighth International Conference on Underwater Education in San Diego, California. The purpose of my paper was to request information about the feasibility of the procedure. Bruce Bassett made me aware that commercial divers do ML diving.

3. D. A or B, but not C. You may determine total bottom time by using equivalent bottom time, which is the amount of bottom time at shallower depth required to attain a repetitive group designation for a deeper depth. Add equivalent time to any additional time spent at the shallower depth. You may calculate the ascent to a shallower depth as a repetitive dive and reduce the no-decompression limit for the new depth by the residual nitrogen time. I prefer equivalent depth calculations.

4. D. Both B and C. ML diving techniques are part of the curriculum for marine technology vocational schools because the procedure is valuable in the work environment and because the activities of commercial divers can be controlled. PADI includes ML diving in its curriculum, but says you may not use conventional dive tables to plan ML dives. The Canadian DCIEM dive tables, which some instructors choose to teach, are designed and tested for ML diving.

5. D. The time spent at one depth should not include the time required to ascend to a shallower depth. Incorrect. You should consider ascent time as time at the deeper depth. When you calculate equivalent time, include the time required to reach the shallower depth. Although the ascent time may be of short duration, it may be enough to cause a different letter group designation.

6. D. Trained, qualified divers. Diver training organizations offer multi-level diving specialty courses. Any diver may do ML diving, but only those who are properly trained should attempt deeper ML dives. There are several methods of ML diving. You should understand the advantages and disadvantages of each and learn essential safety practices.

7. A. Single dives only. Theory supports repetitive ML diving, but my personal recommendation is to limit deeper ML dives to a single, carefully-planned dive. Repetitive ML dives compound your risk of decompression sickness, which seems inappropriate for recreational purposes.

8. C. Step (deep to shallow). Some parts of your body fill rapidly with gas at deeper depths, but can outgas at shallower depths. Other body parts require longer times.

9. B. False. Dive computers continuously calculate nitrogen levels during dives and are effective ML diving tools when used correctly. PADI trains divers to use the circular calculator for ML dive planning. Multi-level diving is the most common dive profile, although most divers do not plan their ML dives.

10. D. None of the above. Entry-level divers can learn and use fundamental ML diving procedures. Deeper ML excursions should be attempted only by divers with additional training. A leadership rating does not automatically qualify a person for ML diving, which is a specialty requiring specific skills and knowledge.

11. D. Educate divers concerning correct technique. Initial articles requested information, posed questions, and challenged the technique. The information published in texts and magazines in recent years emphasizes cautions and procedures. ML diving is an accepted diving technique when done properly.

12. B. False. The 1991 DAN Report on Diving Accidents and Fatalities indicates that ML profile was a characteristic in 56.4% of dives that resulted in decompression sickness and a factor in 54.6% of 1990 accident dives. The percentage has increased annually, especially for dives where the maximum depth exceeded 80 feet.

13. B. False. The idea that ML dives—especially repetitive ML dives—with deep excursions are safe because dive computers allow them is insane. Use common sense in addition to your dive computer display. You outgas some tissues at shallower depths during ML dives, but remember that decompression sickness remains a mystery. We know its statistical probability and symptoms, but little else.

14. B. False. The DCIEM dive tables, recognized by the Canadian government, NAUI, and other organizations, are multi-level tables. The DCIEM tables are an not the only ML tables.

15. B. False. The cumulative effect of depth differences of several feet while ML diving can be significant. Multiple body tissues ingas and outgas at varying rates. A dive team should not share a single dive computer. Your decompression status must be personal.

PRECAUTIONARY DECOMPRESSION

Q:

A precautionary decompression stop—also called a "safety" stop—at the end of dives is a recommended scuba diving practice. When should a stop be made? At what depth? For how long? How should the time spent at the stop depth be counted? How does a stop affect your repetitive group designation? As you can see, there are many questions regarding safety stops. These questions are the basis for the following quiz.

1. Select the incorrect statement. A precautionary decompression stop:
❐ A. Reduces the risk of decompression sickness
❐ B. Prevents decompression sickness
❐ C. Can compensate for an ascent that was too rapid
❐ D. Serves as a safety factor when factors contributing to decompression sickness are present

2. Safety decompression stops should be made at the end of:
❐ A. Any dive in excess of 40 feet
❐ B. Repetitive dives in excess of 40 feet
❐ C. Repetitive dives in excess of 60 feet
❐ D. Every dive, despite the depth
❐ E. The last dive of the day

3. The preferred method for safety decompression is:
❐ A. Hovering
❐ B. Holding onto the anchor line
❐ C. Holding onto a decompression line or bar
❐ D. Following the bottom contour to shallow water

4. When doing a safety decompression stop, it is best to breathe from:
❐ A. Your scuba tank
❐ B. A "hang" tank filled with compressed air
❐ C. A "hang" tank filled with pure oxygen
❐ D. Your buddy's alternate air source

5. The recommended depth(s) for a precautionary decompression stop is:
❐ A. 10 feet
❐ B. 15 feet
❐ C. 10 to 20 feet
❐ D. 10 to 30 feet

6. During a safety decompression stop divers should:
❐ A. Remain as still as possible
❐ B. Exercise mildly
❐ C. Exercise moderately
❐ D. Exercise vigorously

7. The recommended duration of precautionary decompression is:
❐ A. Two minutes
❐ B. Three minutes
❐ C. Two to three minutes
❐ D. Five minutes

8. The time spent at a safety stop:
❐ A. Should be considered part of dive or bottom time
❐ B. May be considered part of dive or bottom time as a safety factor
❐ C. May be considered neutral time that is not part of either dive time or surface interval time
❐ D. Both B and C are correct

9. If precautionary decompression time pushes you past the no-decompression time limit for your dive, you should:
❐ A. Ignore the precautionary stop time
❐ B. Decompress according to the total time spent underwater
❐ C. Double the precautionary stop time
❐ D. Follow the procedures for omitted decompression

10. When surface conditions involve large swells, divers should:
❐ A. Refrain from precautionary decompression
❐ B. Do precautionary decompression at the maximum allowable depth
❐ C. Avoid maximum inhalations during decompression
❐ D. Both B and C are correct

11. Select the least correct answer. When a mild current is present, divers should:
❐ A. Refrain from precautionary decompression
❐ B. Swim into the current during the decompression stop
❐ C. Drift with the current during the decompression stop
❐ D. Have a line to hold during decompression

12. If you surface from a repetitive dive to a depth of 65 feet without precautionary decompression, you should:
❐ A. Carry out the procedures for omitted decompression
❐ B. Determine why the safety stop was omitted
❐ C. Ensure a safety stop is done for any subsequent dives
❐ D. Both B and C are correct

14. If you are nearly out of air at the end of a dive, want to do precautionary decompression, and there is no "hang" tank, you should:
❐ A. Share your buddy's air
❐ B. Ascend directly to the surface
❐ C. Surface, acquire additional air within five minutes, then return to the safety stop depth
❐ D. Remain at the decompression stop until you are out of air

PRECAUTIONARY DECOMPRESSION

 A:

Is there more to precautionary decompression than you thought? Most divers have not given as much consideration to the topic as is contained in this quiz. Safety stops are important because they decrease the risk of injury during ascent. If you scored well on the quiz, but do not make precautionary stops during every dive, you should start doing what you know is right. If you did not score well on the quiz, you now know what you should do and why you should do it. Take the time to increase the safety of your dives.

1. B. Prevents decompression sickness. False. A safety stop cannot ensure a diver will not get decompression sickness (DCS), but will significantly reduce the risk of the bends. While there are no statistics available concerning the risk of DCS following a no-required-decompression dive including a safety stop, there is no question the risk is much less than dives made without precautionary measures.

2. D. Every dive, despite the depth. Why should a safety stop be made at the end of a shallow dive when there is no risk of decompression sickness? The stop should be made to develop or to maintain the ability to make the stop when one is needed. The stop also compensates for ascents at a rate faster than sixty foot per minute (which commonly occurs), helps with buoyancy control, and provides a pause to help ensure the surface area directly above is clear before completing the ascent.

3. C. Holding onto a decompression line or bar. An anchor line is a less than desirable location for a safety stop, although many divers use anchor lines, which tend to rise when divers hold them. Jerking motion caused by the boat at the surface can create hazardous movement of an anchor line. Minimize problems by using proper lines for decompression. You should be able to perform hovering or swimming decompression stops in case you cannot find a line for a stop, but neither of these techniques are the preferred method.

4. A. Your scuba tank. Precautionary decompression should be part of dive planning. Allow air for the stop. It is always better to retain your mouthpiece than to breathe from another air source. Oxygen decompression is beyond the scope of recreational diving and should not be attempted. If you do run short of air during a precautionary decompression stop and there is no "hang" tank available, breathe from your buddy's alternate air source.

5. D. 10 to 30 feet. For many years the depth for a safety stop was ten feet. Diver training organizations established a recommended depth of fifteen feet because logistically it is easier to remain at that depth than at ten feet. At an ascents workshop conducted by the American Academy of Underwater Sciences, experts agreed that any depth between ten and thirty feet is acceptable. Stopping in shallow water to eliminate excess nitrogen is more important than an exact depth.

6. There is currently no correct answer for this question! If you answered either A, B, or C, give yourself credit for a correct answer. For years the policy has been to avoid exercise during decompression, but studies in which divers exercised indicate exercise is beneficial. Since there is no consensus of opinion on this issue, mild exercise is probably a reasonable compromise and is most likely to be the case. It is difficult to remain perfectly still underwater.

7. Either C (two to three minutes) or D (five minutes). Various organizations recommend different times. Suggested times are only guidelines. The greater the amount of nitrogen in your system, the longer the stop should be. If you surface from a repetitive dive near the limits of no-required-decompression, a five minute precautionary stop is appropriate. Instead of accepting recommended times as absolutes, use common sense to increase your safety.

8. D. Both B and C are correct. You should not be penalized for a safety decompression stop because you eliminate nitrogen from all but the slowest compartments. The amount of nitrogen absorbed by a 120 minute compartment in a few minutes in shallow water is negligible. If any contributing factors to decompression sickness are present, it may be wise to include your safety stop time as part of your dive time to provide a margin of safety.

9. A. Ignore the precautionary stop time. If you could have ascended directly to the surface with no stop required, it is only logical that time spent eliminating excess nitrogen with a precautionary decompression stop cannot force you into a situation that requires decompression. A case can be made for answer C—doubling the stop time—because the situation is obviously near the maximum time limit for the dive. Answer A is the most correct answer, however.

10. D. Both B and C are correct. Decompression stops are more difficult when large swells pass overhead. The shallower you are, the more water movement affects you. Turbulence decreases with depth, so a safety stop as deep as thirty feet may be appropriate if surface conditions deteriorate during a dive. Very large swells cause significant pressure changes as crests and troughs rapidly change the depth of the water. Be aware that these pressure changes can cause lung overexpansion injuries. Avoid full inhalations. Breathe continuously. Avoid such conditions whenever possible.

11. D. Have a line to hold during decompression. Swimming into a current is never a wise option, especially when you are suspended between the surface and the bottom in the water column. If currents are likely, prepare for them with specially-rigged decompression lines or carry line on a reel to use as a tether line.

12. D. Both B and C are correct. There is agreement that safety stops should be made. If you missed one, determine the exact cause so you can correct it. Perhaps you had buoyancy problems or your buddy went directly to the surface. Correct the problem, then make it a point to do precautionary decompression during subsequent dives. It has been said that safety stops "cover a multitude of sins." Another good saying to keep in mind is "It is better to be safe than sorry."

14. B. Ascend directly to the surface. The answer to this question is situation dependent, but with only the information contained in the question, B is the most correct answer. If your buddy had plenty of air and an extra second stage, sharing air would be appropriate. If you had to exchange a single regulator to share air and your buddy was also low on air, sharing air would be inappropriate. The best course of action is to plan your dive and dive your plan so you have sufficient air for precautionary decompression.

HYPERBARIC CHAMBERS

$Q:$

Divers should be familiar with chambers and their use, but there is little information about them in recreational texts. It is time to find out how much you know (and what you need to learn). <u>Select all correct answers.</u>

1. An appropriate hyperbaric chamber is a pressure vessel capable of simulating pressures:
❏ A. Up to ten atmospheres
❏ B. Up to six atmospheres
❏ C. Less than one atmosphere
❏ D. From one atmosphere up to five atmospheres

2. The most correct term for the chamber used to treat recreational divers is:
❏ A. Decompression chamber
❏ B. Recompression chamber
❏ C. Hyperbaric chamber
❏ D. High pressure vessel

3. Which of the following diving maladies usually require chamber treatment?
❏ A. Decompression sickness
❏ B. Air embolism
❏ C. Spontaneous pneumothorax
❏ D. Mediastinal emphysema

4. Monoplace chambers are _____ for diving-related injuries.
❏ A. Appropriate
❏ B. Encouraged
❏ C. Discouraged
❏ D. Completely inappropriate

5. The main advantage of a double-lock chamber is that:
❏ A. A casualty can remain under pressure during transfer of materials and personnel
❏ B. The operators can treat two or more injured divers simultaneously
❏ C. The operators can treat different injuries simultaneously by separating the chamber into two compartments

6. The standard gas used to pressurize monoplace chambers is:
❏ A. Compressed air
❏ B. Medical grade oxygen
❏ C. A mixture of helium and oxygen
❏ D. Nitrox

7. The standard gas used to pressurize double-lock chambers is:
❏ A. Compressed air
❏ B. Medical grade oxygen
❏ C. A mixture of helium and oxygen
❏ D. Nitrox

8. The two greatest hazards associated with chamber treatment are:
❏ A. Fire
❏ B. Oxygen toxicity
❏ C. Carbon monoxide toxicity
❏ D. Carbon dioxide toxicity

9. The initial depth equivalent for chamber treatment of decompression sickness is:
❏ A. 60 feet
❏ B. 165 feet
❏ C. 60 to 165 feet
❏ D. Twice the maximum depth the casualty reached

10. The chamber treatment equivalent depth for air embolism victims is:
❏ A. 60 feet
❏ B. 165 feet
❏ C. 60 to 165 feet
❏ D. Twice the maximum depth the casualty reached

11. During chamber treatment casualties breathe oxygen:
❏ A. Continuously
❏ B. Periodically
❏ C. To reduce the size of bubbles in the body
❏ D. To prevent nitrogen narcosis in treatment personnel

12. Principles associated with chamber treatment include:
❏ A. Compression to collapse circulatory bubbles
❏ B. Compression to reduce the size of circulatory bubbles
❏ C. Oxygen breathing to reduce the size of circulatory bubbles
❏ D. High pressure outgassing of desaturated tissues

13. If a casualty requires chamber treatment and the distance is great to the nearest chamber, you should:
❏ A. Provide oxygen first aid
❏ B. Have the casualty decompress in the water
❏ C. Take the casualty to the chamber
❏ D. None of the above

14. Correct terms for diving hyperbaric chambers include:
❏ A. Recompression chambers
❏ B. Hyperbaric chambers
❏ C. Compression chambers
❏ D. PVHO's

15. When you need to identify the nearest operational chamber, you should contact:
❏ A. The Experimental Diving Unit
❏ B. NOAA
❏ C. DAN
❏ D. NAUI

HYPERBARIC CHAMBERS

It is good to be familiar with hyperbaric chambers and treatment principles, procedures, and precautions. Advanced diving courses may include a hyperbaric chamber orientation. It is interesting and fun to learn more about chambers by taking a "ride" in one during training, which is the only way you should ever acquire chamber experience. Remember that prevention is far better than treatment and plan accordingly.

1. B. Up to six atmospheres. Small, single-lock, single-person chambers can be pressurized to a depth equivalent to 60 feet. An appropriate chamber can be pressurized to a depth of at least 165 feet. Chambers capable of pressure less than one atmosphere are hypobaric vessels, which are inappropriate for diver treatment.

2. B. Recompression chamber or C. Hyperbaric chamber. Commercial divers use chambers for decompression, but recreational divers do not. Divers get re-compressed in a recompression or hyperbaric chamber.

3. A. Decompression sickness and B. Air embolism. Both air embolism and decompression can involve blockage of the circulatory system. Recompression is the treatment for both maladies. Pneumothorax and emphysema require medical treatment, but recompression is not appropriate unless the injuries occur in conjunction with arterial gas embolism.

4. C. Discouraged. Monoplace, single-lock chambers are not rated for the pressure required to treat diving injuries. Single-lock chambers do not permit patient access for medical assistance. Monoplace chambers use 100 percent oxygen for treatment, which can lead to oxygen toxicity.

5. A. A casualty can remain under pressure during transfer of materials and personnel. A double-lock chamber has an outer lock and an inner lock. Operators can raise the pressure in the outer lock to equal inner-lock pressure, thereby allowing access to the inner lock. The pressure in the outer lock also may be lowered to allow egress while the inner lock remains at a higher pressure.

6. B. Medical grade oxygen. Operators pressurize small, monoplace chambers with pure oxygen. Physicians use monoplace chambers to treat illnesses such as gas gangrene, carbon monoxide poisoning, and a variety of slow-healing wounds. Single-lock chambers usually are not appropriate for the treatment of serious diving injuries.

7. A. Compressed air. Double-lock recompression chambers usually have vast storage banks of compressed air for emergency pressurization. Operators also use oxygen for treatment inside the chamber, but they supply the oxygen via demand masks or an oxygen hood.

8. A. Fire and B. Oxygen toxicity. Owing to the high oxygen partial pressure in a chamber environment, fire is a serious threat. Fire prevention is an important aspect of chamber operations. A toxic reaction may result from breathing pure oxygen during treatment. Operators interrupt oxygen breathing with air-breathing periods to reduce toxicity risk.

9. A. 60 feet. The initial depth equivalent for bends treatment is about three atmospheres. Chamber operators follow standard treatment tables to decompress patients slowly for up to six hours.

10. B. 165 feet. Chamber operators quickly pressurize air embolism casualties to a depth equivalent of 165 feet. Any diver who loses consciousness after a compressed air ascent receives the same treatment. Unconscious patients must have an open airway during recompression. Squeezes pose problems, but they are not a priority during a serious emergency.

11. B. Periodically and C. To reduce the size of bubbles in the body. Oxygen breathing requires special procedures because it can cause seizures. Breathing oxygen flushes nitrogen from the body and reduces the size of nitrogen bubbles. The partial pressure differential pulls nitrogen from bubbles into blood and tissues. Oxygen first aid is extremely beneficial for pressure-related diving injuries.

12. B. Compression to reduce the size of circulatory bubbles and C. Oxygen breathing to reduce the size of circulatory bubbles. Breathing oxygen can reduce the size of nitrogen bubbles. Compression also reduces bubble size, but the reduction is non-linear because the bubbles are spheres, which are the most efficient geometrical configuration for volume. It requires six atmospheres pressure to reduce bubble diameter by 45%!

13. A. Provide oxygen first aid and C. Take the casualty to the chamber. Oxygen first aid is appropriate for any serious diving injury. Even if it takes a full day or more, take a casualty who requires recompression to an appropriate facility for treatment. In-water treatment can seriously compound the problems.

14. A, B, C, and D. Recompression, compression, or hyperbaric chambers are interchangeable terms that describe vessels used to treat diving casualties. Engineers refer to chambers as PVHO's (Pressure Vessels for Human Occupancy.)

15. C. Divers Alert Network (DAN). DAN provides a valuable service to the diving community. In the event of a diving accident, you can call DAN 24 hours a day and obtain information about the nearest diving physician or hyperbaric chamber.

REPETITIVE DIVING

Q:

Modern divers frequently make more than one dive per day. What are the current procedures for repetitive diving? What repetitive diving situations pose the greatest risk of decompression sickness? When solving repetitive dive problems, refer to U.S. Navy-based dive tables and use the following maximum time limits: 40 ft/130 min, 50 ft/80 min, 60 ft/50 min, 70 ft/40 min, 80 ft/35 min, 90 ft/25 min, 100 ft/20 min. There are several abbreviations in the quiz. Familiarize yourself with the following terms before reading the questions: USN = United States Navy, DCS = Decompression Sickness, No-D = No required decompression, SIT = Surface Interval Time.

1. A repetitive dive is any dive within ____ hours of a previous dive.
- ❏ A. 6
- ❏ B. 12
- ❏ C. 24
- ❏ D. Any of the above

2. The recommended maximum depth limit for repetitive dives is:
- ❏ A. 60 feet
- ❏ B. 80 feet
- ❏ C. 100 feet
- ❏ D. 130 feet

3. The minimum recommended surface interval between recreational dives is:
- ❏ A. 10 minutes
- ❏ B. 30 minutes
- ❏ C. 60 minutes
- ❏ D. 90 minutes

4. For both single and repetitive dives, the DCIEM and the DSAT dive tables are more conservative than the USN dive tables.
- ❏ A. True
- ❏ B. True for the DCIEM tables, but not the DSAT tables
- ❏ C. True for the DSAT tables, but not the DCIEM tables
- ❏ D. False

5. The type of diving most likely to result in DCS is:
- ❏ A. A single No-D dive to a single depth
- ❏ B. Repetitive No-D dives to a single depth
- ❏ C. Repetitive No-D dives to multiple depths
- ❏ D. A single dive with required decompression

6. Which of the following series of dives is most likely to cause DCS?
- ❏ A. 60 ft/25 min, 1:30 SIT, 60 ft/25 min
- ❏ B. 100 ft/10 min, 1:45 SIT, 80 ft/15 min, 2:00 SIT, 60 ft/15 min
- ❏ C. 100 ft/7 min, 0:05 SIT, 100 ft/7 min, 0:05 SIT, 100 ft/5 min

- ❏ D. 100 ft/7 min + 60 ft/15 min, 2:30 SIT, 60 ft/ 20 min + 40 ft/15 min

7. According to the modified USN dive tables, _____ is the minimum SIT that allows a 70 ft/20 min No-D dive following an 80 ft/30 min dive.
- ❏ A. 1:14
- ❏ B. 2:00
- ❏ C. 2:58
- ❏ D. 1:59

8. According to the modified USN dive tables, the maximum No-D time for a group E diver doing a repetitive dive to a depth of 65 feet is:
- ❏ A. 9
- ❏ B. 14
- ❏ C. 20
- ❏ D. 26

9. According to the modified USN dive tables, the maximum depth to which you could dive for at least 30 minutes after a 72 ft/28 min dive and a 1 hour 30 min surface interval is:
- ❏ A. 60 feet
- ❏ B. 50 feet
- ❏ C. 40 feet
- ❏ D. 30 feet

10. Precautionary or safety decompression stops during repetitive dives should be _____ at depths of ____.
- ❏ A. 1-3 min, 10 ft-15 ft
- ❏ B. 2-3 min, 10 ft-15 ft
- ❏ C. 1-3 min, 10 ft-30 ft
- ❏ D. 3-5 min, 10 ft-30 ft

11. List three surface interval actions that help reduce the risk of DCS.
- A. _____
- B. _____
- C. _____

12. State the rule of repetitive diving exemplified by the two series of dives.
- ❏ A. 80 ft/20 min, 2:00 SIT, 70 ft/20 min, 2:00 SIT, 60 ft/20 min
- ❏ B. 60 ft/20 min, 2:00 SIT, 70 ft/20 min, 2:00 SIT, 80 ft/20 min

13. A bounce (short duration) dive to free an anchor after repetitive dives is not a risky venture because you do not absorb much nitrogen.
- ❏ A. True if the time on the bottom does not exceed two minutes
- ❏ B. True if the depth does not exceed 60 feet
- ❏ C. False because the issue is not the absorption of nitrogen
- ❏ D. False because you do absorb a significant amount of nitrogen

14. When you use a dive computer for multiple level repetitive dives, it is essential to consult traditional dive tables.
- ❏ A. True
- ❏ B. False

15. The number of repetitive dives per day recommended currently is:
- ❏ A. 1
- ❏ B. 2
- ❏ C. 3
- ❏ D. Unlimited

REPETITIVE DIVING

 A:

How is your repetitive diving knowledge? If it is not good, you should make only shallow dives. You are more likely to get bent after repetitive dives than after single dives. DCS is a serious illness. Do a precautionary decompression stop for three to five minutes at the end of every dive. Have surface intervals of at least an hour. Always progress from deep to shallow—within each dive and from dive to dive. Avoid bounce dives. If you use a dive computer, use it conservatively. Avoid repetitive dives over 80 feet. Remember the risk of DCS increases with the number of repetitive dives per day. No dive planning device—table or computer—can guarantee that you will not experience decompression sickness.

1. D. Any of the above. The USN considers any dive within twelve hours of a previous dive a repetitive dive. NAUI uses a conservative 24 hours, while Diving Science and Technology (DSAT) uses only six hours for its dive tables. The disparity is confusing unless you keep in mind that decompression sickness is not an absolute science, but a matter of statistical probability.

2. C. 100 feet. The annual accident reports of the Divers Alert Network (DAN) say the likelihood of decompression sickness increases significantly when the depth of repetitive dives exceeds 80 feet. Several diver organizations, such as NAUI and the YMCA, have policies that repetitive dives should not exceed 100 feet. In light of DAN's findings, 80 feet may be appropriate as the maximum.

3. C. 60 minutes. Although the USN Diving Manual states the minimum time between dives (for the dives to be considered repetitive dives) is ten minutes, many decompression experts and some diver training organizations recommend a minimum surface interval of one hour between dives. The less residual nitrogen you have for a repetitive dive, the less likely you are to get bent.

4. B. True for the DCIEM tables, but not for the DSAT tables. The No-D time limits for the DCIEM and DSAT tables are less than the USN time limits for an initial dive, but the DSAT tables allow more No-D time for repetitive dives than either the USN or DCIEM tables. Why the difference? The organizations that tested the tables have different statistics for DCS probability based on the tests they conducted.

5. C. Repetitive No-D dives to multiple depths. According to the DAN 1990 Report of Diving Accidents, "A record number of DCS cases involved repetitive diving within the tables, 80 feet or greater, with multilevel profiles." Since this behavior causes hundreds of divers to get bent each year, take the information into consideration when planning your dives.

6. C. 100 ft/7 min, 0:05 SIT, 100 ft/7 min, 0:05 SIT, 100 ft/5 min. The first dive se-

ries is a moderate repetitive dive sequence. The second series is three dives with decreasing depth—a recommended practice. The fourth series contains a multilevel dive and a repetitive dive, but the nitrogen load is not excessive. The third series may seem innocent because the total dive time for the three dives to 100 feet is only 19 minutes, but the time does not take into consideration the bubble development and growth likely to occur with multiple ascents. Avoid multiple ascents during deeper dives.

7. B. 2:00. A dive to 80 feet for 30 minutes assigns a diver a G letter group. In order to make a repetitive dive of at least 20 minutes to a depth of 70 feet, you must have as a minimum a D letter group. The minimum time to change from Group G to Group D is two hours.

8. B. 14 minutes. Use a 70 foot schedule for a 65 foot dive. The maximum No-D time for 70 feet is 40 minutes. The Residual Nitrogen Time (RNT) for an E letter group at 70 feet is 26 minutes. The adjusted maximum No-D time is 40 minutes (the maximum) minus 26 minutes (the RNT) or 14 minutes.

9. B. 50 feet. Use an 80 foot/30 minute schedule for the dive (When you exceed a number, use the next greater number). You have a G letter group after the dive. After an SIT of 1:30, you have an E letter group. The maximum depth that will allow a dive of at least 30 minutes for an E-group diver is 50 feet, which permits 42 minutes of No-D time.

10. D. 3-5 min, 10 ft-30 ft. The recommendation of the 1989 American Academy of Underwater Sciences (AAUS) Biomechanics of Safe Ascents Workshop is, "A stop in the 10-30 fsw zone for 3-5 min is recommended on every dive." An exact depth, as specified in USN procedures, is not important as long as the depth is shallower than 30 feet.

**11. Surface interval actions that can help reduce the risk of DCS are breathing oxygen in the highest concentration possible, drinking non-alcoholic fluids, avoiding strenuous exercise, and avoiding activi-

ties that increase circulation.** Take it easy between dives and drink lots of fluids.

12. The rule of diving exemplified by both series of dives is to make your deepest dives first. The only difference between the two series of dives is the profile sequencing. Example A is a No-D series. Example B requires decompression. When you dive shallow and then deeper, you carry an RNT penalty for repetitive dives. Make your dive progressions from deep to shallow. You will have more dive time and are less likely to get bent.

13. C. False because the issue is not the absorption of nitrogen. You have bubbles in your body following repetitive dives, but the bubbles are asymptomatic—they do not cause symptoms of bends. Immediately after a dive the capillary beds of the lungs trap many bubbles until the bubbles break up and dissolve their gas into solution for elimination. A bounce dive releases bubbles from the lungs into normal circulation. The bubbles absorb additional nitrogen, expand, and may no longer be asymptomatic when you ascend following the bounce dive.

14. B. False. Those who say to use dive tables as a back-up for computer dives do not understand dive computers. Computers calculate nitrogen absorption in one-foot depth increments in real time and allow multilevel dives that exceed greatly the maximum No-D time that a table allows for a given maximum depth. While you should not accept dive computer time limits blindly—especially for repetitive deep dives—you should not try to limit computer dives to traditional dive table time limits.

15. C. 3. Experts within the Undersea Hyperbaric and Medical Society (UHMS) recommend a maximum of three dives per day. Many decompression experts agree, although one recent study suggests more than three dives per day may be done without incident. The bottom line is that the more you dive the more likely you are to have decompression sickness. No matter how many dives you make per day, it is a good idea to dive conservatively. Don't be a bold, bent diver.

U. S. NAVY DIVE TABLES

Q:

The U. S. Navy Decompression Tables have been the standard dive tables of much of the world for decades. These tables have also been the subject of much discussion, debate, and confusion for the past several years. This quiz address some aspects of the 1988 U. S. Navy tables where there appears to be widespread confusion. See if you really know your tables. Select the best answer for each question.

1. There is a 5% "safety factor" built into the U. S. Navy Decompression Tables.
❏ A. True
❏ B. False

2. There is a high incidence rate of recreational divers getting bent from dives made within the no-decompression limits of the U. S. Navy Tables.
❏ A. True
❏ B. False

3. The letter-group designations of the U.S. Navy Tables are based on the amount of nitrogen contained in the _____ tissue.
❏ A. 40 minute
❏ B. 60 minute
❏ C. 80 minute
❏ D. 120 minute

4. The U.S. Navy Decompression tables were tested for ___ repetitive dive(s).
❏ A. 1
❏ B. 2
❏ C. 3
❏ D. 4

5. U.S. Navy Tables repetitive dive tests were conducted to a maximum depth of:
❏ A. 100 feet
❏ B. 130 feet
❏ C. 150 feet
❏ D. 190 feet

6. The U.S. Navy Decompression Tables were designed and tested for:
❏ A. Multiple-ascent dives
❏ B. Single-ascent dives
❏ C. Single-level dives
❏ D. Multiple-level dives
❏ E. B and C

7. Which of the following factors is likely to cause decompression sickness:
❏ A. Multiple complete ascents during dives to 60 feet or deeper
❏ B. Multiple repetitive dives
❏ C. Repetitive dives to depths in excess of 100 feet
❏ D. All the above

8. Use the U.S. Navy Decompression Tables to back up all dive computer-assisted dives.
❏ A. True in all instances
❏ B. True in some instances
❏ C. False

9. Presently published versions of the U.S. Navy Dive Tables contain errors in the:
❏ A. No-decompression limits and repetitive group designation table
❏ B. Surface interval timetable
❏ C. Residual nitrogen timetable
❏ D. Tables listed in answers A and B

10. You can increase the safety of the U.S. Navy Dive Tables most effectively by:
❏ A. Reducing the no-decompression limits
❏ B. Slowing the ascent rate
❏ C. Doing a five minute safety decompression stop
❏ D. None of the above

11. The U.S. Navy Dive Tables apply to dives made at elevations up to:
❏ A. Sea level
❏ B. 500 feet
❏ C. 1,000 feet
❏ D. 2,500 feet

12. The average depth of all dives conducted by the U.S. Navy is about:
❏ A. 47 feet
❏ B. 64 feet
❏ C. 72 feet
❏ D. 78 feet

13. The "M-values" of the U.S. Navy Tables are:
❏ A. The maximum allowable tissue nitrogen pressures that can be tolerated by a tissue compartment during pressure reduction.
❏ B. Expressed in feet of sea water absolute (FSWA)
❏ C. The basis for the Navy no-decompression limits
❏ D. All the above

U.S. NAVY DIVE TABLES

A:

Many myths and misconceptions about the Navy Decompression Tables exist. I hope this quiz dispelled some of these misconceptions for you. There has been so much information published about the Navy Tables that you probably could not read it in a lifetime. Note, however, that in spite of all the research that has been done, decompression sickness is still not truly understood. There is only a statistical probability that you will not contract the bends if you limit your time at a given depth and ascend at a given rate. Dive conservatively, shallowly and with common sense. The bends can be a very unforgiving disease.

1. False. Original plans for the Navy tables accepted a 5% incidence rate of bends, but during testing the limits were established for a 0% rate. There were no incidence rate statistics for the Navy tables for the first 25 years of their existence, so many guesses were made as to how safe they really were. The Navy's incidence rate for open circuit scuba dives has consistently been less than one half of one percent. There is no "safety factor" built into the Navy tables, but there is no "risk factor" either.

2. False. We do not have an incidence rate for recreational diving because we do not know how many divers there are nor how many dives are made per year. If an extremely conservative estimate of two million recreational dives per year is made, the incidence rate of bends within the Navy tables would be a mere .0006%!

3. D. 120 minute tissue. Various tissues in the body ingas and outgas at differing rates. The Navy initially computed 14 tables to determine the amount of nitrogen contained in various "compartments" (a mathematical equivalent of a theoretical tissue), but realized that using 14 tables would be unwieldy, so the decision was made to base the letter group designations on the amount of gas remaining in the tissue that took the longest to outgas.

4. A. 1. The Navy Tables were only tested for one repetitive dive. Only 62 manned repetitive dives were made for random dive schedules. The multiple-repetitive dives made by many recreational divers venture into uncharted territory as far as the Navy Tables are concerned.

5. A. 100 feet. The reason for this question is to impress upon readers that the Navy tables were never intended to be used the way some recreational divers apply them. It is possible to use the Navy Tables to plan repetitive dives to depths in excess of 100 feet, but the tables were neither intended nor tested for this type of diving.

6. E, B and C. Dives made by Navy divers usually involve a diver going to a set depth and remaining at that depth until the completion of an assigned task. It is common for recreational divers to vary their depths significantly and repeatedly during dives. Multiple complete ascents during dives are common. Both practices have physiological effects that influence decompression sickness and may help explain why a few recreational divers get bent while supposedly diving within the Navy limits. When using the Navy tables, we should try to apply them as much as possible in the manner for they were designed and tested.

7. D. All the above. If you responded correctly to questions 4, 5, and 6, you probably selected the correct answer for this question as well. This summarizes the hazards associated with the risky practices of some divers who liberally and incorrectly interpret the Navy Tables. Experts caution us that we should avoid deep, repetitive, multi-day diving.

8. C. False. You need to have dive tables in addition to a computer, but you might as well not use a computer if you are going to restrict your dives to the Navy table limits, which consider total bottom time for the deepest depth of the dive. Dive computers allow bottom times far in excess of the Navy no-stop limits when you do progressively shallower, multi-level dives. You can and should use tables for single-depth dives made with a computer, especially dives in excess of 100 feet.

9. D. Tables listed in answers A and B. When the "No-Decompression Limits and Repetitive Group Designation Table" was developed, five of the schedules from 30 feet and shallower were somehow shifted one column to the left, which resulted in a letter-group assignment one group too liberal. There are five entries in the Residual Nitrogen Timetable that are incorrect. The two most significant are from Group B to Group A, which should be 3:20 instead of 2:10; and from Group C to Group A, which should be 4:49 rather than 2:29.

10. C. Doing a five minute safety decompression stop. Slowing the ascent rate actually increases the nitrogen loading of some tissues. Reducing the no-decompression limits contributes to safety, but the best possible action you can take to prevent decompression sickness is to perform a five minute safety stop at the end of every dive. The latest recommendation is to stop for one minute at a depth of 20-30 feet followed by a four-minute stop at 10-15 feet.

11. C. 1,000 feet. There is only 0.036 atmospheres of pressure difference between sea level and an altitude of 1,000 feet. This small variation is allowable when using the USN Tables. Use altitude decompression tables for dives at higher elevations. Remember also that the USN tables are based on saltwater dives rather than freshwater dives. Dive more conservatively as elevation increases. Learn the hazards of and procedures for diving at high altitude before attempting to dive there.

12. A. 47 feet. One reason that the incidence rate for the U.S. Navy has been so low for so many years is because the mean depth of all Navy dives is 46.72 FSW. Half of all Navy dives are shallower than 33.5 FSW. We should learn from the excellent safety record of Navy divers and spend our time underwater at depths of 50 feet and shallower. Too many recreational divers are making multiple-day, multiple-repetitive dives to deeper depths and are being afflicted with decompression sickness. Recreational diving is supposed to be fun.

13. D. All the above. The Navy developed the "M-value" in 1965 to simplify the explanation of the maximum tissue pressure for various tissue compartments. The M-value represents the maximum allowable supersaturation ratios for the tissues and is expressed in feet of sea water absolute (FSWA). For example, the critical supersaturation ratio for a five-minute tissue is 3.15, which is equivalent to 104 FSWA, while the surfacing ratio for a 120-minute tissue is 1.55, or 51 FSWA. The surfacing M-values set the limits for no-decompression dives.

SECTION FOUR

□□□□

Diving Physics

Diving Physics

We call the study of natural law "physics." The natural laws that govern the diving environment are different than the laws governing our atmospheric surroundings. Divers must have a thorough understanding of physics fundamentals because the natural laws that affect us while diving can rapidly become threats to our health and even our lives.

The primary natural laws that concern divers relate to matter and energy. Matter composes the universe and energy is the force that works within matter. Divers assign particular importance to the pressure, gases, buoyancy, drag, humidity, and the properties of heat, light, and sound in water.

The bottom line is that water density affects your buoyancy, mobility, heat loss, vision, hearing, body air spaces, air supply duration, dissolved body gases, and more. The more you know, the more the natural laws governing the aquatic realm will trouble you.

Section Four quizzes challenge your knowledge of diving physics. The quizzes are designed to educate as well as evaluate. When you complete this section, you should know much more about the forces affecting you when you dive. More importantly, you should know how to deal with the effects to avoid injury.

Assume the following facts when answering the physics questions:
1. One atmosphere of pressure = 14.7 psi, 33 feet of sea water, and 34 feet of freshwater.
2. Water density = 64 lb./cf (sea water) and 62.4 lb./cf (freshwater). Freshwater is 2.5% less dense than seawater.
3. Temperatures are degrees Farenheit.
4. Water is 800 times more dense than air.
5. 39.2 degrees F is the maximum density of freshwater.

AIR CONSUMPTION

This quiz covers knowledge ranging from entry level to instructor level. The questions are progressively more difficult. See how many questions you can answer without guessing. Select the most correct answer for each question.

1. Air consumption calculations are:
- ❑ A. Necessary when you do not use a submersible pressure gauge
- ❑ B. Useful to gauge breathing rates
- ❑ C. Required for dive planning approximations
- ❑ D. Of no value if you use a submersible pressure gauge

2. Air consumption:
- ❑ A. Increases as depth increases
- ❑ B. Decreases as depth increases
- ❑ C. Remains the same as depth increases
- ❑ D. Varies inversely with depth

3. The two greatest factors affecting air consumption are:
- ❑ A. Depth and breathing pattern
- ❑ B. Lung volume and physical fitness
- ❑ C. Depth and activity
- ❑ D. Lung volume and water temperature

4. Air consumption rates usually are:
- ❑ A. Lower for women than for men
- ❑ B. Higher for new divers than for experienced divers
- ❑ C. Higher in colder water than in warmer water
- ❑ D. All the above

5. The equipment you need to measure air consumption includes:
- ❑ A. Submersible pressure gauge and underwater timer
- ❑ B. Submersible pressure gauge and depth gauge
- ❑ C. Both the above plus an underwater slate and pencil
- ❑ D. All the above

6. For a given air consumption rate, an 80 cubic foot (CF) tank lasts ___ times longer than a 50 CF tank.
- ❑ A. 1.6
- ❑ B. 1.5
- ❑ C. 0.6
- ❑ D. None of the above

7. Recommended techniques to reduce air consumption include:
- ❑ A. Relaxation and minimizing effort
- ❑ B. Holding each breath for a few seconds
- ❑ C. Slow, deep, continuous breathing
- ❑ D. A and C, but not B

8. As a rule of thumb, 100 psi in a 71.2 CF steel tank equals about ___ CF of air at the surface.
- ❑ A. 2.0
- ❑ B. 2.5
- ❑ C. 3.0
- ❑ D. 3.5

9. Divers used to calculate air consumption in ____ ; today divers usually calculate air consumption in ___.
- ❑ A. CF/min., psi/min.
- ❑ B. Psi/min., CF/min.
- ❑ C. Psi/min., psi/min.
- ❑ D. CF/min., CF/min.

10. The depth consumption rate (DCR) of a diver with a 3,000 psi, 50 CF tank who uses 300 psi in 10 minutes at a depth of 10 feet in the ocean is:
- ❑ A. 30 psi/min.
- ❑ B. 23 psi/min.
- ❑ C. 0.5 CF/min.
- ❑ D. A or C, but not B

11. The surface consumption rate (SCR) for the diver in the previous question is:
- ❑ A. 23 psi/min.
- ❑ B. 30 psi/min.
- ❑ C. 0.38 CF/min.
- ❑ D. A or C, but not B

12. The SCR of a diver who uses 1,100 psi of air at 22 minutes at a depth of 20 feet in freshwater is approximately:
- ❑ A. 31 psi/min.
- ❑ B. 55 psi/min.
- ❑ C. 88 psi/min.
- ❑ D. 22 psi/min.

13. A diver who uses 1,000 psi in 20 minutes at a depth of 33 feet in the ocean needs ___ psi of air for the same length of time at a depth of 90 feet provided all factors remain the same except depth.
- ❑ A. 1,925
- ❑ B. 1,865
- ❑ C. 1,805
- ❑ D. None of the above

14. A diver with a 3,000 psi, 80 CF tank and an SCR of 30 psi/min. uses 160 psi to descend to a depth of 60 feet in the ocean, then remains there for 28 minutes. The diver then uses 100 psi to ascend. There is ___ psi remaining in the tank when the diver reaches the surface.
- ❑ A. 388
- ❑ B. 396
- ❑ C. 516
- ❑ D. 542

15. If a diver with a 3,000 psi, 80 CF tank uses 1 CF per minute at a depth of 25 feet in the ocean and starts a dive with a full tank, the diver can remain at a depth of 80 feet in freshwater for ____ minutes provided all factors remain the same except water density and depth. Use 200 psi for descent and 500 psi for ascent and reserve.
- ❑ A. 65
- ❑ B. 25
- ❑ C. 32
- ❑ D. 19

AIR CONSUMPTION

Beginning divers should be able to determine their air consumption and should keep a record until consumption stabilizes. The record helps gauge proficiency and relaxation. Experienced divers probably have little need to make calculations, but highly experienced divers who engage in specialty activities need to be able to make estimates that require advanced and instructor level knowledge. I hope you did well for your training level and that you can safely decrease your air consumption.

1. B. Useful to gauge breathing rate. Before submersible pressure gauges (SPGs), you had to calculate air consumption or use a reserve valve. While calculations are useful for dive planning, the SPG makes calculations unnecessary. It helps to gauge your use rate for comparison to standard rates. It is good to evaluate your breathing rate.

2. A. Increases as depth increases. Your regulator delivers air at ambient pressure. As pressure increases during descent, your regulator supplies more air from your tank. Usage varies directly with depth. You consume twice as much air with each breath at 33 feet compared to the surface, three times as much at 66 feet, etc.

3. C. Depth and activity. The deeper you dive and the more energy you expend, the faster you consume air. Other factors affect use rate, but none are as great at depth and activity. To reduce air consumption, dive shallow and minimize activity.

4. D. All the above. New divers use air about twice as fast as experienced divers. Cold water increases respiration, which—ironically—increases heat loss. Women have a definite advantage over men when it comes to air consumption.

5. D. All the above. To measure air consumption, descend to depth, write down your starting time and air pressure, remain at a constant depth for a period of time, then write down your ending time and air pressure. Other answers explain how to calculate consumption.

6. A. 1.6. Air consumption rates apply to a cylinder of a given size. If you use a different size tank, you can determine the duration of the new tank by using a conversion factors, which are ratios between the volumes of the cylinders.

7. D. A and C, but not B. Proper breathing habits, relaxation, and minimal efforts are effective ways to gain more time under water by reducing air consumption. Holding each breath—skip breathing—causes carbon dioxide build-up or could cause a lung injury. Experts discourage skip breathing.

8. C. 3.0 100 psi in a 71.2 CF tank equals 2.88 CF (X/100 = 71.2/2,475. 2,475X = 7,120. X = 2.88 CF). 100 psi in an aluminum 80 equals 2.66 CF. These numbers are useful for some air consumption and salvage calculations.

9. A. CF/min., psi/min. Prior to SPGs, divers calculated air consumption in CF/min. Gauges measure pressure in psi, so we now calculate consumption in psi/min. because it is easier.

10. D. A or C, but not B. Here are the answers in both psi/min. and CF/min. DCR = Amount divided by time = 300/10 = 30 psi/min. To calculate CF/min., figure the diver used 10% of the air (5 CF) in 10 minutes. DCR = 5/10 = 0.5 CF/min.

11. D. A or C, but not B. The formula for SCR is DCR divided by (Depth + 33/33). SCR = 30 psi/min./(10 + 33/33) = 30/1.3 = 23 psi/min. SCR in CF = 0.5/1.3 = 0.38 CF/min.

12. A. 31 psi/min. The DCR is 1,100 psi divided by 22 min. = 1,100/22 = 50 psi/min. at 20 feet. SCR = 50/(20 + 34/34) = 50/1.59 = 31.4 psi/min. Note that 34 feet of freshwater equals one atmosphere of pressure.

13. B. 1,865. Always convert the consumption rate to SCR before calculating the use rate for a new depth. The divers DCR = 1,000/20 = 50 psi/min. SCR = 50/2 = 25 psi/min. DCR at 90 feet = SCR (90 + 33/33) = 25 X 3.73 = 93.25 psi/min. For 20 minutes at 90 feet, the diver needs 93.25 X 20 = 1,865 psi.

14. A. 388 psi. Determine DCR first. DCR = SCR (Depth + 33/33) = 30 X 2.8 = 84 psi/min. Multiply the DCR times the duration of the dive (28 minutes) to determine the amount of air used at depth (84 X 28 = 2,352). Subtract the air used at depth plus the air used for descent and ascent from the starting pressure (3,000 - 2,352 - 160 - 100 = 388 psi).

15. C. 32. Begin by converting the 1 CF/min. to psi/min. (1/X = 80/3,000 = 37.5 psi/min.). Next, convert DCR to SCR (37.5/1.76 = 21.3 psi/min.). Determine the DCR at 80 feet in freshwater (21.3 X 3.35 = 71.36 psi/min.). Calculate the available air supply at depth (3,000 - 700 = 2,300 psi). Determine how long the 2,300 psi will last at a DCR of 71.36 psi/min. (2,300/71.36 = 32.2 min.).

BODY POSITIONING

The position or attitude of your body in the water is important. How much do you know about "trim" and "drag." Most divers know that a lot of drag is undesirable, but many do not take actions to reduce it. How can you optimize trim and minimize drag? See if you understand the basics of body positioning. Answer the following questions, then check your answers against the correct ones on the following page.

Q:

1. The "trim" of a diver is best defined as:
☐ A. A neat and orderly condition
☐ B. The balance of the body in water by the arrangement of ballast and buoyancy
☐ C. The leveling off of a diver in motion
☐ D. The decorative ornaments on equipment

2. The three states of body positioning for diving are:
☐ A. Positive, neutral, and negative
☐ B. Head up, level, and head down
☐ C. Buoyant, neutral, and sinking
☐ D. Either A or B is correct

3. The five forces affecting a swimming diver are:
A. _____
B. _____
C. _____
D. _____
E. _____

4. The center of gravity and center of buoyancy of a diver are:
☐ A. Usually the same
☐ B. Usually different
☐ C. Always the same
☐ D. Synonymous

5. "Drag" in diving is best defined as:
☐ A. Pulling heavily or slowly
☐ B. Anything that retards forward progress
☐ C. Resistance to motion
☐ D. Transvestite diving attire

6. Drag force is proportional to the:
☐ A. Frontal area of a diver
☐ B. Frontal area of the diver's equipment
☐ C. Weight and buoyancy of the diver's equipment
☐ D. Both A and B are correct

7. The amount of energy required for movement by a diver through water is affected by:
☐ A. The frontal area of the diver
☐ B. The speed of the diver
☐ C. The velocity of the water
☐ D. All of the above

8. Two ways to reduce energy requirements for diver propulsion are to reduce (one word per blank):
A. _____
B. _____

9. A diver is most likely to achieve level positioning while swimming when buoyancy is:
☐ A. Slightly positive
☐ B. Neutral
☐ C. Slightly negative
☐ D. None of the above

10. The best method to keep the legs and feet down when diving with a dry suit is:
☐ A. By using ankle weights
☐ B. By wearing the weighting system lower on the body
☐ C. By wearing weights just above the knees
☐ D. All the above are equally acceptable

11. "Drop weights:"
☐ A. Are appropriate for deep, specialty dives only
☐ B. Are less likely to be needed with a dry suit than with a wet suit
☐ C. Are not required if a diver is weighted properly for a dive
☐ D. Usually have an adverse effect on body positioning when discarded

12. As a diver's speed through water increases, body position becomes more level regardless of buoyancy.
☐ A. True
☐ B. False

13. The amount of air a diver uses to travel a certain distance is inversely proportional to the frontal area of the diver.
☐ A. True
☐ B. False

14. Resistance to movement through water is proportional to the square of the speed of a diver.
☐ A. True
☐ B. False

BODY POSITIONING

Do you see how buoyancy, trim, drag, and energy requirements are all inter-related and why body positioning is important? Take the time to adjust your equipment so your buoyancy is neutral for the depth you dive and your trim is neutral when you are motionless in the water. Streamline your equipment as much as possible to reduce drag. If you answered more than five questions incorrectly, you need to learn more about trim and drag. If you scored well, hopefully you are practicing what you know.

1. B. The balance of the body in water by the arrangement of ballast and buoyancy best describes the term "trim." The energy requirements for a diver with good trim are lower than for a diver with poor trim. Good trim means a diver is level. Poor trim means the diver is in a head up or head down position while moving through the water.

2. D. Either A or B is correct. There are three ways to identify the state of trim for a diver. Positive buoyancy causes head down or negative trim. Negative buoyancy causes head up or positive trim. Correct buoyancy adjustment allows a level position called neutral trim. Both positive and negative trim increase frontal area, which increases drag, which increases the energy needed to move through the water.

3. The five forces affecting a swimming diver are buoyancy, weight, thrust, drag, and lift. Buoyancy is an upward force. Weight is a downward force. Drag is resistance to motion created by the frontal area of a diver. Thrust is propulsion provided by the diver. Lift is the force resulting when buoyancy and weight are not balanced. An overweighted diver has a positive lift component, while an underweighted diver has a negative lift component.

4. B. Usually different. The center of buoyancy of an object depends upon the shape of the outer surface of the object. The center of gravity depends upon the distribution of the weight of an object within its shape. The centers of buoyancy and gravity coincide only when an object has uniform density. Since divers and their equipment do not have uniform density, the centers do not coincide automatically. The centers may be adjusted by moving weight and flotation along the longitudinal axis of a diver. The adjusting process enables a diver to achieve neutral trim.

5. C. Resistance to motion. The drag force water exerts on a diver depends upon the density and velocity of the water and the frontal area of the diver exposed to the water. The denser the water, the greater the velocity of the water, and the greater the frontal area of the diver, the greater the effort required to move through the water.

6. D. Both A and B are correct. If density and velocity are constant, the amount of drag force affecting a diver is proportional to the frontal area of the diver and his equipment. Streamlining equipment and achieving level trim with correct buoyancy adjustment minimize drag force and reduce energy requirements for swimming.

7. D. All of the above. Whether the diver is moving through the water or the water is moving over the diver, the drag effect is the same. The drag force is proportional to the square of the relative speed of the diver. Doubling speed from one half knot to one knot (or maintaining a speed of one half knot while swimming into a one half knot current) increases the drag force (and the effort required) by a factor of four.

8. Two ways to reduce energy requirements for diver propulsion are to reduce <u>frontal area</u> and <u>speed</u>. Frontal area may be reduced with low profile equipment and with buoyancy adjustments to get the diver as close to neutral trim as possible. A diver who exerts less to swim through the water is less likely to become exhausted.

9. D. None of above. Neutral buoyancy alone may not achieve neutral trim. Level positioning occurs only when a diver is neutrally stable along both his lateral and longitudinal axis. Weighting and buoyancy must be adjusted to get the centers of buoyancy and gravity to coincide.

10. B. By wearing the weighting system lower on the body. (See answer number four). The second best answer is C (wearing weights just above the knees). Weights worn on the ankles when swimming move six to eight times farther than weights worn just above the knees. The amount of effort needed to swim with knee weights is much less than that required to swim with ankle weights.

11. B. Drop weights are weights that clip to a weight belt. To compensate for buoyancy loss, some divers leave drop weights at the bottom of the ascent line. **Such weights are less likely to be needed with a dry suit than with a wet suit.** The compression of the suit by pressure is less with a dry suit. The volume of a dry suit can be nearly constant regardless of depth. As a wet suit diver descends, volume (and buoyancy) decrease steadily. The more air a wet suit diver adds to his BC to compensate for suit compression, the more his center of buoyancy shifts. Trim is affected severely by the shift in the center of buoyancy. Drop weights are a good idea, especially for wet suit divers who make dives deeper than 60 feet.

12. A. True. As a diver's speed increases, his state of trim will become more level regardless of buoyancy. A diver who is not trim while motionless can get closer to neutral trim when swimming. The problem, however, is that a diver whose trim is not neutral at the outset must exert more energy to get and remain level than a diver who is trimmed properly in a static position.

13. A. False. The drag force on a diver is directionally proportional to the frontal area of the diver and his equipment. The amount of air a diver uses to travel a certain distance is, therefore, directly proportional to the frontal area of the diver and his equipment. If the frontal area is increased, air consumption is increased. If the distance were inversely proportional, air consumption would decrease as frontal area increased.

14. A. True. Resistance to movement through a liquid is proportional to the relative speed of the object. If you double your relative speed, you increase drag by a factor of four and must increase your effort by the same factor. Increasing speed increases air consumption proportionally. A moderate, steady pace is better than a rapid one.

FUN WITH BUOYANCY

"An object immersed in a fluid is buoyed up by a force equal to the weight of the fluid displaced." The principle of buoyancy is relatively simple, but the application of it can be confusing for some from time to time. Test your knowledge of this important topic while having fun answering (or attempting to answer) these questions.

1. An object floats when it displaces water weighing _____ the weight of the object.
- ❏ A. More than
- ❏ B. As much as
- ❏ C. Less than
- ❏ D. None of these

2. A 64 pound object measuring 6"x12"x24" is tossed into a river. The object:
- ❏ A. Floats
- ❏ B. Sinks
- ❏ C. Remains at any depth placed

3. A penny rests atop a block of wood floating in a bowl. If the penny falls into the bowl, the water level will:
- ❏ A. Rise slightly
- ❏ B. Fall slightly
- ❏ C. Remain unchanged

4. An object 8"x9"x24" weighs 56 pounds. If the object is immersed in seawater, what percentage of the 9"x24" surface will be above water?
- ❏ A. 12.5 percent
- ❏ B. 25 percent
- ❏ C. 50 percent
- ❏ D. 87.5 percent

5. You and your equipment weigh 227 pounds when you are neutrally weighted for ocean diving. How much weight will you need to remove to be neutrally buoyant in freshwater?
- ❏ A. About three pounds
- ❏ B. About four pounds
- ❏ C. About five pounds
- ❏ D. About six pounds

6. How many 50 pound lift bags, weighing two pounds each, will be required to lift a three cubic foot object with a dry weight of 287 pounds from a depth of 102 feet in freshwater?
- ❏ A. One
- ❏ B. Two
- ❏ C. Three
- ❏ D. Four

7. Select all correct answers. Wood has a specific gravity of 0.5. This means wood:
- ❏ A. Is half as dense as water
- ❏ B. Is twice as dense as water
- ❏ C. Will float 50 percent of the time
- ❏ D. Floats 50 percent above the surface
- ❏ E. Is affected by gravity less than water is affected

8. An object five feet square and five feet high is floating in the ocean. Six inches are above the waterline. What is the minimum strength line needed to lift the object?
- ❏ A. 10,000 pound test
- ❏ B. 7,500 pound test
- ❏ C. 6,000 pound test
- ❏ D. 1,000 pound test

9. A ladder with rungs 11 inches apart extends down the side of a ship at low tide. The bottom rung just touches the water. How many rungs will be underwater when the tide rises four feet?
- ❏ A. Two
- ❏ B. Three
- ❏ C. Four
- ❏ D. None of the above

10. An object with a volume of one-half cubic foot, weighing 300 pounds is deeply embedded in mud at a depth of 66 feet in an ocean bay. Which of the following is needed to properly lift the object?
- ❏ A. A line to a boat at the surface
- ❏ B. Four 75-pound liftbags weighing five pounds each
- ❏ C. Three 100-pound liftbags weighing 10 pounds each
- ❏ D. Five 500-pound liftbags and two 100-pound lift bags

11. If you exhale eight pints of air into your BC in the ocean, your buoyancy will increase by about:
- ❏ A. Two pounds
- ❏ B. Four pounds
- ❏ C. Six pounds
- ❏ D. Eight pounds

12. A wet suit requires 16 pounds of weight to be neutrally buoyant at the surface. If its volume is proportional to pressure, how much weight will the suit need to be neutrally buoyant at a depth of 99 feet in the ocean?
- ❏ A. 16 pounds
- ❏ B. 8 pounds
- ❏ C. 5 1/3 pounds
- ❏ D. 4 pounds

13. If one-third cubic feet of air is needed in your BC at 33 feet in the ocean, how much will your buoyancy increase if you ascend 10 feet?
- ❏ A. About 4 pounds
- ❏ B. About 6 pounds
- ❏ C. About 9 pounds
- ❏ D. About 11 pounds

14. An anchor with an underwater weight of 197 pounds is at a depth of 78 feet in the ocean. What is the minimum pressure in an 80-cubic foot, 3000 psi scuba tank required to fill a lift bag to raise the anchor (assuming constant temperature and a lift bag weight of two pounds)?
- ❏ A. 390 psig
- ❏ B. 423 psig
- ❏ C. 425 psig
- ❏ D. 431 psig

15. A 96-pound sea lion is atop a nine cubic foot hatch cover that is floating 20 percent above the surface in a pool of seawater. The dry weight of the hatch cover is:
- ❏ A. 460.8 pounds
- ❏ B. 364.8 pounds
- ❏ C. 268.8 pounds
- ❏ D. None of the above

FUN WITH BUOYANCY

A:

Buoyancy is a simple concept—displaced weight minus dry weight—but the calculations can be either fun or frustrating. It all depends on how much you know about diving physics and how you relate the topic to your diving activity. You can learn more about buoyancy, physics, and many other excellent topics by completing a continuing education course in diving. Remember, a knowledgeable diver is a better diver.

1. A. More than. If the weight of water an object displaces weighs more than the object, the object will be buoyed up by a force equal to the difference in weight between the object weight and the weight of the water displaced.

2. B. Sinks. The volume of the object is one cubic foot (6x12x24=1,728 cubic inches = 1 cubic foot) and its weight is 64 pounds. Since freshwater weighs only 62.4 pounds per cubic foot, the object will not displace its weight and will be 1.6 pounds negatively buoyant.

3. B. Fall slightly. The density of the penny is about nine time greater than the density of water. When the penny is on the wood, it displaces its entire weight, but when it falls into the bowl, it displaces only its volume, which is one-ninth of its weight. With less water displaced, the water level falls.

4. A. 12.5 percent. The volume of the object is one cubic foot (8x9x24=1,728 cubic inches=one cubic foot) and its weight is 56 pounds. Since seawater weighs 64 pounds per cubic foot, the object will float when 56/64ths (seven-eights of a cubic foot) have been displaced. One eighth of the object (12.5 percent) will float above the waterline.

5. D. About six pounds. Freshwater is 2.5 percent less dense than seawater (64.0-62.4=1.6/64=.025). Since you would obtain 2.5 percent less buoyancy in freshwater, you would also need to reduce your total weight by 2.5 percent (227x.025=5.675=6 pounds). You may also determine displacement in the ocean (227/64=3.547 cubic feet), calculate your freshwater displacement (3.547x62.4=221.3 pounds), and subtract the difference in total weight (227-221.3=5.7 pounds).

6. C. Three. The object displaces 187 pounds (62.4x3) and weighs 287 pounds, so its buoyancy is -100 pounds. The liftbags provide 48 pounds of lift each [displacement (50 pounds) - dry weight (2 pounds) = 48 pounds], so the minimum number of bags is three. Always deduct the weight of a lifting device from its lifting capacity.

7. A and D are correct. Freshwater is the reference for density and has a specific gravity of 1.0. Specific gravity is a means of assigning a numerical value to the density of a material, which may then be compared to the specific gravity of water. Objects denser than water sink and those less dense than water float.

8. B. 7,500 pound test. The weight of the water being displaced is 7,200 pounds (5 x 5 x 4.5 =112.5 x 64=7,200).

9. D. None of the above. No rungs will be underwater because the ship will simply rise with the tide! Why this silly question? Read the next answer.

10. A. A line to a boat at the surface. An embedded object can require a force up to 10 times its weight in order to overcome suction. The use of liftbags in this situation is extremely hazardous, so a taut line is rigged to a large surface float, such as a boat, at low tide and the incoming tide is used as "tidal winch" to break the object loose so it may then be lifted safely by displacement. Care must be taken, however, that the combination of the suction and the weight of an object are not great enough to sink the vessel.

11. D. Eight pounds. Water weighs about eight pounds per gallon. Eight pints of air is one gallon, so your buoyancy is increased by about eight pounds. The amount of air most people can exhale is about six to eight pints. This means you can vary your buoyancy by as much as six to eight pounds between a full inhalation and a full exhalation. Varying average lung volume while breathing continuously is an excellent way to control buoyancy and is a skill that should be developed by all divers.

12. D. 4 pounds. The question illustrates wet suit compression during descent. At a depth of 99 feet in the ocean—four atmospheres—the volume is one fourth that at the surface; the amount of water displaced is only one fourth as much as at the surface. The weight needed for neutral buoyancy also is only one fourth at much, or 1/4 X 16 = 4 pounds.

13. A. About 4 pounds. Your increase in buoyancy after ascending 10 feet is a function of increased volume owing to Boyle's Law. The new volume is figured as follows: $V_2 = V_1 \times P_1/P_2$ where P_1 and V_1 are the initial pressure and volume and P_2 and V_2 are the ending pressure and volume. V_2 = .333 cubic feet x 2 atma (atmospheres absolute)/1.7 atma = .392 cubic feet. The initial buoyancy was .333 x 64 = 21 pounds. The buoyancy at 23 feet is .392 x 64 = 25 pounds, so the increase in buoyancy is four pounds. This may be enough to cause a diver to drift toward the surface and lose control, so be careful when swimming over objects while diving. This problem is compounded when people dive overweighted.

14. D. 431 psig. The volume needed to lift the anchor is 3.125 cubic feet (200/64). (200 pounds is used because 197 pounds achieves only neutral buoyancy and because of the weight of the liftbag). The surface equivalent volume is 10.5 cubic feet (3.125 cubic feet x 3.36 atma). Divide the volume by a tank factor of 80/3015 (.0265) to determine the psia needed to provide the 198 pounds of lift, which is 396 psia. Remember, however, that a tank cannot be emptied below ambient pressure at depth, so the ambient pressure (3.36 atma x 14.7=49.4 psia) must be taken into consideration and that 14.7 psi must be subtracted from the total to obtain gauge pressure. So the minimum pressure needed is 396 psia + 49.4 psia - 14.7 psia = 430.7 psig. Whew, that was fun, right?

15. B. 364.8 pounds. At first you may think that there is insufficient information to solve this problem. The hatch cover displaces its own weight plus 96 pounds when 80 percent submerged. We can solve the problem by determining 80 percent of the total displacement of the cover and subtracting the weight of the sea lion. Weight = .8 x 576 - 96 = 364.8 pounds (9 cubic feet x 64 pounds/cubic foot = 576).

DIVER'S MATH

There are a few times when we need to make calculations as divers and other times when it is good to be able to make them. It is good to understand the forces affecting us while we dive. Here are some problems for you to solve. Some problems are practical and some are only to test your understanding.

1. If a diver uses 1,500 psi in 10 minutes at a depth of 68 feet in freshwater, the diver's surface air consumption rate (SCR) is:
- ❑ A. 50 psi/min.
- ❑ B. 75 psi/min.
- ❑ C. 90 psi/min.
- ❑ D. 150 psi/min.

2. If a diver's SCR is 60 psi/min. for a given activity level, a 2,500 psi refill will last approximately ___ minutes for the same activity level at a depth of 75 feet in saltwater.
- ❑ A. 12.75
- ❑ B. 18.35
- ❑ C. 42.08
- ❑ D. 45.00

3. If a one-half cubic foot block of wood weighs 16 pounds, ___ percent of the block remains above water when you immerse the block in the ocean.
- ❑ A. 25
- ❑ B. 33
- ❑ C. 50
- ❑ D. 75

4. If a diver and her equipment weigh 175 pounds when neutrally buoyant in saltwater, the diver needs to add/remove ___ pounds to be neutrally buoyant for freshwater diving with the same equipment.
- ❑ A. Add, 4.4
- ❑ B. Remove, 4.4
- ❑ C. Add, 5.2
- ❑ D. Remove, 5.2

5. If a tank contains 80 cubic feet (CF) at a pressure of 3,000 psi and a temperature of 70 degrees F, the tank will contain ___ CF at the same temperature and a pressure of 650 psi.
- ❑ A. 17.64
- ❑ B. 17.33
- ❑ C. 19.22
- ❑ D. 21.00

6. If a scuba tank contains 80 CF at 3,000 psig and a temperature of 70 degrees F, the tank pressure will be ___ psig when its temperature increases to 125 degrees F.
- ❑ A. 3,327.5
- ❑ B. 3,312.8
- ❑ C. 3,275
- ❑ D. 3,330

7. If a lift bag that weighs two pounds contains 0.6 CF of air at a depth of 60 feet in the ocean, the bag would provide ___ pounds of buoyancy upon reaching the surface provided no air escaped during ascent.
- ❑ A. 110
- ❑ B. 108
- ❑ C. 106
- ❑ D. 104

8. If a diver's tank contains one percent carbon monoxide, the partial pressure of the gas at a depth of 77 feet in the ocean is ___ psia.
- ❑ A. 0.45
- ❑ B. 0.49
- ❑ C. 0.34
- ❑ D. 0.36

9. The length of a capillary depth gauge tube is six inches. The length of the air column in the tube at a depth of 90 feet in saltwater is ___ inches.
- ❑ A. 4.4
- ❑ B. 4.0
- ❑ C. 2.2
- ❑ D. 1.6

10. A diver at a depth of 70 feet in 40-degree F freshwater has two quarts of air in his buoyancy compensator. The diver ascends to 30 feet and passes through a 75-degree F thermocline. If the diver neither adds nor vents aid from the BC, the volume of the air inside the BC will be ___ quarts after it stabilizes at the new temperature.
- ❑ A. 2.00
- ❑ B. 3.02
- ❑ C. 3.48
- ❑ D. 3.75

DIVER'S MATH

A:

By now you must feel that diving is doing instead of knowing or you feel that it is good to have knowledge to back what you do while diving. Whether you feel frustrated or satisfied as a result of this quiz, it is good to review the principles involved. If you would like to handle problems such as these more easily, complete an advanced diver course. You will increase your knowledge as well as your skills. You can never know too much when you venture beneath the surface.

1. A. 50 psi/min. Formulas: SCR = DCR X (33/Depth + 33); DCR = Air used/Time. Legend: SCR = Surface Consumption Rate; 33 = 1 atmosphere of pressure (34 feet of freshwater); Air used = psi; Time = minutes. Calculate DCR first: 1500/10 = 150 psi/min. Use DCR to calculate SCR: 150 X (34/68 + 34) = 50 psi/min.

2. A. 12.75. Use answer #1 formulas and legend. Determine DCR for the new depth: 60/[33/(33 + 75)] = 196 psi/min. Determine Time for the new depth: 2500/196 = 12.75 min. Note: When you solve air consumption problems, always use SCR as the reference consumption rate.

3. C. 50%. Formula: Buoyancy = Displacement Weight - Dry Weight. Displacement = 0.5 CF X 64 lb./CF = 32 lb. when you completely submerge the block. The block will float with 16 pounds of displacement, so it has 16 pounds of excess buoyancy. 16/32 or 50% of the block floats above water.

4. B. Remove, 4.4. Formula: Fresh Water Neutral Buoyancy = 97.5% X Total Saltwater Weight: .975 X 175 lb. = 170.6 lb. 175 - 170.6 = 4.4 lb.

5. A. 17.64. Formula: P1/V1 = P2/V2. Legend: P1 = Initial Pressure Absolute; Absolute Pressure = Gauge Pressure + Atmospheric Pressure (14.7 psi); P2 = Final Pressure Absolute; V1 = Initial Volume (80 CF; V2 = Final Volume (Unknown). Rearrange the equation to solve for V2: V2 = V1 X P2/P1 = 80 X 664.7/3014.7 = 17.64 CF.

6. B. 3,312.8 psig. Formula: P1/T1 = P2/T2. Psig = psia - atmospheric pressure (14.7). Legend: P1 = Initial Pressure (Absolute); P2 = Final Pressure (unknown); T1 = Initial Temperature (Absolute = Degrees F + 460); T2 = Final Temperature (Absolute). Determine the initial and final temperatures: T1 = 70 + 460 = 530. T2 = 125 + 460 = 585. Solve the problem by rearranging the formula and substituting the values: P2 = T2 X P1/T1 = 585 X 3014.7/530 = 3327.5 psia. Psig - 3,327.5 - 14.7 = 3,312.8 psig.

7. C. 106 pounds. Formulas: Buoyancy = Displaced Weight - Dry Weight; P1V1 = P2V2; Pressure = psi/foot X depth. Legend: P1 = Initial Pressure Absolute; V1 = Initial Volume (unknown); V2 = Final Volume (0.6 CF). Determine the initial and final pressures: P1 = 14.7 psia; P2 = (60 X .445) + 14.7 = 41.4 psia. Rearrange the formula and substitute values: V1 = P2 X V2/P1 = 41.4 X 0.6/14.7 = 1.69 CF. Finally, substitute the volume into the buoyancy equation: Buoyancy = (64 X 1.69) - 2 = 106 lbs.

8. B. 0.49 psia. Formulas: Partial Pressure = Percent of Gas X Total Pressure (Absolute); Total Pressure = (Psi/foot X depth) + atmospheric pressure (14.7) = 48.97 psia. Partial Pressure = 0.01 X 48.97 = 0.49 psia.

9. D. 1.6 inches. Formulas: P1L1 = P2L2; Pressure = Psi/foot X Depth) + 14.7. Legend: P1 = Initial Pressure (Absolute) = Gauge + 14.7); P2 = Final Pressure (Absolute); L1 = Initial Column Length (6 inches); L2 = Final Column Length (unknown). Note: Since the cross section of the tube is constant, the air column length is directly proportional to the inner volume. Therefore, you may substitute the column length for volume in the equation. Determine the initial and final pressures: P1 = 14.7 psia; P2 = (.445 X 90) + 14.7 = 54.75 psia. Rearrange and substitute: L2 = P1 X L1/P2 = 14.7 X 6/54.75 = 1.6 inches.

10. C. 3.48 quarts. Formulas: See previous answers. Legend: P1 = Initial Pressure (Absolute); P2 = final Pressure (Absolute); T1 = Initial Temperature (Absolute); T2 = Final Temperature (Absolute); V1 = Initial Volume (2 quarts); V2 = Final volume (unknown). Determine the initial and final pressures: P1 = (70 X .432) + 14.7 = 44.94 psia; P2 = (30 X .432) + 14.7 = 27.66 psia. Determine the initial and final temperatures: T1 = 40 + 460 = 500; T2 = 75 + 460 = 535. Rearrange and substitute: V2 = P1 X V1 X T2/T1 X P2 = 44.94 X 2 X 535/500 X 27.66 = 3.48 quarts.

HUMIDITY

By definition, humidity is the degree of wetness of the atmosphere. The quantity of water vapor in the air affects divers in several ways. It is important to understand humidity's effects and the causes of the effects. Test your understanding with this quiz.

1. The partial pressure of water vapor in a gas is governed entirely by:
❏ A. The temperature of the gas
❏ B. The pressure of the gas
❏ C. The density of the gas
❏ D. All the above equally

2. The relative humidity of a gas is:
❏ A. The ratio of the amount of water actually present to the amount of water vapor that could be present
❏ B. The amount of moisture present compared to the amount of moisture in the surrounding atmosphere
❏ C. The ratio of the amount of water present in the air compared to the standard amount of pressure.

3. Compression raises the relative humidity of a gas, while expanding a compressed gas reduces the relative humidity.
❏ A. True
❏ B. False

4. The amount of humidity in air affects the cooling capability of the human body.
❏ A. True
❏ B. False

5. Scuba diver dehydration:
❏ A. Occurs because you humidify the dry air your breathe
❏ B. Increases the likelihood of decompression illness
❏ C. Should be prevented by frequent fluid ingestion
❏ D. All the above

6. Regulator second stage freezing is likely to occur when:
❏ A. You exhale into your regulator above water when the temperature is below freezing
❏ B. You fail to breathe through your regulator prior to submerging into near-freezing water
❏ C. Your second stage has not been modified with an anti-freeze solution
❏ D. All the above

7. Regulator first stage freezing is likely to occur when:
❏ A. You exhale into your regulator above water when the temperature is below freezing
❏ B. The cooling effect of air passing through the stage freezes water inside
❏ C. You submerge your regulator and then expose it to sub-freezing temperatures
❏ D. B or C, but not A

8. Using an extra second stage (octopus) regulator increases the likelihood of regulator freeze-up in cold water.
❏ A. True
❏ B. False

9. Mask condensation is caused by:
❏ A. Water vapor you exhale into your mask
❏ B. Moisuture evaporating from your face
❏ C. Moisture evaporating from your eyes
❏ D. All the above

10. Mask defogging is effective because:
❏ A. It absorbs moisture from the air inside the mask
❏ B. It prevents water from condensing on the mask
❏ C. It combines with the moisture to form a new compound
❏ D. None of the above

HUMIDITY

As you can see, there is more to humidity and diving than many divers probably realize. Your diving can be safer and more enjoyable when you understand the effects of humidity and the causes of the effects. Few diving texts address humidity in detail, but you can learn more about humidity and other important topics through continued diving education.

1. A. The temperature of the gas. When a given quantity of gas is exposed to the water, evaporation occurs until the air saturates. Warming of the air allows the air to absorb more water. Cooling the air leads to condensation. The phenomenon occurs regardless of the pressure, density, or volume of gas.

2. A. The ratio of the amount of water actually present to the amount of water vapor that could be present. More specifically, relative humidity is the ratio, expressed in percent, of the amount of water actually present in a gas mixture to the amount of water vapor that could be present if the mixture were saturated at the same temperature.

3. A. True. When you compress a moist gas into a constant volume receiver, you will reach a point where the addition of more air causes condensation inside the container. By contrast, expanding compressed gas causes a decrease in the relative humidity and the partial pressure of water vapor. Now you know why air compressors have water traps and why scuba tank air is dry.

4. A. True. Hot, humid climates inhibit body cooling by evaporation. Use caution during dive preparation in tropical areas. When you cannot offset body heat production with heat loss, heat exhaustion or heat stroke can occur.

5. D. All the above. You humidify each breath you take with moisture from your body, thereby reducing your body fluids. The fluid loss can cause blood thickening and lead to decompression illness. Prevent dehydration by keeping your body well hydrated. Drink fluids before and between dives.

6. A. You exhale into your regulator above water when the temperature is below freezing. The relative humidity of exhaled breath is 100 percent. Breath moisture can freeze inside the second stage. To prevent freezing, exhale into the regulator only when you have the regulator submerged.

7. D. B or C, but not A. First stage freezing is not related to humidity like second stage freezing is. The expansion of compressed air lowers the temperature of the air. Sub-freezing temperature air combined with near-freezing water present on the first stage diaphragm can cause ice crystals to form and interfere with first stage operation. Free-flow will begin, further compounding the problem. If you immerse a first stage, then expose it to freezing temperatures, the water inside can freeze. Anti-freeze regulator first stages can prevent both these problems.

8. A. True. Since expanding air cools a regulator first stage, the greater the air flow, the greater the chance for freeze-up. An extra second stage is a good safety practice generally, but if you use an octopus in near-freezing water, be sure your regulator first stage can handle the increased air flow without freezing.

9. D. All the above. Air in a mask absorbs water vapor from any source until the air inside the mask saturates for a given temperature. When you cool the air in the mask during immersion, the lowered air temperature causes condensation on the mask lens.

10. D. None of the above. The cause of fogging is the "beading" of water droplets on a mask lens. Defogging a mask reduces the surface tension of water so it flows off the lens in a thin sheet instead of forming tiny droplets. The water condenses, but flows to the bottom of the mask. The secret of a clear mask is a clean lens.

DIVE NUMBERS

Many numbers have or should have special meaning to divers. The greater your diving knowledge, the more numbers you should be able to recall from memory or calculate without a reference. See how many of the following numbered statements you can match correctly to the lettered clues list. Use each clue only once. Compare your results with the answers on the following page.

Abbreviations:

atm = atmosphere
°C = degrees Centigrade
cf = cubic feet
° F = degrees Farenheit
ffw = feet of freshwater
fpm = feet per minute
fsw = feet of seawater
ft = Feet
fw = freshwater
gal = gallons

hr = hours
°K = degrees Kelvin
kt = knot
lbs = pounds
max. = maximum
min. = minimum
mph = miles per hour
psi = lbs. per sq. inch
°R = degrees Rankine
sw = seawater

Match to lettered clues:

1. One cf fw weighs ____ lbs
2. There are ____ gal in one cf water
3. 70° F = ____ °C
4. ____ psi is a common working pressure for aluminum tanks
5. The three middle digits of DAN's emergency phone number are (919)___-8111
6. The maximum rate of ascent is ____ fpm
7. The working pressure of a plus-rated steel tank is ____ psi
8. One cf sw weighs ____ lbs
9. 60° F = ____ °R
10. One fsw exerts a pressure of ____ psi
11. The common safety stop depth is ____ ft
12. ____ hrs is the min. time before flying after diving
13. The minimum elevation for altitude diving is ____ ft
14. A reciprocal course requires a ____ ° turn
15. The length of a lunar day is 24: ____
16. The VHF emergency frequency is channel ____
17. ____ ft is the maximum recommended recreational diving depth
18. The hydrostatic test pressure for a 3,000 psi tank is ____ psi
19. Air is about ____% nitrogen
20. ____° is the maximum angle of light reflection on water
21. One nautical mile = ____ ft
22. One gal water weighs ____ lbs
23. Water is about ____ times denser than air
24. The minimum tank pressure when diving is ____ psi
25. The approximate weight of 1 cf air is ____ lbs
26. ____ ft is the extreme chamber treatment depth
27. One atm of pressure is ____ psi
28. 17° C = ____ ° K
29. 1 kt = ____ mph
30. ____ ffw = 1 atm
31. ____° is the usual temperature below 60 ffw
32. There is a ____% decrease in the density of water when it freezes
33. ____ fsw = 1 atm
34. One ffw exerts a pressure of ____ psi
35. The speed of sound in water is approximately ____ fpm

Lettered clues:

A. 14.7
B. 62.4
C. 34
D. 12
E. 33
F. 300
G. 1,000
H. 5,000
I. 15
J. 130
K. 16
L. .08
M. 165
N. 39.2
O. 10
P. 1.15
Q. 64
R. .432
S. 8.35
T. 78
U. 48.5
V. 21.1
W. .445
X. 520
Y. 290
Z. 2,475
AA. 3,000
BB. 684
CC. 60
DD. 180
EE. 7.48
FF. 6,080
GG. 50
HH. 800
JJ. 4,400

DIVE NUMBERS

A:

Scoring:

Novice diver:
21-25 Good
26-30 Excellent
31+ Outstanding

Advanced diver:
26-30 Good
31-33 Excellent
34+ Outstanding

Instructor:
28-30 Good
31-34 Excellent
35 Outstanding

1. (B) One cf fw weighs 62.4 lbs

2. (EE) There are 7.48 gal in one cf water

3. (V) 70° F = 21.1 °C

4. (AA) 3,000 psi is a common working pressure for aluminum tanks

5. (BB) The three middle digits of DAN's emergency phone number are (919) 684-8111

6. (CC) The maximum rate of ascent is 60 fpm

7. (Z) The working pressure of a plus-rated steel tank is 2,475 psi

8. (Q) One cf sw weighs 64 lbs

9. (X) 60° F = 520°R

10. (W) One fsw exerts a pressure of .445 psi

11. (I) The common safety stop depth is 15 ft

12. (D) 12 hr is the minimum time before flying after diving

13. (G) 1,000 ft is the minimum altitude diving elevation

14. (DD) A reciprocal course requires a 180° turn

15. (GG) The length of a lunar day is 24:50

16. (K) The VHF emergency frequency is channel 16

17. (J) 130 ft is the maximum recommended recreational diving depth

18. (H) The hydrostatic test pressure for a 3,000 psi tank is 5,000 psi

19. (T) Air is about 78% nitrogen

20. (U) 48.5° is the maximum angle of light reflection on water

21. (FF) One nautical mile = 6,080 ft

22. (S) One gal water weighs 8.35 lbs

23. (HH) Water is about 800 times denser than air

24. (F) The minimum tank pressure when diving is 300 psi

25. (L) The approximate weight of 1 cf air is .08 lbs

26. (M) 165 ft is the extreme chamber treatment depth

27. (A) One atm of pressure is 14.7 psi

28. (Y) 17° C = 290° K

29. (P) 1 kt = 1.15 mph

30. (C) 34 ffw = 1 atm

31. (N) 39.2° is the usual temperature below 60 ffw

32. (O) There is a 10% decrease in the density of water when it freezes

33. (E) 33 fsw = 1 atm

34. (R) One ffw exerts a pressure of .432 psi

35. (JJ) The speed of sound in water is approximately 4,400 fpm

Ten helpful hints:
1. fw is 2.5% less dense than sw (64 X .975 = 62.4)
2. Since fw is less dense then sw, it takes more (34 vs. 33 ft) to = 1 atm
3. 14.7 psi (1 atm) divided by 34 ffw = .432 psi per ft
4. 14.7 psi (1 atm) divided by 33 fsw = .445 psi per ft
5. °C = (°F - 32) 5/9
6. °F = (9/5 °C) + 32
7. °R = °F + 460
8. °K = °C + 273
9. Hydrostatic test pressure = 5/3 working pressure
10. Plus-rated steel tank allows 10% overfill (2,250 + 225 = 2,475 psi)

PHYSICS PHUN!

$Q:$

It's true divers do not take calculators underwater, but understanding how to solve diving physics problems makes you a better diver because the ability demonstrates familiarity with the concepts that affect your safety. The following questions have two-part answers: the principles and the math. Even if you aren't good at math, you should still be able to outline how to solve the problem. Compare your approach/math answers with those on the following page. REMEMBER, THE FIRST PART OF EACH ANSWER IS A SIMPLE DESCRIPTION OF HOW TO SOLVE THE PROBLEM. THE SECOND PART IS THE ACTUAL MATHEMATICAL SOLUTION.

1. The absolute pressure at a depth of 67 feet in freshwater at an altitude of 3,000 feet (atmospheric pressure of 13.17 psi) is ____ psia.
❏ A. 28.9
❏ B. 42.1
❏ C. 29.8
❏ D. 43.6

2. A wooden raft four feet square, six inches thick and weighing 256 pounds is floating in the ocean and supporting a woman weighing 128 pounds. What percentage of the raft floats above the waterline with the woman on it, and what percentage floats above the water line when the woman is rescued from the raft?
❏ A. 50%, 50%
❏ B. 75%, 25%
❏ C. 25%, 50%
❏ D. 33%, 67%

3. A diver with a full 50 cubic foot, 3,000 psi tank uses 600 psi of air in 12 minutes at a depth of 47 feet in the ocean. The diver's surface air consumption rate is ___ cubic feet per minute.
❏ A. 0.24
❏ B. 0.34
❏ C. 0.54
❏ D. 0.83

4. A buddy team plans to salvage an ingot of lead, which is nine times denser than seawater. The lead ingot measures two by four by 18 inches. The divers have a 50 pound lift bag that weighs one pound. With the lift bag attached to the ingot, which is not embedded in the ocean bottom, the lead will just begin to lift off of the bottom when the lift bag is ___% filled with air.
❏ A. 50%
❏ B. 75%
❏ C. 90%
❏ D. 100%

5. A buoyancy compensator has a lifting capacity of 32 pounds. If the BC is one half full of air at a depth of 99 feet in the ocean, at what depth will the pressure relief valve, which opens with two psi of pressure, begin to release air from the BC assuming no air escapes from the BC until the relief valve opens?
❏ A. 33 feet
❏ B. 28.5 feet
❏ C. 29.5 feet
❏ D. 34 feet

6. A scuba tank holds 80 cubic feet of air at a pressure of 3,000 psi and an internal temperature of 70 degrees F. If the temperature of the tank increases to 85 degrees F and air is released to lower the pressure to 2,100 psi, how many cubic feet of air remain in the cylinder?
❏ A. 54.6 cubic feet
❏ B. 64.0 cubic feet
❏ C. 56.0 cubic feet
❏ D. 68.7 cubic feet

7. A commercial diver uses a gas mixture that contains the sea-level equivalent of 14.7 psi oxygen at a depth of 238 feet in freshwater. What percentage of oxygen is present in this gas mixture at sea level?
❏ A. 14.7%
❏ B. 1.8375%
❏ C. 12.5%
❏ D. 1.56%

8. A neutrally-weighted ocean diver and his equipment weigh 270 pounds. If the diver uses the same equipment for diving in a lake, how much weight must he add or subtract to be neutrally buoyant for freshwater diving?
❏ A. Remove five pounds
❏ B. Add five pounds
❏ C. Remove seven pounds
❏ D. Add seven pounds

9. A diver uses an 80 cubic foot, 3,000 psi scuba cylinder containing 1,600 psi of air to fill a 100 pound lift bag at a depth of 66 feet in the sea. Assuming a constant temperature, that the diver fills the bag completely, and that no air is lost, how many psi of air remain in the tank after the diver fills the bag?
❏ A. 1,500 psig
❏ B. 1,300 psig
❏ C. 1,438 psig
❏ D. 1,423 psig

10. A neutrally-weighted diver has an eighth of a cubic foot of air in his BC at a depth of 68 feet in a lake. The diver finds an anchor weighing 20 pounds (assume no displacement), picks up the anchor and adds air to his BC to achieve neutral buoyancy again. The diver ascends 34 feet without venting any air from the BC, then accidently drops the anchor. How many pounds buoyant is the diver at this point?
❏ A. 40.3
❏ B. 41.7
❏ C. 42
❏ D. 48.1

PHYSICS PHUN!

A:

I hope you see that solving physics problems increases understanding of practical situations in diving and that the ability to solve problems makes you a better diver. If you answered at least half of the questions (both parts) correctly, your understanding is good. If you answered eight or more correctly, congratulate yourself for an above-average ability. We may not use calculators underwater, but we can certainly take the concepts with us in our heads. Good diving.

1. B. 42.1. Part A—Approach: Multiply the pressure per foot of freshwater (34/14.7 = .432 psi/ft.) times the depth and add atmospheric pressure to convert the gauge (water) pressure to absolute pressure. Part B—Math: The pressure at 67 feet in fresh water is .432 lbs./ft. X 67 ft. = 28.94 psig + 13.17 psi = 42.11psia.

2. C. 25%, 50%. Part A—Approach: Determine the volume of the raft, then use the volume to calculate the total displacement possible. Buoyancy is the total displacement minus the dry weight of the raft with the woman aboard, then by itself. Part B—Math: The volume of the raft is 4' X 4' X 0.5' = eight cubic feet. Its displacement is 8 X 64 = 512 pounds, so it will have 512 - (256 + 128) = 128 pounds of excess buoyancy and float 128/512 = 25% out of the water with the 128 pound woman aboard and will have 512 - 256 = 256 pounds of excess buoyancy and float 256/512 = 50% out of the water with no one aboard.

3. B. 0.34. Part A—Approach: Determine the diver's depth consumption rate (DCR). Convert the depth consumption rate to surface consumption rate (SCR). Convert the SCR in psi per minute to cubic feet per minute. Part B—Math: The diver's depth consumption rate is 600 psi/12 mins. = 50 psi per minute. The surface consumption rate is 33'/33' + 47' = 33/80 = .413 X 50 psi/min. = 20.625 psi/minute. Conversion to cubic feet per minute: 50/3014.7 X cfm/20.625. 3014.7 cfm = 1031.25. 1031.25/3014.7 = .34 cubic feet per minute.

4. D. 100%. Part A—Approach: Determine the volume of the lead, then calculate its equivalent saltwater volume based on the density of the lead. The equivalent volume times the weight of seawater per cubic foot tells how many pounds of lift will be needed. An additional one pound of lift—the dry weight of the lift bag—will also be needed. Part B—Math: The volume of the lead is 2" X 4" X 18" = 144 cu. in./1728 = .083 cubic feet, but since it is nine times denser than seawater, it is equivalent to a volume of 9 X .083 = .75 cubic feet. Displacement is 0.75 X 64 = 48 pounds of seawater. The net lift of the lift bag is 50 - 1 = 49 pounds, so the lift bag will need to be 100% filled to lift the 48 pound ingot.

5. B. 28.5 feet. Part A—Approach: Determine the pressure at which the BC will be full, then subtract the depth equal to a pressure of two psi. Part B—Math: The BC contains 16 pounds of air at 99 feet (4 atms.), so it will be full at half of that pressure or a depth of 33 feet (2 atms). An additional two psi of pressure results from ascending 2/.445 = 4.5', so the depth at which the relief valve opens is 33 - 4.5 = 28.5 feet.

6. A. 54.6 cubic feet. Part A—Approach: Convert temperatures and pressures to absolute. Calculate the increased pressure at the higher temperature, then calculate the new volume after the pressure reduction at the higher temperature. Part B—Math: Absolute temperatures must be used, so 460 degrees are added to the starting and ending temperatures. Absolute pressures are also used. The tank pressure at 85 degrees F is 3,014.7 X 545/530 = 3100 psia. If the tank pressure is then lowered to 2,100 psig, the new volume equals 80 X 2,114.7/3100 = 54.6 cubic feet.

7. C. 12.5 percent. Part A—Approach: Determine the partial pressure of the oxygen. Part B—Math: The absolute pressure at 238 feet in freshwater is 238/34 = 7 + 1 = 8 atms. The partial pressure of the oxygen is 14.7/8 X 14.7 = 12.5%. The partial pressure remains constant irrespective of depth, so the correct answer is 12.5%.

8. C. Remove seven pounds. Part A—Approach: Determine the diver's displacement in seawater, then multiply the displacement time the density of fresh water. Since seawater is has greater density than freshwater, subtract from the weight belt the difference in the weights of water displaced. Part B—Math: The diver displaces 270 lbs./64 lbs./cu. ft. = 4.22 cubic feet of water in the ocean. The same volume in freshwater only displaces 4.22 cu. ft. X 62.4 lbs./cu. ft. = 263.25 pounds of water, so the diver will need to remove about seven pounds of weight to achieve proper weighting for freshwater diving.

9. D. 1,423 psig. Part A—Approach: Calculate the volume of air needed for 100 pounds of displacement at three atmospheres. Calculate the starting and ending volumes in the tank, then convert the ending volume to pressure in the cylinder. Part B—Math: One hundred pounds of lift requires 100 lbs./64 lbs. per cu. ft. = 1.56 cu. ft. X 3 atm. = 4.69 cubic feet of air. The starting volume of the tank is 1614.7 psia X 80 cu. ft./3014.7 psia = 42.85 cubic feet. The ending volume is 42.85 cu. ft. - 4.69 cu. ft. = 38.15 cubic feet, so the ending pressure is 1614.7 psia X 38.15 cu. ft./42.85 cu. ft. = 1,438 psia or 1,423 psig.

10. B. 41.7 pounds. Part A—Approach: Determine the amount of lift in the BC at depth and add 20 pounds to it. Calculate the new volume for the shallower depth. Convert the ending volume to pounds of lift. Part B—Math: The diver has .125 X 62.4 = 7.8 pounds of lift in his BC, then adds 20 pounds making a volume of 27.8 lbs./64 lbs./cu. ft. = .446 cubic feet. This volume expands to 3 atm. X .446 cu. ft./2 atm. = .669 cubic feet X 62.4 lbs. = 41.7 pounds of lift and a very dangerous situation.

PHYSICS DEFINITIONS

During entry level training you may not have been exposed to much diving physics theory, or you may have been required only to remember "cause and effect." At some point in your diving education, however, you should become familiar with the laws and principles of physics. You need the knowledge to understand the advanced literature you want to read. Test yourself. Match the terms to the definitions.

Q:

Terms:

A. Absolute Pressure
B. Absolute Zero
C. Ambient Pressure
D. Amonton's Law
E. Archimedes' Principle
F. Amagat's Law
G. Boyle's Law
H. Charles' Law
I. Conduction
J. Dalton's Law
K. Density
L. Gauge Pressure
M. Henry's Law
N. Partial Pressure
O. Pasqual's Law
P. Poiseuille's Law
Q. Pressure
R. Refraction
S. Snell's Law
T. Specific Gravity
U. Specific Heat

Definitions:

1. _____ The pressure of a given quantity of gas at a constant temperature varies inversely with its volume.

2. _____ The volume of a gas at a constant pressure is proportional to the absolute temperature.

3. _____ The pressure of a fixed amount and volume of gas is proportional to the absolute pressure.

4. _____ The pressure exerted by one gas only, in a mixture of gases.

5. _____ The amount of gas that will dissolve in a liquid at a given temperature is proportional to the partial pressure of the gas.

6. _____ The force per unit area.

7. _____ The weight per unit volume of a substance.

8. _____ The pressure of the fluid surrounding an object.

9. _____ The pressure of a gas with a vacuum used as the zero reference.

10. _____ The pressure of a gas with atmospheric pressure used as the zero reference.

11. _____ The lowest possible temperature that a substance can achieve.

12. _____ An object immersed in a liquid is buoyed up by a force equal to the weight of the displaced fluid.

13. _____ Pressure is transmitted in all directions in a confined fluid.

14. _____ The density of a specific substance compared to that of pure water.

15. _____ The amount of heat required to raise the temperature of a specific substance compared to that of pure water.

16. _____ The mathematical ratio expressing the light "bending" effect of a medium.

17. _____ The deflection from a straight path by a ray of light in passing from one medium into another.

18. _____ A formula used to determine the rate at which gas flows through limiting enclosures.

19. _____ The total pressure exerted by a mixture of gases is the sum on the pressures exerted by the gases individually.

20. _____ The transmission of heat by direct material contact.

21. _____ The volume of a mixture of gases is the sum of the volumes of the individual gases and is determined by the pressure and temperature of the mixture.

PHYSICS DEFINITIONS

A:

Advanced divers should be familiar with the concepts contained in this quiz. Since all divers should attain an advanced rating, all divers should understand physics laws and principles. Why? Because an understanding of the theories allows better practical performance. There are many fundamental concepts you needed to learn when you began your diver training. It was not appropriate to relate complex theories to the practical aspects of diving at that time. As an experienced diver, you can and should devote time to learning physics theories because you can and should apply them to practical use.

1. G. Boyle's Law. As pressure increases, volume decreases, and vice versa.

2. H. Charles' Law says the volume varies with temperature. Many divers confuse the laws of Charles and Gay Lussac with Amonton's Law.

3. D. Amonton's Law says the pressure varies with temperature.

4. N. Partial pressure (PP) is the proportion of the total pressure contributed by a single gas in a gas mixture, e. g., oxygen PP in air is approximately 21%.

5. M. Henry's Law says the amount of gas that will dissolve in a liquid at a given temperature is proportional to the partial pressure of the gas.

6. Q. Pressure. Pounds per square inch is an example of force per unit area.

7. K. Density. Pounds per cubic foot, e.g., 64 pounds per cubic foot for saltwater, is an example of density.

8. C. Ambient means "immediately surrounding." We generally use the term to refer to the surrounding pressure or temperature.

9. A. Absolute pressure is the "true" or total pressure exerted at any point and includes atmospheric pressure.

10. L. Gauge pressure is the difference between absolute pressure and a specific pressure being measured. To convert gauge pressure to absolute pressure, add atmospheric pressure.

11. B. Absolute zero. You must convert temperature to absolute zero for gas law calculations. Absolute zero is a hypothetical temperature characterized by complete absence of heat.

12. E. Archimedes' Principle explains the nature of buoyancy and helps us understand how to control it.

13. O. Pasqual's Law. Pressure is transmitted in all directions in a fluid if the fluid is confined.

14. T. Specific gravity. The tendency of a substance to float—or not to float—in water is governed by specific gravity—a number assigned on the basis of the ratio of the density of the substance to the density of freshwater.

15. U. Specific heat is the ratio of the amount of heat transferred to raise a unit mass of a substance one degree to that required to raise a unit mass of water one degree.

16. S. Snell's Law allows mathematicians to calculate refractive index, which is 1.33 for water and 1.5 for glass.

17. R. Refraction. Light travels in straight lines except when it crosses from a medium of one refractive index into a medium of another refractive index, e.g., from air into water. The "bending" of light rays is refraction.

18. P. Poiseuille's Law of laminar flow is used to determine the rate at which gas flows through orifices, hoses, etc., but is useful only in relatively simple systems where flow is laminar.

19. J. Dalton's Law. The total pressure exerted by a mixture of gases is the sum of the pressures that would be exerted by each of the gases if it alone were present and occupied the total volume.

20. I. Conduction. The heating of the handle of a pan on a stove is an example of conduction. Direct material contact transmits heat from the pan to the handle. Water similarly conducts heat away from divers.

21. F. Amagat's Law. Each component of a gas mixture occupies a volume determined by the pressure and the temperature of the mixture regardless of other components involved. See answer 20. Amagat's Law addresses volume, while Dalton's pertains to pressure.

Rating:
   15 correct = Average
   16-18 correct = Very good
   19-20 correct = Excellent

PRESSURE

Divers must deal with pressure during each and every dive. A good understanding of pressure is of the utmost importance. Can you recall the important facts concerning pressure? Test your knowledge by answering the following questions.

1. Select the incorrect statement:
❏ A. Pressure is force per unit area
❏ B. Underwater, pressure is the result of atmospheric and water weights
❏ C. Use gauge pressure for pressure calculations
❏ D. Pressure is equal in all directions at a specific depth

2. The pressure increase per foot of depth in freshwater is:
❏ A. .432 psi
❏ B. .445 psi
❏ C. 1.00 psi
❏ D. 14.7 psi

3. Gauge pressure for divers is:
❏ A. Hydrostatic pressure
❏ B. Atmospheric pressure
❏ C. Hydrostatic pressure plus atmospheric pressure
❏ D. Atmospheric pressure minus hydrostatic pressure

4. The absolute pressure at a depth of 120 feet in the ocean is:
❏ A. 51.8 psia
❏ B. 53.4 psia
❏ C. 66.5 psia
❏ D. 68.1 psia

5. The pressure in a scuba tank increases with a temperature increase. The pressure increase is an example of:
❏ A. Charles' law
❏ B. Dalton's law
❏ C. Boyle's law
❏ D. None of the above

6. A given volume of air in a flexible container expands the most during an ocean ascent from:
❏ A. 132 feet to 99 feet
❏ B. 99 feet to 66 feet
❏ C. 33 feet to the surface
❏ D. All the above equally

7. If a scuba tank contains 80 cubic feet of air at a pressure of 3,000 psig, how much air does the tank contain at 2,000 psig if the temperature remains constant?
❏ A. 52.8
❏ B. 53.3
❏ C. 53.5
❏ D. 120

8. At an altitude of 18,000 feet, the atmospheric pressure is approximately:
❏ A. One half the atmospheric pressure at sea level
❏ B. Twice the atmospheric pressure at sea level
❏ C. One eighteenth the atmospheric pressure at sea level
❏ D. Equal to the atmospheric pressure at sea level

9. If two percent of the air in a scuba tank is carbon monoxide, the partial pressure of the carbon monoxide in air breathed from the tank at a depth of 102 feet in freshwater is:
❏ A. 1.88 psia
❏ B. 1.176 psia
❏ C. 44.2 psia
❏ D. 58.8 psia

10. If you take a sealed, rigid, cubical container measuring ten inches per side to a depth of 20 feet in the ocean, the total crushing force (assume the wall thickness is zero) on the container would be about:
❏ A. 3,560 pounds
❏ B. 5,256 pounds
❏ C. 5,340 pounds
❏ D. 14,076 pounds

PRESSURE

Divers do not have to make pressure calculations to dive, but they must understand the principles involved. If you scored well, you understand the principles and probably enjoy diving academics. If you understand the principles, but can't solve the problems correctly, don't feel badly. Perhaps you will be motivated to study the subject or take a diving continuing education course.

1. C. Use gauge pressure for pressure calculations. False. Use absolute pressure, or zero-based pressure, for calculations because divers are subject to both water and atmospheric pressures. Remember to include atmospheric pressure whenever you do pressure calculations.

2. A. .432 psi. Thirty-four feet of freshwater equals one atmosphere of pressure, or 14.7 psi. One foot of fresh water equals 14.7 divided by 34 = .432 psig (gauge pressure).

3. A. Hydrostatic pressure. Gauge pressure is the difference between a pressure you measure and the surrounding atmospheric pressure. A zero gauge pressure reading is actually an atmosphere of pressure at sea level.

4. D. 68.1 psia. A one-inch square column of saltwater weighs .445 pounds per foot, so the gauge pressure at 120 feet is 120 X .445 = 53.4 psig. To convert gauge pressure to absolute pressure, add 14.7 psi for a total of 68.1 psia (absolute pressure).

5. D. None of the above! It is a misconception that a pressure increase caused by a temperature increase in a scuba tank is due to Charles' Law, which says that the volume of a fixed quantity of gas at constant pressure is proportional to the absolute temperature. The correct law is Guy-Lussac's law, which states, "The pressure of a fixed quantity and volume of gas is directly proportional to the absolute temperature."

6. D. 33 feet to the surface. Use the equation $P1V1 = P2V2$ to calculate the volume change. P1 is the starting pressure, V1 the starting volume, P2 the final pressure, and V2 the final volume. To find V2, rearrange the equation to V2 = P1V1 divided by P2. For answer A, if the starting volume were 10 pints, the ending volume would be 73.44 X 10/58.8 = 12.5 pints. Using the same starting volume, the answers B and C are 13.4 and 20 pints respectively. Note that the greatest volume rate of change occurs near the surface.

7. C. 53.5 cubic feet. Express a scuba tank's pressure/volume relationship $P1/V1 = P2/V2$. Rearrange as follows to solve for V2: V2 = P2V1 divided by P1. V2 = 2,014.7 X 80/ 3,014.7 (use absolute pressures) = 53.46 cubic feet. For general use and practical purposes, you could say the tank was two thirds full.

8. A. One half the atmospheric pressure at sea level. Atmospheric pressure decreases with altitude. 18,000 feet is the point where the pressure is half that at sea level. Note that going from sea level to 18,000 feet is equivalent to going from 33 feet to the surface in water. Special procedures and training are necessary for diving at altitude.

9. B. 1.176 psia. The absolute pressure at 102 feet is 102 X .432 = 44.1 + 14.7 = 58.8 psia. The partial pressure of carbon monoxide is .02 X 58.8 = 1.176 psia. Note that breathing 2% carbon monoxide at 102 feet is equivalent to breathing 8% carbon monoxide at the surface (24.7 X .08 = 1.176) and the physiological effects are the same.

10. C. 5,340 pounds. The total area of the container is 10 X 10 X 6 = 600 square inches. The absolute pressure at 20 feet is .445 X 20 = 8.9 + 14.7 = 23.6 psia. The total pressure on the container is 23.6 X 600 = 14,160 pounds. The pressure on the inside of the container is 14.7 X 600 (same area) = 8,820 pounds. With 14,160 pounds pushing inward and 8,820 pounds offsetting the outside pressure, the crushing force on the container is 5,340 pounds.

PARTIAL PRESSURE

Q:

The indirect effects of pressure result from the partial pressures of the gases we breathe. What is partial pressure? What is the surface equivalent of a gas? How do partial pressures affect divers? Answer the following questions to determine how much you know about an important diving subject. To simplify calculations, assume the composition of air to be 80 percent nitrogen and 20 percent oxygen.

1. _____ Law deals with individual pressures, called partial pressures, exerted by gases that form a gas mixture.
- A. Henry's
- B. Dalton's
- C. Charles'
- D. Amonton's

2. The partial pressure law requires the sum of the partial pressures to always equal the _____ pressure.
- A. Total
- B. Gauge
- C. Absolute
- D. Either A and C

3. The human body regulates respiration primarily by sensing the partial pressure of _____ in the blood.
- A. Oxygen
- B. Carbon dioxide
- C. Hemoglobin
- D. Carbon monoxide

4. A recreational diver is most likely to experience carbon dioxide toxicity as a result of:
- A. Contaminated air
- B. Inhaling the gas from a buoyancy compensator
- C. Inadequate or improper breathing
- D. Excessive "dead space" in equipment

5. Oxygen is likely to become toxic when breathed in concentrations exceeding a partial pressure of 1.6 ATA for durations exceeding:
- A. 6 hours
- B. 4 hours
- C. 3 hours
- D. 1 hour

6. The partial pressure of nitrogen in air at a depth of 76 feet in the ocean is ____ psia.
- A. 6.8
- B. 9.7
- C. 38.0
- D. 38.8

7. The ocean depth at which the partial pressure of oxygen in air equals 1.6 ATA is ____ feet:
- A. 297
- B. 264
- C. 231
- D. 198

8. Assuming a maximum partial pressure limitation of 1.6 ATA, the maximum depth for 32% nitrox air mix is ____ feet of sea water.
- A. 66
- B. 99
- C. 132
- D. 231

9. Assuming 1.6 ATA as the maximum oxygen partial pressure, the maximum depth at which a diver may breathe 100% oxygen is ____ feet of seawater.
- A. 20 feet
- B. 25 feet
- C. 53 feet
- D. 54 feet

10. Assuming a minimum required oxygen partial pressure of 0.16 ATA, the minimum depth at which a commercial diver may use a gas mixture containing 3% oxygen is ____ feet.
- A. 143
- B. 132
- C. 78
- D. None of the above

11. The air you breathe at a depth of 132 feet in the ocean has the same effect as breathing ____% oxygen at the surface.
- A. 20%
- B. 60%
- C. 80%
- D. 100%

12. Breathing 0.5% carbon monoxide at a depth of 132 feet (32 meters) in the ocean is equivalent to breathing ___% carbon monoxide at sea level.
- A. 2.0
- B. 2.5
- C. 0.5
- D. None of the above

13. A gas mixture contains 35% hydrogen, 55% helium, and 10% oxygen. What is the partial pressure of each gas when the total pressure is 9 ATA?
- A. PP Hydrogen = _____ ATA
- B. PP Helium = _____ ATA
- C. PP Oxygen = _____ ATA
- D. PT (Total Press.) = _____ ATA

14. For decompression purposes, breathing a mixture containing 32% oxygen at a depth of 100 feet in the ocean is equivalent to breathing air at a depth of ____ feet.
- A. 53
- B. 80
- C. 99
- D. 111

15. The oxygen partial pressure for a diver breathing Nitrox I (32% oxygen) at a depth of 70 feet in the ocean is _____ ATA.
- A. 1.00
- B. 0.68
- C. 0.80
- D. 0.56

PARTIAL PRESSURE

Partial pressures can be confusing without advanced training. If you can't do the calculations, that's OK, but all divers should definitely understand the effects and potential hazards of increased partial pressures. Do not attempt to use any gas mixture other than compressed air unless you complete specialized training and adhere to all safety recommendations.

A:

1. B. Dalton's. This law states that the total pressure exerted by a mixture of gases is equal to the sum of the pressures that would be exerted by each of the gases if it alone were present and occupied the total volume. Henry's Law deals with the amount of gas that will dissolve in a liquid at a given temperature and partial pressure, Charles' Law with the volume of a gas at a constant pressure and a given temperature, and Amonton's Law with the pressure of a constant volume of gas at a given temperature.

2. D. Either A and C. Dalton's Law refers to the total pressure of a mixture of gases, but total pressure and absolute pressure are synonymous. Always use absolute pressure for pressure calculations. Divers are under the pressure of both the water and the atmosphere and must take both into consideration. Gauge pressure refers to water pressure only and does not include atmospheric pressure.

3. B. Carbon dioxide. While the body uses oxygen for metabolism, the detection of system levels of carbon dioxide provides the primary breathing stimulus. The greater the partial pressure of carbon dioxide in the blood, the greater the stimulus to breathe. Carbon dioxide build-up is a commercial diving concern because the partial pressure of carbon dioxide increases with depth.

4. C. Inadequate or improper breathing. The effects of carbon dioxide become noticeable at partial pressures exceeding 2%. Recreational diving equipment does not contribute to carbon dioxide excess. Deliberately reducing your breathing rate—skip breathing to conserve air—will cause carbon dioxide build-up. Overexertion combined with skip breathing at depth can cause carbon dioxide toxicity with little or no warning. Pace yourself and breathe properly.

5. C. 3 hours. Oxygen toxicity occurs as a product of time and partial pressure. People can tolerate oxygen partial pressures higher than 1.6 ATA, but the exposure time must be less than 3 hours to avoid toxicity. Other pressure-time limits for oxygen during working dives are: 1.76 ATA—150 minutes, 1.91 ATA—120 minutes, and 2.06 ATA—80 minutes.

6. D. 38.8 psia. The total pressure at 76 feet is 3.3 ATA (76 + 33/33), which is 48.5 psia. Nitrogen comprises 80% of the total pressure: 0.8 times 48.5 psia = 38.8 psia. You can also calculate the answer by multiplying the pressure per foot of sea water (0.445 psi) times the depth (76), adding one atmosphere (14.7 psi) to convert gauge to absolute pressure, and multiplying the product by 0.8: 0.445 X 76 = 33.8 psig + 14.7 psig = 48.5 psia X 0.8 = 38.8 psia.

7. C. 231 feet. Assuming oxygen is 20% of one atmosphere, a total pressure of eight atmospheres would yield an oxygen partial pressure of 1.6 ATA. Since the question asks for depth, which is gauge pressure, we need to subtract one atmosphere from the total pressure. Seven atmospheres of pressure occurs at an ocean depth of 231 feet (7 ATA X 33 feet).

8. C. 132 feet. 1.6 ATA divided by 0.32 = 5 ATA total pressure, which occurs at a depth of 132 feet (5 X 33 = 165 - 33). 32% is the oxygen partial pressure for Nitrox I, while Nitrox II contains 36% oxygen. The depth limitation for Nitrox II is 114 feet of seawater (1.6 ATA divided by .36 = 4.44 X 33 = 147 - 33 = 114). The higher the oxygen partial pressure, the shallower the depth limitation.

9. A. 20 feet. Subtract one atmosphere from the total pressure (1.6 ATA) to obtain gauge pressure and multiply the number times 33 feet to obtain the maximum depth (0.6 X 33 = 19.8 feet). Breathing pure oxygen underwater is hazardous and requires special training, equipment, and supervision. Fill scuba tanks with compressed air only—never with oxygen.

10. A. 143 feet. Three per cent of the total pressure must equal 0.16 ATA. Divide both sides of the equation by 0.03 to isolate the total pressure, which is 0.16 ATA divided by 0.03, or 5.33 ATA. Subtract 1 ATA to obtain gauge pressure and multiply the water pressure (4.33 ATA) times 33 (the depth equivalent of 1 ATA) = 142.89 feet. If a commercial diver breathes mixed gas at shallow depths, the diver may lose consciousness, so commercial divers breathe different gas mixtures at various depths.

11. D. 100%. 132 feet is a total pressure of 5 ATA (132 + 33/33). Oxygen is 20% of the total pressure, 1 ATA, or 14.7 psia. Breathing air at a depth of 132 feet in the ocean is the same as breathing pure oxygen at the surface. No problems result from the higher oxygen partial pressure, but the same multiplying effect applies to other gases, which can be hazardous.

12. B. 2.5%. The answer to this question is similar to the answer to the previous question, except that the effect is harmful when you breathe carbon monoxide. A small amount of carbon monoxide can be extremely toxic when you increase its partial pressure. Always obtain air from a reliable source.

13. A = 3.15 ATA, B = 4.95 ATA, C = 0.9 ATA, D = 9 ATA. Each gas exerts a percentage of the total pressure. The sum of the pressures exerted by the gases equals the total pressure.

14. B. 80 feet. To determine the equivalent air depth (EAD) when breathing enriched air nitrox, subtract the oxygen decimal value from 1.00, multiply the remainder times the depth plus 33, divide the product by 0.8 (nitrogen partial pressure), and subtract 33 (to convert to gauge pressure). 1.00 - 0.32 = .68 times 133 = 90.44 divided by 0.8 = 113 - 33 - 80 feet. Nitrox divers with specialized training use EADs to determine their decompression statuses.

15. A. 1.00 ATA. The total pressure at a depth of 70 feet is 3.12 ATA (70 + 33 divided by 33). 32% of 3.12 = .999 ATA. Compare the answer to that of #11. Breathing Nitrox I at a depth of 70 feet produces the same oxygen partial pressure as breathing air at a depth of 132 feet. Nitrox becomes toxic much shallower than air and has an absolute depth limit compared to air's recommended depth limit.

SECTION FIVE

□□□□□

Diving Physiology

Diving Physiology

The branch of biology that deals with the processes, activities, and phenomena of live and living organisms is physiology. Diving obviously affects our body processes and organs, so it helps to understand diving physiology.

When we change our natural environment by submerging, we alter our physiology. Our bodies have limited toleration for altered processes. If we exceed our tolerance limits, we develop dive-related illnesses, some of which can be fatal. It is essential to prevent the serious consequences of excessive physiology alteration. Knowledge and its correct application are the best means to avoid physiological problems while diving.

Do you know as much as you should about nitrogen narcosis, overexposure, seasickness, squeezes and blocks, thermal problems, vertigo, and decompression sickness? It's helpful to understand the basic aspects of anatomy, respiration, circulation, stress, pressure equalization, physical fitness, gas toxicity, and diving illnesses. You need to be familiar with certain medical terms to understand physiology. Learn more about diving physiology by completing this section. You also can attend diving conferences and seminars or take an advanced diver course.

AIR PASSAGES

Q:

Divers need to know more than the average person about the air passages of various cavities in their bodies. You should know the location of the passages, the functions of the various parts comprising the passages, and how health and pressure affect the passages. Determine how much you know by answering the following questions. Do not look at the answers on the following page until you have answered all the questions. I hope you enjoy the double true-false format for questions 7 through 13.

Matching questions. The numbered items may have more than one answer.

1. Pharynx
2. Larynx
3. Epiglottis
4. Trachea
5. Palatum
6. Eustachian

A. The structure that guards the entrance to the trachea
B. A lid-like structure that prevents foreign material from entering the larynx and trachea
C. The tube extending from the larynx and branching into left and right main bronchi
D. The partition separating the nasal and oral cavities
E. The passage between the mouth and nasal cavities and the larynx and esophagus
F. Auditory tubes that connect the nasal and middle ear cavities
G. The throat
H. The voice box
I. The windpipe
J. The palate

Double true-false questions. Answer the stem of each question true (T) or false (F), then select all answers that explain correctly why the statement in the stem of the question is true or false.

7. Avoid diving when you have a cold or upper respiratory infection, when you have chronic congestion that requires medication to open your nasal airways, or for several weeks following the extraction of an upper molar. This statement is True/False because your sinuses:

A. Have airways lined with membranes that may swell and close
B. Are interconnected via a series of airways
C. May be unable to equalize pressure when the effect of a decongestant wears off
D. May have a temporary airway to your mouth after a tooth removal

8. Movement of various anatomical parts of your airways affects your ability to equalize pressure in your ears and sinuses. This statement is True/False because:

A. Your soft palate moves to shield your nasal passageways when you swallow
B. Your Eustachian tubes open when you swallow and when you lift the base of your tongue
C. Your tongue can act as a piston to help equalize ear pressure
D. Voluntary mechanical movements help equalize pressure in your sinuses as well as your ears

9. The middle ear air cavities are isolated from other air spaces except the throat. Body positioning makes no difference when equalizing middle-ear pressure through the two-inch long Eustachian tubes. The statements are True/False because the middle ears:

A. Connect to the mastoid cells
B. Connect to the nasopharynx (upper throat)
C. Are at a higher elevation than the openings of the Eustachian tubes when you are upright
D. Equalize through tubes much less than two inches in length

10. The airways to your lungs do more than serve as a conduit for air and they do not permit gas exchange with your blood. This statement is True/False because the airways to your lungs:

A. Include air passages in your mouth, nose, throat, and chest
B. Have a "dead air space" of about 150 milliliters
C. Help heat and humidify inspired air
D. Help clean inspired air

11. A laryngospasm is an involuntary, spasmodic closure of the larynx that usually causes submerged, non-breathing victims to embolize during ascents. The statement is True/False because a laryngospasm:

A. Relaxes immediately upon loss of consciousness
B. Relaxes when the victim becomes hypoxic (low oxygen level)
C. Does not occur in 90% of drownings and near drownings
D. Prevents air from entering but not exiting the lungs

12. To administer artificial respiration to a non-breathing diver in the water, tilt the victim's head back, clear the airway, turn the victim's head toward you, and administer rapid, forceful breaths. The statement is True/False because:

A. You must do more than tilt the victim's head back to properly open the airway
B. You do not need to clear the victim's mouth before ventilating
C. Turning the victim's head restricts the airway
D. Rapid, forceful breaths may force air into the victim's stomach

13. A near-drowned person is likely to vomit during resuscitation and could suffer severe lung damage from aspiration of vomitus. The statement is True/False because:

A. Stomach acid and debris can seriously damage lung tissues
B. Laryngeal reflex will prevent foreign matter from entering lungs
C. A drowning person usually drinks large quantities of water, filling the stomach
D. The muscles of the larynx and the lower esophagus relax in a near-drowned person

AIR PASSAGES

A:

How much do you know about air passages? There were 47 possible correct answers. If you selected 35 or more correct responses, congratulate yourself. You can dive easier and safer when you understand physiology. If you want to learn more about your body and diving, complete an advanced class or read my book, Scuba Diving.

1. E, G. The pharynx is the throat.

2. A, H. The larynx is a structure that protects your windpipe and has a secondary function as the organ of voice.

3. B. The epiglottis is a flap that closes when you swallow and prevents objects from entering your voice box and windpipe.

4. C, I. The trachea is the windpipe between your voice box and the main bronchi of your lungs.

5. D, J. The palatum is your palate, which separates the cavities of your nose and mouth. The part of your throat above your soft palate is your nasopharynx.

6. F. The eustachian tubes connect the middle ear cavities to the nasopharynx.

7. True, A, B, C, D. The passageways to your sinuses are small and have a mucous membrane lining. Infections and allergies cause the membranes to swell and can prohibit the passage of air. Attempting to dive with plugged air passages can cause injury and spread infection. Use of decongestants may bring temporary relief by reducing membrane swelling, but the "rebound effect" when the medication wears off can close the passageways. The roots of some teeth may extend into your maxillary sinuses. Allow extractions time to heal.

8. True, A, B, C. Several movements of your throat muscles will open your Eustachian tubes, which normally remain closed. Swallowing, yawning, and lifting the base of your tongue are better ways to equalize pressure in your ears than the Valsalva maneuver. Your sinuses equalize pressure automatically when your passageways are clear. Voluntary mechanical movements do not aid sinus equalization.

9. False, A, B, C, D. There are air cells in the temporal bone behind your ear. Infections in your ears can spread into the mastoid cells in the temporal bone. The eustachian tubes, which average about 1 3/8 inches in length, extend from your middle ear cavities forward and downward to your nasopharynx. When you descend feet first, air travels up through the tubes into the middle ears; but when you descend head first, you must force air downward against water pressure to equalize ear pressure. Descend feet first for easier equalization.

10. True, A, B, C, D. When you inspire air through your nose, hairs and mucous remove foreign particles. Tiny, hair-like projections, called cilia, move particle-carrying mucous from your lungs to your esophagus to cleanse your airways. Passageways heat and humidify inspired air. Respiration, or gas exchange, occurs only in the lungs. No respiration occurs in the plumbing of your air passages. Your passageways are "dead air" space, so you must inhale and exhale sufficiently to exchange the air they contain. Shallow breathing is inefficient breathing.

11. False, B, C. A laryngospasm is a strong contraction of the voice box that seals the windpipe passageway completely. While it is possible for an unconscious person to have a laryngospasm, the condition is not likely in a submerged, unconscious diver. Only 10% of near-drowning victims exclude water because of laryngospasm, so nine of ten near-drowning victims do not experience laryngospasm. Of those who do experience laryngospasm, the contractions relax when system oxygen levels decrease soon after loss of consciousness. Submerged, non-breathing scuba divers will not embolize when you rescue them. Their hypoxic condition would negate a laryngospasm, if they should happen to be amongst the 10% experiencing the condition. The involuntary coughing you do when you swallow and irritate your voice box is a laryngeal reflex, not a laryngospasm.

12. False, A, C, D. The statement appears correct at first glance, but it is incorrect. You should lift a victim's jaw to fully open the airway. Failure to lift the jaw allows air to go into the victim's stomach. Rapid, forceful breaths also put air into the victim's stomach. Air in the stomach impedes ventilation and increases the likelihood of vomiting. You may turn the victim's head <u>and</u> body toward you in the water to reduce the effort of rescue breathing, but if you turn only the victim's head you restrict the airway. It's time to re-evaluate many in-water rescue breathing techniques.

13. True, A, C, D. When people drown or nearly drown, they usually drink large quantities of water before aspirating fluid and losing consciousness. Muscles in your gullet normally keep your esophagus closed, but the muscles relax in a hypoxic state. Regurgitated material can cause severe complications if aspirated into the lungs. If a near-drowned victim vomits, turn the patient's head to the side and clear the airway of vomitus before continuing rescue breathing.

RESPIRATION

Experienced divers may not pay much attention to their breathing while diving. They should be more attentive to respiration. There is much more to respiration in and underwater than simply moving air in and out of the lungs periodically. Take a deep breath and test your knowledge of an important subject.

1. When a diver hyperventilates excessively before a breath-hold dive and loses consciousness as a result, blackout is most likely to occur when the diver:
❑ A. Descends
❑ B. Is on the bottom
❑ C. Ascends
❑ D. Is apprehensive

2. A symptom of low oxygen levels in the body is:
❑ A. No symptom at all
❑ B. Tunnel vision
❑ C. Extremity tingling
❑ D. Dizziness

3. An "oxygen debt" means that:
❑ A. A person is not breathing enough oxygen to meet body needs
❑ B. Body circulation is not replacing oxygen consumed by body tissues
❑ C. A person's blood is not receiving an adequate oxygen supply from the lungs
❑ D. The body carbon dioxide level is abnormally high

4. During an emergency swimming ascent, the breathing pattern least likely to cause a lung overexpansion injury is:
❑ A. Continuous exhalation with most of the air expelled at the beginning of ascent
❑ B. Continuous exhalation with most of the air expelled near the surface
❑ C. A normal breathing pattern with attempted inhalations
❑ D. A complete exhalation at the beginning of ascent and breath-holding thereafter

5. The single greatest cause of lung over expansion injuries while scuba diving is:
❑ A. Rapid ascents
❑ B. Lung defects
❑ C. Breath-holding
❑ D. Not understood

6. Higher than normal levels of carbon dioxide in the bloodstream cause a breathing stimulus called:
❑ A. Hypoxia
❑ B. Hypercapnia
❑ C. Hyperpnea
❑ D. Dyspnea

7. Divers can use conditioning and training to elevate the urge-to-breathe trigger point.
❑ A. True
❑ B. False

8. Skip breathing decreases the normal stimulus to breathe.
❑ A. True
❑ B. False

9. Physiological effects of carbon dioxide toxicity may be observed when the percent of carbon dioxide reaches:
❑ A. 10%
❑ B. 8%
❑ C. 4%
❑ D. 0.033%

10. Carbon dioxide toxicity in scuba divers results primarily from:
❑ A. Improper ventilation
❑ B. Breathing resistance
❑ C. Dead air space
❑ D. Contaminated air

11. Which of the following methods safely increases air supply duration?
❑ A. Paced activity
❑ B. Slow, deep, continuous breathing
❑ C. A high level of physical conditioning
❑ D. All the above

12. Higher than normal blood carbon dioxide levels can increase susceptibility to:
❑ A. Nitrogen narcosis
❑ B. Decompression sickness
❑ C. Heart rhythm changes
❑ D. All the above

13. Arrange in order, from greatest to least effect, the following factors that contribute to overexertion.
❑ A. Skip breathing and a high activity level
❑ B. Reduced lung capacity caused by immersion
❑ C. A tight exposure suit and a hard-breathing regulator
❑ D. Dead air space and breathing resistance

14. When a scuba diver experiences air starvation underwater, that is, it feels as if the regulator will not deliver sufficient air when air is available, the problem probably is:
❑ A. A regulator badly in need of service
❑ B. Diver overexertion
❑ C. A regulator malfunction
❑ D. Extremely poor diver fitness

RESPIRATION

Did you answer 11 or more questions correctly? If so, you passed this quiz. If not, read a diving medicine book or complete an advanced scuba course. It is amazing that there are multiple factors that cause carbon dioxide retention and that we can further compound the problem with skip breathing. Hopefully, you now realize carbon dioxide excess is a problem even when you breathe properly. Give yourself a good respiratory margin of safety to deal with any problems that may arise while diving.

1. C. Ascends. Excessive hyperventilation reduces body carbon dioxide to such a low level that a person loses consciousness before breathing stimulus occurs. Increased oxygen partial pressure at depth aids an experienced breath-hold diver. The oxygen partial pressure decreases rapidly during ascent. The low oxygen level causes unconsciousness, or "shallow water blackout." Avoid hyperventilating more than three or four breaths prior to a breath-hold dive.

2. A. No symptom at all. Hypoxia gives no warning. The absence of symptoms is dangerous. Low oxygen levels, such as those you create with excessive hyperventilation or incorrect breathing while exerting strenuously, are hazardous. Always breathe correctly while diving.

3. B. Body circulation is not replacing oxygen consumed by body tissues. When we begin to exercise, body tissues consume oxygen before the heart and circulation begin to function at full capacity. The duration of oxygen-deficit exercise is brief. You must repay the debt to the tissues after exercise or decrease exertion until your circulation can replace the oxygen in the tissues. If you fail to repay the oxygen debt, you will be unable to continue the activity. Avoid overexertion by pacing activity.

4. C. A normal breathing pattern with attempted inhalations. Believe it or not, a diver can embolize while exhaling continuously. A combination of factors can collapse airways and trap air in the lungs. The continuous flow of air in a single direction collapses small airways. An attempted inhalation re-opens a closed airway. Avoid other emergency ascent breathing patterns, especially the old "blow-and-go" technique. Continuous exhalation is better than breath-holding, but not as good as attempting a normal breathing pattern.

5. C. Breath-holding. The common denominator for all lung overexpansion injuries is holding the breath while ascending. A friend ruptured his lung while straining to cock a speargun. He held a large breath, which increased his buoyancy and made him rise while straining to cock the gun. Always keep breathing when you use compressed air under water.

6. B. Hypercapnia. Hypoxia means low oxygen level in tissues. Hyperpnea means rapid breathing. Dyspnea means breathing difficulty. Hypercapnia is an undue amount of blood carbon dioxide, which causes excessive activity in the brain respiratory center.

7. A. True. Physical conditioning enables the body to make efficient use of oxygen while tolerating higher than normal carbon dioxide levels. Diving experience, increased breathing resistance, and high oxygen partial pressure all reduce your normal response to carbon dioxide build-up. The combined effect of many factors can be an extremely high carbon dioxide level before breathing stimulus occurs.

8. A. True. A low breathing frequency and holding each breath maximizes pulmonary gas exchange and reduces breathing effort, but the practice also tricks the body into accepting a higher than normal carbon dioxide level. The major problem with skip breathing is the rapidity with which respiratory distress can occur if a problem develops. Another major problem is that breath-holding while breathing compressed air can lead to a lung overexpansion injury during ascent.

9. C. 4%. Fresh air contains about 0.033% carbon dioxide. When the carbon dioxide level reaches about 4%, respiration rate doubles. An 8% CO_2 level affects vision, causes nausea, and makes a diver feel air starved. Unconsciousness occurs at a 10% CO_2 concentration. While it seems unlikely that carbon dioxide toxicity could occur with open-circuit scuba equipment, the problem does occur owing to factors not related to the equipment.

10. A. Improper ventilation. Neither the breathing medium nor scuba equipment pose problems for scuba divers as they do for commercial divers, but improper breathing does cause difficulty. Some divers breathe rapid and shallowly in response to respiratory demand. Such breathing, called hypoventilation, leads quickly to a high carbon dioxide, low oxygen condition. Unconsciousness may follow. Always breathe deeply while scuba diving.

11. D. All the above. Good physical condition aids divers. Slow, deep breathing without breath-holding is the most efficient underwater breathing pattern. Pacing activity allows respiration to match tissue oxygen needs. It is wise to rest periodically to allow respiratory catch-up. Because the rules that pertain to carbon dioxide change under pressure, you may not be aware that you are nearing an overexertion situation.

12. D. All the above. Excess blood carbon dioxide can temporarily enhance narcosis effects and play a part in decompression sickness. Carbon dioxide comes out of solution rapidly during bubble formation. Excessive carbon dioxide from breath holding causes heart rhythm changes. Avoid undesirable physiological conditions. Breathe properly.

13. A, C, D, B. Exertion without adequate ventilatory response is hazardous, yet divers often overexert and underventilate. Overexertion, with its accompanying feeling of suffocation, hits suddenly and without warning. Recognizing the condition, knowing its cause, and taking appropriate action if it occurs, are extremely important safety measures. Other listed factors contribute to air starvation, but not as much as improper ventilation coupled with strenuous effort.

14. B. Diver overexertion. It is my conviction that overexertion is one of the most important physiological diving topics because it initiates many diving accidents. You should never experience a shortness of breath while underwater. At the first indication of overexertion, cease all activity, breathe deeply, and recover fully before proceeding with the dive.

CIRCULATION

Your cardiovascular system undergoes changes underwater. Awareness of the changes and knowledge as to why they occur can help you better understand what happens to your circulation while diving. Awareness and knowledge can help prevent injury and accidents.

1. The likelihood of a heart attack is no greater while diving than while exercising on land, provided your heart is healthy.
❏ A. True
❏ B. False

2. An increased activity level significantly increases the amount of oxygen the blood carries to your body.
❏ A. True
❏ B. False

3. Pressure on the neck, such as that from a tight hood, causes your heart rate to increase.
❏ A. True
❏ B. False

4. Water temperature is the primary factor affecting the magnitude of the diving reflex in divers.
❏ A. True
❏ B. False

5. Blood pressure is lower underwater than it is on land.
❏ A. True
❏ B. False

6. Your body shunts blood from the extremities to conserve core heat. The shunting persists no matter how cold your extremities become.
❏ A. True
❏ B. False

7. Increased urination (diuresis) occurs when your body shunts blood from the extremities to conserve core temperature.
❏ A. True
❏ B. False

8. Alcohol increases circulation to the skin and increases heat loss.
❏ A. True
❏ B. False

9. Blood plasma can carry enough dissolved oxygen at depth to meet your body's needs even when hemoglobin oxygen-carrying capability has been significantly reduced.
❏ A. True
❏ B. False

10. With frequent exposure, it is possible to improve your tolerance to cold water.
A. True
B. False

11. Medical experts have determined that diving may be unhealthful for the average person due to the adverse circulatory effects of submersion.
❏ A. True
❏ B. False

CIRCULATION

A:

In spite of extensive physiological studies and research, there is more unknown about diving physiology than there is known. Physiology experts do know that good—not just marginal—health is essential. If you will read some of the excellent diving medicine books available, you will find that diving is not just another form of exercise and cannot be compared strictly on the basis of exercise requirements. You should have a physical examination at least every two years; annually if over 40. Request emphasis on your cardiovascular system.

1. A. True. Decreased heart blood supply, less efficient heart muscle contractions, changes in heart rate and rhythm, and increased cardiac work load all occur while diving. A healthy heart can tolerate such stresses, which can cause a heart attack for people with coronary problems. A person with a heart disorder should not dive unless cleared by both a cardiologist and a diving physician.

2. B. False. The blood always carries nearly as much oxygen as it can carry. Exercise increases blood circulation to meet increased tissue oxygen needs and remove waste products. Increased oxygen partial pressure while diving increases the amount of oxygen in your blood, but other cardiovascular changes offset the benefit of dissolved oxygen.

3. B. False. The carotid sinuses, located at the bifurcation of the main arteries on each side of your neck, are sensors for blood pressure and provide information to the brain, which controls your heart rate. When blood pressure increases, the carotid sinuses tell your brain to slow your heart rate. Artificial pressure on the neck, such as a tight hood, slows the heart. If you are exerting and your need for oxygen is high, a slowed heart rate can lead to fainting. Avoid a carotid sinus syndrome.

4. A. True. The diving reflex is much more pronounced in marine mammals than in people, but wetting the face does cause cardiovascular changes. The controlling factor seems to be the temperature of the water in contact with the face. The colder the water, the greater the effect. The effects of the diving reflex are not always beneficial. Diving in extremely cold water strains your circulatory system significantly.

5. B. False. Your body can lose heat rapidly in water. To reduce heat loss, your body restricts blood flow to the extremities. The shunting, called vasoconstriction, causes a greater than normal blood volume in your torso and increases your blood pressure slightly. Weightlessness in water reduces the pooling of blood in your legs. A temporary blood pressure

increase is not a problem except for those who have high blood pressure.

6. B. False. Vasoconstriction in body extremities is one body defense against heat loss. When your skin temperature drops below 55 degrees F, constriction fails and your body attempts to protect the extremities by dilating blood vessels and restoring circulation. Cold-induced vasodilation is undesirable and potentially hazardous because the amount of heat you lose is significant. Minimize vasodilation by insulating your extremities, especially in cold water.

7. A. True. Diuresis occurs in cold water because blood volume in your torso increases. Blood passes through your kidneys in greater than normal amounts, so your need to urinate is more frequent when you are cold. Negative pressure breathing—breathing from a regulator—also is diuretic. If you feel you urinate excessively when you go diving, don't worry. You are only normal!

8. A. True. Alcohol causes vasodilation and opposes your body's heat loss defense. Drinking before diving not only affects judgement, it inhibits your heat loss defense mechanism. Drinking after diving may release nitrogen trapped in extremities and predispose you to decompression sickness. Tee-totaling divers have good justification for their abstention.

9. A. True. Increased partial pressure at depth increases the amount of oxygen in circulation because oxygen molecules can dissolve in blood plasma. A diver who breathes carbon monoxide experiences toxic effects during ascent because the oxygen partial pressure decreases. If you are not feeling well at depth, ascend close to a buddy because loss of consciousness is possible as you approach the surface.

10. A. True. Studies of the Japanese Ama divers prove that people can adapt to cold. Years ago when I spent many hours in the water every week I could tolerate cold much better than I can today. Isn't it nice to know that the more you dive the more comfortable you will be? You now have a

great excuse to justify diving on a regular basis!

11. B. False. While diving does require participants to be in good health, the medical community does not suggest that diving is harmful for average, healthy people. Medical experts do know, however, that people with cardiovascular problems are much more likely to experience difficulties while diving than they would otherwise. Mild heart problems that allow people to exercise on land can prove fatal while diving. If your cardiovascular system is unhealthy in any way, consult a diving physician.

COLD WATER DIVING

Body heat loss in water can create serious problems for a diver because water drains heat many times faster than air at the same temperature. Test your knowledge of an important dive topic.

$Q:$

1. Hypothermia means a lower than normal:
- ❐ A. Total body temperature
- ❐ B. Body core temperature
- ❐ C. Body extremity temperature
- ❐ D. Body skin temperature

2. A thermally unprotected diver becomes chilled unless active when the water is as warm as:
- ❐ A. 70 degrees F.
- ❐ B. 75 degrees F.
- ❐ C. 80 degrees F.
- ❐ D. 85 degrees F.

3. When a diver lacks thermal protection in water colder than 60 degrees F, about half the diver's heat loss occurs in the:
- ❐ A. Head and neck
- ❐ B. Arms and legs
- ❐ C. Hands and feet
- ❐ D. Abdomen

4. Fear, apprehension, illness, and hyperventilation increase body heat loss in water.
- ❐ A. True for inexperienced divers
- ❐ B. True for all divers
- ❐ C. True for thin divers
- ❐ D. False

5. Body heat loss while diving increases the likelihood of:
- ❐ A. Oxygen toxicity
- ❐ B. Nitrogen narcosis
- ❐ C. Decompression sickness
- ❐ D. All the above

6. A diver lacking thermal protection should exercise vigorously underwater to delay the onset of hypothermia.
- ❐ A. True
- ❐ B. False

7. The body's reaction to cold is blood shunting from extremities, so a diver will lose little heat through the hands in cold water once numbness occurs.
- ❐ A. True
- ❐ B. False

8. Blood shunted from body extremities in cold water increases torso blood volume, which causes:
- ❐ A. More frequent urination
- ❐ B. Thicker blood
- ❐ C. Both A and B
- ❐ D. Neither A or B

9. If you have shivered uncontrollably underwater for some time, then stop shivering and do not feel as cold, it is an indication that:
- ❐ A. You have adapted to the water temperature
- ❐ B. Your shivering has produced enough heat to offset the cold
- ❐ C. You are not physically capable of cold water diving
- ❐ D. You are experiencing symptoms of hypothermia

10. Which of the following are early symptoms of hypothermia:
- ❐ A. Loss of tactile sense
- ❐ B. Numbness
- ❐ C. Muscle cramping
- ❐ D. All the above

11. Which of the following are symptoms of severe hypothermia:
- ❐ A. Speech impairment
- ❐ B. Sluggish reactions
- ❐ C. Fixation of ideas
- ❐ D. All the above

12. Cold increases respiration, which increases heat loss and air consumption.
- ❐ A. True
- ❐ B. False

13. The preferred method to rewarm a diver suffering mild symptoms of hypothermia is:
- ❐ A. Exercise in a hot bath
- ❐ B. Warm clothes, environment, and liquids
- ❐ C. A fire, warm clothes, and brandy
- ❐ D. Exercise and hot drinks

14. A hypothermic diver has rewarmed sufficiently when:
- ❐ A. The diver feels warm
- ❐ B. The diver's skin is red and flushed
- ❐ C. Sweating occurs
- ❐ D. The diver's hands and feet feel warm

15. Wind chill:
- ❐ A. Has an additive effect with actual temperature to produce the effect of an even colder temperature
- ❐ B. Does not affect divers because the underwater temperature is constant
- ❐ C. Can be ignored except on days that are extremely cold
- ❐ D. Is a factor only during winter dives in cold climates

COLD WATER DIVING

A:

The effects of body heat loss in and around water can be serious—even life threatening. Dive with appropriate insulation, recognize the symptoms of hypothermia, and have the wisdom to quit diving or refrain from further diving when you are cold. If you missed more than three questions, I suggest you take some time to study hypothermia. If you understand the effects of cold and scored well, may your diving experiences, although some may be chilly, be enjoyable.

1. B. Body core temperature. Tissues deep inside the body must maintain a temperature of at least 97 degrees F. Physiological malfunctions begin to occur at lower temperatures. Your task while diving is to preserve heat in the core of your body.

2. D. 85 degrees F. Water has a capacity for heat that is 1,000 times greater than air. Seemingly warm water drains heat from a diver faster than the person can generate heat. The isothermic temperature for humans—the temperature at which you remain comfortable when unprotected in water—is 91 degrees F!

3. A. Head and neck. As a defense to cold, your body shunts blood from your extremities—except your head. Your head has excellent circulation, poor insulation, and conducts heat rapidly. To preserve body heat in water, you must insulate your head as well or better than the remainder of your body.

4. B. True for all divers. Fear, apprehension, illness, hyperventilation, and other mental and physiological factors all contribute to body heat loss. Thinking and feeling abnormally can bring on hypothermia much faster than normal. If you do not feel right or are not confident about a situation, abort the dive, especially when the water is cold.

5. C. Decompression sickness. After a diver surfaces, nitrogen may remain trapped in the tissues near the body surface and in the extremities. The body reduces circulation to the skin and extremities to preserve heat. Nitrogen absorbed at depth and trapped in tissues could cause decompression sickness if released quickly. Following long, cold, deep dives you should avoid exercise, hot showers and baths, alcohol, and anything that stimulates circulation.

6. B. False. Exercise underwater increases circulation to your extremities, which lose heat rapidly. When you exercise in water colder than 60 degrees F. you lose more heat than you would if you remained motionless. When you are insulated against heat loss, moderate exercise can delay hypothermia.

7. B. False. The body restricts circulation to hands and feet until skin temperature reaches 55 degrees F. At that temperature, the body restores circulation until the extremity temperature reaches 85 degrees F! You lose a great amount of heat unless you insulate your hands and feet adequately.

8. C. Both A and B. When your body reduces extremity circulation, it also removes blood fluid to compensate for increased blood volume in your torso. The thicker blood that results can contribute to decompression sickness. Drink fluids between dives to hydrate yourself as much as possible.

9. D. You are experiencing symptoms of hypothermia. Prolonged shivering is a serious symptom. Get out of the water when you cannot suppress sporadic shivering with voluntary movements. When you shiver uncontrollably, you approach a serious situation.

10. D. All the above. Shivering following the symptoms listed are all signs of hypothermia. When shivering occurs in gross bouts, it is time for you to terminate you dive.

11. D. All the above. Shivering, increased respiration, numbness, and no sense of touch are early symptoms of hypothermia. As body core temperature falls below 96 degrees F, loss of muscle control, difficulty speaking, amnesia, sluggish thinking and reactions, fixation of ideas, and hallucinations occur. You must respond to danger signs to prevent cold from affecting your central nervous system.

12. A. True. Cold causes an initial increase in respiration. You can lose from 15 to 24 percent of your heat-producing capability via respiration. As respiration increases from the effects of cold, you can experience air starvation even though your equipment functions properly. Rapid breathing in cold water may cause some regulators to freeze.

13. B. Warm clothes, environment, and liquids. When you are cold after diving, get out of the wind, get dry, don warm clothes, get into warm surroundings, and drink warm, non-alcoholic drinks. Hot baths or showers, exercise, and alcoholic drinks may warm you too rapidly and cause decompression sickness.

14. C. Sweating occurs. Cold water exposure studies report that people feel warm soon after they cease shivering when rewarming is less than 50 percent complete! The onset of sweating is a simple indicator that the body is warm and has excess internal heat.

15. A. Has an additive effect with actual temperature to produce the effect of an even colder temperature. Protect against exposure when you are out of the water as well as when you dive. A 30 mph wind at an actual temperature of 0 degrees F produces an effective temperature 48 degrees colder. You need protection against wind at your dive sites.

DECOMPRESSION ILLNESS

Getting injured while diving is no laughing matter, but at times divers' attitudes and actions indicate a disregard for the seriousness of decompression illness (DCI). All divers need to know the causes, effects, symptoms, first aid, and prevention of decompression illness. See if you know all you should concerning an important topic. Select the most correct answer to each question.

1. Decompression illness can result from:
- ❏ A. Bubble formation and growth in body tissues
- ❏ B. A lung overexpansion injury
- ❏ C. Either of the above
- ❏ D. None of the above

2. Which of the following is not likely to cause DCI?
- ❏ A. Ascending faster than 60 feet per minute
- ❏ B. Omitted decompression
- ❏ C. Altitude shortly after diving
- ❏ D. All the above may cause DCI

3. During ascent, you eliminate excess nitrogen from your body via:
- ❏ A. Exhaled air
- ❏ B. The pores of your skin
- ❏ C. Chemical combination
- ❏ D. All the above

4. Symptoms of cerebral arterial gas embolism usually manifest themselves within ____ .
- ❏ A. One to five minutes
- ❏ B. Five to 60 minutes
- ❏ C. One hour
- ❏ D. One to 24 hours

5. The median onset time for bends symptoms is ____ after diving.
- ❏ A. 20 minutes to two hours
- ❏ B. One to 12 hours
- ❏ C. One to 24 hours
- ❏ D. Two hours to days

6. Local pain is a common symptom in the ____ of recreational diving bends cases and the pain is usually in the ____.
- ❏ A. Minority, shoulders and arms
- ❏ B. Majority, shoulders and arms
- ❏ C. Minority, legs and feet
- ❏ D. Majority, legs and feet

7. Which of the following is likely to cause or aggravate DCI after diving?
- ❏ A. Drinking alcoholic beverages
- ❏ B. A hot shower or bath
- ❏ C. Exercise
- ❏ D. All the above

8. If a diver surfaces from a dive, feels dizzy and nauseous, appears to recover after resting, then develops severe neurological symptoms, the diver has most likely suffered:
- ❏ A. A lung overexpansion injury
- ❏ B. The bends
- ❏ C. Acute seasickness
- ❏ D. Both A and B

9. Which of the following is not a symptom of decompression illness?
- ❏ A. Cyanosis (bluish skin color)
- ❏ B. Weakness
- ❏ C. Extreme fatigue
- ❏ D. Tingling or numb extremities

10. If a diver suffers DCI in a remote location, you should:
- ❏ A. Recompress the diver underwater
- ❏ B. Transport the diver to a treatment facility even if that involves considerable delay
- ❏ C. Provide oxygen first aid and water to drink
- ❏ D. Both B and C are correct

11. If you must evacuate a DCI victim via air transport, advise the pilot not to exceed an altitude of:
- ❏ A. 100 feet
- ❏ B. 500 feet
- ❏ C. 800 feet
- ❏ D. 2,000 feet

12. DCI neurological symptoms usually result from _____ dives while localized pain symptoms generally result from _____ dives.
- ❏ A. Short deep, long shallow
- ❏ B. Long shallow, short deep
- ❏ C. Multi-level, constant depth
- ❏ D. Repetitive, single

13. If you feel abnormal after a dive, you should:
- ❏ A. Wait to see if your symptoms improve
- ❏ B. Immediately contact a treatment facility
- ❏ C. Breathe oxygen and remain under observation
- ❏ D. B and C are correct

14. The preferred first aid position for a diver suffering DCI is on the back or side with the:
- ❏ A. Head lower than the hips and legs
- ❏ B. Body flat
- ❏ C. Head and torso flat and the legs elevated
- ❏ D. Either B or C are correct

15. A diver suffering from DCI should breathe the highest possible oxygen concentration because:
- ❏ A. Oxygen first aid may make recompression treatment unnecessary
- ❏ B. Oxygen vasodilatation can free blocked arteries
- ❏ C. Oxygen first aid may relieve symptoms and enhance recompression treatment
- ❏ D. All the above

DECOMPRESSION ILLNESS

Years ago we separated air embolism and decompression sickness. We now know that bubble trouble is much more complicated than we thought it was. Next to drowning, DCI is the diver's greatest concern. Adhering to safe diving practices minimizes the risk of any injury while diving. If you act responsibly, the risk of DCI or any other diving injury is extremely low. Do all you can to prevent injury, but be prepared to handle emergencies.

1. C. Either of the above. An arterial gas embolism can trigger decompression sickness that would not occur otherwise. Arterial bubbles entering the brain or spinal cord can expand rapidly from excess system nitrogen. The illnesses can occur separately, but the symptoms of decompression sickness and arterial gas embolism are similar. First aid and treatment are almost identical for both diseases. The term "decompression illness" includes both "bubble trouble" maladies.

2. D. All the above may cause DCI. Rapid ascents can cause bends even when you are within established time limits. Unfortunately, a University of Washington study indicates that the typical ascent rate of recreational divers is 120 to 200 feet per minute! Omitted decompression can definitely cause bends. Decreased ambient pressure at altitude, either from mountain driving or flying after diving, can cause bends.

3. A. Exhaled air. Breathing is the only means by which you absorb and eliminate gas from your body. When pressure increases, your blood absorbs additional nitrogen and carries the nitrogen to the tissues of your body. When pressure decreases, it takes time for your blood to carry excess nitrogen from your tissues back to your lungs. Breathing habits and physical activity affect nitrogen ingassing and outgassing. Pace yourself. Breathe slowly and deeply while diving.

4. A. One to five minutes. The median onset time for cerebral arterial gas embolism (CAGE) is one minute. A diver may experience symptoms while in, and even, underwater. It is not uncommon for CAGE to cause drowning or near drowning.

5. A. 20 minutes to two hours. Bends signs and symptoms develop more gradually than those of CAGE. In a few cases, symptoms may be delayed. Be alert for any suspicious feeling after diving—even hours or days after diving. If you do not feel right, consult a diving physician. The longer you delay medical evaluation and treatment, the greater the odds that you will have residual symptoms from your injury.

6. B. Majority, shoulders and arms. More than 85% of bends cases involve local pain, which occurs most frequently in divers' shoulders and elbows. A joint may have initial ill-defined discomfort, which movement may relieve. A deep, dull ache usually develops within an hour. Movement aggravates the pain at that point in time. Bending the joint provides the position of greatest comfort.

7. D. All the above. Alcohol causes skin capillary dilation, which may allow nitrogen—trapped in your extremities by blood shunting caused by cold—to release suddenly into your circulation. Circulation stimulation resulting from hot baths or exercise can trigger bends. Take it easy after a dive or series of dives that near the maximum time limits.

8. D. Both A and B. See answer #1. An air embolism during ascent can produce neurological symptoms, but more importantly, may trigger decompression sickness that would not have occurred if the diver had not embolized. Avoid rapid ascents. Prevent panic. Prevent out-of-air emergencies. Don't be a victim of decompression illness.

9. A. Cyanosis. A person is cyanotic when the surface of the body becomes blue because of insufficient aeration of the blood. DCI, except for extreme cases, does not interfere with blood gas exchange in the lungs. A cyanotic condition occurs when an injured person is deprived of oxygen.

10. D. Both B and C are correct. Never attempt to treat bends in the water. Bends casualties need medical support in addition to recompression. Oxygen and fluids can help relieve symptoms until you obtain medical aid. Have DCS treated even if your treatment is delayed. Plan in advance for diving emergencies. Be prepared. Know what to do, who to call, and where to go.

11. C. 800 feet. As altitude increases, ambient pressure decreases. DCI bubble size and symptoms increase proportionately. Although ambient pressure does not increase much during the first 1,000 feet of altitude, 800 feet is the recommended altitude limit unless you can transport a casualty in a portable recompression chamber.

12. A. Short deep, long shallow. Short deep dives create a high nitrogen load in well-perfused body tissues. Long shallow dives dissolve nitrogen into "slower" tissues, such as the joints. Bends in fast tissues cause neurological damage, while bends in joints produce pain. Multiple-day, multiple-depth dives also predispose divers to neurological bends. Dive conservatively.

13. D. B and C are correct. The average delay before calling for assistance after onset of DCI symptoms is 18 hours! Do not delay medical assistance because you do not believe your symptoms are serious. Don't procrastinate because you may be concerned about treatment expense. What amount of money is worth residual symptoms? Have dive accident insurance, be prepared for an accident, and seek medical aid promptly.

14. D. Either B or C are correct. Medical experts no longer recommend the old, modified Trendelenberg position that placed an injured diver in a head-down position. The modified-T position was based on theory and, in reality, exacerbated an injured diver's condition. The modern first aid saying is, "Supine (on the back) is fine." Slight leg elevation is acceptable to treat for shock, but not essential.

15. C. Oxygen first aid may relieve symptoms and enhance recompression treatment. When an injured diver breathes a high oxygen concentration, the partial pressure gradient between nitrogen in bubbles versus lung nitrogen cause system bubbles to outgas and shrink. Dramatic recovery is possible. No matter how much a casualty improves, medical evaluation is mandatory. Recompression may be required. Do not allow injured divers to sit or stand just because they feel better.

STRESS AND PANIC

Divers learn about the effects of pressure and how to deal with them, but do not learn nearly as much about stress and panic, which are factors in nearly all dive accidents. Find out if you know you should about these important topics.

1. Stress is:
- ❏ A. A psychological and physiological state that evokes effort to maintain or restore equilibrium
- ❏ B. Fear or apprehension you experience in the face of real or imagined danger
- ❏ C. An imbalance between perceived demand and perceived capacity to respond to a situation
- ❏ D. A or C, but not B

2. Select the incorrect statement:
- ❏ A. Some individuals enter rapidly into a stress state
- ❏ B. Some individuals show increased alertness and improved performance when stressed
- ❏ C. Some individuals are immune to the stress-producing qualities of environmental conditions
- ❏ D. None of the above statements are correct

3. The number one factor causing diving stress is:
- ❏ A. Cold
- ❏ B. Workload
- ❏ C. Fitness
- ❏ D. Fluid balance

4. Which of the following items is not a sign of stress:
- ❏ A. Irritability
- ❏ B. Repetitive behavior
- ❏ C. Increased respiration rate
- ❏ D. All the above are signs of stress

5. Psychological effects of stress include:
- ❏ A. Impaired analysis
- ❏ B. Decreased perception and awareness
- ❏ C. Dependence on most recently acquired skills
- ❏ D. A and B, but not C, are correct

6. Optimum performance for complex tasks usually occurs when stress is:
- ❏ A. Low
- ❏ B. Extremely low
- ❏ C. Neither extremely high nor extremely low
- ❏ D. High

7. Arrange into proper sequence the following physiological effects of stress:
- ❏ A. Increased pulse and respiration rates
- ❏ B. Adrenaline secretion
- ❏ C. Repetitive behavior
- ❏ D. Trembling or jerky movements

8. When a problem occurs while diving, a three-event cycle can ultimately cause panic. Select the three events and arrange them in sequence.
- ❏ A. Mental narrowing and physiological changes
- ❏ B. Stress
- ❏ C. Uncontrolled respiration
- ❏ D. Single-thought fixation

9. Arrange the following stress-control procedures into the correct sequence:
- ❏ A. Establish controlled, deep breathing (if air available)
- ❏ B. Correct the problem causing the difficulty
- ❏ C. Minimize physical activity
- ❏ D. Identify the problem
- ❏ E. Analyze the problem

10. Panic is:
- ❏ A. Sudden, extreme, unreasoning fear
- ❏ B. Total loss of logic and mental control
- ❏ C. The ultimate effect of unmanaged stress
- ❏ D. All the above

11. Select two actions that are most likely to minimize stress and panic:
- ❏ A. Good, well-maintained equipment
- ❏ B. Awareness and analytical thinking
- ❏ C. Controlled activity and respiration
- ❏ D. Favorable environmental conditions

12. Panic can result from real or imagined dangers and can lead to either active (struggling) or passive (frozen) behavior either gradually or instantaneously.
- ❏ A. True
- ❏ B. False

13. Select the false statement:
- ❏ A. An unexpected problem is more likely to cause stress or panic than one that a diver expects
- ❏ B. A lone diver experiences more stress than a diver with a buddy
- ❏ C. Advance problem solving using mental visualization is an ineffective method of problem management
- ❏ D. Fear caused by the consequences of a problem may be eliminated by concentrating on the solution to the problem

14. Task relevant instructional self talk (TRIST) can help prevent panic. Select all items that are TRIST components.
- ❏ A. Relax and think
- ❏ B. Encourage yourself and others
- ❏ C. Monitor and counteract distorted thinking
- ❏ D. Use skill and task relevant statements
- ❏ E. Phrase instructions positively

15. The leading factor contributing to scuba diving fatalities is:
- ❏ A. Insufficient air
- ❏ B. Buoyancy problems
- ❏ C. Entrapment
- ❏ D. Panic

STRESS AND PANIC

A:

Were you afraid that you would not select the correct answers as you read the questions? Did your heart and breathing rates increase? Did you feel the effects of stress? If you understand stress, recognize its symptoms, anticipate problems and prepare to manage them, and maintain control during difficulties, you can avoid accidents. The quiz addresses only a few aspects of a comprehensive topic. I encourage further study of these important subjects.

1. D. A or C, but not B. People confuse anxiety with stress. Anxiety is the fear or apprehension that you experience when confronted with either real or imagined danger. Stress requires effort to control an anxious reaction to fight or flee the stressor.

2. D. None of the above statements are correct. All the statements are, in fact, correct. Some people stress easily, while others experience improved performance. Some individuals, such as the astronaut whose heart rate increased only six beats per minute during a launch, are immune to stress.

3. A. Cold. Cold exposure is so routine for divers that they accept it and ignore its potential for harm. Cold affects mental and physical ability and distracts divers. Mental and physical errors create problems that may be avoided and easily corrected by a diver who is not hypothermic. Minor problems and the inability to manage them leads to stress and, ultimately, panic.

4. D. All the above are signs of stress. Increased respiration and heart rates are a person's initial reactions to stress. Mood extremes are common tension symptoms. Repetitive behavior, especially incorrect behavior, signals serious mental narrowing and a significant performance capability degradation.

5. D. A and B, but not C, are correct. As stress builds, mental narrowing occurs. As perceptual narrowing occurs, analysis narrows, response narrows, and control weakens. Mental narrowing can initiate a degenerative cycle that can lead to panic. The need to think, analyze, and retain control when in difficulty is paramount to diving safety.

6. C. Neither extremely high nor extremely low. A moderate amount of stress may enhance performance. Professional athlete performance benefits frequently from the effects of moderate stress. A high state of stress rarely enhances performance. A high level of stress is detrimental and undesirable.

7. B, A, C, D or B, A, D, C. The main point to note is that fear or concern causes adrenaline secretion, which causes increase heart and respiration rates. Rapid breathing is detrimental to divers. You need to control respiration to control stress. Any erratic behavior by a diver should arouse a suspicion of stress.

8. B, C, A. Fear causes the physiological changes described in the previous answer. The changes lead to a respiration control loss, which increases anxiety and compounds the problem. Loss of control establishes a cycle that a diver must interrupt or it will repeat itself until the thought process reduces to a single thought, e. g., getting to the surface. Panic will result. The cycle need not occur and may be arrested.

9. C, D, A, E, B. Control stress by stopping all activity, thinking about the situation, and concentrating on breathing. Mind over matter applies literally in the presence of stress. After you confirm a problem and have your breathing under control, think of possible options to overcome your difficulty, select the best possible option, and take action. Divers often compound difficulties by attempting immediate action before thinking.

10. D. All the above. Panic is one of your worst enemies. Panic displaces analysis, perception, and control. Panic limits response to instinctive reactions. A panicked person is convinced doom is immediate and loses all mental and physical control. Panic is not self-curable; you must prevent it.

11. B. Awareness and analytical thinking, and C. Controlled activity and respiration. The key to preventing stress and panic is control of mind and body. The advice to "get hold of yourself" when tension mounts is a sound recommendation. Recognizing what is happening and taking charge of both mental and physical functions should be the goal of anyone facing a stressful situation.

12. A. True. A person can reach a state of panic gradually from the stress cycle or instantly if the individual experiences sud-

den and extreme fear. Avoid visualizing dangers mentally because your body reacts to events imagined vividly the same as if the event were real. Passive panic, although rare, can occur to divers. Consider passive panic if a diver freezes in one position and is unresponsive.

13. C. Advance problem solving using mental visualization is an ineffective method of problem management. The foregoing statement is incorrect. Positive mental visualization can be effective. Just as envisioning dangers and their consequences is detrimental, anticipating problems and visualizing correct response is beneficial. Pre-visualization allows extended time for analysis and produces confidence. Mental rehearsals reduce stress when a previously anticipated problem arises.

14. All the listed items are TRIST components. Ellis (1962), Maultsby (1968), Beck (1976), and Asken (1993) address "self talk" and its benefits. It is important to understand that your reaction to stress depends much more on your self talk than the situation. Divers learn to identify stress and take physical actions to manage difficulties, but they also need to learn the critical self talk skills.

15. A. Insufficient air. It is a widespread belief that panic is the diver's number one enemy. While an uncontrolled reaction to a problem is extremely serious, running out of air, a lack of ability to control buoyancy, and entrapment are the primary factors affecting diving fatalities. No matter how well you manage stress and prevent panic, you may not be able to deal with some diving risks. To maximize diving safety, avoid and be prepared for no-air emergencies, develop a high degree of buoyancy control, and avoid entrapment situations.

DRUGS AND DIVING

Modern medicine has thousands of medications to bring relief from illness. Which medications are safe to use while diving? Are there hazards associated with the use of non-prescription drugs? What happens when you combine pressure and medication? Are social drugs hazardous in the diving environment? See if your thinking agrees with the findings of diving physicians and various studies on the subject.

Note: Select all correct answers. Some questions have more than one correct response.

1. The effect of pressure on drugs taken by divers can cause:
- A. An intensification of the drug's effect
- B. A reversal of the drug's effect
- C. Unforeseen effects to occur
- D. No change in the drug's effect

2. As long you can tolerate a decongestant without effects above water, you may use it for diving and not have problems.
- A. True, provided the medication is non-prescription
- B. True, as long as you do not exceed the recommended dosage
- C. False, because the medication may lose its effect underwater
- D. False, because decongestants predispose people to seizures under pressure

3. Select the true statement(s) concerning alcohol. A person who consumes alcohol:
- A. Either before or after diving is more likely to get bent than someone who abstains
- B. Before diving is more likely to become chilled than someone who abstains
- C. Is less susceptible to narcosis than someone who abstains
- D. Is less likely to experience respiratory distress than someone who abstains.

4. Select the false statement(s) concerning diving while under the influence of marijuana.
- A. The effects are radically different in cold water than in warm water
- B. Marijuana use increases breath-hold ability
- C. Marijuana makes divers feel warmer in cold water

- D. Marijuana effects include overwhelming anxiety and fear fixation

5. Which of the following, in large quantities, can cause dangerous variations in heart rhythm?
- A. Pain relievers
- B. Cigarettes
- C. Coffee
- D. Decongestants
- E. Motion sickness medication

6. Generally speaking, antihistamines _____ and decongestants _____. Therefore, you should avoid the use of _____ when diving.
- A. Stimulate, sedate, decongestants
- B. Sedate, stimulate, decongestants
- C. Stimulate, sedate, antihistamines
- D. Sedate, stimulate, antihistamines

7. When you use drugs in combination under pressure, the increased pressure:
- A. Makes the drugs' effects completely unpredictable
- B. Intensifies the effect of each drug
- C. Intensifies the effect of one drug or the other
- D. Nullifies the effect of both drugs

8. Select the true statement(s) concerning motion sickness:
- A. Most prescription medications for motion sickness produce undesirable effects for divers
- B. Over-the-counter motion sickness medications are acceptable for use by divers
- C. It is better to risk motion sickness than to risk the side effects of medication for the illness

9. Smoking reduces diver performance capability by:
- A. Reducing the blood's oxygen-carrying capability
- B. Increasing the risk of an air expansion injury
- C. Reducing breath-holding ability
- D. A and B, but not C, are correct

10. Antibiotics increase susceptibility to:
- A. Vomiting
- B. Nitrogen narcosis
- C. Sunburn
- D. Decompression sickness

11. Potential side effects of antimalarial drugs at tropical dive locations include:
- A. White blood cell production suppression
- B. Anemia
- C. Eye damage
- D. Vertigo
- E. Coordination disturbances

12. Potential problems from the use of pseudoephedrine (Sudafed) while diving include:
- A. Sudden death
- B. Localized tolerance to the drug
- C. Ascent barotrauma
- D. None of the above

13. The use of oral bronchodilators to relieve airway obstruction makes divers susceptible to:
- A. Pulmonary barotrauma
- B. Decompression illness
- C. Panic and drowning
- D. All the above

14. Caffeine from coffee, tea, cola, and chocolate drinks:
- A. Stimulates urine production
- B. Can cause heart rhythm disturbances
- C. Predisposes a diver to decompression illness
- D. All the above

DRUGS AND DIVING

Diving physiology is complex, as are the physiological effects of medication. Drugs mask symptoms, but do not eliminate the illness producing them. Illness causes body chemistry changes. The body is not normal when under the influence of drugs. Why complicate the situation by exposing yourself to the effects of higher pressure in combination with medications when the risk is avoidable? The worst scenario is the voluntary use of mind-altering drugs, which severely affect judgement and motor skills. The best "trip" you can take is a natural high that you experience when diving in good health.

1. C. Unforeseen effects to occur. Pressure's effects on drugs are unpredictable. Effectiveness may be lost completely, or may disappear sooner than expected. Even worse, the effect may intensify to a dangerous level. For example, it is not uncommon for a diver to lose consciousness underwater while under the effect of a drug that produces drowsiness above water. Caution, discretion, and medical advice are in order.

2. C. False because the medication may lost its effect underwater. Pressure, perhaps because of increased oxygen partial pressure, causes the effects of some drugs to wear off more quickly than on land. For example, when a decongestant loses it effectiveness underwater, air can be trapped in air spaces and a serious reverse block can result during ascent. There also is the "rebound" effect, where congestion is worse when the medication wears off than it was prior to taking the drug.

3. A and B are correct, and perhaps C. Alcohol causes skin vasodilatation, which increases nitrogen ingassing and outgassing and susceptibility to decompression illness. And, alcohol's effects may mask bends symptoms. Increased circulation to the body's surface also causes increased heat loss, which is undesirable. Resistance to narcosis usually parallels a person's alcohol tolerance, but one absolutely should not be under alcohol's influence when diving.

4. B and C are false. Marijuana's influence may reduce breath-hold ability by as much as 75 percent. Heat loss tolerance may reduce by as much as 90 percent. The effects of marijuana vary greatly with water temperature, but are always extremely hazardous. "Joints" and diving, just like alcohol and diving, do not mix.

5. All the answers are correct. Normal diving causes some heart rhythm changes, but drugs and diving may cause dangerous dysrhythmias. Even seemingly harmless activities, like heavy smoking or the consumption of large quantities of coffee, can cause problems. Decongestants stimulate the heart and predispose to heart rhythm disturbances. Pain relievers and stimulant drugs can vary heart rhythm dangerously.

6. D. Sedate, stimulate, antihistamines. The desire to dive with a stuffy head causes many divers to resort to a variety of medications that open clogged airways. Pressure can increase the sedative effect of some antihistamines. Avoid any drug that causes drowsiness. Antihistamines can reduce mucus production, blur vision, and cause rebound congestion. Postponing diving until airways are healthy is a far better option than using antihistamines.

7. A. Makes the drugs' effects completely unpredictable. The interaction of drugs under pressure is complex and unpredictable. The late Dr. Charlie Brown expressed the problem well by stating that drug interactions can defy imagination. He further stated, "A decongestant that raises blood pressure might instead lower it if compazine is aboard. Most interactions are not understood, and testing them in the water is a form of Russian roulette."

8. All the statements are true. Although divers generally tolerate non-prescription motion-sickness medications, such as Merezine and Bonine, quite well, all motion illness drugs can produce undesirable effects for divers. Two or three ginger root capsules—a natural and harmless herb—may help prevent or relieve motion sickness. Do not risk throwing up underwater. If you can't prevent motion sickness without drugs, consider a new leisure time activity.

9. D. A and B, but not C, are correct. Reduced tissue oxygenation results when carbon monoxide from cigarette smoke combines with blood hemoglobin. Smoking affects the circulatory system in other undesirable ways. The risk of air expansion injuries in the polluted lungs of smokers is well known. Divers need all the physical resources available, and smoking reduces ability, except for breath-holding (smokers adapt to high levels of carbon dioxide in their systems). People should not smoke, but divers absolutely should not smoke.

10. A. Vomiting and C. Sunburn. Tetracyclines may cause photosensitivity—increased sensitivity to sunlight. Many antibiotics increase your susceptibility to vomiting. Divers marginally able to cope with motion sickness may become ill if taking antibiotics. The condition for which you take an antibiotic is often of greater concern than the potential problems of a drug. Be well when you dive.

11. All answers are correct. Antimalarial drugs are fallible and can cause serious side effects, such at those listed in the answers. The effects of many drugs can cause diagnostic problems when a diver requires medical treatment. If you plan to visit an area where malaria is a concern, seek expert medical advice from a diving physician who understands the possible interactions of prescribed drugs and diving.

12. A, B, and C are correct. Nasal decongestant tablets and sprays all have a disruptive effect on the heart's conduction system and may cause sudden death, especially in the water. See answer #2 for additional details about congestion problems.

13. D. All the above. Divers with active airway obstruction difficulties should not dive. Individuals with asthma are susceptible to pulmonary barotrauma, breathing difficulties that can cause them to panic and suffocate or drown. Some oral bronchodilators cause pulmonary vasodilatation that permits "silent" venous bubbles to pass through the lung capillary beds—that normally trap bubbles—to arterial circulation and cause severe decompression illness.

14. A and B are correct. Caffeine is an innocent drug that is common in many drinks and foods. Excessive caffeine can cause heart rhythm disturbances and stimulate urine production. Avoid caffeine or consume it in moderation.

EAR CLEARING TECHNIQUES

Problems with pressure equalization in the ears probably plague divers more than any other physical difficulty. Additionally, permanent ear damage can result if divers do not handle pressure properly. Ear clearing knowledge and skill are among the most important diving education topics. Find out what you know about ears and their equalization.

Q:

Note: Select all correct answers. Several questions have more than one correct response.

1. You should initiate pressure equalization in your ears:
❏ A. Prior to beginning a descent
❏ B. At the beginning of a descent
❏ C. Before reaching a depth of ten feet
❏ D. When you feel pain in your ears

2. Ear pressure equalization is easiest during descent when you position your body:
❏ A. Vertical with the head up
❏ B. Vertical with the head down
❏ C. Horizontal
❏ D. At a 45 degree angle with the head up
❏ E. At a 45 degree angle with the head down

3. The equalization method(s) that will not open the eustachian tubes is/are:
❏ A. Attempting to blow against closed nose and mouth
❏ B. Swallowing
❏ C. Lifting the back of the tongue and thrusting it forward while yawning
❏ D. Wiggling the jaw back and forth
❏ E. All the above methods open the eustachian tubes

4. Outer ear pressure equalization can be affected by:
❏ A. A cold
❏ B. Ear plugs
❏ C. An internal ear infection
❏ D. A tight-fitting hood
❏ E. Plugged Eustachian tubes

5. If you have difficulty equalizing pressure in your ears while descending, you should:
❏ A. Return to the surface and re-initiate the descent
❏ B. Ascend three feet and attempt equalization
❏ C. Ascend until you relieve the pressure effects and attempt equalization

❏ D. Stop and wait until the discomfort subsides
❏ E. Continue to the bottom and equalize the pressure

6. A forceful Valsalva maneuver can result in:
❏ A. A ruptured ear drum
❏ B. A ruptured round window in the middle ear
❏ C. Permanent tinnitus (ringing ear)
❏ D. A reduction in hearing ability
❏ E. An improved ability to equalize pressure

7. Which of the following practices should you discourage and avoid?
❏ A. Diving with a cold
❏ B. Head-first descents
❏ C. Decongestants before diving
❏ D. Diving after major dental work
❏ E. Frenzel equalization maneuver

8. Which of the following statements concerning ears and equalization are true?
❏ A. Your eustachian tubes are closed about 85% of the time
❏ B. Air in the middle ear gets absorbed into the blood stream
❏ C. Vertigo always results when an ear drum ruptures underwater
❏ D. When you feel pain in your ears during descent, pressure is holding the eustachian tubes shut
❏ E. Adolescents have more equalization problems than adults

9. When pressure does not equalize in your ears during an ascent:
❏ A. Pain and injury are likely to occur
❏ B. A sudden release of pressure can cause vertigo
❏ C. Inhaling against closed nose and mouth may help
❏ D. You probably are at fault for diving while congested

10. A person with a perforated ear drum:
❏ A. Should not dive even after the injury has healed

❏ B. May experience vertigo if the perforation occurs underwater
❏ C. May dive with special equipment that excludes water from the ears
❏ D. May dive only with ear plugs
❏ E. None of the above answers are correct

11. You must ascend when you feel ear pain during descent because:
❏ A. It is no longer possible to equalize your middle ear spaces
❏ B. Ear drum rupture is imminent
❏ C. Forceful equalization attempts can damage your inner ears
❏ D. Your eustachian tubes are locked shut

12. Practicing ear clearing techniques on land increases the ease of ear clearing underwater.
❏ A. True
❏ B. False

13. When a diver ascends and the air in one ear escapes easily but remains trapped inside the other ear, the diver may experience:
❏ A. Vertigo
❏ B. Infection
❏ C. Hearing loss
❏ D. All the above

14. A reverse block occurs when:
❏ A. The external pressure on the ears is greater than the pressure in the middle ears
❏ B. The internal pressure in the middle ears is greater than the external pressure
❏ C. A diver experiences vertigo from a sudden pressure drop in one ear during ascent
❏ D. A diver wears ear plugs and the ear drums rupture outward

15. The preferred equalization method during descent is:
❏ A. Forcefully and frequently
❏ B. Gently and frequently
❏ C. Forcefully and infrequently
❏ D. Gently and infrequently

EAR CLEARING TECHNIQUES

If just one diver can equalize pressure more easily or prevent an ear injury, this quiz has served its purpose. If you are a certified diver, you should have answered at least 12 questions correctly. A lower score indicates a need to increase your knowledge. When it comes to pressure, the subject must be perfectly clear.

1. A or B. I like to "pump up" my ears gently prior to starting a descent. It is important to keep ahead of ambient pressure increases. If the outside pressure exceeds internal ear pressure, the differential will hold the eustachian tubes closed and make equalization impossible. You can prevent the effect, known as the trap door effect, by equalizing early and often.

2. A. We may be weightless underwater, but gravity still affects us. Increased blood pressure in the head during inversion engorges capillaries surrounding airways, decreases airway diameter, and reduces equalizing ability. A feet-first descent allows better orientation and buddy contact and helps prevent air swallowing. Disorientation can occur during a 45 degree head-down descent owing to the positioning of the semi-circular canals in your inner ears.

3. E. All the above methods open the eustachian tubes. The Valsalva maneuver (described in Answer A) is the best known equalization method, but it is a forceful maneuver that can cause damage. Swallowing and jaw wiggling are less forceful and work well for many divers. Tilting the head to the shoulder opposite an ear that won't clear while you attempt equalization can help open a stubborn eustachian tube. The best ear clearing technique is the Frenzel maneuver—thrusting the jaw and tongue forward while keeping your throat closed.

4. B Ear plugs, and D a tight-fitting hood. Pressure does not cause problems in the external ear canals unless you close off the canals. Closed canals do not allow pressure in the ear canal to increase during descent and match ambient pressure. Although the middle ear space may equalize, the outer ear cannot. The ear drum will bulge outward and may rupture. Keep your external ear canals open and clear.

5. C. Ascend until you relieve the pressure effects and attempt equalization. As explained in the answer to question one, the trap door effect actually prohibits equalization. You must reduce the pressure before you will be able to open the eustachian tubes and clear your ears. Pain is a signal that you must ascend before you can equalization. Continuing a descent after pain occurs will only result in tissue damage and may cause a ruptured ear drum.

6. A, B, C, and D. You can rupture an ear drum outward by blowing too hard! Although the process has a complex physiological explanation, you can rupture an inner ear round window with an overly forceful Valsalva maneuver. Needless to say, injuries can permanently damage the ears. Avoid blowing hard against a closed nose and mouth.

7. A, B, C, and D. Head-first descents and colds reduce airway diameters. Decongestant use may be permissible with medical approval. Dental work especially involving top molars, can affect sinus cavity equalization. As mentioned in answer three, the Frenzel maneuver is effective and less likely to cause injury than a Valsalva.

8. A, B, C, D, and E. The blood stream does absorb gas from your ears, so you must replace the air from time to time. Your eustachian tubes are normally closed. That's why your equalization requires effort. Youngsters may have a difficult time with ear clearing, but their ability usually improves as they mature.

9. A, B, C, and D. Pressure in the ears must equalize during ascents as well as during descents. The Valsalva maneuver may help reduce pressure if a reverse block occurs. When a pressure build-up releases suddenly, vertigo may result. The dizziness, known as alternobaric vertigo, passes quickly. Slow or stop your ascent if you feel pressure in your ears or in one ear. Equalization problems during ascent are uncommon because it is much easier for air to get out through your eustachian tubes than it was for the air to get into your middle ears.

10. B or C. A perforation of the ear drum is a temporary, but not usually a permanent problem. A perforation, although serious because infection is possible, needn't end a dive career once healed. See a diving physician. Vertigo may occur if cold water enters the middle ear after a rupture, but dizziness does not always take place. Special equipment will allow a person to dive who has a permanently perforated ear drum. Never wear ear plugs while diving.

11. A, B, C, and D. When you feel pain in your ears, the trap door effect has occurred. The ends of your Eustachian tubes, which are buried in soft tissue, are locked shut by ambient pressure. Equalization is impossible. You must ascend to reduce the pressure and allow equalization.

12. A. True. Equalization is a natural process that takes place without thought when you swallow and yawn. Making the process voluntary so we can cope with pressure increases underwater requires training muscle groups we are not used to controlling. By working the muscles of the throat and tongue, we can learn to control them and open our eustachian tubes voluntarily.

13. A. Vertigo. A sudden pressure decrease in one ear disturbs equilibrium. Alternobaric vertigo is the term for pressure-related dizziness. Fortunately, the malady is uncommon. The trend toward slower ascents today should help minimize ascent vertigo.

14. B. The internal pressure in the middle ears is greater than the external pressure. If you feel pain in your ears during ascent, slow or stop your ascent and try sucking gently against closed nose, mouth, and throat.

15. B. Gently and frequently. The old saying, "Equalize early and often," is sound advice. Slightly overpressurizing your ears just prior to descent can help you keep ahead of increasing pressure. The first ten to 15 feet is the most difficult and critical equalization zone. Don't ignore ear discomfort.

DIVE FITNESS

Q:

What is fitness? How fit for diving are you? What do you have to do to become and remain fit? How can you improve your level of fitness? What are the benefits of fitness? Divers should be able to answer these questions because they need to be fit for diving. Find out what you know about fitness and, more importantly, find out about your level of fitness.

1. Select the incorrect answer. Fitness for diving involves:
- A. Physical health
- B. Physical conditioning
- C. Mental health
- D. Strength and stamina
- E. Physical health and strength only

2. A medical examination for diving is recommended when learning to dive and:
- A. Every year thereafter
- B. Every other year thereafter
- C. Every other year thereafter until age forty
- D. Annually after age forty
- E. Answers C and D are both correct

3. Diving with a cold is:
- A. OK as long as air spaces can be equalized
- B. OK if decongestants have no adverse effects
- C. Something that can and should be avoided
- D. Commonly done even though discouraged
- E. Answers C and D are both correct

4. The two most significant difficulties proper fitness for diving are likely to prevent are:
- A. Exhaustion and panic
- B. Fatigue and physical injury
- C. Apprehension and anxiety
- D. Stress and panic
- E. Apprehension and physical injury

5. Select the most correct answer. The attribute(s) most likely to prevent diver injury is/are:
- A. Muscular strength and stamina
- B. Cardio-vascular stamina
- C. Diving within physical limitations
- D. Physical flexibility
- E. Application of proper lifting techniques

6. Select all correct answers. A good fitness conditioning program for divers consists of:
- A. Stretching
- B. Weight training
- C. Swimming
- D. Frequent diving
- E. Continuing education

7. Fitness is best developed with a program that steadily and gradually increases:
- A. Endurance
- B. The exertion level
- C. Muscular strength
- D. Cardio-vascular stamina
- E. The mental attitude

8. "Transfer of fitness" implies:
- A. The ability of one person to influence the performance of another
- B. The degree to which fitness from training is transferred to actual use
- C. The ability to transfer the effects of a level of fitness in the past to the present
- D. All the above
- E. None of the above

9. Experienced divers exert less energy than novice divers while diving because experienced divers have:
- A. Skill proficiency
- B. Better fitness
- C. Better equipment
- D. Confidence
- E. Adaptation

10. Fitness for an activity is enhanced by skill proficiency achieved by:
- A. Experience and knowledge
- B. Knowledge and strength
- C. Strength and endurance
- D. Endurance and attitude
- E. None of the above

11. Fitness is a measure of how well your body can:
- A. Supply oxygen to tissues
- B. Use oxygen in the tissues
- C. Respond to stimulus
- D. Tolerate resistance
- E. Answers A and B are both correct

12. A benefit of increased fitness is:
- A. Improved circulation
- B. A slower heart rate
- C. A feeling of general well being
- D. Increased stamina
- E. All of the above

13. Fitness for diving can be developed in ____ weeks. Decreased fitness is apparent after ____ week(s).
- A. Six, one
- B. Six, two
- C. Four, one
- D. Four, two
- E. Four, three

14. To develop fitness for diving, it is best to follow a program of:
- A. Gradually increasing the exertion level
- B. Attempting the desired final results at the outset
- C. Repeating the same activity daily
- D. Repeating the same activity on a more frequent basis
- E. Stretching, lifting, running, swimming, and cool down

15. Fitness for diving is <u>not</u> affected by:
- A. Diet
- B. Rest
- C. Confidence
- D. Non-prescription drugs
- E. Fitness <u>is</u> affected by all the above

DIVE FITNESS

Now that you know what fitness is, the final question is, "Are you fit to dive?" While you may be fit for one type of diving, or for diving in certain conditions, you are probably not fit for all types of diving or diving conditions. An important aspect of fitness is to know your limitations and dive within them. Dive readiness, physical fitness, and good judgment are like a three-legged stool—you need all three legs to maintain balance. A balanced approach to diving minimizes risks and maximizes enjoyment.

1. E. Physical health and strength only. This answer is incorrect. Fitness involves everything required to meet the demands of a particular activity. Good physical and mental health, a confident attitude, skill proficiency, and physical strength and stamina are all diving fitness requirements.

2. E. Answers C and D are both correct. It is a good idea to have a physical examination for diving when learning to dive. Examinations also are recommended every two years until age forty, when annual physical exams become appropriate.

3. E. Answers C and D are both correct. Body air passages are obstructed when a person has a cold. The blockage interferes with pressure equalization. The use of decongestants is ill-advised. Many divers dive with colds, but they should heed the advise of expert diving physicians. If not well, don't dive.

4. A. Exhaustion and panic. Divers lacking fitness for diving tend to waste energy and lack stamina. These factors coupled with the aquatic environment cause a high degree of stress that frequently results in panic. To maintain mental control, you must be able to control yourself physically while diving.

5. C. Diving within physical limitations. Strength, stamina, and flexibility are desirable, but knowing your capabilities and diving within them are more likely to prevent a diving accident than a high degree of physical fitness. Good judgment will prevent more accidents than brute strength.

6. All answers are correct. Fitness includes knowledge, confidence, and skill proficiency. Physical fitness alone is not sufficient to meet the demands of diving. A regular routine to maintain physical fitness combined with frequent diving and continuing education is the best possible way to maintain a high level of dive fitness.

7. B. The exertion level. It takes time to develop fitness. Attempting too much too soon can cause an injury. Begin a fitness development program slowly. Consult your doctor first if you have been inactive for a long period of time. Each time you exercise, attempt to increase the workload of the activity. Also, avoid trying to match past performance at the beginning of a fitness program.

8. B. The degree to which fitness from training is transferred to actual use. The degree of transfer to actual use depends largely on the similarity between the training exercise and the actual activity. As similarity increases, so does the transfer of fitness. The closer your exercise program resembles diving, the more you will benefit from your exercise when you dive.

9. A. Skill proficiency. A novice at any activity usually exerts several times more energy than an experienced participant. The experienced person saves energy by making only necessary movements and moving efficiently. Knowledge also increases proficiency. Combine study and skill practice with exercise to optimize dive fitness.

10. A. Experience and knowledge. This question and answer underscore the previous question and answer. Knowing the easiest way to perform skills and practicing the skills until their performance is almost automatic contributes to your overall fitness for diving—your ability to meet the demands of diving.

11. E. Answers A and B are both correct. Fitness is a measure of how well your body can use oxygen and how well your lungs, heart, blood, and circulation can supply the oxygen. Your knowledge and experience affect your attitude, which affects your willingness to achieve physical fitness.

12. E. All the above. Increased fitness develops your body's means to supply oxygen to tissues. Fitness improves circulation, slows your heart rate, increases your stamina, and produces a feeling of general well being. Be fit and feel great!

13. A. Six, one. Although it takes six to eight weeks to develop fitness for an activity, efficiency deteriorates rapidly with inactivity. The only way to maintain a level of fitness is to continue the training activity several times weekly. It is easy, however, to maintain a level of fitness with regular exercise that approximates the desired activity.

14. A. Gradually increasing the exertion level. See answer number seven. To increase fitness, you must push the limits of endurance for an activity. A training program where each workout is a slight improvement over previous improvement is recommended.

15. E. Fitness is affected by all of the above. Anything that affects your body or your mind affects your fitness for diving. If you are tired, stressed, under the influence of drugs, ill, or lack proper nourishment, you lack adequate fitness to dive. Take care of yourself so you can enjoy diving safely.

GAS TOXICITY

Several gases that divers breathe or may breathe become toxic if the gas concentration is great enough. It is important to know when and how these gases can affect us. Check your knowledge of gas toxicity by answering the following questions.

1. The percentage of oxygen needed in a gas mixture to maintain consciousness at sea level is:
- ❑ A. 5 percent
- ❑ B. 10 percent
- ❑ C. 16 percent
- ❑ D. 21 percent

2. Oxygen becomes toxic when breathed in concentrations where its partial pressure approaches:
- ❑ A. 1 atmosphere (atm)
- ❑ B. 1.5 atm
- ❑ C. 2.0 atm
- ❑ D. 3.0 atm

3. Diving with oxygen-enriched breathing gas:
- ❑ A. Permits longer bottom times
- ❑ B. Allows deeper dives to be made
- ❑ C. Requires specialty training
- ❑ D. A and B, but not C

4. Normal air contains approximately ____ carbon dioxide, which causes unconsciousness at a level of ____ at sea level.
- ❑ A. .03 percent, 3 percent
- ❑ B. .03 percent, 10 percent
- ❑ C. .003 percent, 10 percent
- ❑ D. .003 percent, 3 percent

5. Carbon dioxide toxicity is least likely to occur in recreational diving as a result of:
- ❑ A. Skip breathing
- ❑ B. Dead air space in equipment
- ❑ C. Faulty regulator
- ❑ D. Overexertion

6. Hemoglobin (oxygen-carrying blood component) has an affinity for carbon monoxide that is ____ times greater than its affinity for oxygen.
- ❑ A. 10
- ❑ B. 50
- ❑ C. 100
- ❑ D. 200

7. Carbon monoxide becomes toxic when its partial pressure exceeds ____ at sea level.
- ❑ A. .1 percent
- ❑ B. .25 percent
- ❑ C. 1 percent
- ❑ D. 5 percent

8. Signs and symptoms of carbon monoxide toxicity closely approximate those of:
- ❑ A. Hypoxia
- ❑ B. Carbon dioxide toxicity
- ❑ C. Oxygen toxicity
- ❑ D. Nitrogen narcosis

9. Exertion accelerates carbon dioxide toxicity.
- ❑ A. True
- ❑ B. False
- ❑ C. True only at depth
- ❑ D. True only at sea level

10. Treatment for carbon monoxide toxicity ranges from ____ hour(s) to ____ hours depending on the procedure used.
- ❑ A. 1/2-5+
- ❑ B. 1-8+
- ❑ C. 4-12+
- ❑ D. 24-48

11. The most likely source of carbon monoxide for divers is:
- ❑ A. Improperly located intake on air compressor
- ❑ B. Improperly maintained air compressor
- ❑ C. "Flashing" of oil vapors in the air compressor
- ❑ D. Any of the above

12. Headache, dizziness, nausea, vomiting and confusion are signs and symptoms of:
- ❑ A. Carbon dioxide toxicity
- ❑ B. Carbon monoxide toxicity
- ❑ C. Oxygen toxicity
- ❑ D. A and B, but not C

13. Breathing air containing one percent carbon monoxide at a depth of 132 feet is equivalent to breathing air at the surface containing ____ percent carbon monoxide.
- ❑ A. One
- ❑ B. Two
- ❑ C. Four
- ❑ D. Five

14. Unconsciousness from carbon monoxide toxicity is most likely to occur to a diver:
- ❑ A. During descent
- ❑ B. While on the bottom
- ❑ C. During ascent
- ❑ D. After diving

GAS TOXICITY

A:

When you know the problems of gas toxicity, you are better able to avoid them. Be sure to take all recommended precautions to avoid the serious consequences of gas toxicity.

1. B. 10 percent. Normal air contains approximately 21 percent oxygen, which is more than the 10 percent needed to maintain consciousness. This is why artificial respiration is possible. Oxygen levels can be lowered in scuba tank air through the corrosion process when air is stored for long periods in steel tanks that also contain water. Have only a few hundred psi of air in tanks being stored and have the tanks visually inspected regularly.

2. C. 2 atm. If pure oxygen is breathed at depths greater than 25 feet or if air is breathed at depths approaching 300 feet, seizures from oxygen toxicity are likely to result.

3. C. Requires specialty training. The use of oxygen-enriched breathing mixtures is inappropriate for recreational divers unless they complete a specialty course and adhere to all recommended safety procedures.

4. B. .03 percent, 10 percent. People can tolerate nearly 100 times the amount of carbon dioxide normally found in air. This is because we are able to adjust to carbon dioxide variations that result within us from exercise, breath-holding, etc. The problems with carbon dioxide for recreational divers nearly always result from metabolic production of the gas combined with improper breathing habits.

5. B. Dead air space in equipment. The problems of rebreathing air from equipment apply to commercial divers rather than scuba divers. Recreational divers do not use helmets and full-face masks, which have large amounts of dead air space. Skip breathing—holding each breath for a few seconds to reduce air consumption—is bad because it can lead to carbon dioxide excess. This condition, when combined with exertion, can produce carbon dioxide toxicity. The remaining answers also contribute to carbon dioxide excess. Avoid the situations described.

6. D. 200. Hemoglobin in the blood is 200 times more likely to combine with carbon monoxide than with oxygen. This is particularly bad because the hemoglobin re-

mains combined with the carbon monoxide for many hours instead of the seconds involved with oxygen. As more and more hemoglobin is occupied with carbon monoxide, the blood's oxygen transporting capabilities are reduced proportionally. This deprives the body of oxygen and leads to a hypoxic state than can result in unconsciousness and even death.

7. A. .1 percent. Carbon monoxide is quite dangerous because very small amounts produce serious effects. The standard for air purity for diving is measured in parts per million (ppm). As you will see, the problems of carbon monoxide are compounded by pressure. Contaminated air should be considered extremely hazardous because it can and has contributed to diving accidents.

8. A. Hypoxia or B. Carbon dioxide toxicity. Headache, dizziness, nausea, vomiting and confusion accompany several respiratory difficulties. Bright red lips and nail beds may result from carbon monoxide toxicity, as may shortness of breath. If high concentrations of the poisonous gas are present, the gradual progression of signs may be bypassed and the person may lose consciousness quickly. Remember that hyperbaric chamber treatment and the administration of oxygen are in order for any diver losing consciousness.

9. A. True. Since exertion increases circulation and since carbon monoxide molecules combine with the blood, exertion accelerates carbon monoxide toxicity as the blood circulates through the body more frequently than when not exerting. Working hard while breathing contaminated air at depth is the worst possible situation for a diver. Exertion at depth should be avoided for this and other reasons.

10. 1/2-5+. Treatment for carbon monoxide toxicity ranges from one-half hour in a hyperbaric chamber to about one hour when pure oxygen is breathed to five or more hours when fresh air is breathed. Divers are encouraged to have oxygen available for the treatment of this and

several other diving maladies. For severe cases of carbon monoxide poisoning, artificial respiration may be necessary.

11. D. Any of the above. The most likely source of carbon monoxide in breathing air is the fumes from an internal combustion engine being sucked into the air intake of a compressor, although the problem can be caused by the other answers as well. Your best bet is to have your tanks filled only at professional facilities that have their compressors well maintained and their air tested regularly for purity.

12. D. A and B, but not C. Fast, labored breathing is a sign of carbon dioxide excess, while shortness of breath is a symptom of carbon monoxide excess. Red lips or nails or red blotches on the skin may also identify carbon monoxide toxicity. Otherwise, the signs and symptoms produced by these two gases are quite similar.

13. D. Five. Owing to partial pressure, a one percent concentration of carbon monoxide in air (a very large amount) produces an effect at 132 feet (five atmospheres absolute pressure) equivalent to five percent at sea level. This "surface equivalent" effect is a primary reason why carbon monoxide is so dangerous for divers.

14. C. During ascent. At the higher pressures encountered underwater, oxygen can be dissolved in and carried by blood plasma. This can keep a diver conscious even when the hemoglobin is combined with carbon monoxide. Unfortunately, as a diver ascends, the lower resulting pressure will not dissolve the oxygen into the blood and unconsciousness results from hypoxia. The longer the diver remains submerged, the greater the danger. Be sure to surface at once if contaminated air is suspected.

THE LUNGS

Breathing is an important element of diving. You know that you should not hold your breath when breathing compressed air underwater, but you also should know the physical limitations of your lungs and how depth affects your ability to breathe. Test your level of knowledge about lungs.

Matching: (Match Three Columns)

Capacity	Definition	Average Volume
1. Resting Tidal Volume	A. Air that remains in your lungs after complete exhalation.	V. 5 Liters
2. Vital Capacity	B. The max. amount of air that you can inhale after a complete exhalation.	W. 0.5 Liter
3. Expiratory Reserve	C. The volume of air passing in and out of your lungs with each breath.	X. 1 Liter
4. Residual Volume	D. Volume of air that you can exhale after a normal expiration.	Y. 2.75 Liters
5. Inspiratory Reserve	E. Volume of air that you can inhale after a normal inspiration.	Z. 1.75 Liters

Matching:

6. Pneumothorax
7. Mediastinal emphysema

8. Air embolism
9. Subcutaneous emphysema

A. Air obstruction in the circulation
B. Air between the lungs and behind the sternum
C. Air beneath the skin around the neck
D. Air in the pleural cavity

10. The conditions of questions 6 through 9 almost always are caused by:
❏ A. An ascent that is too rapid
❏ B. Holding the breath during ascent
❏ C. Lung abnormalities
❏ D. All of the above

11. The physical structure of the lungs approximates most closely that of a:
❏ A. Balloon
❏ B. Plastic bag
❏ C. Sponge
❏ D. Tree

12. The elasticity of the lungs approximates most closely that of a:
❏ A. Balloon
❏ B. Thin plastic bag
❏ C. Paper bag
❏ D. Plastic bottle

13. Lung rupture can occur with over pressurization in water as shallow as:
❏ A. Four feet (1.2 m)
❏ B. Eight feet (2.4 m)
❏ C. Ten feet (3 m)
❏ D. Twelve feet (3.6 m)

14. The best action to take to prevent a lung injury if you must make an emergency swimming ascent while scuba diving is to:
❏ A. Exhale fully at the bottom and keep exhaling all the way to the surface.
❏ B. Exhale a small amount of air all the way to the surface.
❏ C. Attempt to maintain a normal breathing pattern even though air may not be available to breathe.
❏ D. None of the above

15. The purpose of surfactant, a lipoprotein substance within the lungs, is to:
❏ A. Humidify inspired air
❏ B. Reduce alveolar surface tension
❏ C. Seal tiny leaks in capillary beds
❏ D. All of the above

16. When you become an adult, your lung volume is constant and you cannot increase your maximum lung capacity.
❏ A. True
❏ B. False

17. Swollen lung tissues may follow the use of breathing apparatus that has high inspiratory resistance.
❏ A. True
❏ B. False

18. Overbreathing caused by anxiety increases your capacity for work at depth.
❏ A. True
❏ B. False

19. Resistance to the flow of air in body airways severely impairs the ability of a diver to exercise at a depth of 100 feet (30 m).
❏ A. True
❏ B. False

20. Diving medical experts agree that lung squeeze is a significant problem that can affect breath-hold divers and non-breathing divers.
❏ A. True
❏ B. False

THE LUNGS

There are many misconceptions about the lungs. What many divers learn about breathing resistance, lung squeeze, and lung problems may not be correct. If information in this quiz was new to you, you might want to study some diving medicine books and learn more about your wonderful lungs and the mechanics of breathing. Knowledge helps increase your safety while diving. Hopefully you are aware that overexertion at depth is a serious problem and one you must avoid. Now that the test is over, take a deep breath and relax.

1. C, W
2. B, V
3. D, Z
4. A, X
5. E, Y
6. D
7. B
8. A
9. C

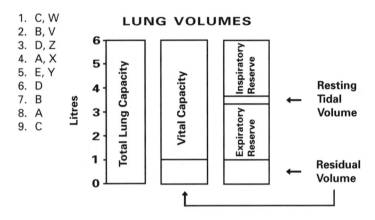

10. B. Holding the breath during ascent. Lung abnormalities rarely cause lung over expansion injuries. If you hold your breath while ascending after breathing compressed air, you will rupture your lungs and the escaping air may go into one or more areas of your body. If you do not hold your breath, your rate of ascent is not a factor as far as lung expansion is concerned.

11. C. Sponge. Many people visualize the lungs as balloon-like bladders hanging inside the chest cavity. Your airways branch many times until they reach tiny, sponge-like lung tissues. The total surface area of the inside of your lungs exceeds that of a tennis court! Your lungs are amazing structures.

12. B. Thin plastic bag. A thin plastic bag does not stretch when it reaches its maximum capacity. Additional pressure inside the bag causes the bag to rupture instead of increase in size. Your lungs behave similarly. They are not elastic and can withstand only a slight amount of over pressurization.

13. A. Four feet (1.2 m). If you inhale fully while lying on the bottom in water only four feet deep, hold your breath, and stand up, you could suffer a lung over expansion injury. Lung physiology and the rapid pressure changes in water are the reasons that avoiding breath-holding is the number one rule of scuba diving.

14. C. Attempt to maintain a normal breathing pattern even though air may not be available to breathe. When you exhale, you collapse airways in your lungs temporarily. Unless you reverse the pressure, air on the lung side of the restriction can expand and cause an injury although you are exhaling. Try to maintain your normal breathing pattern. If you are out of air at depth, you can get additional air to breathe as you ascend.

15. B. Reduce alveolar surface tension. Without surfactant, your lungs would not inflate completely. Surfactant keeps the tiny air sacs in your lungs expanded, even at low lung volumes. When water contacts surfactant, foam results. The reaction is the source of the foam seen in near-drowning incidents.

16. B. False. Most people do not use their full lung capacity enough. If you exercise regularly, you can expand unused portions of your lungs and increase your capacity up to 25%. Breath-hold divers have higher than average lung capacities not so much because they were born with them, but because they use their lungs to their full capacity on a regular basis. If you want to be a better diver, increase your level of physical fitness.

17. A. True. Breathing hard to maintain adequate lung ventilation during exercise may damage small veins and allow fluid seepage into lung tissues. You should pace your diving activity to avoid situations underwater that require strenuous respiratory effort. Symptoms of lung edema, which clear without treatment in about a day, are coughing and shortness of breath.

18. B. False. Trying to exceed the maximum flow rate of breathing resistance due to air density wastes expiratory effort and reduces your capacity for other work. You can move air through your airways at a certain speed and volume for a given depth. If you try to move the air faster, the effort to do so increases dramatically and you waste energy.

19. B. False. According to Strauss, your maximum flow rate at a depth of 100 feet (30 m) is half the surface rate, but since you use only half your respiratory capacity at the surface, there should be no ventilation-imposed exercise limitation at that depth assuming your equipment does not add significantly to your breathing resistance. Overexertion problems underwater result when divers exert strenuously, then try to exceed the flow rate limitation imposed by resistance. When you exercise underwater, do so slowly and steadily, and avoid heavy breathing.

20. B. False. There is information about thoracic squeeze in many diving medicine books, but the ailment is theoretical. Apparently there is one documented case of lung squeeze, although some experts question the diagnosis of that instance. It seems that a lung squeeze is at best an extremely rare malady and may not be a valid concern for recreational divers .

Rate your score:

14-15 correct answers—Basic diver level

16-18 correct answers—Advanced diver level

19-20 correct answers—Instructor level

MEDICAL TERMINOLOGY

Medicine is a prominent scuba diving subject. You encounter many medical terms in texts, articles, and presentations. It helps divers to understand medical terms. Test your knowledge by matching each list of terms to each list of the definitions. Use each definition only once. The precise medical definition may vary somewhat from those provided because I have phrased the definitions for the average diver.

List A: Anatomy

1. Alveoli
2. Bronchus
3. Carotid
4. Epiglottis
5. Eustachian
6. Larynx
7. Mediastinum
8. Pleura
9. Pulmonary
10. Sternum
11. Thorax
12. Trachea
13. Tympanic
14. Viscera
15. Xiphoid

A. Windpipe
B. Lowest sternum segment
C. Windpipe subdivision
D. Protects larynx and trachea
E. Membrane covering lungs and chest walls
F. Voice box above trachea
G. Chief artery to the head
H. Middle of the chest
I. Breastbone
J. Area between neck and abdomen
K. Internal organs of the body
L. Lung air cells
M. Pertaining to the lungs
N. Tube between throat and middle ear
O. Membrane forming the ear drum

List B: Physiology

16. Anoxia
17. Apnea
18. Asphyxia
19. Bradycardia
20. Diuresis
21. Dyspnea
22. Hypercapnia
23. Hyperpnea
24. Hyperventilation
25. Hypoglycemia
26. Hypoxia
27. Narcosis
28. Necrosis
29. Tachycardia
30. Vertigo

P. Respiration in excess of need
Q. Death of body tissues
R. Dizziness
S. Total lack of oxygen
T. Difficult or labored breathing
U. Slowed heart rate
V. Rapid, shallow breathing
W. Suspension of breathing
X. Excessive urine excretion
Y. Insufficient tissue oxygen
Z. Low blood sugar level
AA. Excessive heart rate rapidity
BB. State of stupor or arrested activity
CC. Oxygen lack and carbon dioxide excess
DD. Excess carbon dioxide in the blood

List C: Maladies

31. Aerodontalgia
32. Aerotitis
33. Barotrauma
34. Ciguatera
35. Convulsions
36. Cyanosis
37. Dermatitis
38. Edema
39. Embolism
40. Emphysema
41. Hemorrhage
42. Hypothermia
43. Pneumothorax
44. Subcutaneous
45. Syncope

EE. Loss of blood from vessels
FF. Bluish skin discoloration
GG. Tooth pain caused by gas pocket
HH. Fluid accumulation in tissues
II. Low body core temperature
JJ. Fainting
KK. Ear squeeze
LL. Arterial circulation blockage
MM. Pressure-related injury
NN. Air in the pleural space
OO. Under the skin
PP. Violent, uncontrolled muscle contractions
QQ. Fish poisoning
RR. Skin inflammation
SS. Swelling from gas in any body tissue

MEDICAL TERMINOLOGY

Did you feel challenged by this quiz or overwhelmed? If you did not do well, consider the quiz a learning experience. You do not need to know all the terms to be a good diver, but knowing them can help you dive better. The more you learn about diving, the more you discover all that you do not know. Enjoy your diving. Keep discovering what you do not know.

List A: Anatomy

1. Alveoli — L. Lung air cells
2. Bronchus — C. Windpipe subdivision
3. Carotid — G. Chief artery to the head
4. Epiglottis — D. Protects larynx and trachea
5. Eustachian — N. Tube between throat and middle ear
6. Larynx — F. Voice box above trachea
7. Mediastinum — H. Middle of the chest
8. Pleura — E. Membrane covering lungs and chest walls
9. Pulmonary — M. Pertaining to the lungs
10. Sternum — I. Breastbone
11. Thorax — J. Area between neck and abdomen
12. Trachea — A. Windpipe
13. Tympanic — O. Membrane forming the ear drum
14. Viscera — K. Internal organs of the body
15. Xiphoid — B. Lowest sternum segment

List C: Maladies

31. Aerodontalgia — GG. Tooth pain caused by gas pocket
32. Aerotitis — KK. Ear squeeze
33. Barotrauma — MM. Pressure-related injury
34. Ciguatera — QQ. Fish poisoning
35. Convulsions — PP. Violent, uncontrolled muscle contractions
36. Cyanosis — FF. Bluish skin discoloration
37. Dermatitis — RR. Skin inflammation
38. Edema — HH. Fluid accumuilation in tissues
39. Embolism — LL. Arterial circulation blockage
40. Emphysema — SS. Swelling from gas in any body tissue
41. Hemorrhage — EE. Loss of blood from blood vessels
42. Hypothermia — II. Low body core temperature
43. Pneumothorax — NN. Air in the pleural space
44. Sybcutaneous — OO. Under the skin
45. Syncope — JJ. Fainting

List B: Physiology

16. Anoxia — S. Total lack of oxygen
17. Apnea — W. Suspension of breathing
18. Asphyxia — CC. Oxygen lack and carbon dioxide excess
19. Bradycardia — U. Slowed heart rate
20. Diuresis — X. Excessive urine excretion
21. Dyspnea — T. Dificult or labored breathing
22. Hypercapnia — DD. Excess carbon dioxide in the blood
23. Hyperpnea — V. Rapid, shallow breathing
24. Hyperventilation — P. Respiration in excess of need
25. Hypoglycemia — Z. Low blood sugar level
26. Hypoxia — Y. Insufficient tissue oxygen
27. Narcosis — BB. State of stupor or arrested activity
28. Necrosis — Q. Death of body tissues
29. Tachycardia — AA. Excessive heart rate rapidity
30. Vertigo — R. Dizziness

NITROGEN NARCOSIS

Q:

Modern divers venture into greater depths on a more frequent basis. Whether or not this is a good idea is a controversial issue, but it is a fact that narcosis takes effect during deep dives. Do you know all you should about nitrogen narcosis? This quiz focuses on the cause, signs, symptoms, and remedy for the strange malady of narcosis.

1. All divers feel the symptoms of nitrogen narcosis at depths greater than 100 feet.
❑ A. True
❑ B. False

2. Nitrogen narcosis affects all divers at depths greater than 100 feet.
❑ A. True
❑ B. False

3. It is possible to accurately predict the signs and symptoms of nitrogen narcosis with depth.
❑ A. True
❑ B. False

4. The effects of nitorgen narcosis are constant for a diver from day to day.
❑ A. True
❑ B. False

5. The cause of nitrogen narcosis is best understood with:
❑ A. The Myer-Overton theory
❑ B. Pascal's law
❑ C. Behnke's "window" effect
❑ D. Toricelli's experiment

6. The degradation of performance caused by narcosis is the primary reason for the recommended recreational depth limit of 130 feet.
❑ A. True
❑ B. False

7. The higher mental functions, such as the ability to reason, make decisions, remember recent events, learn new tasks, and concentrate are first affected by nitrogen narcosis.
❑ A. True
❑ B. False

8. In cold, turbid water, divers may feel euphoric from narcosis, while in warm, clear water divers may develop a sense of impending doom.
  A. True
  B. False

9. Short term amnesia is a common after-effect of narcosis.
❑ A. True
❑ B. False

10. Symptoms of narcosis tend to develop:
❑ A. Quickly and progress with time
❑ B. Slowly and stabilize with time
❑ C. Quickly and stabilize with depth
❑ D. Slowly and stabilize with depth

11. Symptoms of narcosis tend to depart:
❑ A. Slowly with decreased depth
❑ B. Quickly with decreased depth
❑ C. Suddenly at a specific shallower depth
❑ D. Slowly at a specific shallower depth

12. Select _all_ correct answers. The severity of narcosis is aggravated by:
❑ A. High carbon dioxide levels
❑ B. Anxiety and apprehension
❑ C. Cold and fatigue
❑ D. Medications and alcohol

13. Nitrogen narcosis begins to affect the average diver at a depth of:
❑ A. 70-80 feet
❑ B. 80-90 feet
❑ C. 90-100 feet
❑ D. 110-130 feet

14. You may use motivation, concentration, and acclimatization to reduce the effects of narcosis.
❑ A. True
❑ B. False

15. Divers using seasickness medication patches may experience narcosis at depths as shallow as 60 feet.
❑ A. True
❑ B. False

NITROGEN NARCOSIS

Narcosis is serious and not something to play around with. Divers who want to get "high" at depth or see what it feels like to get "narked" can get into serious trouble. If you want to dive deep, first take a deep diving specialty course, then increase your depth ten feet at a time. Dive with those who have a lot of experience at deeper depths. On any dive when you feel narcosis, ascend until the symptoms are relieved. If you want to take chances with narcosis, become a commercial diver. Then at least you will be paid for the risk you take.

1. B. False. Studies have shown that some divers do not feel symptoms of nitrogen narcosis. This does not mean they do not get "narked," just that they do not feel the symptoms. Not feeling symptoms is a liability rather than an asset because the diver receives no warnings. Short term memory loss frequently occurs from narcosis. Some divers who claim they are not affected by narcosis simply do not remember being affected by it.

2. A. True. Everyone is affected by narcosis when breathing compressed air at depths greater than 100 feet. Some are able to tolerate it and overcome it to a greater extent than others, but all are affected. Only fools say they do not get narked during deep dives.

3. B. False. The effects of narcosis vary from individual to individual and within an individual from day to day. I have felt narcosis at the same depth on two occasions, and the symptoms were different each time. The only thing you can count on is that you will get narked if you go deep and that you cannot predict the effects of the narcosis.

4. B. False. While the effects of narcosis do change, some adaptability is possible with frequent exposure. Narcosis still occurs, but the ability to deal with it increases. Unfortunately, the adaptation ceases to exist after only a few weeks of not diving. Making lots of deep dives to increase tolerance to narcosis is only a good idea if you are a commercial diver.

5. A. Myer-Overton theory. This theory suggests that any inert gas will cause an anesthetic effect if enough of it is dissolved in the fatty tissues of the nervous system. The heavier the gas, the more quickly the narcotic effect will occur. It is believed the dissolved gas short-circuits the nerves. The exact cause is not understood.

6. A. True. Many divers believe the 130 foot limit is based upon decompression limitations. While no-decompression diving is strongly encouraged by all diver training organizations, narcosis is a major consideration for safety at depths in

excess of 100 feet. If you want to dive below 90 feet and are inexperienced at greater depth, you should dive with a professional who can tolerate narcosis so you will have someone to help you cope with narcosis.

7. A. True. Mental functions are affected before mechanical functions. Reasoning and short-term memory are affected before motor coordination. Delayed response to things seen and heard are usually the first symptoms of motor function degradation, but these may not be noticed by a narked diver. The inability to reason clearly is the primary reason narcosis is a diving hazard.

8. B. False. The opposite is usually the case. In warm, clear waters, a diver may feel euphoric from narcosis. In cold, turbid waters, the same diver may feel impending or foreboding doom. Many factors in addition to the water temperature and visibility combine to determine the effects of "rapture of the deep."

9. A. True. Immediate memory can be affected at depths as shallow as 100 feet. I watched a diver use a knife during a deep dive, lay the knife down and swim away, and then claim after the dive he had lost his knife. Not only did he did not recall laying the knife down, he did not recall even using it!

10. C. Quickly and stabilize with depth. The U. S. Navy Diving Manual states, "Onset of narcosis is rapid. The condition often is more severe on first reaching depth, and may then be followed by a relatively stable level." The times I have experienced narcosis, the onset has been immediate upon reaching depth.

11. B. The onset of narcosis is rapid, but thankfully, recovery is equally rapid with ascension to a shallower depth. Just because narcosis tends to stabilize at depth does not mean a recreational diver should accept the condition. If you feel narked, you should ascend, even if you have dived to the same depth previously.

12. A, B, C, D. All of the items listed in the answers affect the severity of narcosis.

Carbon dioxide does not cause narcosis as some people believe, but high levels of carbon dioxide aggravate narcosis. The more excited you are, the more you will be affected. If you are tired and/or cold, you will be more affected by the malady. Any medication that makes your mouth dry, including decongestants and seasickness medicine, will increase the severity of narcosis. Alcohol and its aftereffects combined with depth is an especially poor combination.

13. C. 90 to 100 feet. Some novices may be affected at shallower depths, but nearly everyone is affected to some extent at depths greater than 90 feet. Some divers tend to think narcosis is not a significant factor until much greater depths are reached, but as soon as impairment begins, narcosis has a significant effect upon the safety of a buddy team.

14. A. True. Divers who truly need to accomplish something at depth are often able to get the job done, especially if the task has been practiced repeatedly. Experience at depth can enable a diver to increase his or her concentration, which is believed to be the basis for what is termed to be "adaptation" to narcosis. This helps explain why commercial divers, who have specific tasks to accomplish, are able to make deep dives using compressed air.

15. A. True. Motion sickness medication and deep diving are not compatible. Narcosis at depths as shallow as 60 feet has been documented. If the drug makes your mouth dry or your vision blurry, find another type of medication to prevent seasickness.

OVEREXPOSURE

Because divers are exposed to the elements—heat, cold, sun, wind, and water—they should know the effects of overexposure and how to deal with them. Do you know all you should about this important safety topic?

1. While standing in the sun in a full wet suit, your buddy perspires profusely, is weak, and has pale and clammy skin. Your buddy probably suffers from:
❏ A. Heat stroke
❏ B. Heat exhaustion
❏ C. Chilblains
❏ D. Sunburn

2. Which of the following statements concerning heat stroke is not true?
❏ A. The skin is hot.
❏ B. Heat stroke is an extremely serious condition.
❏ C. The pulse is rapid.
❏ D. Perspiration is profuse.

3. Which of the following overexposure conditions is a medical emergency?
❏ A. Heat stroke
❏ B. Heat exhaustion
❏ C. Heat cramps
❏ D. Heat rash

4. Which of the following statements concerning sunburn is true?
❏ A. Sunburn will not occur while you are in the water.
❏ B. There is little danger of sunburn on overcast days.
❏ C. Suntan oil prevents sunburns.
❏ D. All the statements are false.

5. Bright sunlight and glare may reduce:
❏ A. Peripheral vision
❏ B. Night vision
❏ C. Depth perception
❏ D. Visual acuity

6. Uncontrollable shivering is a danger sign in cold water exposure. The statement is:
❏ A. True, and you should exercise vigorously to generate body heat
❏ B. True, and you should terminate the dive immediately
❏ C. False. Shivering is merely an early warning sign
❏ D. False. Shivering generates body heat to prevent hypothermia

7. Which of the following contribute to body heat loss while diving:
❏ A. Drinking alcohol before a dive
❏ B. Smoking before a dive
❏ C. Exercising vigorously during a dive
❏ D. All the above cause body heat loss

8. Which of the following statements concerning frostbite is true?
❏ A. Firmly massage a body part that you think may be frostbitten.
❏ B. A frostbite victim usually is aware of the condition.
❏ C. Immerse a frostbitten area in warm water.
❏ D. Circulation restriction reduces the chance of frostbite.

9. A wind blowing 10 mph at 0 degrees F is equivalent to ___ degrees F on exposed flesh under calm conditions.
❏ A. -5 to -10
❏ B. -10 to -15
❏ C. -15 to -20
❏ D. -20 to -25

10. Prolonged exposure to saltwater can lead to inflammation, welts, peeling or splitting skin, rashes, or other skin disorders.
❏ A. True, and the affliction can be incapacitating.
❏ B. True, but the affliction is only discomforting.
❏ C. False because only minor irritation can result.
❏ D. False because skin disorders only occur in polluted water.

OVEREXPOSURE

Sunburn, hypothermia, heat exhaustion, dehydration, frostbite, dermatitis, and other maladies are possible while diving unless you exercise caution. The intent of this quiz is to educate and stimulate more than to test knowledge. Divers need to know the cause, effects, signs and symptoms, and first aid for overexposure. Minimize your risk by maximizing your knowledge.

1. B. Heat exhaustion. Harmful effects can occur when the body cannot eliminate excess heat. Reactions usually result when you lose large amounts of water, salt, or both through profuse perspiration.

2. D. Perspiration is profuse. Heat stroke actually blocks the body's sweating mechanism. The skin is hot, red, and dry during heat stroke. You must take immediate measures to cool a casualty's body temperature quickly.

3. A. Heat stroke. Damage to brain cells may result unless you provide prompt relief. You must lower a casualty's body temperature as rapidly as possible. Have the casualty see a doctor as soon as possible.

4. D. All the above statements are false. You can get sunburned in the water, on overcast days, and while wearing suntan oil. Brief sun exposures, use of sun screen lotion, and protective clothing all help prevent a painful experience. Beware of the sun in tropical climates because the rays are more intense than in temperate regions.

5. B. Reduce night vision. Your eyes have different parts (rods and cones) for day and night vision. Bright light and glare reduce the capability of the parts you use to see at low light levels. Protect your eyes from glare and you will be able to see better at night (and at low light levels underwater).

6. True, and you should terminate the dive immediately. Further heat loss may lead to reduced mental capacity, muscular weakness, and cramps. You can lose the ability to function safely. When you start to shiver uncontrollably, stop diving. Rewarm yourself until you perspire before you dive again.

7. D. All the above cause body heat loss. Alcohol dilates skin capillaries, smoking increase the heart rate 15 to 20 beats per minute, and vigorous exercise circulates blood to the extremities where you lose heat rapidly.

8. C. Immerse a frostbitten area in warm water. Get a person suffering frostbite indoors, provide a warm drink, and rewarm the frozen part in warm (100 to 105 degrees F) water. Encourage the casualty to see a doctor promptly.

9. D. -20 to -25 degrees F. According to the U.S. Army Wind Chill Index, a 10 mph wind at 0 degrees is equal to -22 degrees F under calm conditions. Beware of the danger of wind chill.

10. A. True, and the affliction can be incapacitating. Continuous exposure to saltwater, especially in tropical climates, can cause serious skin disorders (dermatitis). Freshwater showers, dry clothing, and antiseptic powder can help prevent skin problems that diving may cause.

SEASICKNESS

There are many jokes about motion sickness and many people find them humorous—until they become ill. Motion sickness is no laughing matter for divers and ruins wonderful dive opportunities. Since all divers eventually are exposed to situations that can cause motion sickness, knowledge about the illness and its prevention is valuable.

1. Seasickness is caused primarily by:
☐ A. Visual and olfactory (sense of smell) stimulation
☐ B. Vestibular (sense of balance) stimulation
☐ C. Visual and vestibular stimulation
☐ D. None of the above
☐ E. All the above

2. Select the least effective means to combat seasickness:
☐ A. Reading
☐ B. Sleeping
☐ C. Keeping busy
☐ D. Watching the horizon
☐ E. Eating lightly

3. Aboard a boat, the best location for seasickness prevention is:
☐ A. On the bow
☐ B. On the stern
☐ C. Amidships
☐ D. On the bridge
☐ E. Below decks

4. When you use medication to prevent seasickness, you should take the medicine:
☐ A. An hour before exposure to stimulation
☐ B. At the first symptoms of illness
☐ C. The day before exposure to stimulation
☐ D. In doses proportional to the planned depth

5. Which of the following effects caused by seasickness medication should cause diving postponement:
☐ A. Dry mouth and nasal passages
☐ B. Blurred vision
☐ C. Drowsiness
☐ D. All the above
☐ E. None of the above

6. Divers usually are more susceptible to seasickness:
☐ A. Aboard boats
☐ B. In the water
☐ C. Underwater
☐ D. Than the average person
☐ E. After diving

7. If nausea leads to vomiting while aboard a boat, an ill person should empty the stomach:
☐ A. Over the windward rail
☐ B. Over the leeside rail
☐ C. In the head (rest room)
☐ D. At any convenient location
☐ E. As completely as possible

8. Which of the following foods should you avoid to reduce the chances of seasickness:
☐ A. Fats
☐ B. Carbohydrates
☐ C. Proteins
☐ D. All the above
☐ E. None of the above

9. Select the true statement: Seasickness susceptibility:
☐ A. Decreases with age
☐ B. Is greater in women than in men
☐ C. Decreases with experience
☐ D. All the above
☐ E. None of the above

10. Select the false statement(s):
☐ A. Drugs you may use to prevent seasickness can aggravate narcosis.
☐ B. Seasickness reduces your ability to recognize and cope with problems underwater.
☐ C. If you must vomit underwater, it is best to throw up through your regulator.
☐ D. Seasickness is contagious in that one person's illness can cause others to develop the illness.
☐ E. About one third of the general population is highly susceptible to seasickness.

SEASICKNESS

It was not easy to deal with some of the unpleasant aspects of this topic, but I hope you learned a few tricks to make your boat dives more pleasant. Those who scored well are probably those most affected by seasickness. If you did well on this quiz, but are not generally a sufferer, please share your knowledge with novices who are trying to find their sea legs. Let's make diving as enjoyable as possible for everyone.

1. C. Visual and vestibular stimulation. Motion generates signals to the brain via several senses—sight, vestibular stimulation (utricles, saccules, and semi-circular canals in the ears), and propriocepter nerve endings that detect distortion in the skin and tendons. While the exact cause of seasickness is not known, physiologists believe that conflicting information to the brain from the various senses triggers the illness. The primary conflict stems from what you see compared to what you feel.

2. A. Reading. Based on the answer to question #1, it should be apparent that focusing visually on a nearby object while the rest of the world is in motion about you increases your motion sickness susceptibility. Closing your eyes helps, but sleeping is best because it takes you mind off thoughts of illness.

3. C. Amidships. The extremes on a boat are the areas of greatest movement. While fresh air on the bow may help in one respect, the amplified motion may lead to illness. The ideal location is at the center line of a boat at its mid point and as close to the water line as possible while still getting fresh air. Bracing your head against something while seated also seems to help.

4. A. An hour before exposure to stimulation. It is correct that you should try medication in advance to determine if the medicine causes bothersome side effects, but you should test the medicine well in advance of its anticipated need. Taking seasickness medication a day in advance to adjust to the drug may reduce the medicine's effectiveness.

5. D. All the above. Remember that the effects of drugs, especially drugs in combination and under pressure, are largely unknown and often aggravated. Consult a diving physician for advice if you require any medication for diving.

6. A. Aboard boats. Many divers are encouraged to get into the water if not feeling well owing to mal de mer. While it is true that some people obtain relief under water, you must use discretion when you make the decision to dive while feeling seasick. Vomiting underwater can be dangerous. Rushing to get underwater when you are ill may be unwise.

7. B. Over the leeside rail. All boat divers should be familiar with nautical terms. Use of any rail is acceptable, but the lee rail is preferred because it is down wind. The sheltered location makes a person's plight less messy and less offensive to others on board. Throwing up in the head is a fine way to anger the crew, worsen your condition, and cause others to become ill.

8. A. Fats. There are many theories about diets and seasickness. One theory suggests a full stomach, while another recommends eating lightly. Crackers, hard candy and other specific foods are suggested frequently. The best diet is the one you find to work. Avoid fatty and acidic foods, however. Light meals of proteins and carbohydrates usually work best to minimize motion sickness.

9. All the above. Seasickness susceptibility decreases with age with one exception—babies do not have problems at sea. It is comforting to know that we can adapt to motion and become more tolerant with increased experience on the water. Unfortunately, it does seem that women are more susceptible than men, but this is probably owing to less experience with the conditions that cause the illness. Women's susceptibility should decline as more females gain boat diving experience.

10. C. If vomiting occurs underwater, it is best to throw up through your regulator. No so. Don't stay underwater if you are ill and vomiting is likely to occur. If struck with sudden and acute nausea, avoid throwing up through your regulator because you might clog it. Removing the mouthpiece can lead to difficulties from involuntary gasping after throwing up. Do remove the regulator, but place it at the corner of your mouth and keep the purge button depressed to create a free flow. You can vomit and still get air. Thanks to Harry Larigione, who shared the idea with me years ago.

SINUS PROBLEMS

The sinuses are a source of concern and possible discomfort for many divers. An understanding of sinus anatomy and physiology and how pressure affects your sinuses can increase your diving comfort. Test your knowledge.

1. Sinuses are best described as:
❏ A. Flexible air spaces in the head
❏ B. Rigid air spaces in the head
❏ C. Enlarged areas in certain arteries
❏ D. Mucus producing organs in the head

2. How many pairs of sinuses does a person have?
❏ A. Two
❏ B. Four
❏ C. Six
❏ D. Eight

3. You normally achieve sinus pressure equalization:
❏ A. By blowing against closed mouth and nose
❏ B. By swallowing, yawning, or wiggling your jaw
❏ C. By transfer of blood in capillaries
❏ D. Automatically through normal breathing

4. A sinus squeeze during descent can cause hemorrhaging due to:
❏ A. The sinus being compressed by increased external pressure
❏ B. Capillary rupturing from insufficient internal sinus pressure
❏ C. A diver failing to use proper clearing techniques
❏ D. None of the above

5. Diving with a cold is:
❏ A. Acceptable
❏ B. Acceptable with proper medication
❏ C. Permissible to 30 feet or less
❏ D. Unacceptable

6. Medication taken to relieve sinus congestion:
❏ A. Can open sinus passages to allow diving activities
❏ B. Can cause increased congestion when the effects wear off
❏ C. Helps divers who have colds or sinus problems
❏ D. A and B, but not C, are correct

7. A symptom of a sinus squeeze is:
❏ A. A general ache in the head
❏ B. An intense pain in one area
❏ C. A stuffy feeling during descent
❏ D. A pulling sensation on the eyes

8. Your sinuses normally drain by:
❏ A. Gravity, which affects all sinuses
❏ B. Gravity, which affects all sinuses except one pair
❏ C. Wave-like action of hair-like projections in all sinuses
❏ D. Wave-like action of hair-like projections in all sinuses except one pair

9. Bleeding from the nose following a dive usually indicates:
❏ A. A person should not be a diver
❏ B. A diver has been assaulted
❏ C. Sinus injury has occurred
❏ D. Professional medical treatment is mandatory

10. Sinus problems during ascent are:
❏ A. Common and easily relieved
❏ B. Uncommon, but easily relieved
❏ C. Common and difficult to relieve
❏ D. Uncommon and difficult to relieve

SINUS PROBLEMS

Many divers use medication to clear the sinuses for diving. Get approval from a diving physician before you use any medication prior to diving. Diving without drugs should be possible for normal, healthy divers. May the water and your sinuses be clear for all your dives!

1. B. Rigid air spaces in the head. The exact purposes of the sinuses is not understood, but they may be to reduce the weight of the head, to warm and humidify inspired air, and to help trap foreign particles. The sinuses are membrane-lined cavities within the skull. They connect to the nasal passages by small airways.

2. B. Four. The parasinuses consist of the frontal sinuses (above the eyes), the smaller sphenoid and ethmoid sinuses (behind the eyes), and the maxillary sinuses (inside the cheek bones).

3. D. Automatically through normal breathing. The sinuses airways connect to the nasal passages. Normal, healthy sinuses do not require equalization techniques. Head-first descents can increase sinus clearing difficulty because increased blood pressure in the head enlarges passageway lining capillaries and reduces airway diameter.

4. B. Capillary rupturing from insufficient internal sinus pressure. Increasing external pressure on a sinus without increasing internal pressure creates a pressure imbalance. The inequality causes sinus membrane capillaries to bulge into the cavity. If you cannot equalize the sinus, the capillaries will eventually rupture and fill the cavity with blood.

5. D. Unacceptable. Sinus mucous membranes swell and discharge during a cold. Airway swelling and congestion make equalization difficult or impossible. Other effects of a cold also make diving inadvisable.

6. D. A and B, but not C, are correct. The "rebound" effect when medication wears off under pressure can trap air in sinuses. Increased oxygen partial pressures at depth affect any medicines that divers may use.

7. B. An intense pain in one area. Divers who have experienced sinus squeezes often describe the pain "like an ice pick stuck into my head." The most frequent complaints are about the frontal sinuses above the eyes.

8. B. Gravity, which affects all sinuses except one pair. The maxillary sinuses inside the cheek bones do not drain by gravity unless inverted. Divers who get water up their noses may fill the maxillaries with water. Lowering the head allows the water to run out of the nose. Divers sometimes experience the strange sensation when they bend over after a dive.

9. C. Sinus injury has occurred. A small amount of blood from the nose is not uncommon with new divers and is not serious. For severe, prolonged, or repeated bleeding following dives, consult a diving physician to determine the cause of the problem.

10. D. Uncommon and difficult to relieve. Usually sinus problems occur during descent and the pain causes the diver to abort the dive. If air can get into the sinus to equalize the space, the air probably can escape during ascent. If you experience sinus pain while ascending, slow or stop your ascent and allow the air in the sinus to slowly work its way out.

SQUEEZES AND BLOCKS

Q:

All certified divers are aware of the hazards of barotrauma—tissue damage caused by pressure differences. Have you experienced equalization problems? Do you know as much as you should about equalization techniques and difficulties? Do you know how to prevent equalization injuries? Since barotrauma is a serious matter, it is a good idea to make sure you are up-to-date concerning the subject.

1. A physiological condition called a squeeze occurs when:
- ❐ A. The pressure on the inside of an air space is greater than the external pressure
- ❐ B. The pressure on the outside of an air space is greater than the internal pressure
- ❐ C. The pressure on the inside of an air space is increasing to equalize with the external pressure
- ❐ D. None of the above

2. A physiological condition called a reverse block occurs when:
- ❐ A. The pressure on the inside of an air space is greater than the external pressure
- ❐ B. The pressure on the outside of an air space is greater than the internal pressure
- ❐ C. The pressure on the inside of an air space is decreasing to equalize with the external pressure
- ❐ D. None of the above

3. The recommended method to avoid sinus squeezes and blocks is to:
- ❐ A. Only use decongestants that do not produce side effects
- ❐ B. Dive only when your sinuses are healthy and clear
- ❐ C. Forcibly equalize the pressure in your sinuses every few feet
- ❐ D. Ascend and descend slowly to allow gradual equalization

4. The sinuses most often involved in sinus barotrauma are the:
- ❐ A. Frontal sinuses
- ❐ B. Maxillary sinuses
- ❐ C. Ethmoidal sinuses
- ❐ D. Sphenoidal sinuses

5. Select all correct statements concerning sinus squeezes and blocks.
- ❐ A. Sinus barotrauma is twice as common during descent as on ascent.
- ❐ B. Nosebleed occurs in about 60 percent of the cases of sinus barotrauma.
- ❐ C. On ascent, 25 percent of divers with sinus barotrauma may have nosebleed without pain.
- ❐ D. Decongestant use may cause "rebound" congestion in the sinuses.

6. Match the following techniques for equalizing pressure in the middle ears:
- A. Valsalva maneuver
- B. Toynbee maneuver
- C. The Edmonds technique
- D. Frenzel maneuver

- 1. Closing the mouth and nose, then contracting the muscles of the floor of the mouth
- 2. Attempting to exhale against a closed mouth and nose
- 3. Jutting the lower jaw forward while perfomring the Frenzel or Valsalva maneuver
- 4. Swallowing with the mouth and nose closed

7. Which of the following techniques is the least desirable method of equalizing pressure in the middle ears?
- ❐ A. Valsalva maneuver
- ❐ B. Toynbee maneuver
- ❐ C. Frenzel maneuver
- ❐ D. The Edmonds technique

8. The "trapdoor" effect refers to inability to equalize pressure in the _____ during _____.
- ❐ A. middle ears, descent
- ❐ B. middle ears, ascent
- ❐ C. sinuses, descent
- ❐ D. sinuses, ascent

9. Permanent hearing loss and ringing in the ear are most likely to result from a ruptured:
- A. Ear drum
- B. Oval window
- C. Round window
- D. Semicircular canal

10. A rupture in the inner ear is most likely to occur from:
- ❐ A. Failure to equalize pressure during descent
- ❐ B. Forceful attempts to equalize pressure during descent
- ❐ C. Failure to equalize pressure during ascent
- ❐ D. A rapid decrease in pressure during ascent

11. If you have a blocked eustachian tube during ascent, you are likely to experience:
- ❐ A. Vertigo due to increased middle ear pressure
- ❐ B. Ringing in your ear
- ❐ C. Pain due to a bulging ear drum
- ❐ D. All the above

12. The most effective technique for equalizing pressure in a blocked ear during ascent is:
- ❐ A. The Valsalva maneuver
- ❐ B. The Toynbee maneuver
- ❐ C. The Frenzel maneuver
- ❐ D. Any of the above

13. Dental barotrauma is likely to result from:
- ❐ A. Fillings that have undergone secondary erosion
- ❐ B. A tooth cavity with a thin filling
- ❐ C. Seepage of gas into tissues after oral surgery
- ❐ D. Any of the above

14. If you fail to equalize pressure inside your mask during descent, you are likely to suffer:
- ❐ A. Conjunctival hemorrhages
- ❐ B. Swollen eyelids
- ❐ C. Facial hemorrhage
- ❐ D. All the above

15. A lung squeeze is most likely to occur to a:
- ❐ A. Skin diver
- ❐ B. Scuba diver
- ❐ C. Commercial diver
- ❐ D. Any of the above equally

SQUEEZES AND BLOCKS

Do you have a greater appreciation for the seriousness of squeezes and blocks? Are you going to descend and ascend slowly, try different equalization techniques, and refrain from forceful equalization? The purpose of this quiz is to educate you and get you to answer "yes" to the foregoing questions. If you answered all the questions correctly, you have instructor-level knowledge of this month's subject. If you answered less than eleven questions correctly, you should increase your knowledge so you can avoid barotrauma.

1. B. The pressure on the outside of an air space is greater than the internal pressure. A squeeze is not the difference in pressures but the injury that results from the difference. When the pressure outside a body air space is greater than the internal pressure, the result is swelling and hemorrhaging of tissue. The longer the exposure to unequalized pressure, the greater the damage.

2. A. The pressure on the inside of an air space is greater than the external pressure. Reverse blocks are painful, but are rarely as serious as squeezes. A blocked eustachian tube restricts the expansion of air in the middle ear during ascent. Pain, vertigo, and tinnitus (ringing in the ear) may result.

3. B. Dive only when your sinuses are healthy and clear. Your sinuses equalize automatically when your health is good. All you have to do to avoid sinus squeezes is refrain from diving if you have an upper respiratory tract or sinus infection. If you are a smoker and have problems equalizing your sinuses, giving up the smokes will reduce your sinus problems (as well as many others).

4. A. Frontal sinuses. The frontal sinuses have the longest ducts and, according to an article by Fagan entitled "Sinus Barotrauma in Divers," are most often involved in barotrauma. You experience a frontal sinus squeeze when you feel pain above your eyes during descent. You can have squeezes and blocks in all sinuses, however.

5. All of the statements are correct. The answers are direct quotes from Dr. Chris Dueker's fine book, "Scuba Diving in Safety and Health." I included the statements to emphasize the seriousness of sinus barotrauma. Do not dive unless your sinuses are clear.

6. A. Valsalva maneuver: 2. Attempting to exhale against a closed mouth and nose
  B. Toynbee maneuver: 4. Swallowing with the mouth and nose closed
  C. The Edmonds technique: 3. Jutting the lower jaw forward while performing the Frenzel or Valsalva maneuver

D. Frenzel maneuver: 1. Closing the mouth and nose, then contracting the muscles of the floor of the mouth

7. A. Valsalva maneuver. Most divers use the Valsalva maneuver, but it is most likely to cause lasting damage to the ears due to excessive internal pressure. The Frenzel maneuver during a slow descent is best for your ears. If the Frenzel technique does not work, try the Toynbee or Edmonds maneuvers. Only use the Valsalva maneuver as a last resort, and when you use it, avoid forceful equalization.

8. A. middle ears, descent. The throat ends of the eustachian tubes normally are closed. Failure to equalize middle ear pressure during descent allows increasing pressure to add to the effort needed to open your eustachian tubes. When you cannot overcome the pressure holding the tubes shut, you experience the trapdoor effect. You must ascend until you reduce the pressure on the tube ends sufficiently to permit you to open them and equalize your ears.

9. C. Round window. When you experience an ear squeeze, pressure pushes your ear drum inward. Bones between the ear drum and the inner ear transfer the pressure to the oval window in the inner ear. The oval window bulges inward in the inner ear and forces the round window to bulge outward. A rupture of the round window is a serious injury that is likely to cause a permanent high frequency hearing loss and tinnitus.

10. B. Forceful attempts to equalize pressure during descent. If you attempt a forceful Valsalva maneuver while experiencing a trapdoor effect during descent, the force of equalization will be transmitted through your body to your inner ear and add to the pressure causing the round window to bulge. The added pressure of equalization may cause a rupture of the round window. Avoid forceful equalization attempts!

11. D. All of the above. Air in the middle ear obeys Boyle's Law during ascent. If your eustachian tube restricts the expansion of air, the expansion of gas within

the middle ear may cause vertigo due to increased middle ear pressure, i.e., alternobaric vertigo; pain in the affected ear; and tinnitus.

12. B. The Toynbee maneuver. To cope with a block, descend until you no longer feel pressure, then re-ascend slowly, swallowing with your nose and mouth closed. The procedure is the Toynbee maneuver, which some divers also use for equalization during descent.

13. D. Any of the above. If you experience pain in your teeth during and after diving, see your dentist. Diving medical experts also recommend biannual dental examinations and refraining from diving after dental extractions and surgery.

14. D. All the above. To prevent a mask squeeze, simply exhale into your mask during descent. If you fail to equalize your mask, pressure forces your eye and facial tissues into the space. The partial pressure inside the mask hemorrhages the tissues, giving you a red, puffy face and eyelids and red eyes.

15. C. Commercial diver. I do not believe a classic lung squeeze is a matter of concern for recreational divers. The condition occurs rarely to surface-supplied commercial divers. Loss of surface pressure with failure or absence of a non-return valve or failure of the gas supply to compensate for a rapid descent can cause a lung squeeze, but recreational divers do not encounter these circumstances. Pulmonary barotrauma of descent is extremely rare and poorly documented, even for commercial diving injuries.

THERMAL PROBLEMS

Divers are often subject to situations that stress the limits of the body's ability to regulate temperature. We may become overheated before a dive, then become severely chilled during a dive. It is important to understand how your body maintains thermal balance and the factors that affect temperature regulation.

1. The safe range of tolerance for deep core body temperature is plus or minus ____ degree(s) Centigrade.
❏ A. Five
❏ B. Two
❏ C. One
❏ D. 0.25

2. List five methods the human body employs to maintain thermal balance:
A. _____
B. _____
C. _____
D. _____
E. _____

3. Thermal balance in the body is equal to metabolic heat production:
❏ A. Minus respiratory heat loss
❏ B. Minus skin heat loss
❏ C. Plus skin heat production
❏ D. Minus respiratory and skin heat loss

4. Temperature regulation of the human body is controlled by:
❏ A. The carotid sinuses
❏ B. The sympathetic nervous system
❏ C. Thermal proprioceptors
❏ D. None of the above

5. Shivering increases body heat production ____ times the resting rate and is ____ for rewarming a submerged diver.
❏ A. Three, effective
❏ B. Three, ineffective
❏ C. Five, effective
❏ D. Five, ineffective

6. Physical exertion can increase body heat production up to ____ times the resting rate and is ____ for rewarming a submerged diver.
❏ A. Ten, effective
❏ B. Ten, ineffective
❏ C. Twenty, effective
❏ D. Twenty, ineffective

7. Protection against heat loss is <u>essential</u> when the water temperature is less than ____ degrees Fahrenheit.
❏ A. 80
❏ B. 75
❏ C. 70
❏ D. 65

8. Tension, fear, and apprehension affect heat loss from the body.
❏ A. True
❏ B. False

9. When the hands reach a certain temperature, no further heat loss can occur from them because the body conserves heat by shunting circulation from the extremities.
❏ A. True
❏ B. False

10. The temperature regulating capabilities of women usually are ____ than those of men.
❏ A. Greater
❏ B. Less
❏ C. The same as

11. The heat-producing ability of an individual is primarily determined by the person's:
❏ A. Muscle mass
❏ B. Body fat
❏ C. Metabolism
❏ D. All of the above equally

12. Select the most serious situation.
❏ A. A flushed, sweaty diver before a dive.
❏ B. A diver beginning to shiver during a dive.
❏ C. A diver beginning to shiver after a dive.
❏ D. All are equally serious.

13. Body overheating progresses at ____ rate than/as chilling.
❏ A. The same
❏ B. A faster
❏ C. A slower

14. The thermal tolerance of the body in humid climates is ____ as/than the tolerance for drier climates.
❏ A. Less
❏ B. Greater
❏ C. The same as
❏ D. Greater at lower temperatures and less at higher temperatures

15. Divers can acclimate to lowered body temperature.
❏ A. True
❏ B. False

THERMAL PROBLEMS

To be a good cold water diver, you need to keep yourself in good physical condition, be healthy, insulate yourself appropriately, dive frequently, and avoid situations that require exertion or produce anxiety. Thermal imbalance is a serious matter. Avoid both hyperthermia (excessive body core temperature) and hypothermia (lowered core temperature) during your diving activities.

1. B. Two. The body generates heat. If you lose too much heat or cannot dissipate enough heat, the temperature deep inside the body changes from normal and severely impairs the body functions. An increase of only three degrees C in the core temperature of the body will cause delirium. A decrease of three degrees C will cause a coma.

2. Methods used by the human body to maintain thermal balance are metabolism (chemical process within cells to create energy), circulatory control via vasoconstriction and vasodilation, the shunting of blood from body extremities, respiratory control, shivering, and perspiration.

3. D. Minus respiratory and skin heat loss. Depending upon the circumstances, you can lose as much as 25 percent of your body heat through respiration. Breathing air is heated for commercial divers. The primary heat loss problem for recreational divers is heat lost from the surface of the skin. Heat loss via conduction from the body surface is why insulation is so important.

4. B. The sympathetic nervous system. The hypothalmus, a part of the brain that contains vital autonomic (automatic responses) nervous centers, controls thermal balance in the body. The hypothalmus senses blood temperature directly from the blood passing through it and also receives input from skin sensors. The combined input is used to control the body's resources to maintain thermal balance.

5. D. Five, ineffective. Shivering can produce about five times as much heat as you generate at rest. While shivering is an efficient means of generating heat in air, it is inefficient in water. Conduction saps the heat you generate by a shivering while immersed. Shivering in water is a complex and compound problem. When prolonged shivering begins, terminate diving until you begin to perspire, which indicates your body has rewarmed to the point where it has excess heat.

6. D. Twenty, ineffective. Physical exertion produces heat. The harder you work, the warmer you become. If you are not cold in water, moderate activity can help you avoid chilling for a short period of time. If you become chilled, however, exertion is an ineffective means of rewarming while in or under the water owing to conductive heat loss. The only effective way to rewarm is to get out of the water.

7. C. 70 degrees Fahrenheit. Diving in only a bathing suit in water that is 80 degrees F is equivalent to being unclothed in air that is 42 degrees F. While your body will make some adjustments so you do not feel uncomfortable initially, the amount of heat lost to water that feels relatively warm is great owing to the heat capacity and conductive ability of water. Some people have more "natural insulation" than others, but the typical person should wear insulation for nearly all diving activities.

8. A. True. Nearly anything that affects your physiology can increase heat loss. If you become excited or afraid, your respiration and circulation, and therefore, your heat loss increase. Seasickness and other forms of illness also increase heat loss. The problem just described is one good reason for the recommendation to be in good health when you dive.

9. B. False. Blood is shunted from the hands, and they do stop losing heat at least to a point. When the temperature of the hands reaches fifty degrees F, circulation is restored to them for partial rewarming. Since the hands have a large surface area to mass ratio, the warmth supplied to them is lost rapidly. The overall effect is a loss of core temperature through the hands. Even though the hands become numb, they should still be insulated to conserve body heat.

10. B. Less. Women are equal to or superior to men in many ways in diving, but they are at a physiological disadvantage when it comes to maintaining thermal balance. Females usually have a smaller muscle mass and generate less heat. All thermal control recommendations made for divers are doubly important for small people—male or female.

11. A. Muscle mass. Muscle is the source of heat generation. The more muscle you have, the more heat you can produce. Muscle activity explains why physical activity increases body temperature. Fat reduces the loss of heat generated by muscle. A lean, muscular person can generate a large amount of heat, but the heat will be lost quickly in water unless the diver is well insulated.

12. A. A flushed, sweaty diver before a dive. A heavily perspiring diver exerting in an exposure suit prior to a dive can rapidly become a victim of heat exhaustion. Cooling the diver is important to prevent overheating.

13. B. A faster. Body overheating progresses at a more rapid rate than cooling. The more rapid rate is why an overheated diver is a more serious situation than a diver beginning to shiver during or after a dive. Do not tolerate a situation where you feel like you are "cooking" inside an exposure suit. Take action to cool yourself.

14. A. Less. The higher the humidity, the less your ability to rid yourself of excess heat via perspiration and respiration. Keep that fact in mind when diving in tropical areas. Breathing cold, humid air increases heat loss when it is cold. The point of this answer is that climate is a factor that affects your ability to maintain thermal balance.

15. A. True. With frequent exposure to cold water, you can become less sensitive to cold and actually reduce heat loss. Decreased shivering response has been documented as a result of cold water conditioning. Both physiological and psychological adaptation can be achieved. If you do not believe you are as susceptible to cold, you actually lose less heat.

DISORIENTATION AND VERTIGO

Q:

The underwater world is a beautiful place, unless you have an alarming sensation that you do not know where your are. There are many causes of vertigo and disorientation. It is important to know the causes, their effects, and how to deal with them. See if you can orient yourself to the correct answers to the following questions.

1. Diving disorientation is best described as:
❏ A. Loss of one's bearings or perception of relative position
❏ B. Movement hallucination
❏ C. Dizziness and light-headedness
❏ D. Being lost

2. The primary means by which a diver usually orients underwater is by:
❏ A. Proprioceptors
❏ B. Vestibular sense
❏ C. Visual clues
❏ D. Instruments

3. The most dramatic cause of disorientation underwater is:
❏ A. Vertigo
❏ B. Turbid water
❏ C. Darkness
❏ D. Weightlessness

4. List three means available to every diver to determine orientation in dark or turbid water:
A. _____
B. _____
C. _____

5. If you become disoriented between the surface and the bottom in turbid water, the action you should take after regaining orientation is to:
❏ A. Surface and abort the dive
❏ B. Swim quickly to the bottom
❏ C. Surface, obtain a descent line, and continue the dive
❏ D. Surface, abort the dive, and seek medical assistance

6. Vertigo is best described as:
❏ A. A sensation that the world is revolving around you
❏ B. Dizziness
❏ C. A disturbed sense of relationship to space
❏ D. Any of the above

7. A diver can experience vertigo underwater while:
❏ A. Descending
❏ B. On the bottom
❏ C. Ascending
❏ D. Any of the above

8. Vertigo following ear drum rupture is most likely as a result of:
❏ A. Air escaping the middle ear
❏ B. The sudden pressure increase in the middle ear
❏ C. The sudden temperature change in the middle ear
❏ D. None of the above

9. The most likely cause of ascent vertigo is:
❏ A. Decompression sickness
❏ B. A reverse ear block that clears suddenly
❏ C. Carbon dioxide partial pressure reduction
❏ D. A eustachian tube "trapdoor" effect

10. Select the position most likely to cause vertigo during descent:
❏ A. Diver vertical with the head up
❏ B. Diver vertical with the head down
❏ C. Diver at 30 degree angle with the head down
❏ D. Diver position makes no difference

11. The most appropriate action to take if vertigo occurs while diving is to:
❏ A. Swim to the surface and rest
❏ B. Assume a head-down position
❏ C. Grasp a stationary object until vertigo subsides
❏ D. Ascend a few feet and equalize ear pressure

12. During a dive to 100 feet in cold, dirty water, divers could be affected by vertigo owing to:
❏ A. Sensory deprivation
❏ B. Nitrogen narcosis
❏ C. Caloric stimulation
❏ D. All the above

13. In addition to temperature and pressure-induced vertigo, which of the following could also cause the ailment?
❏ A. Motion sickness
❏ B. Contaminated air
❏ C. Excess ear wax
❏ D. All the above

14. The most frequent cause of diving vertigo is:
❏ A. A ruptured ear drum
❏ B. Unequal auto-inflation
❏ C. Unequal ear pressures during ascent
❏ D. Unequal ear temperatures

15. The correct action to take for vertigo that occurs frequently or is prolonged while diving is to:
❏ A. Discontinue diving
❏ B. See an ear specialist
❏ C. Only dive with people who are aware of your problem
❏ D. Use vertigo-suppressing medication

DISORIENTATION AND VERTIGO

A:

Don't be frightened by the information about disorientation and vertigo. As with all diving problems, understanding them and knowing how to deal with them can prevent difficulty. By learning more about vertigo you should be better prepared to keep your underwater world from becoming topsy-turvy. Perhaps you will be a little less dizzy as a result of the information presented!

1. C. Loss of one's bearings or perception of relative position. Disorientation is more serious than just being lost. Disorientation means you do not know where you are in relation to the surface, the bottom, or anything. You literally cannot distinguish up from down. Disorientation is not dizziness; it is a frightening feeling that you must avoid or overcome quickly.

2. B. Vestibular sense. When you can see well and there are visual references, sight can prevent disorientation. Low light levels, limited visibility, and lack of references make you dependent upon your sense of balance for orientation. Proprioceptors (sensory tissue nerves) are largely ineffective in the weightless state of diving.

3. A. Vertigo. Because your primary orientation means underwater is vestibular and equilibrium disturbance causes vertigo, you can instantly become disoriented when the world around appears to spin. You must prevent vertigo to avoid disorientation.

4. Means to determine orientation include the direction of gravitational pull on weights, the angle of water inside a mask, exhaust bubble direction, air shift inside a buoyancy compensator or dry suit, and direction of movement when you increase buoyancy.

5. C is correct, but A is an acceptable response. If you need or want to dive in poor conditions and you have sufficient training and experience do so, you may resume the dive if you use a descent line for reference. Seek medical attention if disorientation is a prolonged or frequent occurrence.

6. D. Any of the above. Vertigo is an illusion of movement. You may feel as though you are revolving in space. Vertigo results from vestibular disturbances and from inner ear diseases. You may be disoriented without being dizzy, but you will always be disoriented when you experience vertigo.

7. D. Any of the above. Causes of vertigo include pressure or temperature differences in one ear compared to the other, decompression sickness (rare), sensory deprivation, carbon monoxide toxicity, nitrogen narcosis, and body positioning. One or more of the causes can trigger vertigo at any point of a dive.

8. C. The sudden temperature change in the middle ear. The organs of balance in the ears must be in equilibrium with respect to temperature and pressure or vertigo occurs. Cold water entering an ear through a ruptured ear drum upsets the balance and causes vertigo. Dizziness will pass when the water warms and ear equilibrium returns to normal.

9. B. A reverse block that clears suddenly. Sudden pressure changes in one ear can produce vertigo. The changes can occur from equalization difficulty during descent (uncommon) or from the sudden release of pressure in one ear during ascent. Be sensitive to pressure changes in your ears. Ascend and descend slowly and keep your ears clear and balanced.

10. C. Diver at 30 degree angle with the head down. The three semi-circular canals in the ear provide reference information to the brain. In a 30-degree head-down position, the canal that provides the horizontal reference information is vertical and the lack of input to the brain can lead to vertigo, especially when you deprive other senses of references. Feet-first descents are most desirable.

11. C. Grasp a stationary object until vertigo subsides. Stay put. Divers have swum down or sideways thinking they were going to the surface. Most cases of vertigo are temporary. Hold a solid object for reference until you regain control. In mid-water, hug yourself for some relief until dizziness passes.

12. D. All the above. Without visual reference or weight sensory input, vertigo can occur without ear problems. Use a descent line for reference in turbid water. Use shallower depths to avoid or correct narcosis-induced vertigo. Water entering your ear canals needs to do so simultaneously. Take care with hoods and avoid ear wax buildup.

13. D. All the above. Dizziness is a symptom of many ailments, seasickness among them. Carbon monoxide toxicity is another cause of vertigo. Avoid seasickness. Use a reputable air source. If bothered by excess ear wax that clogs your ear canals, ask your druggist for a non-prescription solution that reduces wax accumulation.

14. C. Unequal pressures during ascent. According to a 1965 study by Lundgren, most divers complain of ascent vertigo. Further investigation revealed than nearly all the difficulty resulted from alternobaric (changing pressure) vertigo. It is wise to ascend slowly using a reference line whenever possible.

15. B. See an ear specialist. Explain that you are a diver and make sure the physician understands pressure effects. Ideally, the physician should be a diver. Medical attention may correct your problem. Avoid diving until you can prevent vertigo. Disorientation resulting from vertigo can be hazardous.

SECTION SIX

□ □ □ □ □ □

Diving Activities

Diving Activities

Scuba diving is a means to an end. Scuba allows you to remain underwater so you can do something. There are many underwater activities and pastimes. No matter what your end goal in diving, it helps to learn how to do what you want to do. Continuing education specialty diving courses help you quickly and efficiently acquire the knowledge and skills you need to enjoy various activities while minimizing your injury risk.

An entry-level diving certification is a license to learn to dive. Experience is a good teacher, but often gives you a harsh test before providing a lesson. It is much better to complete a diving specialty course before participating in a specialized activity than it is to graduate from the "school of hard knocks."

Here is a partial list of specialized diving activities. Experts recommend training for all the listed specialties:

Advanced buoyancy control
Altitude diving
Cave diving
Cavern diving
Deep diving
Drift diving
Dry suit diving
Enriched-air (Nitrox) diving
Ice diving
Limited visibility diving
Night diving
Rescue techniques
River diving
Search and recovery
Underwater collecting
Underwater environment
Underwater hunting
Underwater navigation
Underwater photography
Underwater videography
Wreck diving

Are you interested in diving at altitude, in a cave or cavern, in wrecks, at greater depths, under ice, in a dry suit, in limited visibility, or at night? Do you want to hunt game, salvage items, use nitrox, or fly after diving? If you answered yes to any of the questions, you will benefit from studying Section Six.

ALTITUDE DIVING

Q:

Divers venture beneath the surface of mountain lakes frequently. There are many differences between diving in the ocean and diving in freshwater at altitude. See if you are aware of the differences and how to handle them.

1. Altitude diving procedures apply to any elevation above:
- ❒ A. 500 feet
- ❒ B. 1,000 feet
- ❒ C. 1,150 feet
- ❒ D. 2,000 feet

2. At an elevation of 8,000 feet, where the atmospheric pressure is 10.92 psia, the depth in freshwater at which the pressure on a diver doubles is:
- ❒ A. 34.0 feet
- ❒ B. 33.0 feet
- ❒ C. 25.3 feet
- ❒ D. 24.5 feet

3. The amount of weight a diver wearing a wet suit needs for neutral buoyancy in a lake at high altitude is:
- ❒ A. Less than the amount needed for ocean diving
- ❒ B. More than the amount needed for freshwater diving at sea level
- ❒ C. The same amount needed for freshwater diving at sea level
- ❒ D. Both A and B are correct, but C is incorrect

4. The least desirable type of depth gauge for diving at altitude is:
- ❒ A. Bourdon tube
- ❒ B. Dive computer
- ❒ C. Capillary
- ❒ D. Diaphragm

5. Select the incorrect statement about depth gauges used at altitude.
- ❒ A. Capillary gauges provide conservative depth readings because they are calibrated for saltwater.
- ❒ B. Capillary gauges provide unconservative information because cold water at depth contracts the air column.
- ❒ C. Some dive computers adjust to reduced atmospheric pressure at altitude automatically.
- ❒ D. Mechanical depth gauges cannot be reset to compensate for reduced atmospheric pressure at altitude.

6. The depth at which a Bourdon tube depth gauge would read zero at an altitude of 10,000 feet (where the atmospheric pressure is 10.11 psia) is:
- ❒ A. 8.77 feet
- ❒ B. 8.5 feet
- ❒ C. 10.6 feet
- ❒ D. 10.9 feet

7. The rate of ascent for diving at altitude is:
- ❒ A. The same as the rate of ascent for diving at sea level
- ❒ B. 3% slower for each 1,000 feet of altitude
- ❒ C. Two feet per second slower for each 1,000 feet of altitude
- ❒ D. Five feet per second less for each 1,000 feet of altitude

8. Upon arrival at altitude, the first dive planning consideration for a diver is:
- ❒ A. Residual nitrogen from sea level saturation
- ❒ B. The equivalent depth conversions for the altitude
- ❒ C. The equivalent decompression stop depths for the altitude
- ❒ D. The equivalent rate of ascent for the altitude

9. When a Bourdon tube depth gauge indicates 70 feet at an altitude of 6,000 feet, the approximate equivalent ocean depth is:
- ❒ A. 72 feet
- ❒ B. 78 feet
- ❒ C. 89 feet
- ❒ D. None of the above

10. When a capillary depth gauge indicates a depth of 33 feet at an altitude of 6,000 feet, the actual depth is about:
- ❒ A. 33 feet
- ❒ B. 27 feet
- ❒ C. 39 feet
- ❒ D. None of the above

11. Dive table calculations for cold water dives at altitude require you to use:
- ❒ A. The time of your dive and the depth indicated by your gauge
- ❒ B. The next greater time and the next greater depth than that indicated by your depth gauge
- ❒ C. The next greater time and the next greater depth than the equivalent ocean depth of the deepest depth of your dive
- ❒ D. The next greater time and the equivalent ocean depth of the deepest depth of your dive

12. Loss of consciousness by divers at altitude is most likely to occur:
- ❒ A. While preparing to dive
- ❒ B. During surface swims
- ❒ C. Underwater
- ❒ D. Upon surfacing

13. The equivalent depth for a 15 foot decompression stop at an altitude of 6,000 feet is:
- ❒ A. 10 feet
- ❒ B. 12 feet
- ❒ C. 15 feet
- ❒ D. 18 feet

14. Assuming a similar activity level, your air consumption rate when diving at altitude is:
- ❒ A. The same as your air consumption rate for the equivalent depth at sea level
- ❒ B. The same as your sea level air consumption rate for the actual depth of the dive
- ❒ C. Less than your sea level air consumption rate for the equivalent depth at sea level
- ❒ D. Less than your sea level air consumption rate for the actual depth of the dive

15. The recommended way to minimize the hazards of diving at altitude is to:
- ❒ A. Dive with experienced altitude divers
- ❒ B. Complete an advanced scuba diver course
- ❒ C. Complete an altitude diving specialty course
- ❒ D. Refrain from diving at elevations above 3,000 feet

ALTITUDE DIVING

Altitude diving is hazardous and technical. You can minimize the risks if you know what to do and do what you know. Training is essential. NAUI publishes an excellent book on the topic. NAUI also offers a handy altitude conversion calculator. If you have not taken an altitude diving course and you did not do well on the quiz, don't feel bad. You should be impressed, however, with the complexity of altitude diving and realize the need for training. If you dive at altitude and did not score well, that's a different story. Increase your knowledge before you injure yourself. You can get high on diving without risking serious injury. Special thanks to altitude expert Bruce Wienke for reviewing this quiz.

1. B. 1,000 feet. The atmospheric pressure at an elevation of 1,000 feet is more than one half psi less than air pressure at sea level. Since the pressure at the surface is less than at sea level, the depth at which the pressure doubles is less. The difference in the surface pressure affects your depth gauge readings, rate of ascent, and decompression stop depths.

2. C. 25.3 feet. Pressure in freshwater is .432 psi per foot of water (14.7 psi divided by 34 feet of water). The depth equivalent to an atmospheric pressure of 10.92 psia is 10.92 divided by .432 = 25.28 feet. If you calculated the problem using the pressure per foot of <u>sea water</u> (14.7 psi divided by 33 feet of water = .445), your answer (which is incorrect) would be 24.54.

3. D. Both A and B are correct, but C is incorrect. You need less weight for fresh water diving than for ocean diving because fresh water is not as dense as salt water. When you take your wet suit to altitude, however, the gas bubbles within the material expand when the atmospheric pressure decreases. Depending on the altitude of your dive, you may require more weight than you would for a freshwater dive at sea level.

4. A. Bourdon tube. A Bourdon tube depth gauge reads zero at an atmospheric pressure of 14.7 psia. As air pressure decreases with altitude, the needle moves, or tries to move, below zero. If there is a zero stop for the needle, the pressure change may damage the instrument. If there is no zero stop, the gauge will be inaccurate.

5. B. Capillary gauges provide unconservative information because cold water at depth contracts the air column. The statement is not completely correct. Temperature does affect the air column in a capillary depth gauge, but the effect is less than difference in density between saltwater and freshwater. The net effect is that capillary depth gauge reading may be used directly for dives at altitude. Several types of dive computers adjust for altitude automatically. Some mechanical depth gauges can be adjusted for altitude.

6. C. 10.6 feet. The difference between atmospheric pressure at sea level (14.7 psia) and the pressure at 10,000 feet (10.11 psia) is 4.59 psia. The gauge needs 4.59 psia of pressure to reach the zero mark. At an increase in pressure of .432 psi per foot, the depth at which the gauge would read zero is 4.59 divided by .432 = 10.6 feet.

7. C. Two feet per second slower for each 1,000 feet of altitude. While there are tables that provide ascent rates for various altitudes, I prefer an easy-to-recall rule-of-thumb. As an example, a dive at 5,000 feet calls for a decrease in ascent rate of 5 times 2 feet per minute = 10 feet per minute slower = 50 feet per minute.

8. A. Residual nitrogen from sea level saturation. If you live at sea level, you are saturated with one atmosphere of nitrogen. When you ascend to a higher elevation, it takes time for you to outgas to reach equilibrium for the new atmospheric pressure. Immediately upon arrival at altitude, consider yourself a repetitive diver. A conservative rule-of-thumb is to use one letter group for each 1,000 feet of altitude, e.g., letter group D for 4,000 feet, unless you wait at least 12 hours at altitude before diving.

9. B. 78 feet. A good rule-of-thumb for mechanical depth gauges is to add one foot of depth for each 1,000 feet of altitude plus 3 percent of the gauge reading. For this problem, you add six feet plus 3 percent of 70. 70 + 6 + (70 X .03) = 78.1 feet.

10. B. 27 feet. A good rule-of-thumb for actual depth calculations with a capillary depth gauge is to subtract 3 percent of the gauge reading for each 1,000 feet of altitude. In this instance, 6 times 3 = 18 percent less depth than that indicated by the gauge or 82 percent or 33 feet, which equals 27 feet. The problem is a theoretical exercise. Because capillary gauges are not easy to read, you should use the depth indicated by the capillary gauge.

11. D. The next greater time and the equivalent ocean depth of the deepest depth of your dive. You must use the equivalent ocean depth of your dive at altitude when planning your dives. A dive to 70 feet at an altitude of 6,000 feet is equivalent to a 90-foot dive in the ocean. Since the water is cold, you should use the next greater time than the time of your dive. Since answer C is more conservative, it is an acceptable response as well.

12. D. Upon surfacing. Oxygen in air is about 21 percent at sea level, but only 14 percent at an altitude of 10,000 feet. If you fail to recover from exertion underwater, surface and breathe air that has a low oxygen partial pressure, you might black out. It is important to avoid exertion and to fully recover from exertion before surfacing when diving at altitude.

13. B. 12 feet. I like rules-of-thumb. A good one for decompression stops at altitude is to decrease the depth by one half foot for each 1,000 feet of altitude. The stop depth at 6,000 feet is 0.5 times 6 = 3 feet less. 15 minus 3 = 12 feet.

14. C. Less than your sea level air consumption rate for the equivalent depth at sea level. Since atmospheric pressure at altitude is less than at sea level, the amount of air you breathe with each breath is less (about 3.2 percent less for each 1,000 feet of altitude). The amount of air you consume at equivalent depths is proportionally less at altitude.

15. C. Complete an altitude diving specialty course. Advanced classes may address altitude diving concerns, but do not prepare you adequately for altitude diving. The activity is a specialty, and you should complete a specialty course if you want to dive at higher elevations.

CAVERN AND CAVE DIVING

If you discover a cavern underwater, is it OK to enter? How much equipment should you have? What is the difference between a cavern and a cave? What are the potential hazards in caverns and caves? Take this quiz to find out the answers to these questions and more.

Q:

1. Cavern diving is defined as:
❑ A. Diving within sight of natural light
❑ B. An area from which an emergency swimming ascent is possible
❑ C. Diving within a rock environment with restricted vertical access
❑ D. Both A and B are correct

2. At night a cavern is considered:
❑ A. A safe dive site
❑ B. A cave
❑ C. A completely unacceptable dive site
❑ D. Both A and B are correct

3. Haloclines in caverns and caves occur due to differences in water _____ and can cause _____.
❑ A. Temperature, hypothermia
❑ B. Salinity, vertigo
❑ C. Density, hyperthermia
❑ D. Movement, turbidity

4. In addition to getting lost and running out of air, hazards of cave and cavern diving include:
 A. _____
 B. _____
 C. _____

5. Select the true statement. You should not attempt to breathe the air from pockets of air in caverns and caves:
❑ A. Under any circumstances
❑ B. Unless the air smells fresh
❑ C. Unless bats are present
❑ D. Until your buddy has tested the air

6. List all of the equipment in addition to standard recreational equipment for open water diving that is recommended for use when diving in a <u>cavern</u>:
 A. _____
 B. _____
 C. _____
 D. _____

7. The most important prerequisite for safe cave diving is:
❑ A. Extensive open water diving experience
❑ B. A complete, extensive set of cave diving equipment
❑ C. A diving leadership rating
❑ D. Sanctioned cave diving training

8. The "one third" rule in cave diving means you should:
❑ A. End your dive with at least a third of a tank of air
❑ B. Penetrate into a cave no further than one third its length
❑ C. Get no further from your buddy than one third of the visibility
❑ D. Decompress for five minutes at a depth equal to one third of your maximum depth

9. The minimum number of lights and cutting devices per diver recommended for cave diving is:
❑ A. Two lights, one cutting device
❑ B. Two lights, two cutting devices
❑ C. Three lights, two cutting devices
❑ D. Three lights, three cutting devices

10. The single greatest hazard encountered by cave divers is:
❑ A. Running out of air
❑ B. Getting disoriented and lost
❑ C. Silt
❑ D. Light failure

11. The preferred number of divers for a cave dive is:
❑ A. A single, highly experienced diver
❑ B. Two trained, highly experienced divers
❑ C. Three trained, highly experienced divers
❑ D. Four trained, highly experienced divers

12. If silt is disturbed and reduces visibility to zero, a cavern or cave diver who cannot locate the guide line should:
❑ A. Remain perfectly still until the silt settles

❑ B. Proceed by feel until clear of the silt
❑ C. Slowly rise to the ceiling using buoyancy control
❑ D. Keep moving until the guideline is located

13. If lost in a cave with 500 psi of air remaining, the best action a diver can take is to:
❑ A. Find an air pocket and rebreathe the air in the pocket
❑ B. Exhale each breath of air into his or her buoyancy compensator and rebreathe the air about a dozen times
❑ C. Keep moving using only the arms for propulsion
❑ D. A or B, but not C

14. Cave and cavern diving training is primarily sanctioned by:
❑ A. The Professional Association of Diving Instructors
❑ B. The National Association for Cave Diving
❑ C. The National Speleological Society Cave Diving Section
❑ D. Both B and C
❑ E. All of the above

15. Divers should not enter into <u>any</u> underwater situation where vertical access to the surface is denied unless they have completed appropriate training, are properly equipped, and have a buddy who is similarly trained and equipped.
❑ A. True
❑ B. False

CAVERN AND CAVE DIVING

Caverns are less hazardous than caves, but you should not enter into a cavern without exercising good judgment and self-discipline. The skills acquired in a cavern diving course are good skills to have for diving in general, and the minimum equipment for cavern diving can also be useful for all dives, so why not complete a sanctioned cavern diving course? You will be a better diver who can safely enjoy the beauties and mysteries of underwater caverns. If that intrigues you, cave diving training can prepare you to safely enjoy deeper penetrations into underwater formations. Trained cavern and cave divers dive and live. Untrained divers who enter underwater labyrinths often do not survive.

1. D. Both A and B are correct. Sanctioning agencies define cavern diving as the area in an underwater cave illuminated at least in part by natural sunlight and from which an emergency swimming ascent is possible. Cavern diving can be an enjoyable activity for all divers who enjoy exploring darkened places, but it can be hazardous.

2. B. A cave. Since natural light is required to qualify a formation as a cavern, what would be a cavern during the day becomes a cave at night. One can easily become disoriented, confused, and apprehensive at night inside a cavern. Excursions into caverns should be limited to daytime dives only except for trained and properly equipped cave divers.

3. B. Salinity, vertigo. A halocline is the transition between two layers of water of differing salinities. Vision can be affected when the boundary is disturbed and a mixing of the waters occurs. Although a halocline disturbance may be only a few feet deep, if a diver remains within the area for more than a few seconds, disorientation can occur. Pass through halocline regions quickly.

4. According to NAUI standards for cavern diving, special emphasis during training is required for silting, entanglement, and disorientation. Divers who enter caverns need to be able to make their way safely back out of the formations. Training for this purpose includes body positioning (trim), buoyancy control, emergency procedures, line following, and propulsion techniques.

5. C. Unless bats are present. It can be very dangerous to breathe the air from pockets inside caves and caverns. The air may be devoid of oxygen or may even be toxic. When bats are present, however, it is an indication that the structure has an outlet to fresh air because bats breathe air the same as divers.

6. Some experts feel no special equipment is required to explore a cavern. Others feel a guideline is necessary, but that no light should be used. Without a light, divers are forced to remain within the area illuminated by natural light. The author feels a light should be used in order to enjoy the wonders and life inside a cavern. A line should also be used, but its length should not exceed 50 feet. A knife and back-up line-cutting device are recommended whenever line is being used underwater. Cavern divers do <u>not</u> need double tanks, special tank manifolds, or redundant regulators.

7. D. Sanctioned cave diving training. No amount of open water diving experience or equipment can substitute for proper education in cave diving techniques. No matter how skilled or accomplished one may be as a diver, no matter what rating one may possess, a person is a fool to believe that he or she can safely venture into caves without completion of a sanctioned cave diving course. Training is an absolutely essential prerequisite for safe cave diving.

8. A. End your dive with at least a third of a tank of air. For cave dives, one third of the air supply is used to penetrate the formation, one third is used to exit from the structure, and one third is allowed as a reserve to provide a margin of safety. Frequent monitoring of the air supply is crucial to safety because an emergency swimming ascent is not possible in a cave and because sharing air reduces safety for a pair of divers.

9. C. Three lights, two cutting devices. These are the minimums. Cave divers carry two back-up lights in addition to a primary light, which should have a minimum power rating of 30 watts. A small knife attached to the BC or strapped to the arm for easy access is recommended plus a small line cutter carried in the BC pocket in case the knife is dropped or lost.

10. C. Silt. Trained and properly equipped cave divers are able to avoid running out of air, getting disoriented or lost, and being plunged into total darkness. They may not be able to prevent a "silt-out," however, and this can be nightmarish. Clouds of silt can reduce visibility in crystal clear water to zero in seconds and it can require hours for the silt to settle. If this is a major problem for trained divers, imagine the consequences for the untrained.

11. C. Three trained, highly experienced divers is the optimum number for cave diving. A two-man team may not have sufficient air to assist a third team member with an air supply problem. Training allows three-man cave diving teams to coordinate as effectively as a typical two-man team in open water.

12. C. Slowly rise to the ceiling using buoyancy control. This action should be taken if the guideline cannot be immediately located. Often silting only occurs near the floor of a cave or cavern. By rising gently to the ceiling, you may pass out of the silt. Also, the ceiling will be the first area to clear. It is much better to prevent a silt-out than it is to cope with one.

13. B. Exhale each breath of air into his or her buoyancy compensator and rebreathe the air about a dozen times. If low on air and trapped underwater, a good diver can extend the duration of the air supply by rebreathing each breath. Learn to rebreathe air from your BC, but use the technique for emergencies only. At least one cave diver has survived by conserving his air in this manner.

14. D. Both B and C. There are two nonprofit, educational agencies in the United States that are the primary organizations for cavern and cave diving instruction. The organizations are the National Association for Cave Diving (NACD) and the National Speleological Society Cave Diving Section (NSS-CDS). NAUI sanctions cavern and cave diving courses provided the training conforms to the standards of NACD or NSS-CDS. PADI sanctions cavern diving only.

15. A. True. It may seem safe to go into a small cavern to chase lobster, spear fish, or to explore; but such action can be unwise and may even prove fatal. Untrained divers die every year because they naively venture into caves, caverns, wrecks, and beneath ice. If you have not been trained to dive in these situations or if you are not equipped and prepared to enter an overhead environment, stay out!

DEEP DIVING

Diving leaders discourage deep recreational diving, but many divers go deep for a variety of reasons. Although I support the concept of refraining from deeper dives, it is important to address correct procedures for those who feel the need to reach deeper depths. See if your knowledge of this specialty area is up to what it ought to be before you go down.

1. Deep Diving is defined as dives of:
☐ A. 150 feet and deeper
☐ B. 130 feet and deeper
☐ C. 100 feet and deeper
☐ D. 60 feet and deeper

2. Which of the following reasons for deep diving is unacceptable:
☐ A. To explore unique formations
☐ B. To accomplish a specific task
☐ C. To see what it is like
☐ D. To set a record

3. List four hazards of deep diving:
  A. _____
  B. _____
  C. _____
  D. _____

4. The minimum number of people recommended to carry out a deep dive with minimal risk is:
☐ A. Two
☐ B. Three
☐ C. Four
☐ D. Six

5. List four items of personal equipment <u>required</u> for deep diving that are not necessarily required for dives to shallower depths.
  A. _____
  B. _____
  C. _____
  D. _____

6. The amount of weight worn for deep diving should be:
☐ A. The same as the amount of weight worn for regular diving
☐ B. Greater than the amount of weight worn for regular diving
☐ C. Less than the amount of weight worn for regular diving
☐ D. Adjusted for the planned depth

7. List three reasons why air consumption is greater on deep dives than it is on shallow dives:
  A. _____
  B. _____
  C. _____

8. The recommended way to avoid decompression sickness on deeper dives is to:
☐ A. Use a diving computer
☐ B. Use the U.S. Navy Dive Tables conservatively
☐ C. Always make a safety decompression stop
☐ D. B and C, but not A

9. The maximum number of no-decompression dives to depths in excess of 100 feet recommended for a single 24 hour period is:
☐ A. One
☐ B. Two
☐ C. Three
☐ D. Unlimited as long as you do not exceed the no-decompression limits

10. List four post-dive activities that should be avoided following deep dives.
  A. _____
  B. _____
  C. _____
  D. _____

11. If you become very cold during a deep dive, your dive schedule should be:
☐ A. The next greater time
☐ B. The next greater depth
☐ C. The next greater time and depth
☐ D. None of the above

12. Which of the following is the currently recommended method for safety decompression:
☐ A. Five minutes at ten feet
☐ B. Five minutes at 20 feet
☐ C. One minute at 20 feet and four minutes at 10 feet
☐ D. Four minutes at 20 feet and one minute at 10 feet

13. Extreme fatigue is nearly always associated with which of the following diving maladies:
☐ A. Air embolism
☐ B. Decompression sickness
☐ C. Nitrogen narcosis
☐ D. Carbon dioxide toxicity

DEEP DIVING

As you can see, deep diving is serious diving, and should not be attempted by going deeper with standard diving equipment. You need additional equipment, training and supervision to increase safety as you gain experience and adapt to new sensations. Do not attempt deep dives without these essential elements. Do not base your diving prowess on how deep you have dived. If you have a need to dive deeply, approach it the right way. Otherwise, stick to depths less than 60 feet and enjoy the longer bottom time and reduced risk that the shallower water offers.

1. D. 60 feet and deeper. Although 60 feet doesn't sound deep, this depth has been identified by several agencies as the beginning depth for deep diving. Equipment requirements, experience and procedures are different for deeper diving, so if you dive to depths of 60 feet or deeper, you should be using deep diving techniques.

2. D. To set a record. It is perfectly acceptable for a diver to make an excursion to 100-130 feet under the right circumstances just to see what it is like. Many divers avoid repeating the experience once their curiosity has been satisfied. Certain wrecks and underwater formations in deeper water can only be explored and enjoyed by deep divers.

3. Hazards of deep diving include nitrogen narcosis, decompression sickness, possible respiratory difficulty, rapid air supply depletion, disorientation, and increased problems with emergencies. Deep diving is everything diving has to offer, and less—less light, less warmth, less life, less time, less safety, etc.

4. B. Three. The minimum number of people recommended to make a deep dive with minimal risk is a buddy team with a surface support person who is based aboard a boat. Deep diving from shore is generally unwise. Perhaps an even better number of people is five—two dive teams that alternate diving plus a surface support person. The more experienced dive team should stand by to lend assistance if needed while the less experienced team makes a dive, then the more experienced team can make their dive.

5. Items of personal equipment required for deep diving include complete instrumentation—two depth gauges per diver, two timers per diver, a compass, an alternate source of air, a BC low pressure inflator, an underwater slate with a contingency matrix, and waterproof dive tables. Several of these items are recommended for all dives, but not required like they are for deeper dives.

6. A. The same as the amount of weight worn for regular diving. This is not an easy question to answer due to varying situations and philosophies. The rationale is simply that you must be able to arrest your ascent to perform a safety decompression stop at the end of your dive and can not count on using the "down line" to handle buoyancy problems. A hovering decompression stop may be necessary, and you need enough weight to be able to perform the task with less than a full tank of air. You can learn a lot about buoyancy control and weight distribution in a deep diving specialty course.

7. Air consumption is greater on deep dives due to increased air density—simply breathing in more molecules of air with each breath, colder temperatures in deeper water, and anxiety. When stressed divers become cold, respiration increases, which increases heat loss, which further increases respiration. Stress also affects respiration in a degenerative manner. Check your submersible pressure gauge much more frequently than normal when making deeper dives.

8. D. B and C, but not A. The dive computer manufacturers may not agree, but I believe nearly all of the currently available computers allow multiple deep dives when the dive tables will not permit such dives. Repetitive dives to depths greater than 100 feet in a single 24 hour period should be avoided completely, even if your computer says it is all right to make the dive. Computers are fantastic for multi-level diving where you progress from deep to shallow and where repetitive dives are progressively shallower. Use computers where they excel, but use the dive tables and safety decompression stops for deep dives.

9. A. One. Divers tend to take the information provided by a computer or the numbers in the U.S. Navy tables at face value. If the device or the tables say a dive can be made, then it is assumed it is OK to make the dive. This is incorrect. The inadequacy of most computers for multiple deep dives was explained in the previous answer. The U.S. Navy tables were never tested for repetitive dives in excess of 100 feet! There was very little testing of the Navy tables for repetitive diving. The Navy simply uses "clean" divers when a situation requires more diving. We are not Navy divers. We must use prudence and common sense to avoid injury.

10. Post-diving activities to be avoided following deep dives include exercising, bathing (hot baths and showers), drinking alcoholic beverages, and going to higher elevations (flying, driving up into the mountains). The best action is to take it easy after deep dives. Let others do work like pulling the anchor or carrying equipment. Don't risk decompression sickness.

11. A. The next greater time. According to the NOAA Diving Manual, "if a dive was particularly cold or strenuous, use the next longer bottom time schedule." There is certainly nothing wrong with using the next greater time and depth, which is more conservative. Remember that becoming chilled results in the shunting of circulation to your extremities and that nitrogen in these areas is essentially trapped there until circulation is restored. Prevent heat loss as much as possible, make extended safety decompression stops, and dive conservatively.

12. C. One minute at 20 feet and four minutes at 10 feet. Any form of safety decompression is helpful, but it is felt that stopping at 20 feet for a minute provides mechanical and physiological advantages. It allows you to stop and get your buoyancy under control at a depth where volume changes do not occur with changes in depth as quickly as they do at 10 feet. The brief 20 foot stop may allow a high degree of outgassing with less bubble formation than would occur if you proceeded directly to 10 feet.

13. B. Decompression sickness. Most divers think the bends involves pain in the joints. This is only one symptom, but this effect may not be felt initially. Many divers with decompression sickness first notice a feeling of being very tired and weak. They usually attribute the feeling to something other than decompression sickness. If you feel this way after a deep dive, let others know. If a feeling of "pins and needles" in your extremities follows your feelings of fatigue and weakness, contact the nearest recompression chamber.

DRIFT DIVING

Drift diving is a specialized activity requiring an orientation from an experienced diver, preferably an instructor. There are several types of drift diving, and unique procedures and rules for this exciting activity. See what you know or what you need to learn about drift diving techniques. Wait until you have answered all the questions before you peek at the answers.

1. List three acceptable reasons for drift diving.
- A. _____
- B. _____
- C. _____

2. The preferred method for a boater to maintain contact with drift divers is to:
- ❏ A. Have the divers tow a surface float
- ❏ B. Have the divers hold onto a down line or anchor line
- ❏ C. Watch the divers' bubbles
- ❏ D. Rendezvous at a known point

3. Select the least desirable method for initiating a drift dive:
- ❏ A. Assemble on trail line behind boat
- ❏ B. Assemble on lead or grab lines beside boat
- ❏ C. Assemble at depth of 15 feet on down line or anchor line
- ❏ D. All enter at once and descend together

4. List four potential environmental causes of separation from buddy, group or boat by drift divers.
- A. _____
- B. _____
- C. _____
- D. _____

5. Complete the following specifications for a surface float to be used for drift diving:
- A. Line length should be ___ times maximum expected depth.
- B. Buoyancy should be from _____ to _____ pounds.
- C. Line diameter should be _____ Thin, moderate, thick).
- D. Line should be controlled by means of a _____.

6. List four items of extra equipment recommended for drift diving.
- A. _____
- B. _____
- C. _____
- D. _____

7. List four procedures to be followed by the divers and the boaters in the event a team of drift divers becomes separated from the cover boat.
- A. _____
- B. _____
- C. _____
- D. _____

8. List the maximum number of divers recommended for each type of drift dive:
- A. Float drift = _____ divers maximum
- B. Anchor drift = _____ divers maximum
- C. Free drift or "Live-boating" = _____ divers maximum

9. Describe the main difference in conditions for an anchor drift dive versus a float drift dive.
_____
_____

10. The number one rule for anchor drift diving is:
_____

11. Use of a trail line from the cover boat is recommended for:
- ❏ A. Float drift dives
- ❏ B. Anchor line drift dives
- ❏ C. Free drift dives
- ❏ D. All the above

12. The most common method of drift diving is _____ drifting, and the difficult and hazardous method of drift diving is _____ drifting.
- ❏ A. Float, free
- ❏ B. Float, anchor
- ❏ C. Free, anchor
- ❏ D. Anchor, free

13. List three recommended procedures to be carried out immediately upon surfacing from a float drift dive.
- A. _____
- B. _____
- C. _____

14. When picking up drift divers, a boat should be positioned:
- ❏ A. Upwind and down current
- ❏ B. Upwind and up current
- ❏ C. Down wind and up current
- ❏ D. Down wind and down current

DRIFT DIVING

A:

Were you aware of the different types of drift diving and the different procedures for each form? Has an experienced drift diver actually showed you how to drift correctly? If you guessed at answers and passed the test, but do not have drift diving training, please don't think you are ready to jump into a current. Logic alone can never replace supervised experience. Any time you do not know how to go about an activity in diving, get an expert—a professional—to show you the correct procedures. Sanctioned drift diving specialty courses are available in areas where drift diving is popular.

1. Acceptable reasons for drift diving include desirable dive sites located in moving waters, desire to dive in sediment-free area, observe more and larger life forms, ability to explore a large area with minimal effort, and enjoyment of an exhilarating experience.

2. A. Have divers tow a surface float. Communication between a cover boat and divers drifting underwater is difficult. A float provides the best means for a boater to monitor the position of the divers beneath the surface. Since the divers surface near the float, the boat can avoid them. Watching bubbles is difficult when the surface is choppy, and poses a dilemma if separation occurs. As you will soon read, there are more problems when a diver holds onto the boat's anchor line than when holding onto a float line. A rendezvous is "chancy" and should be avoided.

3. D. All enter at once and descend together. This is not recommended because everyone needs to maintain contact with the boat in some way during the initiation of a drift dive. The only way the group can expect to remain together is to descend together along the same line. Free descents while drift diving are not recommended except "live boat" drifts where the boat follows divers who drift with no line or float. Drift diving must be controlled by the least capable person in a group.

4. Potential environmental causes of separation from buddy, group or boat include eddies, still-water areas behind rocks and in gullies, underwater formations, entanglement, and fog at the surface. Learn as much as possible about potential problems in advance, and develop a plan of action for dealing with them. Separation can occur within a few seconds when drift diving, and reunions without surfacing are improbable. Prevention is paramount.

5. The length of the float line should be at least two times the expected depth, and the line should be thin to minimize drag. Heavy fishing line with a test strength of 50 to 100 pounds works very well. The line should be controlled by means of a quality reel, so you can quickly let out or reel in the line. The float should be large enough to be visible, it should be bright in color, and should have buoyancy ranging from 25 to 50 pounds.

6. Items of extra equipment recommended for drift diving include a surface float, line and reel; a whistle; a mirror; a telescoping signal flag or long, thin signal buoy; waterproof flares; smoke bombs. Note that these items are all signaling devices. Not all of them are required. A recall system and a marker buoy for the cover boat are also recommended. The purpose of the recall system is obvious. The buoy should be deployed by the boater as a last-known point of reference in the event the boat becomes separated from the divers.

7. In the event divers become separated from the cover boat, the castaways should assure buoyancy at the surface, establish and maintain physical contact with each other, conserve remaining air, remain calm and attempt to attract attention. If within reasonable distance of shore, divers adrift should attempt to reach it. The boater should deploy a reference buoy and patrol the area down current from the last-known location of the divers. All procedures should be discussed and agreed upon in advance.

8. The maximum number of divers recommended for float drifting is 14; the maximum for anchor drifting is six; and the maximum for free drifting is eight. This is the maximum number for seasoned drift divers who have experience drifting together, and includes at least one leader or divemaster. More reasonable numbers for less than highly-experienced divers are eight for float drifting, and four for anchor or free drifting.

9. Current is present throughout the water column when float drifting, but only at the surface during an anchor drift. With a float drift dive, the water and the boat move at nearly the same speed; but during an anchor drift dive, the boat is pushed by the wind and moves faster than the water and, therefore, the divers.

10. The number one rule for anchor drift diving is, "Don't let go of the line." As indicated in the previous answer, the boat moves faster than the water, so if the diver releases the line, he or she probably will not be able to catch it. Separation will result. Do not tie yourself to the line or wrap it around you, however. If your hands become tired, you may hook your arm around the line. Just don't let go.

11. B. Anchor line drift dives. The boat is drifting without power. Any diver losing contact with the line should be able to surface and maintain contact with the boat. A trail line is not recommended for float drift dives or free drift dives because the boat must be free to maneuver and cannot risk entanglement of the trail line in the prop.

12. A. Float, free. Float drifting is by far the most common method of drift diving. It works very well for a fairly large group of experienced drift divers. Free drifting is the most difficult and hazardous method because the only link between the boat and the divers is the bubble pattern of the divers. Free drifting requires more planning, experience and expertise than tethered forms of drift diving.

13. Immediately upon surfacing from a float drift dive, which should be done directly along the line to the float, a buddy team should establish positive buoyancy, locate the boat and signal "OK" with one or both arms, and then move away from the float so the boat can approach them for pickup.

14. D. Down wind and down current. A pick-up boat positioned up wind or up current from divers in the water can literally run over the divers in the water. When the boat is down wind or down current from divers in the water, the vessel can be maneuvered very well until the divers can establish contact.

DRY SUIT DIVING

Q:

Many divers in temperate waters have discovered that diving is much more enjoyable when they can avoid getting cold underwater and have made the transition from wet suits to dry suits. Have you dived in a dry suit? Are you considering a dry suit? Do you know what you need to know to use a dry suit? See how you do with the following questions. Do not peek at the answers until you have made all of your selections.

1. Select the <u>incorrect</u> statement. Training for the use of a dry suit is:
❏ A. Essential
❏ B. Mandatory
❏ C. Recommended
❏ D. Desirable

2. Buoyancy compensators should be worn in conjunction with all dry suits and used for surface flotation only.
❏ A. True
❏ B. False

3. Select the <u>incorrect</u> statement. The exhaust valve for a dry suit should be:
❏ A. Self-venting
❏ B. Located in the chest area
❏ C. A constant-volume valve
❏ D. Well maintained

4. A dry suit diver should dive with:
❏ A. Another dry-suit-equipped diver
❏ B. A buddy who understands the dry suit
❏ C. Divers who can tolerate cold
❏ D. Two buddies

5. The maximum amount of air that should be maintained in a dry suit at depth is the minimum amount necessary to:
❏ A. Prevent suit squeeze
❏ B. Maintain neutral buoyancy
❏ C. Offset loss of buoyancy for items collected underwater
❏ D. A and B, but not C are correct

6. Except for foam neoprene suits, all dry suit and undergarment configurations will be too heavy to allow a diver to swim to the surface if the suit is completely flooded at depth.
❏ A. True
❏ B. False

7. True or false: Most dry suits require at least fifteen pounds more weight than a full one quarter inch wet suit requires.
❏ A. True
❏ B. False

8. The worst possible buoyancy configuration for a dry suit is:
❏ A. "Woolly bear" undergarments under a foam neoprene suit
❏ B. "Woolly bear" undergarments under a crushed neoprene suit
❏ C. "Radiant insulation" undergarments under a shell suit
❏ D. "Thinsulite" undergarments under a foam neoprene suit

9. The fit of a dry suit is not particularly important as long as the suit is large enough for the diver to move freely.
❏ A. True
❏ B. False

10. The correct amount of weight for dry suit diving is:
❏ A. Enough to sink the diver after a complete exhalation when all air has been exhausted from the suit
❏ B. Enough to sink the diver while holding an average breath when all air has been exhausted from the suit
❏ C. Enough to allow the diver to hover at a depth of ten feet when all air has been exhausted from the suit and the diver's cylinder pressure is 300 to 500 psi
❏ D. None of the above are correct

11. Arrange the following in order of priority. If diving in a dry suit and you feel yourself floating up feet first, you should:
❏ A. Flare out to slow the rate of ascent
❏ B. Swim down hard and grab hold of something on the bottom
❏ C. Invert yourself and vent the suit at a seal
❏ D. Invert yourself and vent the suit using the exhaust valve

12. Ascents with dry suits should be:
❏ A. At the same rate as when diving with a wet suit
❏ B. Slower than when diving with a wet suit
❏ C. Made by stopping every ten feet to vent the suit
❏ D. Made with negative buoyancy

13. Which of the following situations will cause the most serious buoyancy problem for a trained dry suit diver?
❏ A. Depth variations while diving
❏ B. A flooded suit
❏ C. A manual exhaust valve
❏ D. Overweighting offset with air in the suit

14. In addition to more warmth, an advantage of a dry suit over a wet suit is:
❏ A. Near-constant insulation regardless of depth
❏ B. Less maintenance
❏ C. Less initial cost
❏ D. Less resistance to movement through the water

DRY SUIT DIVING

A:

How is your dry suit knowledge? Did you furrow your brow or raise your eyebrows at some of the answers? The information in this quiz is the latest available and represents the best recommendations of dry suit manufacturers and diver training agencies. If you are a dry suit diver and disagree with some of the policies, it may be a good idea to reconsider your practices. If you are not yet a dry suit diver, please get training and adopt the correct procedures if you do become one.

1. B. Mandatory. Training for dry suit diving is not mandatory, but it is essential, desirable, and recommended by training agencies and dry suit manufacturers. Experience alone can not qualify you to handle the special situations you may encounter while diving with a dry suit. If you use or plan to use a dry suit, get training.

2. A. True. Some dry suit divers, especially those with foam neoprene suits, disagree with the need for a BC. Others disagree that the BC should be used for surface flotation only. The recommendations are agreed upon by the manufacturers of dry suits, however, and have been adopted by NAUI. It is not a good idea to have two means of buoyancy to control underwater.

3. B. Located in the chest area. The exhaust valve for a dry suit does not necessarily have to be located in the chest area. Some suits have the valve positioned on the upper arm or on the forearm, and it is easier to make your arm the highest point in the suit than it is to elevate your chest. The valve should definitely be a self-venting, hands-free type.

4. B. A buddy who understands the dry suit. It is important to check all valves, hoses, zippers, and seals before each dive. A buddy familiar with a dry suit can assist with the inspection. A buddy who knows the potential problems of dry suit diving can help prevent them while diving or can recognize a problem and assist in overcoming it.

5. D. A and B, but not C are correct. Maintain as little air as possible in a dry suit underwater. Add just enough to avoid suit squeeze and to maintain neutral buoyancy. Large quantities of air result in air shifts within a suit when a diver changes position in the water. Such shifts of air can be hazardous and must be minimized by limiting the amount of air in the suit. It is also hazardous to use suit buoyancy to offset the weight of items picked up while diving.

6. B. False. Tests conducted by Steven Barsky and John Heine demonstrated that negative buoyancy results with nearly all dry suits if the suits are completely flooded, but that the test divers could swim to the surface. Also, by depressing the inflator valve and raising the arms, it was (and is) possible to trap enough air to create a positive buoyancy situation.

7. B. False. The amount of weight required is affected by many factors, but generally a person should not require more than an additional ten pounds when changing from a wet suit to a dry suit. The point of the question is that many divers believe a great deal more lead is needed for dry suit diving, and that is an incorrect concept which can produce a dangerous situation.

8. A. "Woolly bear" undergarments under a foam neoprene suit. Both the suit and the undergarments compress under pressure, producing a severe loss of buoyancy. To compensate for the loss, large amounts of air must be added to the suit, which can cause hazardous air shifts when the diver's feet are raised higher than the head. A shell-type dry suit with radiant insulating material for undergarments requires the least amount of weight and is affected the least by pressure changes.

9. B. False. Excess space forms air pockets that require extra weight, make the diver more prone to air shifts, make folds that can pinch, and increase resistance to movement through the water. Avoid oversized, baggy suits so you can dive more safely and save energy. Suits can be modified to fit.

10. C. Enough to allow the diver to hover at a depth of ten feet when all air has been exhausted from the suit and the diver's cylinder pressure is 300 to 500 psi. This is the correct weighting for any modern diver, but is especially important for a dry suit diver, who needs to be able to arrest an ascent for a precautionary decompression stop. This means the diver will be slightly (3-4 pounds) heavy at the beginning of the dive, but in control at the end of the dive.

11. B., D., C., A. For a small amount of excess buoyancy in a feet first ascent, try to swim to a horizontal position, then arch your back to get into a head-up position to vent the suit. For greater buoyancy, power to the bottom vertically and anchor yourself (if possible) while inverting. Once inverted, reasonable quantities of excess air can be vented with the exhaust valve, but large quantities should be dumped by pulling on a wrist seal or the neck seal. If completely out of control, flare out in a spread eagle position to create maximum drag to slow your ascent. (Prevention is better than all of the above techniques combined.)

12. B. Slower than when diving with a wet suit. It takes time for air inside a dry suit to migrate to the exhaust valve. Ascend slowly enough to allow for the migration of the air. Slow ascents with automatic exhaust valves can be very effective and allow more control than faster ascents with periodic manual venting.

13. D. Overweighting offset with air in the suit. Trained or not, overweighting is the biggest single problem for any dry suit diver. The air expands with changes in depth or with changes in body position. The air also moves inside the suit, always seeking the highest point. A properly weighted, trimmed, and trained dry suit diver can deal with other suit problems, including a stuck inflator valve, a stuck exhaust valve, and even a flooded suit.

14. A. Near-constant insulation regardless of depth. A wet suit loses insulating capability as depth increases, but a dry suit can retain as much as 85 percent of its ability to retain heat. This makes dry suits especially valuable for deeper dives in cold or temperate waters. Dry suits do cost more than wet suits, and require more maintenance, but they can last many years with proper care.

ICE DIVING PREPARATION

Ice diving is one of the most complex activities in which divers can engage. It provides challenge and enjoyment for thousands of divers annually. See for yourself how involved this pursuit can be by answering the following questions that pertain only to the preparation required for ice diving.

1. The minimum level of training for safe participation in ice diving activities is:
❏ A. Advanced scuba diver
❏ B. Master scuba diver
❏ C. Ice diving specialty
❏ D. Either A or B plus C

2. The minimum number of participants recommended for ice diving is:
❏ A. Two
❏ B. Four
❏ C. Six
❏ D. Seven

3. The minimum ice thickness for safe ice diving activity is:
❏ A. Two inches
❏ B. Three inches
❏ C. Four inches
❏ D. Five inches

4. Four items of diving equipment in which freeze-up is likely to affect safety include:
A. _____
B. _____
C. _____
D. _____

5. Three important items of equipment needed by line tenders are:
A. _____
B. _____
C. _____

6. Eight items of equipment needed to prepare a site for ice diving include:
A. _____
B. _____
C. _____
D. _____
E. _____
F. _____
G. _____
H. _____

7. The preferred shape of the hole in the ice for ice diving is _____, and the minimum size of the hole is ____ feet per side.
❏ A. Triangular, four
❏ B. Triangular, five
❏ C. Rectangular, four
❏ D. Rectangular, five

8. Three actions to take with the block of ice cut from the hole when ice diving include:
A. _____
B. _____
C. _____

9. Which of the following items of diving equipment is not recommended for use while ice diving:
❏ A. Snorkel
❏ B. Full-face mask
❏ C. Line-attachment harness
❏ D. Extra second stage
❏ E. Dive knife

10. Three recommended characteristics of a safety line used by ice divers include:
A. _____
B. _____
C. _____

11. The length of line used by ice divers should not exceed ____ feet in length.
❏ A. 100
❏ B. 125
❏ C. 150
❏ D. 200

12. Three differences in the line used by safety divers compared to the line used by ice divers are:
A. _____
B. _____
C. _____

13. An ice diver's safety line should be tied to his or her:
❏ A. Tank valve
❏ B. Wrist
❏ C. Waist
❏ D. Harness

14. Three recommended precautions to prevent regulator freeze-up include:
A. _____
B. _____
C. _____
D. _____

15. Stand-by divers should be prepared to ____ in the event of an ice diving emergency.
❏ A. Suit up
❏ B. Enter the water immediately
❏ C. Enter the water within two minutes
❏ D. Summon emergency medical assistance

ICE DIVING PREPARATION

A:

Is there more to ice diving preparation than you thought? There is even more involved with the procedures for ice diving. If you are interested in diving beneath water upon which you can walk, be sure you have completed an ice diving course, are properly prepared for the activity, and abide by all recommended safety practices. Ice diving can be fun when done properly.

1. C. No one should attempt ice diving without completion of an ice diving specialty course. No amount of talking or reading can replace supervised experience. Ice diving is a hazardous diving activity that is very unforgiving. It must be done correctly. Specialty training is essential for safety. The prerequisites for an ice diving specialty course vary from one training agency to another.

2. C. The minimum number of participants for a properly conducted ice dive is six: Two divers, two tenders, and two stand-by divers. The divers can rotate roles so everyone can make a dive, but the role of stand-by divers is a difficult one for divers who are wet. Complete second sets of dry equipment are helpful.

3. D. Five inches. Ice diving concentrates a lot of weight in a small area. The ice must be at least five inches thick to support all of the people and the equipment. Remember that ice is thicker near shore than in the middle of a body of water. Don't risk crashing through ice that is too thin to support proper operations.

4. Items of diving equipment likely to freeze and affect diving safety include the regulator (both stages), the buoyancy compensator (bladder, hose, inflator), dry suit valves, caribiners (for line attachment), and wet exposure suits. Emphasis must be placed upon the prevention of freeze-ups. All equipment must be thoroughly dry inside and out at the outset. Water inside valves (regulator, BC, dry suit) can render them inoperative. Water inside a BC can cause the sides to freeze together.

5. Important items of equipment needed by line tenders are warm boots, a pallet to stand on, waterproof gloves, and a pair of hand spikes. The hands must be kept dry when handling wet line. The feet must be kept warm with good boots and with separation from the ice (purpose of pallets). Hand spikes should be carried by everyone in the party so each can get out of the water in case he or she falls through the ice.

6. Items of equipment needed to prepare a site for ice diving include an **ice auger** to drill holes in the ice, an **ice saw** for cutting holes in the ice, **waterproof clothing** to keep dry while cutting holes, **ground cover, a wind break, shovels** to shovel spoke lines and arrows to indicate the direction to the hole, **sticks** to anchor the ice block, **ice spikes** to tether the safety lines, and a **toboggan or sled** to haul all of the equipment to the site.

7. A. triangular, four. The narrow angles of the corners of a triangular hole provide good leverage to allow divers to exit the water easily. There is also one less side to cut with a triangular shape than with a square or rectangle. A hole four foot per side is the smallest size that allows two divers to enter or exit at the same time.

8. Actions to take with the block of ice from the hole cut in the ice include **drilling two holes through the block (best if done before block is cut), pushing the block beneath ice adjacent to the hole, pinning or tying the block so it cannot slip and block the opening, putting the block back into place when diving is completed, and marking the location** to warn others of the weakened area.

9. A. Snorkel. Ice divers do not need snorkels. It is a myth that a diver trapped under the ice can chip a hole in the ice and breathe through a snorkel or can breathe from air pockets beneath the ice. A snorkel can also snag on the safety line and cause the mask to be dislodged. A full-face mask is a desirable item for ice diving, but those using it must be familiar with how to use one. An extra second stage and a dive knife are essential items.

10. Recommended characteristics of the **safety line used by ice divers include a diameter of 3/8 to 1/2 inch, non-floating, brightly colored, and marked (color-coded) to indicate various distances.** Remember that wet line can freeze, so care must be exercised when handling safety lines. It is not an easy job to be a good ice diving tender.

11. B. 125 feet. Divers should limit excursions beneath the ice to a lateral distance of 100 feet. The additional 25 feet of line is for securing the end of the line above the water. The free end must be secured to an ice spike. Attaching a large float to the above-water end of the line is also a good idea in case the ice spike should come loose.

12. Differences in the lines used by safety divers compared to the lines used by ice divers include the **use of floating line by the safety divers versus non-floating line by the divers, the use of lines of different colors than those of the divers, and lines twice as long as those used by the divers.**

13. D. Harness. A safety harness is an essential item for ice diving. A secure point of attachment is needed. A harness allows a line to be attached or detached quickly and easily. Knots are difficult to deal with when diving, and can freeze in place.

14. Recommended precautions to prevent regulator freeze-up include **not breathing into the regulator before a dive, keeping the entire regulator submerged continuously when in the water, avoiding rapid breathing while diving, and keeping the regulator warm as long as possible before use.**

15. C. Enter the water within two minutes. Safety divers should need only to don their scuba units (which should be kept warm), fins, and masks if assistance is needed by a diver beneath the ice. It is not a good idea for safety divers to be completely outfitted while standing by.

LIMITED VISIBILITY

Limited visibility diving exists when a buddy diver cannot be discerned at a distance greater than 10 feet. To dive safely in turbid water requires preparation and skills beyond that required for clear water diving. See how well prepared you are for limited visibility (LV) diving by listing answers to the following questions.

1. List five factors that can cause underwater visibility to become limited.
A. _____
B. _____
C. _____
D. _____
E. _____

2. List five items of diving equipment, other than standard open water gear, that are recommended for diving in limited visibility.
A. _____
B. _____
C. _____
D. _____
E. _____

3. List ten potential hazards of limited visibility diving.
A. _____
B. _____
C. _____
D. _____
E. _____
F. _____
G. _____
H. _____
I. _____
J. _____

4. List five methods by which you can prepare to dive in limited visibility.
A. _____
B. _____
C. _____
D. _____
E. _____

5. List five skills that should be well developed before diving in limited visibility.
A. _____
B. _____
C. _____
D. _____
E. _____

6. List three procedures concerning movement along the bottom in limited visibility.
A. _____
B. _____
C. _____

7. List the meaning of each of the following line pull signals:
A. One pull =
B. Two pulls =
C. Three pulls =
D. Four pulls =
E. Five+ pulls =

8. List three acceptable reasons for diving in limited visibility.
A. _____
B. _____
C. _____

9. List three unacceptable reasons for diving in limited visibility.
A. _____
B. _____
C. _____

10. List three rules for tethered diving.
A. _____
B. _____
C. _____

11. List three procedures for use of a buddy line.
A. _____
B. _____
C. _____

12. List three means of communicating in limited visibility.
A. _____
B. _____
C. _____

13. List three rules for signaling in limited visibility.
A. _____
B. _____
C. _____

LIMITED VISIBILITY

 A:

Limited visibility diving is a specialty requiring training and supervised experience. Many aspects of diving in turbid water can be learned by completing a night diving course. Dirty water diving and navigation are often included in advanced scuba courses. Know the area or dive with someone who does when visibility is poor. Plan well, dive carefully and examine the small things. The water doesn't need to be clear for diving to be enjoyable.

1. Factors that produce limited underwater visibility: **storms, surf, rough weather, rain, run-off, river heads, pollution, sewage outfalls, plankton, algae, upwellings, currents, tidal changes, stirring up a silty bottom.**

2. Equipment for limited visibility diving: **compass, dive light, buddy line, tender line, tether harness, descent line, helmet, leather gloves, small, sharp arm-mounted knife.**

3. Potential hazards of limited visibility diving: **cuts, infections, anxiety, apprehension, panic, increased air consumption, vertigo, overhangs, disorientation, entanglement, buddy separation, control of ascents, head injuries, hazardous animals.**

4. Methods of preparation: **night diving class, advanced diving class, blacked-out mask exercises, familiarization with site during good visibility, dives with more experienced buddy, study of literature on the topic.**

5. Skills for limited visibility diving: **navigation, buddy system techniques, acute sense of buoyancy, signaling, use of tender line, diving primarily by touch, "blind" problem solving.**

6. Procedures for moving along the bottom in LV: **Extend one hand in front. Move slowly and carefully. Back out of entanglements. Check buddy frequently. Check orientation frequently. Check tank pressure frequently. Avoid contact with the bottom except with extended hand.**

7. Line pull signals: **A. 1 pull = OK? OK. B. 2 pulls = go. C. 3 pulls = stop. D. 4 pulls = surface, come here. E. 5+ pulls = emergency.** Any signal except five pulls should be answered by repeating the signal when received.

8. Acceptable reasons for diving in limited visibility: **typical local conditions, training, specific objective and properly prepared and equipped, qualified for LV diving, want to dive and other conditions good.**

9. Unacceptable reasons for diving in limited visibility: **rough water, surf, surge, strong currents, swift water, traveled a long distance to do diving, because other divers are doing it, to "try it" without training or supervision.**

10. Rules for tethered diving: **Be trained in procedures. Know and practice signals. Attach line only to a special harness. Wear line harness under other equipment. Avoid slack line.**

11. Procedures for diving with a buddy line. **Practice in good conditions first. Know and rehearse signals. Do not tie line to self. A rubber loop around wrist is OK. Keep line taut. Establish a procedure to deal with line snags that might occur.**

12. Means of communicating in limited visibility: **line pulls, squeezes, light signals, audible signals, hand signals, messages on a slate.**

13. Rules for signaling: **Agree on signals in advance, rehearse them before the dive, give signals clearly and distinctly, always acknowledge signals received.**

Diving at night is exciting and beautiful. You should be trained to dive at night, but many divers who lack training dive in the darkness. As you will see when pondering the following questions, training is valuable.

1. Select the preferred sequence for gaining experience:
- ❏ A. Night diving before limited visibility diving
- ❏ B. Limited visibility diving before night diving
- ❏ C. Logging 25 dives before night diving
- ❏ D. The sequence doesn't make any difference

2. Night diving should be done:
- ❏ A. Anywhere the water is clear and calm
- ❏ B. At high tide on moonlit nights
- ❏ C. In known locations when conditions are good
- ❏ D. All the above

3. The most important consideration before a night dive is:
- ❏ A. The environmental conditions
- ❏ B. The equipment you will use
- ❏ C. Who will be diving
- ❏ D. All are equally important

4. Select the most important skill for night diving:
- ❏ A. Air sharing
- ❏ B. Underwater navigation
- ❏ C. Repetitive dive calculations
- ❏ D. Using a dive light

5. Select the night diving practice that experts discourage:
- ❏ A. Attaching a chemical glow light to the tank valve or the snorkel
- ❏ B. Waving a dive light up and down to get a buddy's attention
- ❏ C. Shining a light on another diver's chest to gain attention
- ❏ D. Using a line for descents and ascents

6. Diving at night is more difficult than diving during the day. The most significant problem for a diver at night is:
- ❏ A. Buddy separation
- ❏ B. Judging the ascent rate
- ❏ C. Disorientation
- ❏ D. Marine life hazards

7. The total number of lights (above and below water types) for a buddy team diving at night from shore in an unlighted location is:
- ❏ A. Two
- ❏ B. Four
- ❏ C. Six
- ❏ D. Eight

8. Select the incorrect statement:
- ❏ A. Red light disturbs marine life less than white light does.
- ❏ B. 30 minutes of adaptation to low light levels before a night dive improves a diver's vision.
- ❏ C. Bright, glaring light entering the eyes during the day can reduce your ability to see at night.
- ❏ D. All the statements are false.

9. The well-equipped night diver has:
- ❏ A. A compass and a whistle
- ❏ B. Extra weight and a low-pressure BC inflator
- ❏ C. An alternate air source
- ❏ D. All the above

10. White strobe lights are particularly useful for:
- ❏ A. Marking exit locations
- ❏ B. Dive boat relocation when suspended beneath a boat
- ❏ C. Emergency signaling at the surface
- ❏ D. B and C, but not A

11. The minimum injury risk occurs when you dive at night from:
- ❏ A. A boat
- ❏ B. The shore
- ❏ C. A dock
- ❏ D. A jetty

12. To maintain buddy contact during night dives, divers typically use:
- ❏ A. Physical contact
- ❏ B. A buddy line
- ❏ C. Light signals
- ❏ D. Audible signals

13. The preferred exit point reference for a night dive is:
- ❏ A. A large bonfire
- ❏ B. A pair of steady lights
- ❏ C. A pair of flashing lights
- ❏ D. One flashing light

14. When ascending at night, gauge the rate by shining your light on:
- ❏ A. Your bubbles
- ❏ B. Your gauges
- ❏ C. Another diver
- ❏ D. None of the above

15. To keep track of divers at the surface at night, it is best for each diver to use:
- ❏ A. A night light that shines continuously
- ❏ B. A chemical glow light that is visible at the surface
- ❏ C. Reflective tape on the snorkel tip
- ❏ D. All the above

NIGHT DIVING

A:

Was some of the information in the answers new to you? Diving at night is easier, safer, and more enjoyable when you complete a night diving specialty course. Expand your opportunities to dive by completing night diving training. If you did not score well, don't remain in the dark.

1. A. Night diving before limited visibility diving. A night dive under good conditions is a good method to gain experience for diving in turbid water with limited visibility. Some divers hesitate to dive at night, but they should not because a good night dive is far better than a bad dive during the day.

2. C. In known locations when conditions are good. Do not attempt night dives in strange areas or under poor conditions. Diving at night in rough or turbid water is hazardous. Seek ideal conditions when you dive at night.

3. A. The environmental conditions. Your primary concern at night is the dive site conditions. Check the weather forecast, water movement, and water visibility in advance. Dive only at well-known sites. Dive the area during the day first whenever possible.

4. B. Underwater navigation. At night you must rely on your compass and navigational skills for orientation. Develop your navigational skills before attempting night dives. Reduce the distance you swim at night.

5. B. Waving a dive light up and down to get a buddy's attention. An up-and-down motion with a light is a standard signal that means something is wrong. To gain attention, wave your light rapidly from side to side. Another standard light signal is a large "O" to signify OK.

6. C. Disorientation. In water, your sense for spatial orientation is impaired. You rely heavily on visual input for reference. Visual deprivation can lead to a sensation of not knowing up from down and may cause vertigo. The problem is greatest when you are between the surface and the bottom. Using a descent line helps prevent disorientation.

7. D. Eight. Use dive lights only while in the water. Each diver needs a small, above-water flashlight for dive preparation. Mark the exit point with two flashing lights aligned one above and behind the other. Each diver should have primary and back-up dive lights.

8. D. All the statements are false. No, all the statements are true! A red filter on a light makes the light less bothersome to marine life. Dark adaptation for at least a half hour enhances your vision. Bright light temporarily disrupts parts of your eyes you use to see in low light levels.

9. A. A compass and a whistle. All divers should have an alternate air source. No recreational diver should dive with excess weight. A low-pressure inflator is highly desirable because it allows one-hand buoyancy control. A whistle is an effective surface signaling device at night.

10. D. B and C, but not A. White flashing lights above the water are emergency signals and can be seen for miles on the water. You could cause marine navigation confusion. A small strobe light beneath the surface is an excellent marker for a boat dive. A strobe is a good emergency signaling device. You can carry a small, inexpensive strobe in your BC pocket.

11. A. A boat. A boat supplies surface support, serves as a base of operations, and can come to you if you require assistance. Boat entries and exits are quick and easy. A well-lighted boat is easy to locate at the end of a dive. Be sure to dive against any current.

12. C. Light signals. The use of your hands is limited when you hold a light. A buddy line can get tangled in your light. With reasonable visibility you can keep track of your buddy easier at night than during the day because you can see the glow from your partner's light. Review and agree on light signals before you dive.

13. C. A pair of flashing lights. From a distance all lights on shore look similar. Use distinctive lights to mark your exit point. Flashing amber lights with one positioned above and behind the other form a "range," that will guide you along the correct exit route. Do not use white, red, or green lights because they are nautical signals.

14. B. Your gauges. Shining light on your bubbles causes confusion. Use a line for ascents whenever possible. If you do not have a line or cannot find the line, watch your gauges, ascend slowly, and keep one hand above your head to avoid overhead obstructions. Avoid buoyant ascents.

15. B. A chemical glow light visible at the surface. You may be able to see better at the surface at night if you turn your dive light off. Usually there is sufficient light to allow you to see distant objects. You need to be visible, however, so attach a glow light to your snorkel or to your regulator first stage.

Diving with gas mixtures containing higher levels of oxygen than air contains is somewhat new to recreational diving. This type of diving commonly is called enriched-air nitrox diving or nitrox diving. Enriched-air nitrox has advantages over air, but also poses greater hazards. What do you know about nitrox? Learn more about the subject by studying and answering the following questions

1. Nitrox is a gas composed of ___% nitrogen and ___% oxygen.
- A. 79, 21
- B. 68, 32
- C. 64, 36
- D. All the above

2. The ideal depth range for enriched-air nitrox diving is:
- A. Between 130 feet and 190 feet (39 and 58 meters)
- B. Between 60 and 190 feet (18 and 58 meters)
- C. Between 50 and 130 feet (24 and 39 meters)
- D. Between 30 and 90 feet (9 and 27 meters)

3. Three advantages of enriched-air nitrox as a breathing gas are:
- A. _____
- B. _____
- C. _____

4. Three disadvantages of enriched-air nitrox as a breathing gas are:
- A. _____
- B. _____
- C. _____

5. The partial pressure limit for oxygen in Nitrox I is:
- A. 2.0 atma for 30 minutes
- B. 1.58 atma for 45 minutes
- C. 1.39 atma for 150 minutes
- D. B and C are correct, but A is incorrect

6. The greatest physiological hazard of enriched-air nitrox is:
- A. Nitrogen narcosis
- B. CNS oxygen toxicity
- C. Hypoxia
- D. Hypercapnia

7. Which of the following renders a scuba regulator incompatible for use with enriched-air nitrox?
- A. Teflon seats
- B. Silicon grease
- C. Neoprene diaphragm
- D. All the above

8. The recommended color coding for an enriched-air nitrox cylinder is:
- A. Yellow with a green band on the neck
- B. Yellow with a green neck
- C. Green with a yellow band on the neck
- D. A or B, but not C

9. Select the most correct statement:
- A. Cleaning by itself may not qualify a regulator for use with enriched-air nitrox.
- B. An enriched-air nitrox mixture should be analyzed immediately prior to use.
- C. The depth limit for enriched-air nitrox diving is 130 feet (39 meters)
- D. All of the statements are correct.

10. Enriched-air nitrox experts generally recommend that recreational divers breathing nitrox use ____ to determine dive time limits:
- A. The equivalent air depth (EAD)
- B. The actual depth of the dive
- C. The average of the actual depth and the EAD
- D. None of the above

11. The treatment of decompression sickness is less effective if the patient has been breathing enriched-air nitrox.
- A. True
- B. False

12. The least desirable method for filling a scuba cylinder with enriched-air nitrox is with ____ and an oil-free compressor.
- A. The weighing method
- B. The partial pressure method
- C. A continuous nitrox mixer
- D. A gas tumbler

13. The use of enriched-air nitrox diving currently is regulated by:
- A. The Compressed Gas Association
- B. The Department of Transportation
- C. The Interstate Commerce Commission
- D. None of the above

ENRICHED-AIR DIVING

It is too soon to determine if nitrox will become a common alternative breathing mixture for recreational diving. The day may come when you will have your choice of "regular" or "ethyl" at air fill stations. Whether you decide to use enriched-air nitrox now or in the future, do it correctly. Be trained, be properly equipped, and follow all recommendations for safety. Explosions are unforgiving. Seizures that occur underwater are unforgiving. As with any highly specialized activity involving risk, the hazards are minimized if the activity is done correctly.

1. D. All the above. Nitrox is any mixture of nitrogen and oxygen. Air is called normoxic nitrox because it contains the normal concentration of oxygen. SafeAir is a copyrighted term that signifies any nitrox mixture with an oxygen concentration between 22 percent and 50 percent. Nitrox I contains 68 percent nitrogen and 32 percent oxygen; Nitrox II contains 64 percent nitrogen and 36 percent oxygen. Only Nitrox I is approved for recreational use.

2. C. Between 50 and 130 feet (24 and 39 meters). When used at depths between 50 and 130 feet, enriched-air nitrox allows as much as twice the amount of dive time without required decompression when compared to air. The following are the Nitrox I time limits compared to the U. S. Navy Standard Air Decompression time limits.

Depth Limit	Air Time Limit	Nitrox I Time
50 ft.	100 minutes	200 minutes
60 ft.	60 minutes	100 minutes
70 ft.	50 minutes	60 minutes
80 ft.	40 minutes	50 minutes
90 ft.	30 minutes	40 minutes
100 ft.	25 minutes	30 minutes
110 ft.	20 minutes	25 minutes
120 ft.	15 minutes	25 minutes
130 ft.	10 minutes	20 minutes

3. Advantages of enriched-air nitrox as a breathing gas (when compared to air) are **decreased likelihood of decompression sickness, decreased nitrogen narcosis, reduced residual nitrogen times, shorter surface interval times, reduced decompression time if maximum time limits are exceeded, reduced surface intervals between diving and flying, and reduced air consumption.**

4. Disadvantages of enriched-air nitrox as a breathing gas are the **requirement for specialized training, the requirement for equipment dedicated for use with enriched-air nitrox only, increased oxidation of scuba cylinders, possible deterioration of equipment parts, fire hazards, the risk of oxygen toxicity, the inability to use air-based dive computers, and the potential for nitrox mixing and filling problems.**

5. D. B and C are correct, but A is incorrect. The partial pressure limit for oxygen (using a Nitrox I mixture) is depth dependent and cumulative as follows:

Depth	Pressure	Max. Exposure
130 ft.	1.58 ATA	45 minutes
120 ft.	1.48 ATA	120 minutes
110 ft.	1.39 ATA	150 minutes
100 ft.	1.29 ATA	180 minutes
90 ft.	1.19 ATA	210 minutes

6. B. CNS oxygen toxicity. Convulsive seizures caused by high concentrations of oxygen can cause death by drowning. Susceptibility to oxygen poisoning varies among individuals. Exertion and immersion hasten the onset of a seizure. The effects of breathing oxygen are cumulative, so either a repetitive dive with an enriched-air mixture or oxygen decompression at the end of a nitrox dive can lead to oxygen toxicity. There may be no warning that a seizure is imminent, or the time between symptoms and a seizure may too short to take any action. Oxygen toxicity is a serious diving illness that must be prevented.

7. D. All the above. The materials listed in the answers are incompatible for a pressurized system containing elevated oxygen pressures. Some materials are a fire hazard and can ignite explosively. Substances that do not burn or are not easily ignited must be used for oxygen systems. Standard scuba regulators and low pressure inflator valves are not compatible for use with enriched-air nitrox.

8. D. A or B, but not C. Cylinders containing enriched-air nitrox must be color coded and tagged. The Compressed Gas Association (CGA) recommends the cylinder body be yellow with a four-inch wide green band on the neck or with the entire neck of the cylinder painted oxygen green. Each cylinder should have an enriched-air nitrox ID tag that provides specific information about the gas mixture.

9. D. All of the statements are correct. A regulator must be cleaned for use with high pressure oxygen, but also must have only materials that are compatible with oxygen. Elevated oxygen breathing mixtures must be analyzed immediately prior to use. Nitrox is not a gas for deep dives. Enriched-air nitrox may not be used below a depth of 130 feet (39 meters).

10. B. The actual depth of the dive. There is a procedure to convert the nitrogen partial pressure of a nitrox mixture at one depth to the nitrogen partial pressure of air at another depth, which is called the Equivalent Air Depth (EAD). This is not recommended for recreational diving. By using the actual depth of a dive, an automatic safety factor is added and there is no need for calculations, which may produce an error.

11. A. True. The treatment for decompression sickness is the breathing of pure oxygen under pressure. Since susceptibility to oxygen toxicity is cumulative, administering pure oxygen to a bends patient who was diving with enriched-air nitrox could cause convulsive seizures. Physicians can be restricted in providing treatment.

12. B. The partial pressure method. The "home brew" approach to mixing gases is hazardous. Putting pure oxygen into a scuba cylinder and adding compressed air to obtain an enriched-air mixture can cause explosions and lead to oxygen toxicity. This technique, called the partial pressure method, should be avoided. Cylinders should be filled with a continuous nitrox mixer.

13. D. None of the above. Like all aspects of scuba diving, the use of enriched-air nitrox is self-regulated. If we do not want the government to intervene in diving, then we must develop and abide by reasonable practices that ensure a high degree of safety. The standards and procedures for enriched-air nitrox diving have been developed. Every diver interested in using nitrox has a responsibility to abide by all standards and recommendations pertaining to its use.

Q:

Sooner or later all divers have a need to search for something underwater, either something they have lost or something someone wants them to find. Professional search and recovery operations demand comprehensive training, organization and preparation. The following quiz pertains only to informal searching by a buddy team of recreational divers. See if you know the appropriate procedures for finding an object underwater.

1. The three primary rules of searching are: (1) Define the area to be searched, (2) Select the optimum search pattern, and (3):
- ❏ A. Search a known area
- ❏ B. Keep track of areas previously searched
- ❏ C. Avoid stirring up the bottom
- ❏ D. Use the best possible search equipment

2. The single, most-important factor affecting the success of underwater searches is:
- ❏ A. Defining the areas to be searched
- ❏ B. Selection of the search pattern
- ❏ C. The number of searchers involved
- ❏ D. The diving conditions

3. State the number one rule for all underwater search activities.

_____

4. The best way to ensure proper execution of an underwater search pattern is:
- ❏ A. Select the simplest possible pattern
- ❏ B. Always use the same pattern
- ❏ C. Walk through the pattern before the dive
- ❏ D. Be certified as a search and recovery diver

5. When searching for an object underwater, a diver's buoyancy should usually be:
- ❏ A. Neutral
- ❏ B. Slightly positive
- ❏ C. Slightly negative
- ❏ D. Very negative

6. List five items of equipment—other than standard diving equipment—recommended for effective underwater searching.
- A. _____
- B. _____
- C. _____
- D. _____
- E. _____

7. The most accurate patterns for underwater searching are:
- ❏ A. Directed by a tender from the surface
- ❏ B. Gang sweeps
- ❏ C. Circular sweep patterns
- ❏ D. Compass patterns

8. List three rules for sending and receiving line pull signals.
- A. _____
- B. _____
- C. _____

9. Match the correct meaning to the following line pull signals.

Signal	Meaning
1. One pull	__ A. Surface or surfacing
2. Two pulls	__ B. Go or OK
3. Three pulls	__ C. Come here quickly
4. Four pulls	__ D. Stop
5. Five pulls	__ E. No meaning assigned

10. Select the optimum search pattern for each situation.

Pattern	Situation
1. Grid	__ A. Dive mask in kelp bed
2. Circular sweep	__ B. Outboard motor on sand bottom
3. Semi-circular sweep	__ C. Tackle box alongside pier
4. Diver's sled or two bar	__ D. Weight belt in river
5. Contour	__ E. Earring in a harbor
6. Straight line	__ F. Fishing pole at exactly 60' in a lake
	__ G. Speargun from anchored boat
	__ H. Wreck or reef

11. List three ways to improve the accuracy of a straight-line search.
- A. _____
- B. _____
- C. _____

12. The minimum number of people required for a proper search in a dirty, swift-moving river is:
- ❏ A. Two
- ❏ B. Three
- ❏ C. Four
- ❏ D. Five

13. List two reasons to avoid stirring up the bottom when searching for an object underwater.
- A. _____
- B. _____

14. The optimum way to spot an object underwater during a swimming search is to:
- ❏ A. Look for the color of the object
- ❏ B. Look for the overall shape of the object
- ❏ C. Look at every square inch of the bottom
- ❏ D. Use peripheral vision rather than scanning from side to side

15. List two benefits resulting from completion of a search and recovery specialty course.
- A. _____
- B. _____

SEARCH TECHNIQUES

Just how effective do you feel you are in the art of the search? Hopefully you have completed at least an advanced scuba diver course and are familiar with the basics of finding an object underwater. Even if you did well on this quiz, however, please don't consider yourself an expert on search techniques unless you also have training and experience as a search and recovery diver. Also, avoid becoming involved with the recovery of evidence, bodies, etc. unless you are a professional with the need and training for such activities. Finally, good luck with your informal searches for lost items.

1. B. Keep track of areas previously searched. A search will rarely be successful unless the searchers begin with the best possible information regarding the point of loss and then precisely define the primary and secondary areas to be searched. Selection of the means of search is also critical to success, as is keeping track of areas already searched. Notice that preparation comprises two thirds of the required procedures.

2. A. Defining the areas to be searched. This point is being re-emphasized because it is so very, very important. The best possible search pattern executed perfectly in the wrong place is completely ineffective. Searchers should gather as much information as possible to pinpoint as precisely as possible the location of the loss. People seldom know exactly where something was lost in water, but they usually believe they know.

3. The number one rule for all underwater searching activities is to ensure the safety of the participants. People's safety comes first. Nothing is worth finding at the cost of health or life. Searchers tend to risk decompression sickness and overexposure. Greater-than-normal diving risks are inappropriate and foolish when looking for a material object.

4. C. Walk through the pattern before the dive. Training is recommended and definitely helpful, but nothing helps as much as practice just prior to execution of a pattern. Problems with common understanding, coordination, signals, etc. can be prevented or overcome during a "dry run" conducted in advance of an underwater search. The use of a familiar search pattern also helps, but even if the searchers have used the pattern before, they should still rehearse it prior to the dive.

5. B. Slightly positive. An over-weighted diver or even a neutrally-buoyant diver stirs up silt and sediment when swimming along the bottom. With slight positive buoyancy a diver is forced to assume a head-down position to remain at the bottom. This directs finning action upward and helps keep the bottom from being disturbed. To ascend in this situation, use breath control to drift six to eight feet from the bottom, assume an upright position, achieve near-neutral buoyancy, and perform an ever-so-slightly-buoyant ascent.

6. Recommended equipment for underwater searching includes floats (with dive flags), lines, line reels, anchors or weights, marker buoys, slates, dive lights, heavy gloves (for groping in low visibility). Emergency equipment, tools and spare parts are also recommended, but these should be considered part of standard equipment for diving.

7. A. Directed by a tender from the surface. A surface tender can control the size of the area being searched, can direct the diver via signals while constantly observing surface reference points, can determine the area searched by watching the diver's bubbles, and generally has a superior perspective of the situation compared to any means employed underwater.

8. Rules for sending and receiving line signals: **Keep the line taut. Deliver all signals slowly and deliberately. Acknowledge all signals. Review and agree upon all signals in advance. Use standard signals rather than "homemade" ones.**

9. Line pull signals recommended in "The Art of The Search" article contained in Skin Diver magazine:
  1. **One pull = Stop (D.)**
  2. **Two pulls = Go or OK (B.)**
  3. **Three pulls = No meaning assigned (E.)**
  4. **Four pulls = Surface or surfacing (A.)**
  5. **Five pulls = Come here quickly (C.)**

10. Optimum search patterns:
  1. **Grid pattern for earring in harbor (E.)**
  2. **Circular sweep for outboard motor on sandy bottom (B.)**
  3. **Semi-circular sweep for weight belt in river (D.) and speargun from an chored boat (G.)**
  4. **Diver's sled or tow bar for wreck or reef (H.)**
  5. **Contour pattern for fishing pole at 60' in a lake (F.)**
  6. **Straight line pattern for dive mask in kelp bed (A.) and tackle box alongside pier (C.)**

11. Ways to improve the accuracy of a straight-line search include **use of a stretched, weighted reference line; use of a compass board; orientation to sand ripples on the bottom; and one member of dive team navigating while other diver concentrates on searching.**

12. B. Three. A searching diver, a tender and a stand-by diver are recommended for river searches. A tended diver is safer in these conditions than a buddy pair. The stand-by diver is fully equipped and ready to enter the water at a moment's notice. This type of diving requires training, experience and a knowledgeable person in charge.

13. Reasons to avoid stirring up the bottom when searching for an object underwater include **preserving underwater visibility and preventing silt from covering the object being sought.** A layer of silt or sediment over an item greatly increases the difficulty of the search.

14. B. Look for the overall shape of the object. Items can be spotted more easily underwater when the searchers impress the shape or contour of the object in their minds and then scan for the shape rather than for the exact item. Even partially-hidden objects seem to "jump" to the attention of a searcher when sought in this manner.

15. Benefits from completion of a search and recovery specialty course include **increased knowledge of search options, increased safety during searches, less confusion and fewer coordination problems while searching, and generally more effective operations.** Enthusiasm or need is no substitute for training, which is always recommended for any special aspect of diving.

It is common for divers to find objects underwater that merit recovery, but it is not as common for the divers to use safe, correct procedures when salvaging the items. Raising objects to the surface can be quite dangerous if correct procedures are not followed. See what you know about the principles of and procedures for recovering objects underwater. Answer all of the following 15 questions before consulting any answers.

1. The maximum recommended weight of an object that may be carried to the surface by hand is:
- ❏ A. 5 pounds
- ❏ B. 10 pounds
- ❏ C. 20 pounds
- ❏ D. Variable

2. The maximum recommended capacity of a lift bag for recreational purposes is:
- ❏ A. 50 pounds
- ❏ B. 100 pounds
- ❏ C. 500 pounds
- ❏ D. 1,000 pounds

3. The most important safety feature of a lift bag is a:

_____

4. Three items of recovery equipment recommended for object recovery are:
- A. _____
- B. _____
- C. _____

5. The two knots most useful for the rigging of objects to be recovered are:
- ❏ A. Sheetbend and bowline
- ❏ B. Bowline and clove hitch
- ❏ C. Two half hitches and bowline
- ❏ D. Clove hitch and two half hitches

6. Arrange in order of priority the following concerns regarding the rigging of an object to be recovered.
- ❏ A. Attaching object so it will not flip over
- ❏ B. Attaching object so it will not come free
- ❏ C. Attaching object so it can be easily untied
- ❏ D. The rigging will support the weight of the object

7. Four acceptable methods of breaking the suction of an object embedded in the bottom are:
- A. _____
- B. _____
- C. _____
- D. _____

8. Which of the following methods of inflating a lift bag is the preferred and recommended procedure? The bag should be inflated:
- ❏ A. Slowly and continuously
- ❏ B. Rapidly, but with short bursts of air
- ❏ C. Rapidly at first, then slowly as object begins to rise
- ❏ D. Slowly with short bursts of air

9. An object being lifted during recovery should be positioned a few inches from the bottom to take several actions before ascending. Four recommended actions include:
- A. _____
- B. _____
- C. _____
- D. _____

10. The single most important rule for the lifting phase of object recovery is to:

_____

11. List four appropriate, acceptable actions that may be taken by the buddy of a diver controlling a lift.
- A. _____
- B. _____
- C. _____
- D. _____

12. What single action should be taken at the first possible opportunity after an object has been raised to the surface and before it is removed from the water?

_____

13. How many psi of air from an 50 cubic foot, 3,000 psi tank will be required to fully inflate a 50 pound lift bag at a depth of 99 feet in saltwater (assume constant temperatures)?
- ❏ A. 47 psi
- ❏ B. 140 psi
- ❏ C. 187 psi
- ❏ D. 374 psi

14. Training for object recovery techniques is:
- ❏ A. Necessary for novice divers
- ❏ B. Necessary for recovering objects heavier than 100 pounds
- ❏ C. Necessary for recovering objects heavier than 10 pounds
- ❏ D. Very difficult to obtain

LIGHT SALVAGE

Are you a light salvage expert? If you scored well on the exam, but have not completed training in recovery techniques, don't be too proud. Salvage techniques employ a lot of common sense, so you may have been able to determine the answers through reasoning. The thinking process is different underwater, though, and nothing can replace supervised experience for learning correct techniques. If you have common sense coupled with training, the best possible situation exists. Be trained for whatever you want to do as a diver. Your activities will then be much safer and a lot more enjoyable.

1. B. 10 pounds. When a diver picks up extra weight, extra air must be added to the BC or the diver must exert to support the extra weight during ascent. Both situations are hazardous and should be avoided. If the weight exceeds ten pounds, a lift bag should be used. I routinely carry a rolled-up lift bag with me while diving. This has helped me recover many weight belts and anchors over the years.

2. A. 50 pounds. This does not seem like very much weight, but this is a good limit for recreational purposes. Remember that objects weigh less in water. A significant problem is that pleasure divers tend to have only one lift bag available. This means a large bag could be used to lift a small object, and this is unwise. A 50-pound bag can be easily controlled. A larger object can be marked with a buoy and a line can be attached to it so it can be pulled to the surface.

3. The most important safety feature of a life bag is a means to vent the air that expands inside the bag during ascent. A manually-controlled dump valve allows expanding air to be vented from the bag so the lift will not accelerate to the surface in an out-of-control manner. There are also lift bags available that are designed to automatically vent excess air. This is an excellent and desirable feature.

4. Recovery equipment recommended includes **a marker buoy; a lift bag; a separate air source for inflating the lift bag; lines or straps for rigging; clips or carabineers; and a boat, float or surface support station.** A rolled-up lift bag with attached rigging, a marker buoy, and a "Spare Air" unit can easily be carried during all dives. This minimal gear permits the safe recovery of many objects found while diving for pleasure.

5. C. Two half hitches and bowline. Two Half Hitches are easy to tie and hold a load securely. They are even more effective when a "round turn" is employed before tying the hitches. Half hitches can be difficult to untie, but "old salts" know a trick that lessens the effort required. A bowline is widely accepted as the most useful of all knots. It is used to form a loop at the end of a line. A bowline is easy to tie and to untie and will not slip.

6. D, B, A, C. All of the concerns should be considered when rigging an object, but the most important ones are those related to the load coming free. The next consideration is preventing the load from shifting or flipping over. How difficult it will be to untie the load is not of great concern because that can be handled after the object is removed from the water.

7. Acceptable methods of breaking the suction of an object embedded in the bottom include **rocking the object back and forth, prying the object loose with a lever, attaching a taut line at low tide and allowing the incoming tide to act as a "tidal winch," and using a similar technique with passing waves to form a "surge lift."** A lift bag should not be used to break an object free because many times the weight of the item may be required and the lift could rocket away when the object breaks loose.

8. D. Slowly with short bursts of air. Water is dense, so there is a delay in the effect of buoyancy. If air is added until an object begins to ascend, the lift will contain too much air. When air is added in short bursts with time between bursts allowed to note effect, the exact amount of air needed can be determined and the lift more easily controlled. The first goal of lifting an object is to get it neutrally buoyant at the bottom, and that is very difficult to do when the lift bag is inflated continuously.

9. Actions to take with an object positioned a few inches from the bottom just before a lift include **testing the rigging to ensure the object being recovered will not slip or shift, coordination of ascent initiation with your dive buddy, allowing your buddy to collect the extra air source and any other recovery equipment on the bottom, adjusting personal buoyancy for the ascent, and checking the position of the line of the marker buoy attached to the object being recovered.**

10. The single most important rule for the lifting phase of object recovery is to <u>stay clear of the area below a lift</u>. There are many ways in which a lift can fail. Serious injury can occur if an object falls out of control and strikes a diver.

11. Appropriate, acceptable actions that may be taken by the buddy of a diver controlling a lift include **taking care of extra equipment used, keeping the marker buoy line clear and free, acting as extra eyes and hands for the diver controlling the lift, and maintaining a position in which continuous observation by the person controlling the lift is possible.**

12. The action that should be taken at the first possible opportunity after an object has been raised to the surface and before it is removed from the water is **to tie the item to a float, boat or surface support station.** If air escapes from the lift bag, the object could be lost. Prevent this from occurring by securing the object at the surface, but first be certain the surface flotation will support the weight of the object!

13. C. 187 psi. Fifty pounds of lift equals .78125 cubic feet (50 lb./ 64 lb. per cu. ft.) at 99 feet. The surface equivalent volume is four times this amount (99' equals 4 atmospheres of pressure) = 3.125 cubic feet. The tank provides one cubic foot of air for each 60 psi of pressure (3,000 psi/ 50 cu. ft. = 60 psi/cu. ft.). Sixty psi/cu. ft. X 3.125 cu. ft. = 187.5 psi of air required. Light salvage frequently requires buoyancy and air requirement calculations.

14. C. Necessary for recovering objects heavier than 10 pounds. Since a lift bag should be used for objects in excess of ten pounds, and since training and supervised practice with lift bags is strongly recommended, essentially all divers should be trained in recovery techniques. This training is part of advanced diver courses and search and recovery specialty courses.

Q:

Hunting was originally the primary activity of recreational divers. Many divers today eagerly pursue game underwater. Game has become sparse in many areas, however, and conservationists are promoting bans on hunting. Should divers hunt? If so, how should they hunt? This quiz reflects the general consensus opinion about this controversial issue. Although the quiz reflects value judgments, see if your views of underwater hunting are consistent with those of the general diving community.

1. Divers today should refrain from underwater hunting.
❏ A. True
❏ B. False
❏ C. The answer is situation-dependent.

2. If divers do choose to hunt, it is best for them to take:
❏ A. The largest game possible.
❏ B. Moderate sized game.
❏ C. The minimum legal sized game.

3. It is best to hunt underwater:
❏ A. Anywhere desired except preserves and sanctuaries.
❏ B. At infrequently dived areas.
❏ C. During morning hours only.
❏ D. At night.

4. Underwater hunters should take:
❏ A. Only what can be personally consumed.
❏ B. Only what is personally wanted.
❏ C. Only the legal limit.
❏ D. What is allowed while the game is still available.

5. If an undersized animal is killed by mistake, an underwater hunter should:
❏ A. Retain the animal for consumption.
❏ B. Leave the animal for the crabs to eat.
❏ C. Improve the ability to estimate size.
❏ D. Both answers B and C are correct.

6. Underwater hunters should not take undersized game nor take game out of season because:
❏ A. It is illegal.
❏ B. It affects the reproduction of the species.
❏ C. It portrays a poor image of hunting.
❏ D. All the above.

7. When spearfishing, a hunter should shoot only if certain of a kill shot.
❏ A. True
❏ B. False

8. If a hunter takes game and then decides he or she does not want to fuss with it, it is best for the hunter to:
❏ A. Toss the game back into the water.
❏ B. Give the game to someone.
❏ C. Throw the game away.
❏ D. Resolve not to take game next time unless use is certain.

9. Explain the potential hazard for each of the following spearfishing situations.
❏ A. A diver has a loaded and cocked speargun at the swim step of a charter boat.
❏ B. A diver has just speared a 200-pound fish that is facing the diver head-on.
❏ C. A diver sticks a large speargun into a rocky hole and fires the gun.
❏ D. A breath-hold diver has speared a large fish that has holed up in rocks.

10. It is unsportsperson-like to hunt underwater using scuba equipment.
❏ A. True
❏ B. False
❏ C. The answer is situation-dependent.

11. Fish that may be poisonous and should not be eaten include:
❏ A. Pufferfish
❏ B. Barracuda
❏ C. Moray eels
❏ D. All the above

12. The best possible arrangement for spearfishing is to:
❏ A. Have the sun behind the hunter.
❏ B. Drift with the flow of a current.
❏ C. Dive in early morning hours during high tide.
❏ D. All the above.

13. Select the true statement.
❏ A. Spearfishing is permitted at the mouths of rivers, but not in the river.
❏ B. The spearing of any fish in fresh water is prohibited.
❏ C. Clams and mussels should be taken on the West Coast of the United States only in months that do not contain the letter "R."
❏ D. Female lobsters with eggs attached should not be taken.

14. Fish and game regulations are primarily intended to:
❏ A. Handicap recreational divers to preserve game for commercial fishing.
❏ B. Provide a sustained yield of game.
❏ C. Provide a basis for money to be generated through fines.
❏ D. Ensure the reproductive cycles of animals.

15. Divers desiring to engage in underwater hunting should:
❏ A. Complete an underwater hunting specialty course.
❏ B. Set a good example as a reasonable, responsible hunter.
❏ C. Learn as much as possible about the life and characteristics of the animals being hunted.
❏ D. All the above

UNDERWATER HUNTING

Some readers do not agree with the hunting ethic presented. Many divers today are opposed to killing anything in the water, but many dedicated hunters consider conservationists to be extremists. The hunters ignore the pleas and oppose bans. As long as there are animals to hunt and hunting is legal, some divers will hunt. This quiz reflects a reasonable set of attitudes and values for responsible hunting. The position appears to be the feeling of the diving community in general. If you choose to hunt, learn how to do it, respect the environment, take only what you personally need, and always keep the future in mind.

1. C. The answer is situation-dependent. There are situations where a diver should absolutely not hunt and situations where responsible hunting is acceptable. The primary consideration is for divers to have the knowledge and discipline to limit hunting activities to appropriate situations.

2. B. Moderate size game. Large animals are the fittest of the species. They are the breeding stock that can help ensure perpetuation of the species in an area. Large animals also may contain toxins, parasites, etc. Small animals may not have had a chance or may have had only a few opportunities to reproduce.

3. B. At infrequently dived areas. When game is depleted in an area, it can take years to recover, or the area may never recover. Instead of taking everything possible from popular dive sites, responsible hunters take only a few animals from remote, infrequently-dived areas. This helps ensure continued availability of game.

4. A. Only what can be personally consumed. Game has become so limited it is now considered irresponsible behavior to give game away. Giving away animals taken denies future game-taking opportunities to other underwater hunters. The practice also promotes the concept of hunting for the sake of killing instead of hunting for food.

5. D. Both answers B and C are correct. In most areas, it is illegal to keep undersized game. Although it seems inappropriate to allow an animal to go to waste, it should be left in the environment and become part of the food chain. The most important thing, however, is for the diver to avoid a repetition of the situation. Make certain an animal exceeds the minimum legal size before injuring or killing it.

6. D. All the above. Not only is it usually illegal to take small animals of a species, it is also irresponsible. Hunters who take "baby" game seriously affect future hunting in the area by taking game before it has reached maturity and reproduced and by suggesting through their behavior that taking small animals is acceptable.

7. B. False. Shooting only if certain of a kill shot is an ineffective method of hunting. On the other hand, random and wild shooting is not only unsafe, but often injures animals that get away and die. Reasonable behavior lies somewhere between these two extremes. A hunter should have a reasonable chance of scoring a good hit when taking a shot at an animal.

8. D. Refrain from taking game unless use is certain. What a person does with unwanted game the first time is not nearly as important as the realization that the practice is irresponsible and inappropriate today. Sometimes at the end of a dive trip the task of cleaning game is unappealing to hunters. Keep this in mind when enthusiastic about taking game at the beginning of the trip. Unless you are certain about personally consuming the game, refrain from taking it.

9. A. A loaded and cocked speargun at the surface around people can result in someone getting speared. A speargun is a dangerous weapon and should be treated as such.
B. If a hunter spears a large fish facing the diver head on, there is a danger the fish will rush forward and impale the diver on the end of the spear protruding from the fish.
C. If a hunter sticks a large speargun into a rocky hole and fires the gun, the spear may impact within a few inches, then push the gun itself rapidly toward the diver.
D. A breath-hold diver trying to extricate a large, speared fish from a rocky hole may become entangled in the line from the speargun and become trapped beneath the surface.

10. C. The answer is situation-dependent. It is unsportspersonlike to take easily-approached game in shallow water unless the game is essential for food. On the other hand, hunting halibut at a depth of 70 feet using scuba is reasonable and acceptable. As with most controversial issues, the answer is not black nor white, but gray.

11. D. All the above. While not all barra-

cuda contain poison that cannot be easily detected, divers should not take a chance. Other fish, such as groupers, can also contain poison at times. Check with local fisherman to learn the fish you should avoid taking and eating. Moray eels can be poisonous. Only eat animals known to be safe for consumption.

12. D. All the above. The point of this question is that divers who choose to hunt have a responsibility to know how to do it. There is more to hunting than going underwater and trying to kill something. Accomplished hunters have a great deal of knowledge about the animals they hunt and know how to hunt them effectively.

13. D. Female lobsters with eggs attached should not be taken. All hunters must be familiar with local fish and game regulations. Ignorance of the law is no excuse. Stiff fines are often assessed to recreational divers who violate fish and game regulations. You should be a law-abiding as well as a responsible hunter if you decide to engage in underwater hunting.

14. B. Provide a sustained yield of game. The purpose of game management is to ensure the continued availability of the game. Size limits, bag limits, and seasons are established by state agencies to help ensure game for the future. Legal limits have, at times, proven to be too generous to accomplish the purpose of the regulations. Don't be hung up on getting the limit of something. Take only what you actually need.

15. D. All the above. Hunters should know how to hunt, should have extensive knowledge about the environment and the animals being hunted, and should be good role models. Currently anyone who wants to hunt can obtain a fishing license and hunt. We should encourage and promote the idea that hunting without hunting skills and knowledge is irresponsible. Let's educate instead of legislate.

Q:

Flying affects people, but flight affects divers more. The effects of flying pose concerns before diving as well as after diving. Are you aware of the problems of flight? Do you know what actions you should take before, during, and after flying to minimize the effects of your flight? Since most divers fly, dive, and fly again, you should know the answers to the following questions.

1. The humidity in the cabin of a commercial aircraft at altitude is about:
- ❏ A. 30%
- ❏ B. 25%
- ❏ C. 15%
- ❏ D. 8%

2. The amount of cabin air recirculated in a commercial aircraft at altitude is about:
- ❏ A. 30-40%
- ❏ B. 40-60%
- ❏ C. 60-80%
- ❏ D. 70-85%

3. You are more likely to develop an upper respiratory infection after flying in a commercial aircraft than after eating in a restaurant.
- ❏ A. True
- ❏ B. False

4. Select all true statements concerning circulation while flying.
- ❏ A. Altitude increases circulatory stress
- ❏ B. Eating heavy meals increases circulatory stress
- ❏ C. Inactivity at altitude can cause numbness and pain in extremities
- ❏ D. Flying can cause blood clots in the lungs and arteries

5. If you experience nausea, headaches, and irritability while flying, the symptoms are most likely due to:
- ❏ A. Hypoxia
- ❏ B. Dehydration
- ❏ C. Bad food
- ❏ D. Cigarette smoke

6. If you wear contact lenses and plan to fly, you should:
- ❏ A. Remove the lenses for long flights
- ❏ B. Wear only soft lenses during flight
- ❏ C. Irrigate your eyes frequently during flight
- ❏ D. Remove, clean, and replace the lenses at altitude

7. Which of the following fluids are appropriate to drink when flying (choose all that are appropriate)?
- ❏ A. Diet soda
- ❏ B. Coffee or tea
- ❏ C. Water
- ❏ D. Unsweetened apple juice
- ❏ E. Beer or wine

8. According the Undersea Hyperbaric and Medical Society (UHMS) and the Divers Alert Network (DAN), the minimum time before flying following no-required-decompression dives with less than two hours total accumulated dive time in the last 48 hours is:
- ❏ A. The time required to attain letter group "D"
- ❏ B. 12 hours
- ❏ C. 24 hours
- ❏ D. 48 hours

9. According to UHMS and DAN, the minimum time before flying following no-required-decompression, multiday, unlimited diving is:
- ❏ A. The time required to attain letter group "A"
- ❏ B. 12 hours
- ❏ C. 24 hours
- ❏ D. 48 hours

10. According to UHMS and DAN, the minimum time before flying following dives that require decompression (when the diver has no symptoms of decompression sickness) is:
- ❏ A. 12-24 hours
- ❏ B. 24-36 hours
- ❏ C. 24-48 hours
- ❏ D. 36-48 hours

11. At the end of a dive trip, the final dives you make before waiting to fly home should be:
- ❏ A. Long, deep dives
- ❏ B. Short, deep dives
- ❏ C. Short, shallow dives
- ❏ D. Long, shallow dives
- ❏ E. Long, deep-to-shallow, multilevel dives

12. Three actions you should take while flying to minimize the effects of altitude are:
- A. _____
- B. _____
- C. _____

13. Three actions you should take after a long flight and before scuba diving are:
- A. _____
- B. _____
- C. _____

14. If you are in a foreign country and suspect you have symptoms of decompression sickness, you should:
- ❏ A. Wait to see if the symptoms improve before you fly
- ❏ B. Seek immediate treatment at a local hyperbaric facility
- ❏ C. Fly home and seek treatment at a hyperbaric facility
- ❏ D. Breathe oxygen for several hours before your flight

15. It may take up to three days for you to feel "normal" following a long, international flight. The long period of adjustment is probably due to (select all that apply):
- ❏ A. Cigarette smoke in the aircraft cabin
- ❏ B. Ozone exposure
- ❏ C. Circadian rhythm (your biological clock)
- ❏ D. Altitude illness

FLYING AND DIVING

When you board a plane and do what most passengers do—remain seated, drink dehydrating drinks, and eat heavy foods—you exercise poor judgment. Whether you scored well or learned from the questions and answers, you know what you should do before, during, and after flying to minimize the detrimental effects of elevation. Enjoy your next air journey to an exotic diving destination and follow the recommendations contained in this quiz.

1. D. 8%. The low relative humidity inside an aircraft at altitude poses one of the greatest problems for passengers—especially scuba divers. The effect of the low humidity is dehydration. You must drink plenty of fluid to keep your blood and tissues well hydrated. One of the worst effects of dehydration is blood sludging—something divers must avoid.

2. B. 40-60%. The problem with recirculated air is two-fold: (1) The air contains bacteria, perspiration and, during international flights, cigarette smoke; and (2) the filtration systems aboard aircraft do not remove the contaminants. The pilot has some control of the amount of air recirculated, so it helps to request maximum fresh air for the cabin.

3. A. True. Bacterial colony counts of aircraft air contain more than 25 times more bacteria than air from restaurants and libraries. There are many people in a small space breathing recirculated air. Many people develop respiratory infections a few days after flying. If you are sensitive, wear a mask over your mouth and nose during flights.

4. All the statements are true. You get 16-20 percent less oxygen with each breath aboard a commercial aircraft at altitude, so your body works harder to meet your metabolic needs. Eating fatty foods can increase circulatory stress by as much as 15 percent. Dehydration causes blood sludging that can cause blood clots to form. Numbness and pain in extremities may cause concern about decompression sickness.

5. A. Hypoxia. Ozone exposure may produce some of the symptoms listed in the question, but altitude sickness from reduced oxygen partial pressure is the most likely reason for nausea, headaches, and irritability when flying. Some people are more susceptible to problems from higher elevations than others.

6. A. Remove the lenses for long flights. If the duration of your flight exceeds two and a half hours, remove your lenses. The low humidity of the cabin can cause corneal ulcerations. I experienced this problem years ago when flying from Australia to the United States. Ozone exposure and cigarette smoke on international flights aggravate the problem. Soft lenses pose more of a problem than hard lenses.

7. C. and D. All fluids that contain salt, sugar, caffeine, or alcohol cause dehydration when your body processes the fluids! Drink a minimum of eight ounces of water or unsweetened apple juice every hour when flying. An additional benefit is that all the fluids necessitate numerous trips to the rest room, and movement helps increase circulation to your extremities.

8. B. 12 hours. Waiting to reach letter group "D" is insufficient. Twelve hours is the minimum time before flying after diving. It is better to wait more than 12 hours. According to the UHMS, "Because of the complex nature of decompression sickness and because unverifiable assumptions are involved in decompression schedules, there can never be a flying-following-diving rule that is guaranteed to prevent bends completely."

9. C. 24 hours. The more dives you make before flying, the longer you should wait before flying. DAN also recommends you refrain from diving for one day following three days of repetitive diving. A day off in the middle of a week of diving helps reduce nitrogen tensions in slow compartments and will certainly reduce nitrogen loads for your flight home.

10. C. 24-48 hours. If you had to decompress during a dive within the past 48 hours, you must delay flying for at least 24 hours and, if possible, 48 hours. If necessary, reschedule your return flight. Don't gamble with the problems of dehydration, reduced oxygen partial pressure, and circulatory stress triggering decompression sickness at altitude.

11. B. Short, deep dives. Times at depth are limited by the halftimes of theoretical mathematical compartments, which saturate or desaturate in six halftimes. A five-minute compartment, representing tissues in the body that have good circulation, ingasses and outgasses in 30 minutes, but a 120 minute compartment takes 12 hours. Faster compartments limit dives of 80-100 feet and outgas quickly. Deeper, no-required-decompression dives leave less nitrogen in your body before flying than long, shallow dives leave.

12. Actions you should take while flying to minimize the effects of altitude are **drinking copious amounts of appropriate liquids, eating light foods, and moving about the cabin frequently to increase circulation to your extremities. You may also request the maximum amount of fresh air.**

13. Actions to take after a long flight and before scuba diving include sleeping uninterrupted until you awake naturally, drinking large quantities of appropriate fluids, and refraining from scuba diving for a day. Exercise after flying is good. Swimming and snorkeling are good activities for divers when they first arrive at their destination.

14. B. Seek immediate treatment at a local hyperbaric facility. If you think you may have symptoms of decompression sickness, two of the worst actions you can take are to delay diagnosis and treatment and worsen the condition with reduced atmospheric pressure at altitude. Don't take chances with your body. You could suffer permanent injury.

15. A, C, and D. Symptoms of ozone exposure usually disappear within two to four hours after termination of the exposure. But managing the effects of breathing second-hand cigarette smoke, time changes, and altitude sickness may require up to 72 hours. If you feel lethargic, irritable, and unable to concentrate when you reach your destination, wait until you feel normal before you engage in diving.

WRECK DIVING

Mystery, excitement and the thrill of adventure attract divers to wrecks. Diving safely on wrecks requires knowledge and preparation. See how well prepared you are for wreck diving.

1. List three typical wreck configurations:
- A. _____
- B. _____
- C. _____

2. List six equipment requirements specified for wreck diving:
- A. _____
- B. _____
- C. _____
- D. _____
- E. _____
- F. _____

3. List three types of lines recommended for use when wreck diving:
- A. _____
- B. _____
- C. _____

4. Describe the effect of a wreck on a diving compass.

_____
_____

5. List seven common risks associated with wreck diving:
- A. _____
- B. _____
- C. _____
- D. _____
- E. _____
- F. _____
- G. _____

6. List three recommended practices for wreck penetration dives:
- A. _____
- B. _____
- C. _____

7. List five hazards of penetration diving:
- A. _____
- B. _____
- C. _____
- D. _____
- E. _____

8. List three hazards associated with wrecks deeper than 80 feet:
- A. _____
- B. _____
- C. _____

9. Describe three recommended ways to free yourself from an entanglement plus one action to be avoided:
- A. _____
- B. _____
- C. _____
- D. _____

10. List four factors that affect on which part of a wreck a dive should be made:
- A. _____
- B. _____
- C. _____
- D. _____

11. List three considerations that should be made before removing artifacts from a wreck:
- A. _____
- B. _____
- C. _____

12. List three methods of relocating the anchor line at the end of a wreck dive:
- A. _____
- B. _____
- C. _____

13. List six sources of information about wrecks:
- A. _____
- B. _____
- C. _____
- D. _____
- E. _____
- F. _____

14. List three ways to learn wreck diving procedures and number the ways from the least desirable to the most desirable.
- A. _____
- B. _____
- C. _____

WRECK DIVING

Wreck diving poses more hazards than regular diving, especially when penetration is involved. The worst mistake a diver without the proper training and equipment can make is to succumb to the temptation to enter a wreck. Too many divers do not understand the hazards of wreck diving, cave diving, ice diving, deep diving or other higher-risk diving activities. These types of dives can be made safely, but only when made properly by divers who know the proper techniques, have the proper equipment, and follow established safety practices for the specific activity.

1. List three typical wreck configurations:
   A. Surface/semi-submerged
   B. Submerged with super structure near the surface
   C. Submerged in deep water

2. List six equipment requirements specified for wreck diving:
   A. Small, sharp knife
   B. Large, heavy duty knife with sawtooth serrations
   C. Dive light
   D. Chemical light
   E. Strobe beacon
   F. Alternate air source
   G. Gloves
   H. Underwater slate and pencil
   I. Long-range surface signalling equipment (whistle, mirror, etc.)

3. List three types of lines recommended for use when wreck diving:
   A. Descent/ascent line or anchor line
   B. Stern line from surface vessel
   C. Penetration line

4. Describe the effect of a wreck on a diving compass: **Compasses frequently swing wildly on wrecks because wrecks contain iron.**

5. List seven common risks associated with wreck diving:
   A. Sharp metal edges
   B. Entangling wires and lines
   C. Entrapment
   D. Collapse
   E. Water movement (currents, surge)
   F. Silt-out or low visibility
   G. Hazardous cargo
   H. Hazardous marine life

6. List three recommended practices for wreck penetration dives:
   A. Be trained and equipped for penetration dives
   B. Move slowly and carefully
   C. Use "rule of thirds" for air supply
   D. Enter only areas large enough to turn around and exit

7. List five hazards of penetration diving:
   A. Getting lost
   B. Running out of air when vertical access is restricted
   C. Becoming entrapped due to shift-

ing or collapse of the wreck
   D. Kicking up silt and reducing visibility to zero
   E. Apprehension and panic
   F. Darkness

8. List three hazards associated with wrecks deeper than 80 feet:
   A. Decompression sickness
   B. Nitrogen Narcosis
   C. Colder water
   D. Darkness

9. Describe three recommended ways to free yourself from an entanglement plus one action to be avoided:
   A. Stop, think, then act.
   B. Attempt to back out of the entanglement.
   C. Remove the snared item and clear it.
   D. Avoid turning or twisting.

10. List four factors that affect on which part of a wreck a dive should be made:
   A. Objective of the dive
   B. Depth
   C. Strength of current
   D. Training and experience of divers
   E. Equipment

11. List three considerations that should be made before removing artifacts from a wreck:
   A. Is it legal to remove an artifact from this particular wreck?
   B. Do I have the ability to restore and preserve the artifact?
   C. Should the artifact be left for others to enjoy?
   D. Could the artifact be of historical significance?

12. List three methods of relocating the anchor line at the end of a wreck dive:
   A. Using natural navigation "landmarks" on the wreck
   B. Locating a strobe beacon tied to the anchor line about 10 feet above the wreck
   C. Following a hand-held line tied to the anchorline. Use a line for low visibility wreck dives.

13. List six sources of information about wrecks:

   A. Wreck diving books
   B. Wreck diving specialty courses
   C. Encyclopedias of ships
   D. Magazine articles
   E. Historical societies
   F. Maritime museums
   G. Naval archives
   H. Newspaper articles on micro fiche
   I. Wreck diving clubs
   J. Charter boat captains

14. List three ways to learn wreck diving procedures and number the ways from the least desirable to the most desirable.
   A. Gaining wreck diving experience on your own.
   B. Diving with an experienced wreck diver.
   C. Completing a Wreck Diving specialty course.

SECTION SEVEN

❑ ❑ ❑ ❑ ❑ ❑ ❑

Diving Safety

Diving Safety

Safety should be the foremost concern for all divers. The adage that "There are old divers and there are bold divers, but there are no old, bold divers" is, unfortunately, quite legitimate. Unlike commercial divers, who are paid to take risks, we dive for pleasure. We should do all we can to minimize the risk of injury. Safety is paramount.

There are widely-recognized diving safety practices. All certified divers learn the buddy system, dive planning, safety rules, and how to manage underwater difficulties. All to many divers fail to maintain skill proficiency, take unnecessary risks, and disregard accepted safety procedures.

The dive community has promoted and encouraged the "Responsible Diver" program for several years. Here are a few of the program's safety slogans:

"Only fools stretch the rules"

"When in doubt. . . get out"

"It doesn't matter which dive tables you don't use"

The point of the Responsible Diver program is that you are responsible for your actions and safety. Diving has an excellent safety record for those who adhere to recommended practices. Scuba diving is similar in many ways to flying an aircraft. If you go when the weather is good, use well-maintained equipment, are sober, and follow recommended safety practices, odds are excellent that you will not have an accident. Both diving and flying can be quite unforgiving if you violate the established safety procedures.

Safety practices include communications, the buddy system, dive planning, flags, problem solving, and more. This section should increase your diving safety knowledge. Hopefully Section Seven also will motivate you to dive more responsibly.

BUDDY AND SOLO DIVING

Some divers today dive alone. Others adhere to the traditional buddy system. Some divers dive with multiple buddies. Which techniques are acceptable, and what are the correct procedures for buddy and solo diving? Compare your thoughts on this timely subject by answering the following questions.

1. The maximum recommended separation distance between buddy divers underwater is:
❒ A. Touching distance
❒ B. Ten feet
❒ C. The limit of visibility
❒ D. Dependent upon circumstances

2. The most desirable relative position for diving buddies is _____ , and the least desirable position is _____ .
❒ A. Side-by-side, above and behind
❒ B. Leader-follower, side-by-side
❒ C. Side-by-side, leader-follower
❒ D. Leader-follower, leap frog

3. If you become separated from your partner while buddy diving, you should:
❒ A. Remain still until your buddy relocates you
❒ B. Surface at once and wait for your buddy
❒ C. Look for your buddy for not more than one minute, then surface
❒ D. Look for your buddy underwater until you find him or her

4. The <u>first</u> action you should take if unable to reunite with your dive buddy after separation is to:
❒ A. Call for help
❒ B. Begin a more extensive search
❒ C. Take a "fix" on the last known location
❒ D. Check to make sure your buddy has not exited the water

5. Diving alone (solo diving) is safer than diving with a buddy because only one person can get into trouble.
❒ A. True
❒ B. False

6. Solo diving is a practice now recognized and accepted by diver training agencies and commercial diving operators.
❒ A. True
❒ B. False

7. Select the correct statement. A diver:
❒ A. Can and should be physically restricted from diving alone.
❒ B. Has the right to dive alone any time he or she wants to do so.
❒ C. Should act responsibly and assume all risks if diving alone.
❒ D. Both answers B and C.

8. The most likely cause of a serious diving accident for an experienced diver diving alone is:
❒ A. Panic
❒ B. Running out of air
❒ C. Entanglement or entrapment
❒ D. None of the above

9. Diving in groups of three is:
❒ A. Discouraged
❒ B. Acceptable for advanced divers
❒ C. Acceptable for leadership-level divers
❒ D. Prohibited

10. Six topics to be discussed by dive buddies prior to making a dive include:
A. _____
B. _____
C. _____
D. _____
E. _____
F. _____

11. The single, most important requirement for maintaining contact with a buddy while diving is:
❒ A. A buddy line
❒ B. A pre-dive plan
❒ C. A familiar diving partner
❒ D. None of the above

12. Select the correct statement:
❒ A. The leader of a buddy team should always be the most experienced diver
❒ B. The least experienced member of a buddy team should be allowed to lead, but may be overruled by the more experienced diver

❒ C. Leadership of a buddy team should alternate during a dive
❒ D. Divers should agree in advance who will be the decision-maker for the buddy team during the dive

13. When you use a buddy line to maintain buddy contact in limited visibility, three pulls on the line is the standard signal for:
❒ A. Stop
❒ B. OK
❒ C. Come here
❒ D. Emergency

14. "Do not dive alone" is considered a cardinal rule of diving.
❒ A. True throughout the entire diving industry
❒ B. True for the recreational diving community
❒ C. True for "technical" and commercial divers
❒ D. False because many divers dive alone

BUDDY AND SOLO DIVING

A:

What are your buddy diving practices? Do you begin your dives with a buddy, but usually finish them alone? Do you frequently dive in threes? Have you ever had a buddy do something for you while diving that you could not have done for yourself or could have done only with great difficulty? You may choose different diving practices than those identified in the answers to this quiz, but you should be aware of what is acceptable and what is not acceptable and how to behave responsibly around other divers and diving leaders. Hopefully, you had a good score on the quiz to indicate that you know what is expected concerning buddy diving.

1. D. Dependent upon circumstances. The maximum distance between buddies should obviously be different for clear, calm, shallow water than for a deep dive in cold, turbid water. Two good rules of thumb for separation distance are to reduce the distance as the depth increases and to stay close enough to your buddy that you can reach him or her and gain attention with only a partial breath of air.

2. A. Side-by-side, above and behind. Buddy divers can remain together best when they dive abreast of each other and maintain the same position relative to one another throughout the entire dive. When this is done, each diver can check on the other by simply looking from side to side while moving forward. Leap-frogging can be an effective technique for experienced buddy divers, but this is not the most effective method.

3. C. Look for your buddy for not more than one minute, then surface. Discuss reunion procedures in advance with your dive partner. If you and your partner will agree on a direction to go until you both agree on a new heading, if will be easier to relocate your partner if you become separated. If unable to find your buddy initially, try ascending about ten feet from the bottom and looking for your buddies bubbles while slowly turning around.

4. C. Take a "fix" of the last known location. If you cannot find your dive partner after looking for him or her and surfacing, take bearings to mark your location before you move from the spot. This can be done with line-ups on shore, with a marker buoy, or by noting your location in relation to a boat or float. This simple act may assist rescuers and could save your buddy's life.

5. B. False. People do dive alone, but diving alone is not necessarily safe, which means literally "without risk." It is true that only one person can get into trouble, but it is also true that if the individual gets into trouble, there will be no one available to assist or rescue him or her. There are circumstances in which experienced, self-reliant divers choose to dive alone. When they do this, they are accepting the possibility that something could go wrong. Accepting a risk does not mean an activity is safe.

6. B. False. While solo diving does have a following and divers do dive alone, the practice is not recognized, accepted, nor condoned by diver training organizations nor by nearly all commercial diving operators. This is simply due to the legal problems associated with supervised diving activities. Until the legal issues are resolved, those who desire to dive alone will probably have to engage in non-commercial diving activities.

7. D. Both answers B and C are correct. A person definitely has the right to dive as he or she chooses, but it would be irresponsible to go diving alone in the presence of novice divers. If you desire to dive alone, this should only be done with other experienced divers. Everyone present should be aware of your intentions and informed that you are aware of the risks of diving alone and that you are willing to accept those risks and be completely responsible for anything that might happen to you. You have a responsibility to make sure that others cannot be held responsible for your actions.

8. D. None of the above. A calm, confident, experienced, self-reliant diver can cope with nearly any "standard" emergency in diving. The one hazard that can cause a serious accident is loss of consciousness, which can and does occur for many different reasons. This is the greatest risk facing the solo diver, and a very unforgiving one. Before you decide to become a solo diver, think what would happen to you if you blacked out or were knocked out underwater. Accident reports show unconsciousness in and under the water occurs more frequently than you might think it does.

9. A. Discouraged. People dive in threes. This is not a good practice because it is demanding to keep track of one other diver, let alone two. There are times when you must dive with two other divers or abstain from diving. Whenever possible, strive to dive with just one other diver. If you absolutely must dive with two part-

ners, discuss procedures and techniques for double-buddy diving before entering the water.

10. Topics to be discussed by dive buddies prior to making a dive include the **dive objective, entry and exit locations, signals, emergency procedures, reunion procedures, the pattern of the dive, relative positioning, and limits for depth, air, and distance traveled.**

11. D. None of the above. The single most important requirement for maintaining buddy contact is the desire to do so. If you do not want to remain with a dive buddy, you will not. Your buddy must also want to remain with you. When you meet a new dive buddy, first ask if he or she plans to abide by the buddy system. If not, you must convince him or her it is a good idea or find a new partner.

12. D. Divers should agree in advance who will be the decision-maker for the buddy team during the dive. If the most experienced diver is always the leader, how will the lesser experienced diver gain any experience as a leader? A good practice is to alternate leadership for each dive with the most experienced diver being the leader for the first dive.

13. A. Stop. Standard line pull signals are one pull = OK, two pulls = Go, three pulls = stop, four pulls = up, and five or more pulls = help. Be sure to review all signals—hand, line pull, or light signals—prior to diving with a new partner.

14. B. True for the recreational diving community. The first rule of diving is "Don't hold your breath when breathing compressed air." and the second rule is still "Don't dive alone." While the new breed of "technical" divers recognize solo diving, this type of diving is very adventurous and beyond the scope of mere recreation. The buddy system continues as an important safety concept for recreational diving.

COMMUNICATIONS

There are many ways for divers to communicate and many signals that are used by divers. Communication means "common understanding." See if you have a common understanding of the ways and means of this quiz topic.

Q:

1. The three primary means of communication for divers are:

A. _____

B. _____

C. _____

2. Ten means of communication between divers underwater are:

A. _____

B. _____

C. _____

D. _____

E. _____

F. _____

G. _____

H. _____

I. _____

J. _____

3. Six ways to signal distress at the surface are:

A. _____

B. _____

C. _____

D. _____

E. _____

F. _____

4. The two basic rules for the use of hand signals are to:

A. _____

B. _____

5. Two signal flags commonly used in diving are:

A. _____

B. _____

6. Eight devices divers in the water can use to communicate include:

A. _____

B. _____

C. _____

D. _____

E. _____

F. _____

G. _____

H. _____

7. Describe how to send each of the following light signals:

A. "OK" _____

B. "Attention" _____

C. "Assistance" _____

8. If you hear a recall signal while underwater, you should:

❏ A. Swim to the boat underwater

❏ B. Remain on the bottom until the "all clear" signal is given

❏ C. Surface and swim to the boat immediately

❏ D. Surface and look to the boat for instructions

9. List the meaning for each of the following number of line pull signals.

A. One pull means _____

B. Two pulls mean _____

C. Three pulls mean _____

D. Four pulls mean _____

E. Five pulls mean _____

10. The emergency communications channels and frequencies are:

A. CB Channel _____

B. VHF Channel ____ or ____ Mhz

C. SSB ____ Mhz

11. When receiving a signal underwater, a diver should first:

❏ A. Repeat the signal to demonstrate understanding

❏ B. Acknowledge that the signal is understood

❏ C. Decide if the indicated action is appropriate

❏ D. Pass the signal along to other divers

12. If trapped underwater with no one in sight, a good way to signal for help would be to _____.

13. When finger spelling "invisible" letters on the palm of your hand to communicate underwater, write _____ and use _____ letters.

14. Diving charter vessels should be equipped with an "EPIRB," which stands for:

E _____

P _____

I _____

R _____

B _____

15. Pounding on the chest with a fist means _____, while a slashing motion across the throat with an open hand means _____.

❏ A. Low on air, out of air

❏ B. Out of air, low on air

❏ C. Give me air, out of air

❏ D. Out of air, give me air

COMMUNICATIONS

A:

What did you learn from this quiz? If you were impressed that there are many ways to send signals, that you need to discuss them with your buddy and agree upon them, and that you should carry with you several means of signaling, you have received the quiz's message. You can acknowledge by taking the actions listed in the preceding sentence. Improved communications means increased enjoyment and safety. Can we get a big "OK" on that?

1. The three primary means of diver communication are audible, visual, and tactile (seeing, hearing, feeling). All forms of diving communications fit into these basic categories.

2. Ten means of communication between divers underwater include hand signals, written messages, sign language, acoustical devices, electronic systems, line pulls, hand squeezes, light flashes, tank tapping, and clicking devices. There are many ways to communicate besides hand signals and tank tapping.

3. Ways to signal distress at the surface include use of the "emergency" hand signal, four or more short bursts with a whistle, calling for help, the firing of a flare, the use of a dye marker, the use of a flashing strobe light at night, the flashing of "S. O. S." with a mask lens or pocket mirror, use of a "rescue tube" or "safety sausage." Throwing water high into the air is also a good method for gaining the attention of people aboard vessels. Smoke bombs can be used, but it is not a good idea for divers to carry these devices.

4. The two basic rules for use of hand signals are to present all signals slowly, clearly, and deliberately and to acknowledge that a signal has been received and understood. It is also recommended that signals to be used while diving be reviewed and agreed upon before diving.

5. The signal flags commonly used in diving are the standard dive flag (red with a white diagonal stripe) and the blue-and-white, swallow-tailed "Alpha" flag. Consideration was given to the recall flag (letter "P"), but a recent survey failed to find any divers who have seen the recall flag used.

6. Devices divers in the water can use to send signals include a **slate and pencil, a whistle, a scuba tank (tapping), a "rescue tube," a signal flare, a marker buoy, a buddy line, a mask lens or mirror (flashes), a dive light, and a strobe light.** One diver can also signal another who is deeper by dropping a small object onto or past the deeper diver.

7. The "OK" signal with a light is a large circle with the light. "Attention" is signaled by moving the light rapidly from side to side. The signal for "assistance" is to move the light rapidly up and down. The vertical distance should be exaggerated when signaling for assistance to distinguish the signal from any bobbing that might occur at the surface.

8. D. Surface and look to the boat for instructions. Charter boats frequently use the recall signal to alert divers when the anchor has slipped and the boat must be moved for reanchoring. The crew wants to make sure all divers are clear of the boat before starting the engine(s). When you hear a recall signal underwater, go directly to the surface rather than going back to the boat underwater.

9. Line pull signals vary. One commonly used set uses one pull to signal "stop," two pulls to signal "OK" or "go," does not use three pulls at all, and uses four pulls to indicate "trouble" or "Come to sender." Another line pull set uses one pull to signal "OK," two pulls to indicate "Go," three pulls to signal "stop," four pulls to signal "up," and five or more pulls to signal "help." What the pulls mean is not as important as agreeing upon them prior to use.

10. Emergency communications channels and frequencies are Channel 9 on CB radio, Channel 16 on VHF (156.8 Mhz), or 2182 Mhz on Single Side Band radio. If a radio is available, make sure it is operable and that you know how to use it in the event of an emergency.

11. B. When a signal is received underwater, the receiver should first acknowledge that the signal is understood. Acknowledgment is indicated by immediate, observable action. The action may be as simple as an "OK" sign or as involved as the donating of air.

12. If trapped underwater with no one in sight, a good way to signal for help is to tap "S.O.S." on your tank. Another way would be to deploy a marker buoy and bob "S.O.S." with the marker. A "rescue tube" from your BC pocket could also be partially inflated, tied off, and sent to the surface. The message is that you should carry several items with you while diving to improve your chances for dealing with various situations.

13. When finger spelling "invisible" letters on the palm of your hand to communicate underwater, write <u>slowly</u> and use <u>large</u> letters. A better alternative is to learn and use the deaf alphabet.

14. "EPIRB" stands for "Emergency Position Indicating Radio Beacon." These devices are designed to float free of a sinking vessel and to transmit an emergency signal when they invert in the water.

15. A. Pounding the chest with a fist means "low on air," while a slashing motion across the throat with an open hand means "out of air." Pointing to the mouth with regulator removed means "give me air." The "out of air" and "give me air" signals are often used in combination.

DIVE PLANNING

You have probably heard the phrase, "Proper planning prevents poor performance," which certainly applies to diving. What is proper planning? How familiar are you with the essentials of the topic? Here are some thought-provoking questions for you.

1. Four problems you can prevent with good dive planning include:
   A. _____
   B. _____
   C. _____
   D. _____

2. Four dive planning benefits are:
   A. _____
   B. _____
   C. _____
   D. _____

3. The first three items to determine when planning a dive are:
   A. _____
   B. _____
   C. _____

4. Arrange in order—from worst to best—the following dive times:
   ❏ A. High tide
   ❏ B. Mid tide on the ebb
   ❏ C. Mid tide on the flood
   ❏ D. Low tide

5. Complete: Dive planning begins when _____ and ends when _____.

6. After determining where you will dive, you and your buddy should:
   ❏ A. Select an alternate dive site
   ❏ B. Check the weather forecast
   ❏ C. Discuss equipment needs
   ❏ D. All the above are correct

7. The time of day you select to dive:
   ❏ A. Can affect visibility and other diving conditions
   ❏ B. Can affect the planned activity
   ❏ C. Can influence site selection
   ❏ D. All the above are correct

8. To prevent equipment problems at the dive site, you should:
   ❏ A. Inspect all equipment in advance
   ❏ B. Pack all equipment using a check list to ensure completeness
   ❏ C. Inspect and inventory equipment at the dive site prior to a dive
   ❏ D. Both A and B, but not C, are correct

9. Just prior to leaving home for a dive, you should:
   ❏ A. Leave information about where you are going and your expected time of return
   ❏ B. Determine where you will be diving and the purpose of the dive
   ❏ C. Make a final check of weather and water conditions, if possible
   ❏ D. Both A and C, but not B, are correct

10. Upon arrival at the dive site, buddies who follow proper dive planning procedures will first:
   ❏ A. Discuss hand signals and communications
   ❏ B. Partially suit up for the dive
   ❏ C. Evaluate the dive conditions
   ❏ D. Discuss emergency procedures

11. Before entering the water for a dive, buddies should:
   ❏ A. Review communications
   ❏ B. Select entry and exit points and the course to be followed
   ❏ C. Discuss buddy system procedures
   ❏ D. All the above are correct

12. Select the false statement. Dive buddies should:
   ❏ A. Agree on limits for time, depth, and air
   ❏ B. Agree on emergency procedures for loss of air supply
   ❏ C. Have different objectives to minimize interference
   ❏ D. Be trained and prepared to handle a dive accident

13. If a dive is well planned and conditions at the selected site are unfavorable, divers should:
   ❏ A. Abort the dive until another day
   ❏ B. Check the conditions at an alternate site
   ❏ C. Either of the above
   ❏ D. None of the above

14. The activity you select for a dive affects the:
   ❏ A. Dive site selection
   ❏ B. Equipment needed
   ❏ C. Dive buddy selection
   ❏ D. All the above

15. Complete: Planning your dives is actually planning your _____.

DIVE PLANNING

Dive planning is important and can make your dives enjoyable, but need not be a large task. By developing habits and using check lists, you can properly plan dives quickly and easily. If you are not already applying the techniques presented in the quiz, try them and see the difference. Always plan your dive, then dive your plan.

1. Problems you can prevent with good dive planning include **accidents, frustration, wasted time, equipment problems, disorientation, separation, and surprises.**

2. Dive planning benefits include **safety, enjoyment, confidence, knowledge of what to expect, and a good success ratio.** The better you plan, the better your chances for success.

3. The first three items to determine when planning a dive are: **(1) The selection of a buddy,** which affects many other decisions. Choose carefully. **(2) Objective,** which is a prime factor. What is the activity? What is the goal? **(3) Location.** Base site selection on team capability, dive objective, season, and water conditions. Select an alternate site also.

4. The best time for a dive (worst to best) is B, C, D, A. Tidal currents are strongest at mid tide. An ebb (outgoing) tide usually carries sediment. A flood (incoming) tide brings cleaner water, but currents may cause problems. Low tide may adversely affect entries, exits, and visibility. High tide usually is the best time. There is no current and visibility is at its best.

5. Dive planning begins when you decide to dive and ends when the dive ends. The plan doesn't end when you enter the water. You use information you receive to plan navigation, exit technique, and more. Always think ahead and anticipate upcoming steps.

6. D. All the above are correct. Select an alternate site you can probably dive if conditions are poor at your primary site. Check the long-range weather forecast. Determine the equipment you need. Agree who will supply common equipment, such as a float, dive flag, and first aid kit.

7. D. All the above are correct. The time of day can affect visibility, water movement, entry and exit techniques, and more. When you plan your dive, consider tides, wind, boat traffic, and sun angle.

8. D. Both A and B, but not C, are correct. If you wait until you reach the dive site to inventory and inspect your equipment, you may discover a problem you cannot solve at the site. A primary purpose of dive planning is to prevent such problems.

9. D. Both A and C, but not B, are correct. File a "float plan" and include information about what to do if you do not return by a certain time. If possible, check conditions at the last minute to prevent a needless trip to the dive site.

10. C. Evaluate the dive conditions. Upon arrival at the dive site, the first step is to check the dive conditions to determine whether or not you should dive. Unless both you and your buddy feel good about the planned dive, seek pleasure elsewhere.

11. All the above are correct. A buddy team should agree on the general pattern of the dive; how they will maintain contact underwater; limits for time, depth, and air; and emergency procedures for loss of air supply. Also review signals and communications.

12. C. Have different objectives to minimize interference. Incorrect. You should have similar objectives so you can remain together and increase your enjoyment by sharing a common interest. The buddy system fails when each diver has a different goal.

13. C. Either of the above. If you can't find a site where conditions are favorable for diving, then postpone the dive until another day or use the time to have fun doing something else. Make all dive experiences enjoyable.

14. D. All the above. The activity you choose, e. g., spear fishing, determines where you will dive, what special equipment you need, and who you select as your dive buddy. The dive objective is a priority topic when you plan a dive.

15. Planning your dives is actually planning your fun, enjoyment, or pleasure. Safety is an acceptable answer. Proper planning helps ensure enjoyment and safety.

DIVING SAFETY RULES

The following safety rules are from diving texts and manuals. Test your safety knowledge by seeing how many of the rules you can complete correctly. Use one word for each blank line.

Complete following sentences. Use one word for each blank line.

1. Never dive _____ .
2. Have scuba tanks and regulators inspected _____ .
3. Know your _____ and dive within them.
4. Begin dives against the _____ .
5. _____ your dive, then dive your _____ .
6. Treat _____ as dangerous weapons.
7. Equalize pressure _____ pain is felt.
8. Display the _____ _____ while diving.
9. Be prepared for _____, which could occur at any time.
10. Know the location of the nearest _____ _____ .
11. Always secure your weight belt with a _____ _____ .
12. Do not use _____ or _____ before diving.
13. Make all recreational scuba dives _____ dives.
14. Do not _____ excessively before breath-hold dives.
15. The maximum recommended depth for recreational dives is _____ feet.
16. Do not _____ or _____ unknown underwater creatures.
17. Have a _____ _____ kit available at the dive site.
18. When ascending with scuba, do not _____ _____ _____ .
19. When in doubt about the symptoms of an illness after diving, consult a _____ _____ .
20. Never attempt to _____ a barotrauma casualty in the water.
21. Do not ascend faster than _____ _____ _____ .
22. Keep track of _____ and _____ to avoid required decompression.

Choose your answers from the following list. You will not use all the choices.

petted, eaten
kick
dive shop
when
begin, reef
intermittently
alone
current
limitations
before
equipment
dive flag
recompression chamber
alcohol, drugs
hyperventilate
touch, disturb
look, listen
recompress
your smallest bubbles
30' per minute
buoyancy compensator
medical facility
time, depth
deep
skipper
storms
belt buckle
sight seeing
100
130
drop weight belt
resuscitate
dive buddy
face mask
current, environment
annually
plan, plan
spearguns
equipment
emergencies
quick release
no-required-decompression
first aid
spare parts
right-hand release
diving physician

DIVING SAFETY RULES

A:

Is your score is greater than 80 percent, you have an excellent knowledge of safety rules. If your score is 70 percent or less, consider a refresher course to review the rules and practices for diving safely.

1. Never dive alone. Dive and remain with a buddy. Always discuss dives in advance with a buddy. Agree on signals, emergency procedures, and limits for time, air, and depth.

2. Have scuba tanks and regulators inspected annually. Maintain your equipment well. Use correct, complete equipment. Have your equipment serviced by qualified technicians.

3. Know your limitations and dive within them. Use good judgment and common sense when you plan dives. Allow a margin of safety. Set reasonable limits for depths, times, and activities. Only dive when you feel well.

4. Begin dives against the current. Know the dive area and conditions. Avoid dangerous places and poor dive conditions. Obtain an orientation to any new dive environment.

5. Plan your dive, then dive your plan. Be prepared. Coordinate emergency procedures. Inform someone of your activity and estimated return time. Discuss final details on location.

6. Treat spearguns as dangerous weapons. Only load and unload spearguns beneath the surface. Do not point a speargun at anyone. Cover spear tips when out of the water. Do not shoot if the spear can travel further than you can see. Use the safety until ready to shoot. Avoid powerheads.

7. Equalize pressure before pain is felt. Equalize pressure early and often. Descend slowly while controlling buoyancy. Never use ear plugs when diving. Do not allow hoods to seal your ears. If you feel pain, ascend until you can equalize pressure.

8. Display the dive flag while diving. Mark the dive area. Dive near your flag. Surface cautiously near your flag. Only display the flag while diving.

9. Be prepared for emergencies, which could occur at any time. Be trained in first aid, CPR, and dive rescue techniques.

Have a dive first aid kit at the site. Have emergency phone numbers. Know how to place an emergency call.

10. Know the location of the nearest medical facility. The Divers Alert Network (DAN) recommends you take an injured diver to a medical facility instead of a recompression chamber because a chamber may not be operational or staffed.

11. Always secure your weight belt with a right-hand release. Have the releases for your scuba unit and weight belt open in opposite directions. Avoid excessive belt length and do not tie or tuck the free end. Pull your weight belt clear of your body for ditching.

12. Do not use drugs or alcohol before diving. Be in good physical condition when you dive. Do not dive if feeling poorly or soon after an illness, operation, or tooth extraction. Learn the adverse effects of drugs and alcohol under pressure and in cold water.

13. Make all recreational scuba dives no-required-decompression dives. Have dive planning devices readily available and use them to avoid required decompression. Know the time limits for the planned time and depth, and the next greater time and depth.

14. Do not hyperventilate excessively before breath-hold dives. Alternate breath-hold dives with a buddy. Avoid holding your breath to the maximum. Test your breath-hold limits cautiously. Maintain a reserve safety margin.

15. The maximum recommended depth for recreational dives is 130 feet. Limit dives to 60 feet. Know the effects of narcosis. Have a specific objective if you dive deep. Recognize the senselessness of depth record attempts. Have redundant breathing equipment for deeper dives.

16. Do not touch or disturb unknown underwater creatures. Be especially careful of anything that is beautiful or ugly. Obtain an orientation to aquatic life in any new environment. Do not injure large animals capable of attacking you.

17. Have a first aid kit available at the dive site. Know what you may need for diving first aid, have the items available, and know how to use them. Be trained in standard first aid and diving first aid. (Second choice: spare parts)

18. When ascending with scuba, do not hold your breath. Always breathe continuously when scuba diving. Be able to do an emergency ascent. Maintain a normal lung volume during an emergency ascent.

19. When in doubt about the symptoms of an illness after diving, consult a diving physician. (Second choice: medical facility.) Do not rationalize ill feeling or pain after diving. Call a local diving physician or the Divers Alert Network. Decompression illness symptoms may occur days after diving.

20. Never attempt to recompress a barotrauma casualty in the water. If possible, have the casualty breathe oxygen and drink water. Obtain medical assistance. Monitor the casualty constantly. Keep a record of times and events.

21. Do not ascend faster than 30' per minute. Thirty fpm is now the maximum rate—slower is better. Time your ascents and learn to gauge the correct rate. Control your buoyancy. Use a reference whenever possible.

22. Keep track of time and depth to avoid required decompression. Keep track of surface intervals also. Know your gauge accuracy. Do not push the maximum time limits.

RESPONSIBLE DIVER PROGRAM

Are you a responsible diver? Are you familiar with the Responsible Diver program? Can you explain the purpose of the program, which a group of concerned leaders introduced to our community in 1991? Can you recall the well-publicized program slogans? Test your knowledge of a program that merits the support of all recreational divers.

Q:

1. The purpose of the responsible diver program is to:
❏ A. Encourage responsible behavior by recreational divers
❏ B. Regulate the behavior of recreational divers
❏ C. Restrict recreational diving activities
❏ D. A and C are correct, but B is incorrect

2. Select all correct statements. The goals of the Responsible Diver program include:
❏ A. Preserving the underwater environment
❏ B. Helping divers understand and assume diving risks
❏ C. Increasing diving safety and enjoyment
❏ D. Encouraging diver training

3. A certified diver's safety is primarily the responsibility of:
❏ A. The instructor who trained the diver
❏ B. The diving operation providing diving services
❏ C. The certified diver
❏ D. All the above equally

4. Complete: As a responsible diver I should dive within the _____ of my ability and training.

5. Complete: I should _____ the conditions before every dive and make sure they fit my personal capabilities.

6. Complete: I should be familiar with and check my _____ before and during every dive.

7. Complete: I should _____ my diving skills under supervision if I have not been diving recently.

8. Complete: When in _____, get out.

9. Complete: Let's respect it, not _____ it.

10. Complete: Never dive deeper than the depth of your _____.

11. Complete: The best regulator on the market is _____ _____ (two words).

12. Complete: Living reefs are _____ not to be touched.

13. Complete: Be aware.... check your _____.

14. Complete: Coral reefs hate _____ _____ (two words).

15. Complete: Only fools _____ the rules.

16. Complete: Just because you are certified doesn't mean you are _____.

17. Complete: Be a reef lover, always _____.

18. Complete: A diver in poor health may be moments away from _____ _____ (two words).

19. Complete: Diving safety is _____ _____ (two words).

RESPONSIBLE DIVER PROGRAM

A:

Do you understand what it means to be a Responsible Diver? Do you support and abide by the program principles? Do you accept the fact that your ultimate safety is your responsibility? It's up to you to make sure that you are in good hands. The best way to ensure that you are in good hands is to be responsible for your diving behavior. Help improve diving's image and safety record. Be a Responsible Diver.

1. A. Encourage responsible behavior by recreational divers. The regulation of recreational diving should be self-regulation. While divers have the right to take risks, they also have a responsibility to understand and assume all the risks associated with their activities and behave in a responsible manner.

2. A, B, C, and D. The dive industry leaders who developed the Responsible Diver program want divers to understand and assume diving risks, be trained and properly equipped for the conditions in which they dive, be healthy and fit when diving, dive within the limits of training and ability, and avoid damaging the underwater environment. The program goals contribute to increased diving safety and enjoyment.

3. C. The certified diver. When you participate in a diving activity, you are under your care, custody and control. Do not blame others for your mistakes. You can refrain from diving when the conditions are beyond your training and ability. You can abort a dive when you feel stressed. It is your duty to monitor your air pressure, decompression status and location. Your safety is your responsibility.

4. As a responsible diver I should dive within the limits of my ability and training. It is all too common for divers to dive deeper than they have been trained or qualified to dive, or to dive in areas or conditions for which they are not trained. Safe diving is no accident. Diving within the limits of your training minimizes the risk of a diving accident.

5. I should evaluate the conditions before every dive and make sure they fit my personal capabilities. When you allow adventure, economics, or peer pressure to make you dive when you know the conditions exceed your abilities—either physical or emotional—you greatly increase the chance of being injured or killed. You take risks when you dive, but you should avoid foolish risks.

6. I should be familiar with and check my equipment before and during every dive. Diving with unfamiliar, ill-fitting, malfunctioning, or incomplete equipment is an excellent way to get into serious trouble while diving. Know your equipment. Be sure it works and fits properly. Use all required and recommended equipment.

7. I should refresh/renew my diving skills under supervision if I have not been diving recently. Many dive operations require supervised dives when a diver has not dived within the past year. A refresher course is a quick, easy way to renew your basic skills. Professional athletes review the basics every year at training camp. CPR skills require annual renewal. Diving safety requires periodic skill updates.

8. When in doubt, get out. When a situation exceeds your capabilities or if you are concerned that it may, abort the dive. Surface, establish buoyancy, and get out. We should commend divers who choose not to dive. Make them feel good about their decision.

9. Let's respect it, not collect it. There are too many divers to support souvenir or specimen collecting at popular dive sites. Many diving destinations today have a look-but-don't touch policy. If every diver took one object per trip, the effect would be environmentally devastating. If you love diving, leave the environment intact.

10. Never dive deeper than the depth of your experience. Dive accidents occur when divers attempt to dive deeper than they are qualified to dive. Recreational divers should not dive deeper than 130 feet and should not dive deeper than 60 feet without training beyond the entry level. After training, increase depth capability in ten foot increments with at least ten logged dives at each depth.

11. The best regulator on the market is common sense. If you want diving to remain a self-regulated activity, regulate your behavior. Avoid deep dives, diving in caves when you are not trained and equipped, and doing repetitive deep dives just because your dive computer says you can. Exercise common sense and be responsible.

12. Living reefs are dying not to be touched. Coral grows slowly. A moment of damage requires years of recovery. Many dive operations now require and enforce no-contact diving. Control your buoyancy, your fin kicks, and your equipment to avoid damaging any living organism while you dive. Do not touch or handle aquatic animals.

13. Be aware. . . . check your air. Running out of air is a leading cause of dive accidents. Excuses for running out of air while diving are as poor as those for running out of gas while driving. Monitor your air supply and remind your buddy to monitor his or hers. Increase the frequency of air supply checks as you increase the depth of your dive.

14. Coral reefs hate standing ovations. See answer #12. Learn to hover, to hold your position without holding on, and to push off with just one carefully-placed finger. Reef wreckers are irresponsible divers.

15. Only fools stretch the rules. A fool, by definition, is one who lacks understanding and reason or lacks powers, which when developed, make for intelligence. Don't be a diving dolt! Seek understanding and develop intelligence through continuing education.

16. Just because you are certified doesn't mean you are qualified. There are enormous differences between certification and qualification. Every day divers with entry-level certifications dive deeper than 60 feet. They are certified to dive, but they are not qualified for deeper diving.

17. Be a reef lover, always hover. See answers #12 and #14.

18. A diver in poor health may be moments away from no health. Health is one of the most important diving considerations. Consider your health and fitness for every dive. Avoid diving under the influence of drugs and medications. Diving enjoyment does not include injuries.

19. Diving safety is no accident. Nearly all accidents are preventable. Learn what to do, then do what you have learned.

OCEAN SURVIVAL

It is common for divers to be in situations where they may need ocean survival skills. Those who seek good dive sites could end up adrift in a boat or in the water. Test your survival techniques knowledge.

1. Select the most important ocean survival item:
- ❏ A. Food
- ❏ B. Water
- ❏ C. A signaling device
- ❏ D. A knife

2. Which of the following is most helpful for dehydration prevention?
- ❏ A. Avoiding seasickness medications
- ❏ B. Refraining from eating unless you have drinking water
- ❏ C. Drinking small quantities of saltwater daily
- ❏ D. All the above practices are helpful

3. Select the signal equipment group that is most desirable for a diver adrift in the ocean:
- ❏ A. Day/night flares, a whistle, and a sea dye marker
- ❏ B. A whistle, flares, and a dive light
- ❏ C. A mirror, a whistle, and a strobe light
- ❏ D. A strobe light, a whistle, and a sea dye marker

4. The most serious in-water problem for a diver stranded in the Caribbean is:
- ❏ A. Exhaustion
- ❏ B. Dehydration
- ❏ C. Hypothermia
- ❏ D. Sharks

5. Which of the following statements concerning fish is correct?
- ❏ A. If a fish swells up, has a box-like shape, or is spiny, you should not eat it
- ❏ B. If fish meat stings your mouth, you should not eat it
- ❏ C. It is safe to eat the skin, head, and roe of all edible fish
- ❏ D. Statements A and B, but not C, are correct

6. Select the incorrect statement:
- ❏ A. All birds are potential food.
- ❏ B. Most seaweed is inedible.
- ❏ C. Eat only small amounts of edible seaweed.
- ❏ D. The juice of fish meat is a food.

7. If you are swept away from shore by a strong current, your best action is/are:
- ❏ A. Establishing buoyancy and waiting for assistance
- ❏ B. Getting neutrally buoyant and tacking across the current while swimming to shore
- ❏ C. Establishing buoyancy, discarding heavy equipment, and waiting for assistance
- ❏ D. Establishing buoyancy, conserving energy, and signaling for assistance

8. Which of the following dive equipment items is not useful for an ocean survival situation?
- ❏ A. The scuba unit
- ❏ B. The weight belt
- ❏ C. Face mask
- ❏ D. All the above items can be useful

9. In the event your boat sinks, you should not:
- ❏ A. Get down wind from the craft to collect debris
- ❏ B. Remain in the vicinity until there is no wreckage visible from the air
- ❏ C. Try to construct a life raft from debris
- ❏ D. All the above statements are correct

10. The single most important factor affecting long-term ocean survival is:
- ❏ A. The water supply
- ❏ B. The food supply
- ❏ C. The will to live
- ❏ D. Exposure protection

OCEAN SURVIVAL

Hopefully you will never have to apply your ocean survival knowledge, but you never know. Always leave a "float plan" with someone. Tell a friend where you are going (exactly), your estimated return time, and what to do if you fail to make contact within a reasonable period of time. (Be sure to contact your friend when you return!) It helps a great deal in a survival situation to know that help will be forthcoming. It is a good idea to keep a small survival kit in your gear bag.

1. B. Water. People can survive for weeks without food, but you become dangerously dehydrated after only a few days without water. If you have a choice of items to take, always choose drinking water. A diver abandoning a boat can put a gallon of water into a buoyancy compensator, which can provide both flotation and drinking water.

2. B. Refraining from eating unless you have drinking water. The U. S. Air Force recommends refraining from food unless you drink two quarts of water per day. Food increases your need for water. The Air Force also has determined that saltwater upsets the body's balance and increases the need for freshwater. Do use seasickness medications if you are prone to motion sickness because vomiting depletes precious body fluids.

3. C. A mirror, a whistle, and a strobe light. All listed signaling devices are valuable. I selected a mirror because reflected light can be seen from a great distance; a whistle because a dehydrated person cannot shout; and a strobe light because the flash can be seen from a great distance at night.

4. C. Hypothermia. The answer depends upon what the diver wears, but the typical diver seldom wears adequate insulation for long-term exposure. The difference between body temperature and water temperature slowly drains heat from an individual and saps life. Learn the Heat Escape Lessening Position (HELP), which minimizes heat loss by protecting vulnerable body areas.

5. D. Statements, A and B, but not C, are correct. Be careful when you eat fish. If you believe a fish is edible, eat only a sliver and wait an hour to see if you have any reaction. If not, eat a small amount and wait 12 hours. If you do not have any symptoms, you may eat the remainder of the fish.

6. B. Most seaweed is inedible. Not so! Two thirds of all seaweed are edible, and most inedible ones taste bad or are indigestible. Test seaweed the way you test fish. If you determine seaweed to be ed-ible, avoid large quantities because seaweed can be violently cathartic. Remember that many edible creatures hide in seaweed.

7. D. Establishing buoyancy, conserving energy, and signaling for assistance. Hopefully someone knows your approximate location and your expected return time. Signal for help before you get swept out of sight. Use the chrome or glass of your mask to reflect sunlight. If you can see people, use whistle blasts to attract attention. A "Dive Alert" air horn accessory is an excellent audible signal.

8. D. All the above items can be useful. The answer is situation dependent. Obviously you should discard heavy items if they cause exhaustion. Whenever possible, however, retain everything. There are scores of survival uses for dive gear. Use your imagination!

9. A. Get down wind from the craft to collect debris. Stay up wind from the wreckage to avoid fuel on the water. Collect everything possible. Construct a raft so you can get out of the water. Some divers have been able to salvage their sunken vessels!

10. C. The will to live. Will power varies from person to person, but often it is the deciding factor in the face of overwhelming odds. People have perished while in relatively good condition just because they gave up hope too soon. Others have survived apparently hopeless situations because they "hung on." Be determined to make it and you will have a better chance of survival.

PRACTICAL PROBLEM SOLVING

Q:

There are numerous problems that can occur while diving. These situations may be deemed emergencies by those who are uninformed or unprepared, but are considered merely nuisances by those who know how to handle them. See how well you can handle the problems contained in this quiz.

1. Your regulator begins free flowing while you are underwater and cannot be stopped. You should:
- ❒ A. Make an emergency swimming ascent
- ❒ B. Make a shared air ascent with your buddy
- ❒ C. Breathe from your free flowing regulator while ascending
- ❒ D. Remove your tank and regulate airflow with the tank valve while ascending

2. Arrange in order, starting with the most desirable, the following options for a loss of your air supply at a depth of 70 feet in cold water. You are wearing a full wet suit and your buddy is 10 feet away looking under a ledge.
- ❒ A. Buddy breathing (sharing one regulator)
- ❒ B. Using buddy's alternate air source (octopus)
- ❒ C. Controlled emergency swimming ascent
- ❒ D. Buoyant emergency swimming ascent

3. Your dive computer is shut off accidentally before its outgassing period is completed and you do not know how much time remained. To continue diving, you should:
- ❒ A. Wait at least 12 hours
- ❒ B. Wait at least 24 hours
- ❒ C. Switch to use of the dive tables
- ❒ D. Wait for the computer outgassing period to expire

4. You begin shivering while diving in cold water. You should:
- ❒ A. Terminate the dive
- ❒ B. Increase activity to increase heat production
- ❒ C. Decrease activity to decrease respiratory heat loss
- ❒ D. Ascend to shallower water to increase insulation

5. The low pressure inflator on your buoyancy compensator (BC) sticks in the open position. The best action is to:
- ❒ A. Disconnect the low pressure inflator hose
- ❒ B. Hold the BC deflator valve open while your buddy turns off your air
- ❒ C. Flare out to increase drag and slow your ascent
- ❒ D. Get a firm hold on a secure object immediately

6. Your BC develops a leak at the dive site and will not hold air. To continue diving, you should:
- ❒ A. Alternate dives using your buddy's BC
- ❒ B. Adjust weight for neutral buoyancy at planned depth
- ❒ C. Obtain another BC from the nearest source
- ❒ D. Make a temporary repair to your BC

7. You surface from a cold dive two miles from an uninhabited island and your charter boat is nowhere in sight. You should:
- ❒ A. Wait for the boat to return
- ❒ B. Swim slowly and steadily toward the island
- ❒ C. Swim slowly against a mild current to maintain position
- ❒ D. Signal for help

8. You surface in a thick fog after a shore dive from the coast. It was clear and sunny when you descended. List at least four natural aids to navigation that would indicate the direction of shore.
- A. _____
- B. _____
- C. _____
- D. _____

9. You rent a BC and discover at the dive site that your low pressure inflator hose does not match the BC inflator connector. You should:
- ❒ A. Obtain another BC before diving
- ❒ B. Proceed to dive and manually inflate the BC
- ❒ C. Alternate dives using your buddy's BC
- ❒ D. Temporarily attach your buddy's BC inflator hose to your BC when inflation is required while diving

10. Select all correct answers and arrange them in order. While diving from a charter boat you become separated from your buddy and cannot locate him after searching briefly on the bottom and then surfacing. You should:
- ❒ A. Mark the last known location of your buddy
- ❒ B. Alert the boat that your buddy is missing
- ❒ C. Remain at the surface until your buddy is located
- ❒ D. Continue searching underwater

PRACTICAL PROBLEM SOLVING

You can minimize problems through proper dive planning and preparation, but you cannot avoid them completely. You need to be prepared to cope with difficulties. Continuing education is an excellent means of increasing your preparedness. Completion of an advanced or specialty course will make you a better diver in many ways and help you solve problems.

1. C. Breathe from your free flowing regulator while ascending. A free flowing regulator can overpressurize your lungs if the regulator is left in your mouth, but if it is removed, it is possible to breathe from it safely by pressing your lips lightly against the mouthpiece. Breathe only what you need while allowing the excess air to escape.

2. B, A, D, C. An alternate air source permits a normal ascent. A buddy breathing ascent is preferred as the second option if you and your buddy are proficient with this skill. Otherwise the next best option is a buoyant emergency ascent. A controlled emergency swimming ascent is the least desirable option owing to the depth and circumstances. Since the option varies with the situation, it is important to discuss and agree upon emergency procedures prior to each dive.

3. D. Wait for the computer outgassing period to expire. Some dive computers require as long as 18 hours for outgassing. To be safe, you should not dive again for the length of time specified by the manufacturer for the computer to outgas completely. Since computers continuously calculate multi-level dives, switching to dive tables is not feasible.

4. A. Terminate the dive. This is a basic rule of diving. Shivering is a sign of significant drop in the core temperature of your body. This heat cannot be replaced with continued diving, but will, in fact, result in further heat loss and lead to more severe symptoms of hypothermia. When shivering starts, diving stops.

5. A. Disconnect the low pressure inflation hose. This the best choice listed. An even better action is to hold the BC deflator up and open while disconnecting the hose. Eliminating the inflation source is much safer than dealing with a lot of excess buoyancy.

6. C. Obtain another BC from the nearest source. Repairs to BCs should be made only by professionals. A BC is a required piece of equipment for scuba diving. Alternating dives using your buddy's BC is not safe or practical. No matter how great

the inconvenience, you should get another BC before diving.

7. A. Wait for the boat to return. If you swim to the island, the returning boat may not locate you. Swimming against even a mild current wastes energy you may need later. Signaling for help is futile given the circumstances. The best action is to wait. If, after several hours, the boat does not return, you should then opt to swim to the island.

8. Fog moves toward a land mass. Shore sounds or breaking surf may be heard. Swells move landward. If you have air remaining, you can redescend and check the surge, which is stronger in the direction of shore. The slope on sand ripples is sharper on the side toward shore. Depth tends to decrease toward shore.

9. B. Proceed to dive and manually inflate the BC. Basic training includes oral inflation of a BC. Divers manually inflated BCs for many years before low pressure inflators were available. Inflator mechanisms make diving easier and safer and are strongly recommended for use, but you should not become so dependent upon them you cannot dive without one.

10. A, B. When your buddy cannot be located, first take a "fix" of his or her last known position. This is important because you may drift away from the area while trying to gain the attention of the boat. Next, alert the crew that your buddy is missing. You should not do any more searching underwater alone. If you remain at the surface until your buddy is located, you may have a very long wait. Follow instructions given by the boat captain.

DIVING SAFETY

How safe a diver are you? The following self-evaluation quiz serves as a review of safety practices and allows you to rate yourself. Additionally, the quiz reminds us of actions we should take or avoid. Check for each question the response that best describes your usual behavior. Compare your conduct to that of the average diver. Be honest with yourself.

Indicate the frequency with which you:

	Never	Seldom	Usually	Always
1. Exercise regularly to maintain diving fitness	❑	❑	❑	❑
2. Practice and review basic diving skills	❑	❑	❑	❑
3. Practice and review diving emergency procedures	❑	❑	❑	❑
4. Upgrade your knowledge and certification level	❑	❑	❑	❑
5. Dive with a buddy and remain together underwater	❑	❑	❑	❑
6. End a dive at a pre-determined point	❑	❑	❑	❑
7. Inspect your equipment prior to going diving	❑	❑	❑	❑
8. Inspect your buddy's equipment before a dive	❑	❑	❑	❑
9. Learn and renew first aid and CPR skills	❑	❑	❑	❑
10. Have your equipment serviced as recommended	❑	❑	❑	❑
11. Fly the dive flag while diving	❑	❑	❑	❑
12. Are confident of a dive and dive within your abilities	❑	❑	❑	❑
13. Abort a dive when conditions are unfavorable	❑	❑	❑	❑
14. Get an orientation to a new dive site	❑	❑	❑	❑
15. Plan a dive with your buddy	❑	❑	❑	❑
16. Dive your plan	❑	❑	❑	❑
17. Make a safety decompression stop at the end of a dive	❑	❑	❑	❑
18. Acquire local emergency contact information	❑	❑	❑	❑
19. Dive neutrally weighted	❑	❑	❑	❑
20. Surface when unable to locate your buddy	❑	❑	❑	❑
21. End a dive with more than 300 psi in your tank	❑	❑	❑	❑
22. Dive with back-up equipment for out-of-air situations	❑	❑	❑	❑
23. Keep an accurate record of bottom time and depth	❑	❑	❑	❑
24. Dive with timer, depth gauge, compass, and SPG	❑	❑	❑	❑
25. Rinse and store your dive equipment properly	❑	❑	❑	❑
26. Consult a dive planning device before a dive	❑	❑	❑	❑
27. Consult weather/water conditions before a dive	❑	❑	❑	❑
28. Dive within the no-required-decompression limits	❑	❑	❑	❑
29. Avoid diving under the influence of alcohol or drugs	❑	❑	❑	❑
30. Avoid ascending faster than 30 feet per minute	❑	❑	❑	❑
31. Dive with an ailment, e. g., a cold	❑	❑	❑	❑
32. Dive deeper than qualified or below 130 feet	❑	❑	❑	❑
33. Push depth time limits to the maximum limit	❑	❑	❑	❑
34. Force equalization of ears or sinuses	❑	❑	❑	❑
35. Experience air starvation from overexertion U/W	❑	❑	❑	❑
36. Dive with a broken or missing equipment item	❑	❑	❑	❑
37. Skip breathe to extend your air supply	❑	❑	❑	❑
38. Dive alone	❑	❑	❑	❑
39. End a dive down current from planned exit point	❑	❑	❑	❑
40. Plan dives that require decompression	❑	❑	❑	❑

EVALUATION - DIVING SAFETY

Diving safety is an attitude more than anything else. The way you feel about safety affects your thoughts on the subject. Your thoughts—in turn—affect your actions. A basic desire to follow established safety practices is a necessary component. When you want to dive safely, doing so is merely a matter of learning what to do and what not to do and putting it into practice. Knowledge and the proper application of knowledge yield the fruits of enjoyable, accident-free dives. You do not need to be a safety "nut" nor wear hard-toed booties to avoid accidents. Much of diving safety is common sense.

Rate yourself as follows: Draw a line between questions 30 and 31. For questions 1 through 30, count the number of Always responses and credit yourself with four points each. Usually responses count two points; Seldom responses one point. You receive no points for a Never answer. Score Questions 31 through 40 in reverse. An Always is zero points; Usually is one point, Seldom two points; and Never four points. Total your points for the quiz, then compare your score to the following chart:

- **81 points or more**—An extremely responsible diver. Congratulations!
- **71-80 points**—A safety conscious diver
- **61-70 points**—An average diver who takes some risks
- **55-60 points**—A daring diver who should reconsider some practices
- **49-54 points**—A probable accident candidate
- **48 points or less**—An accident waiting for a place to happen!

Recommendations:
1. Be prepared to dive—physically, emotionally, and logistically. Regular exercise—something that approximates diving—is important so you can maintain fitness. Have your equipment serviced annually and maintain it carefully. Use all needed equipment for diving. Don't improvise for missing items. Do not loan your scuba equipment to anyone not certified to dive.

2. Be prepared to handle problems. Review skills and emergency procedures periodically. Have current First Aid and CPR training. Have back-up scuba for out-of-air situations. Know your buddy. Discuss and agree upon emergency procedures before you dive together. Inspect each other's equipment and be familiar with its operation. Dive together, decreasing separation distance and depth increases. Let diving be a sharing caring experience. Maximize enjoyment and safety.

3. Consult a dive planning device for all dives deeper than 30 feet. Limit depth according to your training level and experience. Dive shallower than 130 feet. Ascend at 30 feet per minute or less. Al-ways have a margin of safety. Decompress for several minutes as a precaution at the end of every dive. Add your safety stop time to your bottom time as a safety margin.

4. Know the site you dive or get an orientation to the area. Evaluate the diving conditions before each dive and abort the dive if the conditions are hazardous. Know area hazards and how to avoid problems. Respect the environment. Have local emergency contact information.

5. Dive wisely and conservatively. Stick to agreed upon plans. Think ahead. Be aware, consulting your instruments frequently. Fly the dive flag and dive and surface near your flag. Terminate your dive when you are cold or tired. End your dive near the exit point and with at least 300 psi in your tank. Avoid diving overweighted.

6. Breathe properly. Avoid overexertion in and underwater. Absolutely avoid skip breathing and scuba breath-holding. If you experience difficulty, stop all activity, breathe or attempt to breathe, analyze the situation, then calmly follow a plan.

7. Don't dive when ill and don't force equalization. Avoid excessive use of medications, e.g., decongestants. Refrain from alcohol and drug use when you plan to dive. Equalize pressure in your ears every few feet during descents. Avoid forceful equalization attempts. Feel confident about diving. Readiness, health and good planning are accident avoidance essentials.

8. Be trained for specialty activities or environments. Complete a refresher course every two years. Participate in continuing education courses to increase your diving ability, confidence, and enjoyment. Keep current with new developments by reading books and magazines and attending programs.

U.S. DIVE FLAGS

$Q\!:$

Boats injure many divers each year. Have you had any close calls? How good is your knowledge of dive flag regulations and diving procedures? Do you know your local dive flag regulations? How similar are dive flag laws nationwide? To test your knowledge of dive flags and boat avoidance procedures, answer the following questions.

1. The number of states in the United States that have dive flag requirements is:
❒ A. 50
❒ B. 42
❒ C. 34
❒ D. 29

2. According to state regulations, the minimum distance a boat must maintain from a dive flag ranges from ____ to ____ feet.
A. 50, 100
B. 50, 300
C. 100, 200
D. 100, 300

3. According to state regulations, the maximum distance a diver may range from a dive flag is ____ to ____ feet.
❒ A. 25, 100
❒ B. 50, 100
❒ C. 50, 200
❒ D. 25, 300

4. The purpose of the traditional red-and-white dive flag is to:
❒ A. Protect divers from boats
❒ B. Warn boaters there are divers below
❒ C. Warn boaters there are divers in the area
❒ D. Keep boats at least 100 feet from a marked location

5. The purpose of the blue-and-white, swallow-tailed "Alpha" flag is to:
❒ A. Warn boaters there are divers below
❒ B. Warn boaters there are divers in the area
❒ C. Warn boaters that the flagged vessel cannot maneuver
❒ D. Warn boaters of divers in international waters

6. Boating courses routinely teach the meaning of dive flags.
❒ A. True
❒ B. False

7. If you are surfacing from a dive and a boat comes toward you at a speed of ten knots, the length of time from when you could see the boat (assume horizontal visibility of 50 feet) until it passed directly overhead is about:
❒ A. 30 seconds
❒ B. 10 seconds
❒ C. 5 seconds
❒ D. 3 seconds

8. According to the USCG Auxiliary statistics, the average number of recreational boating accidents involving swimmers and divers per year is:
❒ A. 16
❒ B. 32
❒ C. 46
❒ D. 78

9. Most boating accidents involving scuba divers occur when the diver is:
❒ A. Ascending
❒ B. Swimming just beneath the surface
❒ C. Swimming at the surface
❒ D. Both A and B are correct

10. Due to height advantage and exhaust bubbles, boaters can easily see divers beneath the surface of the water.
❒ A. True
❒ B. False

11. List four procedures to avoid being struck by a boat while scuba diving.
A. _____
B. _____
C. _____
D. _____

12. To increase safety for swimmers and divers, the National Boating Safety Advisory Council (NBSAC) has recently recommended to the U.S. Coast Guard that recreational vessels be equipped with propeller guards.
❒ A. True
❒ B. False

13. Many boats used for scuba diving have the traditional red-and-white dive flag displayed at all times. Flying the flag continuously is:
❒ A. Desirable because it informs observers that the boat is a dive boat
❒ B. Desirable because it eliminates the need to hoist and lower the dive flag
❒ C. Undesirable because it reduces the effectiveness of the dive flag
❒ D. Undesirable because it is against federal regulations

14. Fines to divers who fail to abide by dive flag regulations range from $____ to $____.
❒ A. 5, 100
❒ B. 5, 1,000
❒ C. 25, 200
❒ D. 20, 300

15. Your best source of information for dive flag regulations in your area is:
❒ A. Your local diving professional
❒ B. The U. S. Coast Guard District Office
❒ C. The State Department of Boating and Waterways
❒ D. Any of the above

U.S. DIVE FLAGS

We have a dive flag regulation problem in the United States. I believe the regulations are inadequate, are not enforced, and need to be standardized at the federal level by the U.S. Coast Guard. When a boat propeller strikes a diver, severe damage results. Since we are on the receiving end of these accidents, we need to strive to obtain improved boater education about dive flags and improved dive flag regulations. No matter how much you know about dive flags, bear in mind that they do not afford you protection. Use them correctly to warn boaters, but do not rely on them. Surface defensively.

1. B. 42. Based upon surveys by the Minnesota Department of Natural Resources and NAUI, the following states do not require divers to have dive flags: Arizona, Delaware, Georgia, Maine, Maryland, Oregon, Pennsylvania, and Wyoming. (Some states, such as Georgia, say divers may use flags.) If you are aware of dive flag requirements in these states, please send information to me c/o Aqua Quest Publications.

2. B. 50, 300. Eight states have a minimum boat distance of 50 feet; three specify 75 feet; seven specify 100 feet; seven specify 150 feet; two specify 200 feet; and one specifies 300 feet in open water. The diving industry standard is for divers to remain within 100 feet of a dive flag. As you can see, a diver 100 feet from a flag is in jeopardy in at least 18 states.

3. D. 25, 300. New Jersey requires divers to surface within 25 feet of the dive flag except in an emergency. Seven states specify a distance of 50 feet; South Dakota specifies 75 feet; four specify 100 feet; two specify 150 feet. Arkansas allows a maximum diver distance of 300 feet.

4. C. Warn boaters there are divers in the area. The idea that the flag means "Divers below" is inaccurate. Danger to divers is at or near the surface, not on the bottom. Captions in books that specify the meaning must be revised to read, "Divers in the area."

5. C. Warn boaters that the flagged vessel cannot maneuver. The "Alpha" flag means, "I am engaged in underwater operations and cannot maneuver my vessel to comply with the rules of the road." Its meaning is entirely different than that of the traditional red-and-white dive flag. When you dive from a boat, display both flags. When you dive from shore in the U.S., display the red-and-white flag.

6. B. False. There is more information about dive flags in boating books than there used to be, but not all boating course instructors teach the meaning of dive flags. Instructors tell me frequently that they completed boating courses where the flag was not addressed. When

you take a boating course, ask the instructor to include dive flags in the curriculum.

7. D. 3 seconds! One knot is 100 feet per minute, or about 1.67 feet per second. At ten knots, a boat covers about 16.7 feet per second. The point is that looking for oncoming boats while surfacing may not be effective for preventing injury, especially in limited visibility.

8. C. 46. According to the USCG Auxiliary Department of Boating and Consumer Affairs report of recreational boating accidents with swimmer or diver involvement for the years 1985 through 1989, there were 231 accidents with 26 of them fatal. The average of 46 accidents per year does not seem like a significant number except that the Coast Guard estimates, "we receive only 1-10 percent of the nonfatal accident reports." Boating accidents are a serious problem for divers in the United States.

9. D. Both A and B are correct. Of the many accident reports I have reviewed involving divers hit by boats, I know of only one instance in which a diver was injured while swimming at the surface. The worst action a diver can take is to skim—swim just beneath the surface—to avoid surface swimming and extend a supply of air. When you are just beneath the surface of the water, you are difficult to see.

10. B. False. Many factors impede the ability of the operator of a vessel to see a diver underwater. Boat design, glare, surface chop, aquatic plants, and currents that move ascending bubbles are just a few of the problems that boaters encounter. I am aware of several accidents where divers were struck while boating operators were looking for the divers.

11. Procedures you should follow to avoid being struck by a boat while scuba diving are:

  • **Displaying a dive flag**
  • **Surfacing as close to the flag as possible**
  • **Ascending slowly while looking up and around**
  • **Looking and listening for boats while**

making a precautionary decompression stop at a depth of 15 feet
  • **Immediately making a full rotation upon surfacing to scan the area for approaching vessels**
  • **Having neutral buoyancy at the moment of surfacing so you can exhale and sink immediately, if necessary**

12. B. False. NBSAC did submit a propeller guard report to the USCG in November, 1989, but the report recommended the "Coast Guard should take no regulatory action to require propeller guards." There were many reasons cited, but the most convincing one was that use of guards can be "counter-productive and create new hazards of equal or greater consequences."

13. C. Undesirable because it reduces the effectiveness of the dive flag. A flag painted on a boat means the vessel is a dive boat. A flag flying free means divers are engaged in diving operations in the area. Diving boaters should display free-flying dive flags only while people are diving. Boats with hoisted dive flags and underway or tied in a slip reduce the effectiveness of the dive flag.

14. B. 5, 1,000. New Mexico has a diver penalty ranging from $5.00 to $100.00. If you violate dive flag laws in Utah, you may be fined $1,000.00! Seven states also permit jail times ranging from thirty days to six months! You may incur serious penalties if you fail to comply with state regulations. Boaters are subject to similar penalties for violations.

15. C. The State Department of Boating and Waterways. While your local diving professional is a good source of diving information, he or she may not be an authority about dive flag laws. You need to see your state regulations in writing. Request a copy of the regulation from your state boating office. You may be surprised to find that what you are supposed to do is not the local diving practice.

SECTION EIGHT

□□□□□□□□

Diving Skills

Diving Skills

The purpose of training is to impart to divers the knowledge and skills they need to dive and avoid injury. Divers learn basic skills, advanced skills, regional skills, and specialized skills. You have a responsibility to yourself and to the dive community to dive within the limitations of your training. It is not uncommon for divers to dive in conditions and circumstances for which they lack the prerequisite skills.

What skills do you need beyond the basic ones you learned when you were certified? You need to be proficient in buoyancy control, with a variety of entries and exits, emergency skills, navigation, ascents, and self rescue. You may believe you have learned these skills because they are fundamental. Don't be surprised, however, if you do not score well on some of the quizzes in this section because they test a higher level of skill knowledge than that usually taught to beginning divers.

Buoyancy control is perhaps the single most important diving skill. There is much more to controlling buoyancy than wearing enough lead to sink and adding enough air to your BC to achieve neutral buoyancy at depth. Buoyancy control loss causes dive accidents. Adjust your weighting for every new diving situation. Learn to sense buoyancy changes quickly and respond to them effectively without over-reacting.

Acquiring essential skills is only the first step toward diving safety. The second step is to dive regularly. The third step is to practice critical skills frequently to maintain an acceptable proficiency level. The fourth step is to review the skills with each and every new dive buddy. Few divers probably take all four steps on the safety ladder, which is an inverse ladder—the lower you are on the ladder, the harder you land if you lose your grip.

ASCENTS

An ascent is one of the most deceiving diving skills. The task seems simple, but it is one of the most difficult you face as a diver. In my opinion, few divers ascend correctly. Test your knowledge of this important skill by taking the quiz.

Q:

1. Select the statement that best describes the correct rate of ascent for recreational divers.
- ❏ A. Ascend no faster than your smallest bubbles.
- ❏ B. Ascend at a slow rate and make a precautionary ("safety") decompression stop.
- ❏ C. Time your ascent so your progress is no faster than one foot/second.
- ❏ D. The nearer you are to the surface, the slower your rate of ascent should be.

2. The "normal" ascent rate of recreational divers has been found to be:
- ❏ A. 40-60 feet per minute
- ❏ B. 60-80 feet per minute
- ❏ C. 80-120 feet per minute
- ❏ D. 120-200 feet per minute

3. A precautionary decompression stop should be done whenever possible at the end of:
- ❏ A. Every dive
- ❏ B. Every dive in excess of 40 feet
- ❏ C. Every dive in excess of 60 feet
- ❏ D. Any dive that approaches the maximum time limits

4. The more times you surface during a dive to a given depth for a given period of time, e.g., three times during 20 minutes from 100 feet, the more likely you are to develop decompression sickness.
- ❏ A. True because excess nitrogen forms bubbles each time you ascend
- ❏ B. True because the ascent time contributes to nitrogen absorption
- ❏ C. False because the total time spent at depth is the same in both instances
- ❏ D. False because you eliminate excess nitrogen each time you ascend

5. A series of partial ascents during a dive (a sawtooth profile) is:
- ❏ A. Not a factor as long as the depth excursions do not exceed 30 feet
- ❏ B. Desirable
- ❏ C. Undesirable
- ❏ D. Permitted only with British dive-tables

6. List nine actions you should take when doing a correct scuba diving ascent.
- A. _____
- B. _____
- C. _____
- D. _____
- E. _____
- F. _____
- G. _____
- H. _____
- J. _____

7. The correct state of buoyancy throughout a normal scuba diving ascent is:
- ❏ A. Slightly positive
- ❏ B. Neutral
- ❏ C. Slightly negative
- ❏ D. Slightly positive at the beginning and slightly negative at the end

8. The optimum way to maintain the correct state of buoyancy during a scuba diving ascent is to:
- ❏ A. Vent your BC completely before leaving the bottom
- ❏ B. Vent your BC periodically during ascent
- ❏ C. Vent your BC continuously during ascent
- ❏ D. Add air to your BC to initiate your ascent, then vent it during ascent

9. If you are sharing air with another diver during an ascent, you should share air until you:
- ❏ A. Feel confident you can reach the surface alone
- ❏ B. Can breathe again from your scuba unit
- ❏ C. Reach the surface
- ❏ D. Feel like you are not getting enough air

10. If you breathe all the air possible from your scuba cylinder at depth, your breathing during an independent emergency ascent should be:
- ❏ A. A continuous exhalation
- ❏ B. A continuous sound
- ❏ C. As near normal as possible
- ❏ D. A continuous exhalation that increases in volume as the depth decreases

11. During an ascent in which you use a dry suit and a buoyancy compensator you should:
- ❏ A. Vent the BC at the bottom and control the ascent with the air in the dry suit
- ❏ B. Vent the dry suit at the bottom and control the ascent with the air in the BC
- ❏ C. Vent both the BC and the dry suit at the bottom and swim to the surface
- ❏ D. Vent both the BC and the dry suit throughout the ascent

12. The preferred position for two divers to maintain with respect to one another during an ascent is:
- ❏ A. One slightly above the other
- ❏ B. One well above the other
- ❏ C. Both divers at the same level
- ❏ D. Not specified

13. Arrange the following ascent completion techniques in the correct sequence:
- ❏ A. Partially inflate your BC to establish positive buoyancy
- ❏ B. Survey the surrounding area
- ❏ C. Exchange regulator for snorkel
- ❏ D. If diving from a charter boat, give an "OK" signal

14. Arrange the ascents in order from most desirable to least desirable.
- ❏ A. A slow, vertical ascent following an ascent line
- ❏ B. A slow, vertical ascent without a line
- ❏ C. A slow, diagonal ascent following bottom contours
- ❏ D. A slow, diagonal ascent following an anchor line

ASCENTS

A:

If you missed more than five questions, you should study this quiz carefully until you are familiar with the procedures it describes. When you know what to do, practice the techniques until you are able to ascend at the correct rate, with the correct buoyancy, and following all procedures recommended. The most serious injuries of diving occur from improper ascents. When you control your ascents and incorporate the recommended techniques, you increase your safety substantially. If you scored well on the exam and actually follow the practices described, congratulations for being an exemplary diver.

1. B. Ascend at a slow rate and make a precautionary decompression stop. Your ascent rate should not exceed that specified for the computer or dive table you use, but should not be greater than 30 feet per minute. It is difficult to ascend slowly without an instrument to show when your rate is too rapid. Bubbles are not a reliable indicator. A precautionary stop compensates for errors in your rate of ascent.

2. D. 120-200 feet per minute. Years ago the University of Washington did a study of recreational divers and determined an average ascent rate two to nearly four times the maximum recommended rate! My personal observations over the years indicate a slight improvement, but I am confident the majority of divers today still exceed an ascent rate of 60 feet per minute. Slow down!

3. A. Every dive. Unless there is a strong current or the depth of the dive is less than 15 feet, you should do a precautionary decompression stop at the end of every dive. Why should you if there is no decompression obligation? The pause is practice so you will be able to stop when you do need to decompress. The stop also ensures buoyancy control and corrects a rate of ascent that was too rapid.

4. A. True because excess nitrogen forms bubbles each time you ascend. Ascending causes bubble formation. The bubbles usually do not cause decompression sickness when you are within dive time limits. When you form bubbles, redescend, then ascend again, you increase the load of bubbles in your system. Several ascents and descents can give you decompression sickness even though your total dive time may be well within dive time limits. Keep ascents to a minimum during dives.

5. C. Undesirable. Dive planning devices are not designed to accommodate "sawtooth" dives. The best profile is deep to shallow. Dive to your deepest depth first, then work your way progressively shallower during your dive. The British dive tables expressly prohibit sawtooth dives. When you make multiple vertical excursions up and down a reef, wreck, or wall while diving, you cause physiological changes that are beyond the scope of any dive planning device.

6. Actions you should take when doing an ascent as a scuba diver:
   A. Signal the ascent or acknowledge the signal
   B. Hold your BC inflation/deflation controls continuously
   C. Look up
   D. Reach up
   E. Rotate and view the surrounding area
   F. Maintain neutral buoyancy
   G. Maintain buddy contact
   H. Monitor your instrumentation
   J. Pause at a depth between 10 and 30 feet

7. B. Neutral. The most common ascent procedure is periodic venting of the BC. Occasional venting is not the optimum procedure because your buoyancy fluctuates throughout an ascent. An "open valve" BC ascent (see next answer) allows you to maintain neutral buoyancy continuously. Avoid "elevator" (positive buoyancy) ascents. If your buoyancy is correct, you should be able to stop an ascent at any time if you stop swimming and exhale.

8. C. Vent your BC continuously during ascent. If you hold your BC valve open with the mouthpiece pointing down and at the same level as the opening in the shoulder of your BC, expanding air will escape while buoyancy remains constant. An "open valve" ascent is the optimum way to control buoyancy while ascending. Try it!

9. C. Reach the surface. I have reviewed accident reports where an emergency resulted in an injury or fatality because one member of a buddy team broke away while sharing air during ascent. As long as you can obtain air from a buddy, remain with him during a shared-air ascent.

10. C. As near normal as possible. When you exhale continuously during an ascent, you collapse small airways in your lungs and can trap air in portions of your lungs. You could have a lung overexpansion in-jury in spite of continuous exhalation. When you make a sound, your vocal chords reduce air flow by as much as 50 percent. The optimum breathing pattern for an emergency ascent is as close to normal as possible. Exhale slowly, attempt to inhale through your regulator, then exhale again. As ambient pressure decreases, you will be able to breathe some air from your scuba tank.

11. D. (Vent both the BC and the dry suit throughout the ascent) is the optimum procedure if you can do it. You need to have an automatic exhaust valve on your dry suit (manufacturers and training organizations recommend automatic valves) and the valve needs to be located on the upper portion of your left arm. You then can hold your left upper arm up while doing the "open valve" BC ascent technique. You can maintain continuous neutral buoyancy during ascents with a dry suit and a BC.

12. C. Both divers at the same level. Ideally buddies will be eye level to each other throughout an ascent. I am aware of several accidents that occurred because one buddy was ahead of the other while ascending. Buddies can and should observe and caution each other while ascending. You can see things your buddy cannot see and vice versa.

13. B, D, A, C. Divers get injured by boats just before or right after they surface. Before you establish positive buoyancy, turn and survey the water in all directions. If there is a boat approaching, all you have to do is exhale and sink. You can signal you are OK while you turn. When you've determined the area is clear, inflate your BC and switch to your snorkel.

14. C, A, D, B. The point is that ascents with a physical means of control are better than free ascents where you do not have something to aid control. If you can follow gradual, sloping bottom contours for a diagonal ascent to your exit point, that is ideal. A vertical, weighted line—an ascent line—is better than a less stable anchor line. The use of a line is better than a free ascent. Control your ascent whenever possible.

BUOYANCY CONTROL

Q:

For years the diving community has emphasized buoyancy control. Most divers think buoyancy control means maintaining neutral buoyancy. What is the correct way to determine neutral buoyancy? If you are neutrally buoyant, are you doing all you need to do to control your buoyancy? What are the differences in buoyancy control between wet suit diving and dry suit diving? See if your contemporary knowledge of this important subject is what it should be. Answer the following questions before reviewing the answers.

1. The three primary means of buoyancy control are:

A. _____

B. _____

C. _____

2. You should evaluate your weight requirements and adjust for neutral buoyancy when your scuba tank is:

❏ A. Full

❏ B. Half full

❏ C. Nearly empty

❏ D. At any pressure

3. The difference in your weighting requirement for freshwater diving compared to saltwater diving is about 3%:

❏ A. Less than the amount of weight in your weighting system

❏ B. Less than the total weight of you and all your equipment

❏ C. More than the amount of weight in your weighting system

❏ D. More than the total weight of you and all your equipment

4. The air in a scuba cylinder can affect your buoyancy by as much as:

❏ A. 3 pounds

❏ B. 5 pounds

❏ C. 8 pounds

❏ D. 15 pounds

5. True or false. Your level of physical or emotional stress affects your buoyancy significantly.

❏ A. True

❏ B. False

6. For divers trained and experienced with both wet suit diving and dry suit diving, buoyancy control with a dry suit is:

❏ A. More difficult than with a wet suit

❏ B. Less difficult than with a wet suit

❏ C. About the same difficulty as wet suit diving

7. If you have buoyant legs and feet, the best way to keep them down while diving is:

❏ A. Ankle weights worn around the ankles

❏ B. Ankle weights worn just above the knee

❏ C. Wearing the weight system lower on the body

❏ D. All of the above are equally effective

8. For an ascent with buoyancy that is neutral continuously, the exhaust valve on your BC should be:

❏ A. Opened to vent the BC before ascending

❏ B. Open throughout an ascent

❏ C. Opened from time to time during an ascent.

❏ D. Opened momentarily after each 15 feet of ascent.

9. If you find yourself floating to the surface and are unable to vent air from your BC, you should:

❏ A. Invert yourself and attempt to swim down

❏ B. Cut your BC with your dive knife

❏ C. Arch back and flare your body as much as possible

❏ D. Keep breathing and ride out the ascent

10. If your BC power inflation valve sticks when you add air to your BC while underwater, you should:

❏ A. Quickly grasp something on the bottom to hold yourself down while you solve the problem

❏ B. Swim downward while trying to solve the problem

❏ C. Vent your BC continuously while trying to solve the problem

❏ D. Vent your BC while disconnecting the low pressure hose

11. Select all incorrect statements.

❏ A. Buoyancy changes with depth are less for a dry suit diver than for a wet suit diver.

❏ B. If a wet suit diver loses a weight belt at a depth of 30 feet or deeper, the diver will speed to the surface out of control.

❏ C. When making a deep dive in a wet suit you should wear throughout the dive the amount of weight you will need for neutral buoyancy at the decompression stop at the end of the dive.

❏ D. For safety reasons it is essential that the weight a diver wears be contained within one system on one part of the body.

12. The correct amount of weight for scuba diving is:

❏ A. About 10% of your body weight plus four pounds when you wear a full wet suit

❏ B. The amount that enables you to hover motionless at a depth of 15 feet when you have about 300 psi of air in your cylinder and no air in your BC

❏ C. The amount that enables you to float at the surface with a full breath and sink when you exhale when your tank is full and your BC is empty

❏ D. Any of the above

BUOYANCY CONTROL

A:

How is your buoyancy control knowledge? If you answered all 12 questions correctly, you qualify as an expert diver provided you do what you know. If you answered five or more questions incorrectly, consider improving your buoyancy control knowledge and skills. Buoyancy control is critical for your safety and enjoyment and for the preservation of the diving environment. If you want to test and improve your buoyancy control skills, ask your diving retailer for an opportunity to challenge the Buoyancy Training System International "Diamond Reef" buoyancy course.

1. The three primary means of buoyancy control are: (1) the amount of weight you wear, (2) the amount of air in your buoyancy compensator, and (3) the amount of air in your lungs. As you will see in the remainder of this quiz, there are important relationships between these means of buoyancy control. Neutral buoyancy and buoyancy control are not necessarily synonymous.

2. C. Nearly empty. Many divers learned during entry-level training to evaluate buoyancy while wearing a full tank. That method is acceptable as a coarse buoyancy evaluation for training purposes, but certified divers should use a more precise technique. The correct method is to adjust your weighting so you can hover motionless at a depth of 15 feet with about 300 psi of air in your cylinder and no air in your BC. Why? See answer #15.

3. B. Less than the total weight of you and all your equipment. Freshwater (62.4 lb/ft^3) is less dense than saltwater (64.0 lb/ft^3) by 1.6 lb/ft^3. When you and your equipment displace freshwater, you displace a weight of water about 3 percent less than the weight of the same volume of saltwater. If you and your equipment weigh 175 pounds, you will need to remove about 5 pounds from your weight system to be neutrally buoyant for freshwater diving.

4. C. 8 pounds. Air weighs about 0.08 pounds per cubic foot. Scuba tanks contain as much as 104 cubic feet of air. The difference in buoyancy between a full and empty tank of this size is about 8 pounds (104 ft^3 X .08 lb/ft^3 = 8.32 lb). The change in buoyancy is less for smaller cylinders, but the idea that your buoyancy increases as you use air from your tank applies no matter what size tank you use. When you select a scuba cylinder keep in mind that the type and size affects your buoyancy.

5. A. True. When you experience stress while diving, your respiration increases and so does your average lung volume. When your breathing is hard, deep, and frequent, you are likely to have trouble staying down. Emotional stress results from any threat—real or imagined. Over-exertion causes physical stress. To control your buoyancy correctly you need to control your emotions and your exertion level.

6. B. Less difficult than with a wet suit. Except for foam neoprene suits, buoyancy control with a dry suit is easier than it is with a wet suit because suit compression at depth is far less in a dry suit. A good dry suit has an automatic exhaust valve to simplify buoyancy control during ascent. It takes training and experience to learn to control buoyancy in a dry suit, but once you can, the task is easier than it is with a wet suit and you stay warmer in cold water. Your trim (body position in the water) also is better with a dry suit.

7. C. Wearing the weight system lower on your body. Just as you have a center of gravity on land, you have a center of buoyancy in water. You can move your center of buoyancy by moving weight along your longitudinal axis. Several new weighting systems allow you to safely and comfortably wear weights lower than your waist. Think about the effort required to move ankle weights at the end of moving legs. If you must wear weights on your legs, wear them above the knee, if possible, to reduce the distance you have to move the weights when you kick.

8. B. Open throughout an ascent. If you hold the valve open with the mouthpiece pointing down and at the same level as the opening in your BC, expanding air escapes while your buoyancy remains constant. Great technique, isn't it? If you have not tried open valve ascents, you are in for a pleasant surprise.

9. C. Arch back and flare your body as much as possible. Once you are on your way to the surface and cannot vent air, flare yourself to increase your cross sectional area. This position increases drag and slows your rate of ascent dramatically. Preventing an out-of-control ascent is much better than dealing with one. Know how to locate your BC controls quickly.

10. D. Vent your BC while disconnecting the low pressure hose. BC inflator/defla-tor valves are designed so they deflate at a faster rate than they inflate. If the valve sticks, disconnect the hose and leave it disconnected until you have the valve repaired. Control your buoyancy by orally inflating your BC. You should be able to do this skill underwater and at the surface. If it has been a long time since you have practiced oral inflation of your BC, practice the skill on your next dive.

11. None of the statements are completely correct. A. Buoyancy changes for foam neoprene dry suits, especially if the diver wears insulation under the suit, are substantial. Buoyancy changes at depth are less for fabric "shell" dry suits than for wet suits. B. A fully-suited wet suit diver does not rocket to the surface without a weight belt. In fact, a diver who loses a belt and "flares" to achieve maximum cross sectional area, will have a nearly normal rate of ascent except for the last few feet. C. If you wear the amount of weight you need for decompression at the end of the dive, you will be overweighted during a deep dive. Use "drop weights" to descend, leave them clipped to the decompression line, then reattach them at the end of the dive. D. You do not need to have all the weight you require contained within one system on one part of the body. You may not be able to achieve proper trim—another safety concern. You do need to have the bulk of your weight in one system that can be quickly discarded to establish positive buoyancy in an emergency.

12. B. The amount that enables you to hover motionless at a depth of 15 feet when you have about 300 psi of air in your cylinder and no air in your BC. You need to be able to complete a precautionary decompression stop at the end of a dive. If you have to fight to stay down or if you have to rely on a decompression line, you may not complete your stop successfully.

BOAT DIVING

Q:

There is more than you might think to safely exiting the water onto a 50 foot plus charter boat equipped with a large dive platform. While techniques vary with conditions and regions, many procedures are standard. See if you can exit this quiz with a passing score.

1. Arrange in order, from most desirable to least desirable, the following methods for returning to a charter vessel at the end of a dive:
- ❒ A. Surface snorkeling
- ❒ B. Using scuba just beneath the surface
- ❒ C. Using scuba at a depth of 15 feet
- ❒ D. Using scuba on the bottom

2. When surfacing ahead of a charter boat, which of the following methods is least desirable for swimming to the dive platform:
- ❒ A. Swimming under the boat and surfacing at the dive platform
- ❒ B. Swimming under the boat and surfacing beside the dive platform
- ❒ C. Swimming alongside the boat at the surface
- ❒ D. All of the above are equally undesirable

3. Arrange in order from the most desirable to the least desirable the following actions that can be taken if you should happen to surface down current from a charter boat:
- ❒ A. Take a bearing on the boat and navigate to it on the bottom (air supply and bottom time permitting)
- ❒ B. Swim to the current/tag line and pull yourself along it to the boat
- ❒ C. Get buoyant and swim toward the boat to hold your position in the current
- ❒ D. Signal the boat, get buoyant and wait for assistance

4. When waiting your turn to exit the water onto the platform of a charter boat, the recommended location is at the surface and:
- ❒ A. On either side of the platform
- ❒ B. At least six feet behind the platform
- ❒ C. On the current/tag line
- ❒ D. Along the rear edge of the platform

5. If the exit platform should pull away from you as the boat moves sideways during your approach, you should:
- ❒ A. Swim around the platform until you catch up with it
- ❒ B. Wait until the platform stops moving, then swim to it
- ❒ C. Maintain your position and wait for the platform to return to you
- ❒ D. None of the above

6. When holding onto a moving platform when preparing to exit the water, the platform should be held with:
- ❒ A. The arm, fingers and thumb straight
- ❒ B. The arm, fingers and thumb bent
- ❒ C. The arm straight and the fingers and thumb bent
- ❒ D. The arm bent and the fingers and thumb straight

7. When the platform is moving up and down and side to side in rough water, the safest procedure for exiting the water is to:
- ❒ A. Quickly pull yourself onto one side of the platform while it is submerged
- ❒ B. Quickly pull yourself onto the center of the platform while it is submerged
- ❒ C. Wait until the water calms down and the platform is stable
- ❒ D. Exit on a rope ladder on the side of the boat

8. Arrange in order from the most desirable to the least desirable the following procedures for handling accessory equipment (spearguns, cameras, etc.) while exiting the water:
- ❒ A. Place them on the dive platform, exit, then pick up the items
- ❒ B. Hold the items continuously during the exit
- ❒ C. Hand the items to a crew member before exiting, then retrieve them immediately after exiting
- ❒ D. Attach them to pre-placed lines hung over the side of the boat and retrieve them after exiting

9. If equipment must be removed before exiting the water onto the dive platform, which of the following is the recommended order of removal:
- ❒ A. Scuba unit, weightbelt, mask, fins
- ❒ B. Weightbelt, mask, scuba unit, fins
- ❒ C. Weightbelt, scuba unit, mask fins
- ❒ D. None of the above

10. Which of the following actions is not recommended to prevent the loss of weights during boat exits:
- ❒ A. Handling the weight belt by the end without the buckle
- ❒ B. Using keepers to secure weights on the belt
- ❒ C. Using both hands for removal of the belt
- ❒ D. All of the above are recommended actions to prevent loss

11. If an item is dropped from the exit platform, it is likely to:
- ❒ A. Be found directly under the platform
- ❒ B. Be found slightly downstream from the platform
- ❒ C. Either A or B, depending on the current and the object
- ❒ D. None of the above

BOAT DIVING

If you answered eight or more questions correctly, you are well trained and/or highly experienced. I'm sure procedures in some areas differ from those described, but the ones presented apply in most instances, so you can't credit yourself for local variations! This brings us to a good point. No matter how good you are as a diver, always get an orientation to a new area. This is especially important for entry and exit procedures.

1. D, C, A, B. The best technique is to begin and end at the anchor on the bottom, provided the boat is not anchored in depths too deep for safe diving. Following a bearing to the boat at a shallow depth is OK for conserving air, but skimming just beneath the surface is dangerous because you cannot be seen by boaters. Swim at a depth of 15 feet or greater (this is also a form of safety decompression) or snorkel at the surface.

2. C. There is danger at the entry points along the sides of the boat. The best method is to swim wide of the boat until clear of the entry area and then to angle sharply toward the exit platform. A current/tag line should be available for assistance if you are carried slightly past the platform. Avoid surfacing directly under the platform. You could be injured by falling objects.

3. A, B, D, C. C should not even be considered an option. If little or not headway can be made against a current, fighting it is hazardous. Remember that a current is weakest on the bottom, so you can make better progress against it there. Don't swim if a current/tag line is available for use—and one should be.

4. C. On the current/tag line. A line is usually trailed out behind the boat with a float on the end. This line assists divers who end up downstream from the vessel. The line is also useful as a holding area when a number of divers are waiting to exit.

5. C. Maintain your position and wait for the platform to return to you—providing there is no strong current. The boat usually swings in an arc on the anchor line as the wind catches one side and sets the vessel in motion. As the opposite side of the boat swings into the wind, the boat stops, then reverses direction. The stronger the wind, the greater the effect. Don't be alarmed if the boat swings away. As long as there is no current, be patient, and the vessel will come back to you.

6. A. The arm, fingers and thumb straight. If the hand is wrapped around something (especially through a slot), it can get caught when the platform raises. Keep the platform at arm's length with the elbow locked and you will not be struck by the moving platform. If the arm is allowed to bend, you can be pulled beneath the platform when it raises, then struck by the platform when it comes back down. Be careful!

7. B. In rough water, hold onto the platform as described in No. 6 and time the water motion. As the platform comes down, quickly pull yourself onto it. The center is preferred because there is less vertical movement than at the sides.

8. C, D, B, A. Hand items to a crew member or another diver aboard the boat whenever possible. Be sure spearguns are uncocked and handled safely. Don't forget to remove any gear lines from the water before the boat gets underway. (I don't like to use them and some boats don't allow them). Setting items on the exit platform temporarily is a good way to lose them.

9. D. None of the above. The mask should remain in place or be pulled down around your neck until you are aboard the boat. Fins should not be removed until you are on the exit platform. Weights and scuba may be removed in the water in some circumstances, but this should be done only if you are directed to do so by the crew. Otherwise, wear all equipment out of the water and remove only the fins on the exit platform. If removing weights and scuba in the water, remove weights first.

10. D. Weights and weight belts are sometimes dropped at the dive platform because divers do not handle them properly. Falling lead is a good reason to avoid the area directly under the platform. The best procedure is to wear the belt until aboard the boat.

11. D. As described in No. 5, the boat usually swings in an arc. This means an object dropped from the platform can be anywhere along that arc or slightly behind it. It is not very easy to find items dropped from a platform unless the water is quite clear, so be careful and prevent losses.

COMPASSES

In all but the clearest water, a compass is a necessary instrument for keeping track of where you are and helping you get where you want to go. All divers need to understand the compass fundamentals and uses. Advanced divers should have an even higher knowledge and skill level. Find out what you know or don't know about the subject by answering the following questions.

1. Most diving compasses are the _____ type.
❏ A. Direct-reading card
❏ B. Direct-reading needle
❏ C. Indirect-reading card
❏ D. Indirect-reading needle

2. Five desirable features of a diving compass are:
A. _____
B. _____
C. _____
D. _____
E. _____

3. The primary reason a diving compass is liquid-filled is to:
❏ A. Prevent pressure differential problems
❏ B. Dampen needle movement
❏ C. Prevent fogging of the cover
❏ D. Prevent leakage

4. What is the name of the reference line on a diving compass, and where is this line supposed to point?
A. _____
B. _____

5. To obtain a reciprocal heading, add or subtract _____ degrees to a compass heading.
❏ A. 90
❏ B. 120
❏ C. 180
❏ D. 360

6. The greatest factor affecting the accuracy of underwater compass navigation is:
❏ A. The type of compass used
❏ B. The length of the lubber line
❏ C. How the compass is held
❏ D. The underwater visibility

7. List four duties you have when compass navigation occupies your buddy underwater.
A. _____
B. _____
C. _____
D. _____

8. When navigating a triangular (equilateral) course, your turns must be _____ degrees if you want to return to the staring point.
❏ A. 60
❏ B. 120
❏ C. 180
❏ D. 210

9. State when and why you would use a compass board (also called maneuvering board) for diving navigation.
A. _____
B. _____

10. List four actions you should take to prevent damage to a diving compass.
A. _____
B. _____
C. _____
D. _____

11. Which of the following effects is of the greatest concern to a diving navigator?
❏ A. Deviation
❏ B. Variation
❏ C. Declination
❏ D. Inclination
❏ E. All are of equal concern

12. List two compasses useful for diving that are not diving compasses.
A. _____
B. _____

13. To prevent compass error, you must keep all metal objects a minimum of _____ inches from the instrument.
❏ A. 6
❏ B. 12
❏ C. 18
❏ D. 36

COMPASSES

A:

The best way to learn diving navigation is to complete an advanced or specialty course. Boating courses that include navigation can be beneficial. I hope this quiz provided some useful information to help keep you on course.

1. D. Indirect-reading needle. Compasses have either a magnetized disc, called a card, or a magnetized needle. Both the compass needle and the lubber line can indicate headings, depending on the type of compass. The degree bearings on a direct-reading compass ascend in a clockwise direction and the course heading aligns with the lubber line, while the degree bearings of an indirect-reading compass read 0-360 degrees in a counterclockwise direction and the course aligns with the north end of the needle or card. An indirect-reading compass has a rotary bezel with index marks that are used to indicate the course to be followed.

2. Desirable features of a diving compass include a **movable bezel for determining a heading, index marks as a reminder of a heading, luminous markings for use at night and in dark water, and large and easy-to-read markings for easy viewing in dim light.** The compass should also be corrosion resistant, liquid-filled, and read correctly even if tilted slightly from a level position.

3. B. Dampen needle movement. Compasses could be built to withstand pressure and moisture problems, but the housings of compasses are filled with a fluid—usually oil—to dampen the oscillations, or back-and-forth movements, of the needle. The fluid makes the needle respond slowly, but increases accuracy because the needle is not as sensitive to minor movements as it would be if it were suspended in air. You are actually following an average heading when you use a liquid-filled compass.

4. The reference line on a diving compass is called a "lubber line." Point the lubber line in the direction of travel, which is called a "heading." For accurate navigation, it is extremely important that the you align the lubber line precisely with the centerline of your body. There are several "compass lock" positions for holding a compass. All the positions help ensure proper alignment of the lubber line.

5. C. 180 degrees. A reciprocal course is one in the exact opposite direction of an original heading. Since there are 360 degrees in a circle, it is necessary to add or subtract 180 degrees to a heading to obtain a return (reciprocal) course. When your original heading is 180 degrees or less, add 180 degrees; when the original heading is greater than 180 degrees, subtract 180 degrees. If your original direction of travel was a course of 90 degrees, you would add 180 degrees to obtain your reciprocal course of 270 degrees. If your original heading were 210 degrees, you would subtract 180 degrees to obtain your reciprocal course of 30 degrees.

6. C. How the compass is held. A compass can be made to read any heading desired simply by turning the instrument. Unless a compass is properly aligned with the centerline of the body of the user, the desired destination will not be reached even though the compass indicates the proper heading. Some types of compasses are easier to use than others, and the longer the lubber line, the greater the accuracy; but these are minor factors when it comes to navigation compared to the how a compass is aligned with the body.

7. Duties you have when compass navigation occupies your buddy under water include **maintaining contact with your buddy, preventing your buddy from running into obstacles, monitoring and maintaining depth, monitoring the time and your air pressures, and visually scanning the area if searching.**

8. B. 120 degrees. Many people know that the sum of the angles of a triangle total 180 degrees, so they incorrectly assume the angles of an equilateral triangle are each 60 degrees. They do not realize that the diver must make a turn that follows the outside angle of the corner of a triangle rather than the inside angle. If the leg of an equilateral triangle is extended, the new corner created is the complimentary angle of the inside angle, or 120 degrees. Triangular courses are more difficult to navigate than courses with square corners.

9. Use a compass board when you need to navigate long distances underwater. The board extends the length of the lubber line and allows you to hold the compass in such a way that it remains aligned with your centerline. Lengthening the lubber line increases navigational accuracy.

10. Actions you should take to prevent damage to a diving compass include **keeping sand and grit out of your compass, keeping your compass from becoming hot, keeping your compass away from magnetic items and magnetic fields, and avoiding jarring or shocking the instrument.**

11. A. Deviation. A compass error caused by nearby metal or magnetic fields is called deviation. A tragic accident occurred when two ice divers placed their compasses side by side to be sure that they were following the correct heading back to shore. They did not realize the two magnetized needles were attracted to each other and that neither compass was indicating a correct heading.

12. A great deal of diving is boat diving, and a **boat compass** is almost an essential item. It is of interest to note that boat compasses are usually the direct-reading card type. A **hand bearing compass** is useful for taking a "fix" on a position for the purpose of relocation of a specific dive site. Readings taken with a hand bearing compass are much more accurate than those taken with a diving compass or with a boat compass because the hand bearing compass has sights similar to those of a gun.

13. C. 18 inches. To determine what affects your diving compass and to what degree, place your compass on the floor and allow the needle to stabilize, then watch the needle to see if it moves while you pass various pieces of your diving equipment in proximity to the compass. In this manner you can find out which items of gear you need to be concerned with when navigating. Don't forget accessory items such as spearguns and cameras.

EMERGENCY ASCENTS

A subject of interest and concern to divers is how to reach the surface if your scuba unit is inoperative. There are many emergency ascent options and philosophies. What would be your choice for various situations? Compare your choices to the currently recommended procedures by answering the following questions.

Q:

1. The most common recreational diving out-of-air ascent is most correctly termed a/an:
- ❏ A. Free ascent
- ❏ B. Emergency swimming ascent
- ❏ C. Emergency ascent
- ❏ D. Buoyant emergency ascent

2. Arrange in order of preference the out-of-air ascent procedures currently recommended by training organizations:
- ❏ A. Emergency swimming ascent
- ❏ B. Buoyant ascent
- ❏ C. Buddy breathing
- ❏ D. Alternate air source

3. If at 30 feet with your buddy 20 feet away, your best option for an out-of-air situation is:
- ❏ A. An emergency swimming ascent
- ❏ B. Breathing from your buddy's alternate air source
- ❏ C. A buoyant emergency ascent
- ❏ D. A buddy breathing (shared single regulator) ascent

4. If at 70 feet with your buddy 15 feet away, the order of preference for an out-of-air situation is:
- ❏ A. An emergency swimming ascent
- ❏ B. Breathing from your buddy's alternate air source
- ❏ C. A buoyant emergency ascent
- ❏ D. A buddy breathing (shared single regulator) ascent

5. If at 100 feet with your buddy out of sight, the order of preference for an out-of-air situation is:
- ❏ A. An emergency swimming ascent
- ❏ B. A back-up scuba unit
- ❏ C. A buoyant emergency ascent
- ❏ D. An extra second stage

6. The most correct procedure to prevent lung injury during out-of-air ascents is:
- ❏ A. Exhaling completely at the beginning of the ascent
- ❏ B. Continuous exhalation
- ❏ C. Emitting a continuous sound
- ❏ D. Exhaling normally with attempted inhalations

7. Lung volume during an out-of-air ascent should be:
- ❏ A. Nearly full
- ❏ B. Nearly empty
- ❏ C. About half full
- ❏ D. Minimal at all times

8. Pressure-related injuries during ascents are most likely to occur:
- ❏ A. Halfway to the surface
- ❏ B. During the last 10 feet of an ascent
- ❏ C. During the first 10 feet of an ascent
- ❏ D. At all times

9. The ascent rate for an emergency ascent should:
- ❏ A. Be no greater than 60 feet per minute
- ❏ B. Be as rapid as possible
- ❏ C. Vary with the circumstances
- ❏ D. Be rapid at the outset and slow at the end

10. The easiest and quickest way to slow a buoyant ascent is:
- ❏ A. Increasing your frontal surface area
- ❏ B. Venting your buoyancy compensator (BC)
- ❏ C. Exhaling and venting your BC
- ❏ D. None of the above

11. Unconsciousness is likely to occur during an emergency ascent if:
- ❏ A. Your swimming speed is excessive
- ❏ B. You are overweighted
- ❏ C. You overexert just before the loss of air
- ❏ D. Any of the above occur

12. The best overall option for an out-of-air ascent to date is:
- ❏ A. A back-up scuba system
- ❏ B. An extra second stage
- ❏ C. An emergency swimming ascent
- ❏ D. None of the above

13. The most correct and feasible current option for an emergency ascent is:
- ❏ A. An extra second stage
- ❏ B. An emergency swimming ascent
- ❏ C. A back-up scuba system
- ❏ D. Procedures agreed upon before a dive

14. The best possible option for an out-of-air ascent would:
- ❏ A. Be a compact back-up scuba unit
- ❏ B. Be BC rebreathing
- ❏ C. Have to be developed
- ❏ D. Be to limit recreational diving to shallow water

15. Out-of-air ascents can be done effectively if you:
- ❏ A. Maintain ascent skills proficiency
- ❏ B. Reduce the options to a single procedure
- ❏ C. Concentrate on prevention instead of remedies
- ❏ D. All the above

EMERGENCY ASCENTS

Don't feel badly or get upset if you missed quite a few questions. It is quite likely that information in this quiz contradicts what you were taught when you learned to dive. Procedures change with medical discoveries and equipment developments. You need to keep up to date. We commend you for caring about safety by taking this quiz. I hope the information makes you a better diver. You must couple knowledge with skills. Continue and renew your diver training.

1. B. Emergency swimming ascent. A free ascent is a submarine escape procedure with lungs at maximum volume. All out-of-air ascents are emergency ascents. Buoyant ascents lack control, are hazardous to practice, and are not as common as emergency swimming ascents.

2. A, D, B, C. There are independent and dependent options. The best independent option for shallow water is an emergency swimming ascent (ESA). From deep water, a buoyant emergency ascent (BEA) is the preferred independent option. The best dependent option is an alternate air source. The least desirable option is buddy breathing (sharing one regulator).

3. A. An emergency swimming ascent. By the time you reach your buddy and obtain air, you could be at the surface. From shallow depths, your best action is to swim to the surface while controlling expanding air in your lungs.

4. B, C, D, A. An ESA is possible, but questionable. Buoyancy for the ascent is in order if you must ascend independently. From such a depth, obtaining air from your buddy is the appropriate action, especially if you and your buddy are proficient with air sharing procedures.

5. B, C, A, D. For depths greater than 60 feet, an alternate air source (AAS) is recommended. In the absence of an AAS, you must establish buoyancy for a deep water ascent. An extra second stage is of no value to the wearer in the situation described. Swimming should be your last choice for the circumstances.

6. D. Exhaling normally with attempted inhalations. Air trapping can result with continuous exhalations even when lung volume is low! Emitting a sound restricts air flow by 50 percent and can be hazardous. "Blow and go" has been proved dangerous. Exhaling with periodic attempts to inhale is the safest technique.

7. C. About half full. Low lung volume coupled with continuous exhalation can cause collapsed air ways and lung overexpansion. Low lung volume is also a stimulus to breathe. Your lungs should be neither full nor empty.

8. B. During the last 10 feet of an ascent. The closer you are to the surface, the greater the rate of pressure change. For example, volume doubles from 33 feet to the surface, but it takes a 66 foot ascent from 99 feet to double a volume of air. Be especially aware of lung volume as you near the surface.

9. C. Vary with the circumstances. Divers typically exceed 60 feet per minute during normal ascents, so they almost certainly ascend rapidly during an emergency. Ascending as rapidly as possible is incorrect because rapid ascents waste oxygen. Doubling speed in water requires four times as much energy and can trigger the bends. The best approach is to ascend faster than normal, but don't rush.

10. A. Increase frontal surface area. The fastest and most effective means to slow a buoyant ascent is to arch your back and spread your arms and legs. The term for the procedure is "flaring," which is extremely effective owing to the drag you create.

11. D. Any of the above occur. Believe it or not, hypoxia occurs if you ascend too rapidly (see answer #9). A low oxygen situation also results if you are negatively buoyant and must ascend from a depth of 50 feet or more. Pace your activity at the bottom so you will be able to deal with an emergency.

12. A. A back-up scuba system. There is no question this is the best option, but few divers use it regularly. Problems include expense to obtain and maintain, extra bulk, and extra weight.

13. D. Procedures agreed upon before a dive. There are many options and divers have many equipment configurations. The best procedures for an out-of-air situation are those you and your buddy agree upon before you dive. An agreement will be of little value, however, if you are not proficient with the required skills.

14. C. Have to be developed. According to discussions from the Undersea Medical Society workshop on emergency ascents and my research on the subject, a compact re-breathing device with an independent air supply would be the ideal solution. No such device is available on the U. S. market.

15. A. Maintain proficiency in ascent skills. A single option puts all your eggs in one basket and is not a good idea. You need to learn more than one method. It is important to keep proficient with emergency skills. Refresher training is excellent and recommended.

ENTRIES AND EXITS

 Q:

Entries and exits are important parts of every dive. Various aspects of these skills need to be understood for safety and comfort. Test your knowledge of entry and exit skills by answering the following questions.

1. When going through surf to dive off-shore, a diver's float should be:
❐ A. Trailed behind the diver
❐ B. Pushed ahead of the diver
❐ C. Held over the diver's head
❐ D. Kept beneath the diver

2. The preferred entry from the side of a small boat when wearing scuba is a:
❐ A. Giant stride
❐ B. Forward roll
❐ C. Back roll
❐ D. Swan dive

3. Select the preferred entry with scuba from a height of about three feet from a dock or platform.
❐ A. Feet first
❐ B. Forward roll
❐ C. Back roll
❐ D. Half gainer

4. The last thing to check immediately before entering the water from a boat or platform is:
❐ A. Air supply
❐ B. Reserve position
❐ C. Area below
❐ D. Mask adjustment

5. During an entry from a sandy ocean beach, the recommended procedure is to:
❐ A. Put your fins on and walk into the surf
❐ B. Put your fins on and back into the surf
❐ C. Wade into the surf and put your fins on
❐ D. Wade and swim past the surf and put your fins on

6. When preparing to exit from the water into a small boat, the correct order for removal of equipment is:
❐ A. Fins, tank and weightbelt
❐ B. Mask, tank and fins
❐ C. Weight belt, tank, and fins
❐ D. Tank, mask and fins

7. Upon exiting the water onto a dive charter boat, the first actions that should be taken is to:
❐ A. Consult the dive tables and determine your repetitive group
❐ B. Get yourself and all of your equipment clear of the exit area
❐ C. Discuss the details of the dive with your dive buddy
❐ D. Assist the crew members in helping other divers aboard

8. When waiting in the water to exit onto a boat via a ladder, a diver should:
❐ A. Follow his or her buddy up the ladder
❐ B. Remove fins and wait until the ladder is clear
❐ C. Stay clear of the ladder if another diver is on it
❐ D. Climb up the sides of the boat if the ladder is in use

9. When swells are present and you are trying to exit onto rocks or a boat:
❐ A. Wait until the swells subside before exiting
❐ B. Time the swells and use them to help in exiting
❐ C. Swim to another place for a safer exit
❐ D. A and B, but not C are correct answers

10. Divers should check out just before entering the water and check in immediately after exiting the water:
❐ A. On all charter boat divers
❐ B. When there is a divemaster in charge of the dive
❐ C. Only during training dives
❐ D. Whenever it is feasible to do so

ENTRIES AND EXITS

Did you score well? Entries and exits in diving are more than simply getting into the water and getting out again. I would like to emphasize that these skills vary with geographical areas and that an orientation to diving in any new area is in order to assure diving safety. While some entries are standard, varied techniques are frequently called for.

1. A. Trailed behind the diver. Tow the float with a piece of line six to eight feet in length. Push the float ahead during an exit through surf, but if you try this during the entry, problems will be encountered.

2. C. Back roll. A back roll is recommended for use from a low, unstable platform. In a small boat, be sure you and your buddy enter at the same time in order to keep the boat stable. Also, hold your mask front and back during the entry because the water tends to flip the strap up and over your head.

3. A. Feet first. Vertical entries are preferred over rolling entries, which can cause disorientation and equipment displacement. The easiest entry that will get the diver into the water safely—with all equipment in place and properly oriented—is the best entry for a situation.

4. C. Area below. Check all equipment and your buddy, don all final equipment, check out with someone if appropriate, and then check to be sure the area where you will enter the water is clear. Immediately after entering, pick up any items that should be handed in (spear, camera), swim clear of the entry area, and check to make certain all your gear is secure.

5. B. Put your fins on and back into the surf. The surf zone, unless the surf is very small, is an area where divers should spend as little time as possible. Be prepared to pass through it steadily. It is clumsy to walk forward in water with fins on and a diver in the water without fins is at a real disadvantage. Don your fins, back out, and start swimming early.

6. C. Weight belt, tank and fins. Divers attempting to remove their tanks first frequently release and lose their weight belts by mistake, while the tank will not be lost if the waist band is released in error when attempting to remove the weight belt. The fins should be removed only if necessary, as the last item before exiting, and while contact is maintained with the point of exit.

7. B. Get yourself and your equipment clear of the exit area. It is important to prevent congestion and obstructions in the exit area, particularly on a boat. Pick up any and all of your gear, move to the area where you suited up, and stow all gear in your gear bag.

8. C. Stay clear of the ladder if another diver is on it. It is very important to keep clear of ladders, especially the area directly beneath another diver. Weight belts, tanks, and even the diver can and have fallen, and serious injuries can occur.

9. B. Time swells and use them to help in exiting. This is tricky, but necessary at times. As with many situations, let water movement help you rather than fighting it. Around boats, be careful of the up and down motion of the vessel. Keep the boat in front of you at all times and watch it closely. Experience is an excellent teacher of this skill.

10. D. Whenever it is feasible to do so. Checking out and checking in means someone is accounting for you and watching out for you. This person can also record entry and exit times, conditions, and other information that will be valuable for your log. Organized diving is safe diving.

NATURAL NAVIGATION

Magazine articles and books are excellent for increasing diving knowledge, but the knowledge must be exercised in order to be retained. Exercise your natural navigation knowledge by answering the following questions.

Q:

1. List the two primary reasons why navigational skills are important for diving and give an example of each reason.
  A. Reason _____
      Example _____
  B. Reason _____
      Example _____

2. Define a natural navigation "range" and give an example of its use.
  Definition _____
  _____
  Example _____
  _____

3. Define a navigational "fix" and give an example of its use.
  Definition _____
  _____
  Example _____
  _____

4. List five methods of measuring distance underwater and arrange the ways in order from the least accurate to the most accurate.
  A. _____
  B. _____
  C. _____
  D. _____
  E. _____

5. List three methods of relocating a precise position underwater without the aid of a compass.
  A. _____
  B. _____
  C. _____

6. The type of dive pattern not recommended for natural navigation is:
  ❑ A. Square
  ❑ B. Rectangular
  ❑ C. Reciprocal
  ❑ D. Circular

7. List six natural aids to navigation found in the ocean.
  A. _____
  B. _____
  C. _____
  D. _____
  E. _____
  F. _____

8. List five aids to navigation found in freshwater.
  A. _____
  B. _____
  C. _____
  D. _____
  E. _____

9. Contrast "pilotage" and "dead reckoning" and give an example of how each is used for diving navigation.
  A. Pilotage _____
     Example _____
     _____
  B. Dead reckoning _____
     _____
     Example _____
     _____

10. The steepest side of a sand ripple faces:
  ❑ A. Toward shore
  ❑ B. Away from shore
  ❑ C. Perpendicular to shore to the right
  ❑ D. Perpendicular to shore to the left

11. List two methods to estimate the speed of a current.
  A. _____
  B. _____

12. List four methods to determine the direction to shore in a dense fog.
  A. _____
  B. _____
  C. _____
  D. _____

13. The navigational activities of a dive should be controlled by pre-dive planning and:
  ❑ A. The most experienced member of a buddy team
  ❑ B. The least experienced member of a buddy team
  ❑ C. The agreed-upon member of a buddy team
  ❑ D. One buddy for half of the dive and the other buddy for the remainder of the dive

14. List four ways to improve natural navigation skills.
  A. _____
  B. _____
  C. _____
  D. _____

NATURAL NAVIGATION

Hopefully this quiz stimulated some new ideas about natural navigation for you. If you answered 12 or more questions correctly, you really know your way around in the water. If most of this information was new to you, I recommend you consider completing an Advanced Diver course, during which you will learn many techniques to make you not only a better navigator, but a better all-around diver as well.

1. Navigational skills are important for diving safety and enjoyment. Knowing where you are in relation to where you want to go enables you to avoid long surface swims at the end of a dive, and to avoid being down current from your exit point at the end of a dive. A navigational plan helps buddies remain together throughout a dive. Being able to apply navigational skills to relocate a dive site, go where you want to go underwater and avoid anxious situations all make diving more enjoyable.

2. A "range" is a line extending from two in-line objects, and its purpose is to indicate when a navigator is progressing along a specific course. Two in-line lights on shore show the course to the exit point. Two piles of rocks on the bottom can indicate the heading from a known landmark to a specific site, such as a wreck. There are many applications for a "range" in diving.

3. A navigational "fix" is the intersecting point of lines extending from two ranges. A fix is used to accurately locate a surface position directly above a specific dive site, such as a small reef. Two sets of in-line objects on shore are used as lineups. The taller and thinner the objects and the greater the angle between the two ranges, the more precise the fix. Lineups for a fix should be recorded on a slate.

4. Ways of measuring distance underwater include the amount of air consumed, kick cycles, elapsed time, arm spans and line measurements. Air consumption and counting kick cycles are coarse methods of measuring distance; monitoring elapsed time is moderately accurate; counting arm spans is more precise; and the use of a measured line on a reel is the most precise means.

5. To relocate a precise position underwater without the aid of a compass, a diver can: **(1) Use a "fix" of the position, (2) Follow a "range" from a large, easy-to-find underwater landmark, (3) Follow a trail of previously placed markers that lead from the site to a known, easy-to-find underwater landmark, or (4) Follow a "range" to a certain point, descend and** move along the range heading to a known depth, then follow the bottom contour at that depth until the site is encountered.

6. D. A circular dive pattern is not a desirable method of navigation except when employed as a circular sweep during searches, and then a line attached to a tether point is used to control the arcs of the sweeps. Navigational patterns work best with square corners. Triangular patterns may be used, but they are generally not as accurate as a square or rectangular pattern.

7. Natural aids to navigation found in the ocean include **natural formations, current, surge, swells, light and shadows, plants & animals, and sand ripples.** Some animals, such as sea fans and sand dollars, orient themselves perpendicular to the prevailing currents. Sand ripples parallel the shoreline. The bottom is usually an extension of the shoreline. When one pays attention, numerous natural landmarks are available during most dives.

8. Aids to navigation found in fresh water include the **bottom contour, thermoclines, depth, light and shadows, man-made objects and debris.** Conditions are often stable from dive to dive at some fresh water sites, and divers familiar with a location are often able to know their exact position at all times while underwater. The key, again, is awareness of surroundings.

9. Pilotage is confirmation of position by means of visual check points, while dead reckoning is the estimation of position based on distance and direction. Moving along a "range" of markers from one marker to the next underwater is a form of pilotage, while swimming an estimated distance from a known point perpendicular to sand ripples on the bottom is an example of dead reckoning.

10. The steepest side of a sand ripple faces toward shore. Surge—the back-and-forth movement of water beneath the surface resulting when waves enter shallow water—is stronger toward shore than away from shore, so the sides of sand ripples are steeper on the shoreward side. This knowledge can be of great assistance when you become disoriented on a flat bottom.

11. One method to estimate the speed of a current is to measure the time required for an object to travel 55 yards and then to multiply the time in minutes by 32. This results in the time it would take the object to travel one mile. This number is then divided by 60 to obtain the speed in miles per hour. For example, if it takes 2 minutes for an object to travel 55 yards, it would take the object 2 X 32 = 64 minutes to travel one mile. 64/60 = 1.06 miles per hour. **Another method is to measure the time it takes an object to travel 100 feet.** One hundred feet in one minute equals one knot.

12. You can determine the direction toward shore in a dense fog by **listening for noise on the shore or beach; watching swells move toward shore; feeling the surge underwater, which is stronger toward shore; looking at the leading edge of sand ripples on the bottom; or making a loud noise and listening for the echo from bluffs or cliffs.**

13. C. The agreed-upon member of a buddy team. If the most experienced member of a buddy team always leads a dive, the other diver does not develop his or her own navigational skills. Buddies should alternate the lead from dive to dive. The more experienced member of the team can point out things during the dive to assist the less-experienced buddy, but every diver needs opportunities to develop underwater awareness.

14. Natural navigation skills can be improved by completing **continuing education diving courses, applying the skills frequently, discussing methods and problems with buddies, recording information in a dive log, completing boating courses, and reading and studying.**

DIVING NAVIGATION

Knowing where you are underwater requires good navigational ability. The greater your knowledge of navigational terms, the better your navigational ability is likely to be. Test your navigational skills by matching the following terms and definitions. Use each definition only once. You may take the quiz at either an intermediate or an advanced level. For the easier version, refer to the list of terms and match them to the number of the appropriate blank. Use each term only once. Those accepting the advanced level challenge must cover the list of terms and attempt to complete the blanks without referring to the choices.

Q:

To navigate effectively underwater, one must have information about depth, time, direction and (1) _____. Knowledge and practice are essential and are best obtained during training in an (2) _____ diver course. The two main categories of diving navigation are (3) _____ navigation and (4) _____ navigation and good divers use a combination of both.

There are also techniques for navigating at the surface and beneath the surface. Underwater navigation is accomplished using either (5) _____, which is confirmation of a location using visual check points; or (6) _____, which is the estimation of a location based on speed and direction.

Surface techniques require familiarity with a (7) _____, which is similar to a (8) _____, a line extending from two in-line terrestrial objects; and familiarity with a (9) _____, which is a precise location determined when the distance and direction to two or more land-based objects is known. A precise location is also termed a (10) _____ when it is expressed in terms of (11) _____, imaginary lines around the earth parelleling the equator; and (12) _____, periodic imaginary lines extending between the earth's poles. These vertical reference lines are also known as (13) _____.

Compass navigation is possible owing to (14) _____, which is the alignment of a compass needle with the earth's magnetic poles. A compass needle points to (15) _____ rather than to true north. The difference in degrees between where a compass points and true north is termed (16) _____. Metal near a compass can cause (17) _____, and the combined effects of the last two answers is known as (18) _____.

The angular direction to an object expressed in compass degrees is called a (19) _____, while a course being followed or to be followed is called a (20) _____. Several of these (previous answer) may be combined to form a dive (21) _____.

A good diving compass features a (22) _____, which must be aligned with the center line of the user for accurate navigation, and a (23) _____ with index marks for setting a course to be followed.

There are two main types of compasses: the (24) _____ reading type, which requires the reference line to be aligned with the course bearing to be followed and has degree markings that read in a clockwise direction, and the (25) _____ reading type, which has a fixed dial reading 0-360 degrees in a counterclockwise direction. Alignment marks on a rotatable collar are bracketed by the compass needle to indicate the course being followed.

When using a compass for underwater navigation, the diver should look (26) _____ the instrument rather than down on it and should follow a course by navigating from object to object. This technique also helps reduce the amount of error caused by cross currents and known as (27) _____.

Distance may be measured underwater using cylinder pressure, counting kick cycles, using a measured line or monitoring (28) _____. Natural references to assist the underwater navigator include shadows, sand ripples, plants and animals, formations and landmarks and (29) _____.

Good navigational ability is highly desirable because it increases (30) _____ and enjoyment.

Available choices. Use each term only once.

Lubber line
Bezel
Pattern
Position
Direct
Fix
Advanced
Safety
Indirect
Natural
Compass
Across
Bearing
Range
Inclination
Time
Heading
Depth
Magnetic north
Pilotage
Dead Reckoning
Longitude
Compass error
Leeway
Variation
Meridian
Deviation
Latitude
Transit bearing
Distance

DIVING NAVIGATION

A:

It is good to know navigational theory, but it is even better to be able to apply it so you can find your way while diving. If you have trouble keeping track of the boat or your exit point, if you experience frustration trying to relocate a dive site, or if you perform poorly when trying to navigate a dive pattern, your problems can be overcome with training and practice, which are included in an advanced scuba course. Make sure the training consists of more than just a couple of dives with navigational exercises. Boating classes can also help you become a better diving navigator.

To navigate effectively underwater, one must have information about depth, time, direction and **(1) distance**. Knowledge and practice are essential, and are best obtained during training in an **(2) advanced** diver course. The two main categories of diving navigation are **(3) natural** navigation and **(4) compass** navigation and good divers use a combination of both.

There are also techniques for navigating at the surface and beneath the surface. Underwater navigation is accomplished using either **(5) pilotage**, which is confirmation of a location using visual check points; or **(6) dead reckoning**, which is the estimation of a location based on speed and direction.

Surface techniques require familiarity with a **(7) range**, which is similar to a **(8) transit bearing**, a line extending from two in-line terrestrial objects; and familiarity with a **(9) fix**, which is a precise location determined when the distance and direction to two or more land-based objects is known. A precise location is also termed a **(10) position** when it is expressed in terms of **(11) latitude**, imaginary lines around the earth parelleling the equator; and **(12) longitude**, periodic imaginary lines extending between the earth's poles. These vertical reference lines are also known as **(13) meridian**.

Compass navigation is possible owing to **(14) inclination**, which is the alignment of a compass needle with the earth's magnetic poles. A compass needle points to **(15) magnetic north** rather than to true north. The difference in degrees between where a compass points and true north is termed **(16) variation**. Metal near a compass can cause **(17) deviation**, and the combined effects of the last two answers is known as **(18) compass error**.

The angular direction to an object expressed in compass degrees is called a **(19) bearing**, while a course being followed or to be followed is called a **(20) heading**. Several of these (previous answer) may be combined to form a dive **(21) pattern**.

A good diving compass features a **(22) lubber line**, which must be aligned with the center line of the user for accurate navigation, and a **(23) bezel** with index marks for setting a course to be followed.

There are two main types of compasses: the **(24) direct** reading type, which requires the reference line to be aligned with the course bearing to be followed and has degree markings that read in a clockwise direction, and the **(25) indirect** reading type, which has a fixed dial reading 0-360 degrees in a counterclockwise direction. Alignment marks on a rotatable collar are bracketed by the compass needle to indicate the course being followed.

When using a compass for underwater navigation, the diver should look **(26) across** the instrument rather than down on it and should follow a course by navigating from object to object. This technique also helps reduce the amount of error caused by cross currents and known as **(27) leeway**.

Distance may be measured underwater using cylinder pressure, counting kick cycles, using a measured line or monitoring **(28) time**. Natural references to assist the underwater navigator include shadows, sand ripples, plants and animals, formations and landmarks and **(29) depth**.

Good navigational ability is highly desirable because it increases **(30) safety** and enjoyment.

SELF RESCUE

As a diver you have a number of responsibilities. Among them are the responsibility to prevent problems; the responsibility to your buddy; and the responsibility to care for yourself if a difficulty arises. Use the following question to test your self rescue knowledge.

Q:

1. While swimming along the bottom in 40 feet of water you begin to experience air starvation. All your equipment works properly. Select the preferred action:
- ❏ A. Make a normal ascent and rest at the surface
- ❏ B. Stop swimming and rest awhile on the bottom
- ❏ C. Make an emergency swimming ascent
- ❏ D. Stop swimming and breathe rapidly and shallowly

2. While underwater you become extremely nauseated and realize you are going to throw up. You should:
- ❏ A. Hold your regulator tightly in your mouth and vomit through it
- ❏ B. Remove your regulator from your mouth while you are throwing up
- ❏ C. Hold your regulator against your mouth with the purge button depressed
- ❏ D. Pull your mask down over your mouth and throw up into the air space

3. Swallowing can be effective for:
- ❏ A. Overcoming choking
- ❏ B. Extending breath-hold time
- ❏ C. Regulator clearing
- ❏ D. All the above

4. When in difficulty at the surface while diving, which of the following actions should you take first:
- ❏ A. Signal for assistance
- ❏ B. Rest and breathe deeply
- ❏ C. Establish buoyancy
- ❏ D. Notify your buddy

5. If a leg cramp occurs while diving, you should:
- ❏ A. Compress and pound the cramped muscle
- ❏ B. Stretch and massage the cramped muscle
- ❏ C. Wait until the muscle relaxes, then proceed
- ❏ D. Exit the water and treat the cramped muscle

6. When you surface from a dive, your boat is nowhere in sight. The nearest land is miles away and there is a slight current. You should:
- ❏ A. Swim slowly against the current to maintain position and generate body heat
- ❏ B. Get buoyant, drift with the current, and keep activity to a minimum
- ❏ C. Swim slowly and steadily in the direction of the nearest shipping lane
- ❏ D. Get buoyant and swim steadily to ward the nearest land

7. In which of the following situations should a diver's weights be jettisoned?
- ❏ A. Air supply depletion at a depth of 30 feet
- ❏ B. A buddy breathing ascent from 50 feet
- ❏ C. An emergency swimming ascent from 75 feet
- ❏ D. All the above

8. When sudden and severe vertigo occurs underwater, which of the following actions will be the most helpful for overcoming the effects?
- ❏ A. Hugging yourself
- ❏ B. Holding onto a stationary object
- ❏ C. Performing a Valsalva maneuver
- ❏ D. Swimming to the surface

9. While underwater you find yourself alone and entangled. Your initial reaction should be to:
- ❏ A. Remain still and wait for assistance
- ❏ B. Stop, study, and analyze the problem
- ❏ C. Determine the point of entanglement and cut yourself free
- ❏ D. Make one all-out attempt to break free

10. Halfway through a dive you surface and find yourself well down current from your charter boat. You should:
- ❏ A. Get buoyant and signal for assistance
- ❏ B. Use remaining air to navigate back to the boat along the bottom
- ❏ C. Swim toward the boat at the surface as long as possible, then submerge and continue using scuba
- ❏ D. Tack back and forth across the current at the surface until you reach the boat

SELF RESCUE

A buddy can be a valuable asset if a problem arises, but if you are unable to get his or her attention, you need to be self reliant. Many self rescue techniques can be learned in continuing education dive courses. It is also valuable to discuss problem situations with other divers and to share ideas on how to handle the difficulties that can arise while diving. Don't let experience be your teacher. Be prepared and be safe.

1. B. Stop swimming and rest awhile on the bottom. Breathing resistance and partial pressures combine to create a feeling of suffocation when you exert excessively. Avoid overexertion, breathe deeply, and reduce activity at the first symptom of air starvation.

2. C. Hold your regulator against your mouth with the purge button depressed. Vomitus can clog a regulator second stage; gasping can be disastrous when you remove the regulator from your mouth. Don't dive if nauseated, but if you are suddenly overwhelmed, remove the regulator, hold it at one corner of your mouth, and keep the purge depressed while vomiting.

3. D. All the above. A drop of water on your glottis causes choking. Swallowing can help arrest the spasms. The swallowing reflex can override the urge to breathe. And, if all else fails, suck the water from your regulator and swallow it to clear the mouthpiece.

4. C. Establish buoyancy. Nothing is more important than making certain that you will remain at the surface. You can take a number of actions once you establish buoyancy, but if you take another action first, you could become exhausted or panic and unable to get yourself buoyant.

5. B. Stretch and massage the cramped muscle. A cramp is a strong, involuntary contraction of a muscle. It is important to get the muscle stretched out and restore circulation to prevent tissue damage. A twitch in a muscle may signal an imminent cramp. Changing swimming strokes to use different sets of muscles can help prevent cramping.

6. B. Get buoyant, drift with the current, and keep activity to a minimum. Save all the energy possible. Your greatest threat is overexposure—loss of body heat. A fetal position helps reduce heat loss. Even if you shiver, avoid exercise. If you filed a float plan, as recommended, someone will find you within hours.

7. C. An emergency swimming ascent from 75 feet. The various diver training agencies are in agreement that a buoyant ascent is appropriate when it is doubtful that the surface can be reached by swimming. When the weights are ditched, an ascent is no longer controlled. In fact, there are some situations; e.g. cave diving, where a diver is worse off if the weights are ditched. If you can swim up, do it. If not, jettison the weights.

8. B. Holding onto a stationary object. Loss of equilibrium sets the world spinning about you. A reference is somewhat comforting until the vertigo passes. You should stop swimming when dizzy because you can easily proceed in the wrong direction. If there is no object to grasp, answer A is the best alternative.

9. B. Stop, study and analyze the problem. Don't turn around or make sudden moves! Most of the time an entanglement involves the scuba tank. Determine where the entanglement is, and if it is above and behind you, slip out of your tank and clear the snag. Be careful if you use a knife.

10. B. Use remaining air to navigate back to the boat along the bottom. The current is least at the bottom. By following a compass heading straight back to the boat, you should be able to reach it or get close enough to grab the current line strung out behind the boat. Trying to swim into a current is unwise and will quickly lead to exhaustion.

WEIGHT BELT USE

Weight belts frequently do not receive the attention they merit. We tend to view them as a necessary nuisance to help us get down so we can dive. There is, however, much more to weight belts and their use, as you are about to see. The following questions should stimulate your thinking about an important piece of equipment and its usage.

Q:

1. The purpose of a weight belt is to:
❏ A. Establish negative buoyancy
❏ B. Establish neutral buoyancy
❏ C. Offset positive buoyancy
❏ D. None of the above

2. A weight belt should be worn so it can be quickly released:
❏ A. With the wearer's right hand
❏ B. With the wearer's dominant hand
❏ C. With a rescuer's right hand
❏ D. With a rescuer's left hand

3. Select all correct answers. Weights should be prevented from slipping on a weight belt:
❏ A. For safety reasons
❏ B. For aesthetic reasons
❏ C. For physical positioning reasons
❏ D. To avoid loss of the weights

4. To estimate the finished length of a weight belt when adding weight to a belt:
❏ A. Allow two inches of webbing for each weight to be added
❏ B. Allow three inches of webbing for each weight to be added
❏ C. Allow webbing equal to the height of each weight to be added
❏ D. Just guess because you cannot estimate the finished length accurately

5. The following are features and benefits of a _____ weight belt:
❏ A. More comfortable than a standard weight belt
❏ B. Little or no shifting of weights
❏ C. More even distribution of weight than standard belt
❏ D. Less likely to cause damage or injury when dropped

6. To estimate the amount of weight needed when switching from freshwater diving to saltwater diving:
❏ A. Add weight equal to 2.5 percent of the total weight of yourself and your equipment
❏ B. Subtract weight equal to 2.5 percent of the total weight of yourself and your equipment
❏ C. Add weight equal to the difference in weight of the displaced water for saltwater versus freshwater
❏ D. A or C, but not B

7. Suspenders or harnesses to support extremely heavy standard weights are:
❏ A. Necessary when the total weight exceeds 35 pounds
❏ B. Permissible when the total weight exceeds 35 pounds
❏ C. Unacceptable for use by recreational divers
❏ D. Recommended for divers with back problems

8. The weight belt should be the last item of diving equipment donned:
❏ A. True
❏ B. False

9. To discard a weight belt, a diver should:
❏ A. Open the buckle
❏ B. Pull the free end clear of the buckle
❏ C. Pull the weight belt clear of the body
❏ D. All of the above

10. Divers in distress usually do not discard weight belts because:
❏ A. The divers are not properly trained
❏ B. Divers do not maintain proficiency in this skill
❏ C. Of the physical/psychological aspects
❏ D. All of the above

11. Wearing the same amount of weight for all depths in a wet suit is acceptable because you may achieve neutral buoyancy with a buoyancy compensator.
❏ A. True
❏ B. False

12. When donning a weight belt in the water, a diver should:
❏ A. Quickly position the belt across the small of the back
❏ B. Assume a horizontal position
❏ C. Assume a face down position when buckling the belt
❏ D. All of the above

13. When donning a weight belt on land, it is best to:
❏ A. Have your buddy position the belt
❏ B. Hold the belt by one end and swing it around yourself
❏ C. Hold both ends of the belt and step through it
❏ D. A or C but not B

WEIGHT BELT USE

A:

Do you give as much attention to your weight belt as it deserves? Is the excess webbing six inches or less? Are the weights locked in place, yet easily changeable? Are the weights equally divided and placed just forward of each hip? Does your belt compensate for suit compression? Do you always use a right hand release? Do you change the amount of weight for deeper dives or for changes in water density? Can you handle your weight belt in the water as described? Have you practiced weight belt removal and replacement in the water lately? Do you dive with the minimum amount of weight needed to achieve neutral buoyancy? If you can answer yes to all these questions, you did well on this quiz.

1. B. Establish neutral buoyancy, or C. Offset positive buoyancy. Some divers are under the impression that weights are to get them down or hold them down, so they use much more weight than necessary. A properly weighted diver can descend only after a complete exhalation. Avoid excessive weighting.

2. A. With the wearer's right hand. A right hand release is specified for weight belts even if the diver is left-handed. Emergency procedures dictate the need for this standardization. All weight belts should be able to be released in the same way. A good way to ensure a right hand release is to always don a weight belt by holding the end without the buckle held in your right hand.

3. A, B, C and D. It is important to keep weights from shifting because it affects their balance on the diver and can lead to weight belt rotation. This can make it impossible to locate the quick-release and also affects the diver's trim in the water. If weights are not locked onto the belt, they can be lost when handling it. To look and dive better, lock your weights in place.

4. A. Allow two inches of webbing for each weight to be added. The amount of excess strap on a buckled weight belt should not exceed six inches. When setting up a weight belt, allow six inches of excess plus two inches for each weight. This will allow the belt to be set up faster and easier than the trial and error approach.

5. Shot-filled. A shot-filled belt is more comfortable and is less likely to cause damage or injury. Weight keepers are not required and the shot shifts very little owing to the compartmentalized design. A disadvantage of shot filled belts is the inability to easily vary the amount of weight to be worn.

6. A. Add weight equal to 2.5 percent of the total weight of yourself and your equipment, or C. Add weight equal to the difference in weight of the displaced water for saltwater versus freshwater. If a diver and equipment weighing 197 pounds are neutrally buoyant in freshwater, neutral buoyancy can be determined by calculating the diver's displacement (three cubic feet) and figuring the difference in buoyancy for saltwater displacement (five pounds). Or, the difference can be obtained by multiplying 197 by 2.5 percent (the approximate difference in buoyancy between fresh and saltwater).

7. C. Unacceptable for use by recreational divers. Weight belt harnesses are good for commercial applications where air is supplied from the surface, communications are possible and loss of weights is hazardous. These circumstances differ markedly from recreational diving. When a diver requires a large amount of weight, other alternatives, such as weight distribution in a variety of locations, should be considered rather than a weight harness.

8. B. False. "Put the weight belt on last" is an old saying that isn't correct. Divers don mask, gloves and fins as the final items of equipment. With modern jacket-type buoyancy compensators, it is easier to don the belt before donning the scuba unit. This is acceptable. The important criteria is that the weight belt be clear for ditching.

9. D. All of the above. Simply releasing a weight belt may not result in the weights being ditched. As the webbing passes through the buckle, it may pull the flap closed and partially lock the release again. Also, the weight belt can hang up on many items when released. It is important to pull the free end of the belt clear of the buckle and then to pull the entire belt clear of the body before discarding it.

10. C. Of the physical and psychological aspects. When the hands of a diver in distress come up into a "dog-paddle" position, the diver will not put them back down. Instinct replaces reasoning at this point. A diver with a problem must take action to establish buoyancy before logical action is no longer possible. Divers know how to ditch weight belts, but they may not know when. Decide now to establish buoyancy whenever a problem cannot be immediately overcome.

11. B. False. It is not appropriate to wear the same amount of weight for all depths, but it seems that most divers do. Compensating for lost buoyancy owing to suit compression may allow a diver to achieve neutral buoyancy at depth, but trim is incorrect because the air in the BC lifts the diver's head and forces him or her to plow through the water at an angle. Weight yourself for the dive. Use clip-on weights for deeper dives and leave them on the anchor line at depth.

12. D. All of the above. A good diver handles equipment well. To look good, learn how to roll into your weight belt in the water. Once the belt is in place, assume a horizontal, face-down position. This keeps tension off the release while you secure it. Learn how to thread the end of the belt through the buckle without looking and while wearing gloves. If you are unfamiliar with these techniques, an instructor can teach you the procedures in your next continuing education course.

13. D. A or C but not B. The recommended way to don a weight belt on land is to hold one end of it in each hand and step through it. This prevents twists in the belt, allows it to slip naturally into place as you bend forward, etc. An acceptable alternative is for your buddy to position the belt for you and hold the weights in place while you secure the release.

SECTION NINE

□□□□□□□□□

Diving Emergencies

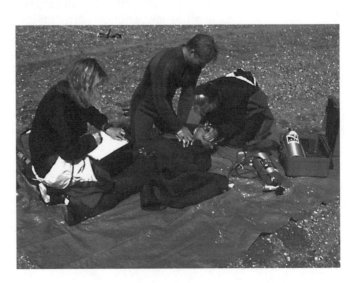

Diving Emergencies

Safe diving is no accident. The foregoing play on words is an excellent statement. When we follow all recommended safety guidelines and practices, the chances of an accident are minimal. Accidents do happen, though, and divers should be prepared to manage them.

Emergency preparedness for scuba diving encompasses several facets: Rescue, first aid, and emergency procedures. You need to know the common causes of diving accidents, the signs and symptoms of diving injuries, and all the necessary procedures to rescue, save, and evacuate an injured diver.

The minimum recommended emergency training for divers is standard first aid, cardio-pulmonary resuscitation, rescue techniques, and oxygen first aid. How many of these certifications do you have? Are they current? When was the last time you rehearsed rescue, first aid, and emergency procedures?

This book can't test your emergency skills, but it can test your knowledge. This section includes quizzes on the subjects of accident management, air evacuations, aquatic rescue breathing, emergency communications, marine life wounds, near drowning, oxygen first aid, rescue techniques, signs and symptoms of diving injuries, and sudden diving fatalities. A prepared diver should be able to pass the quizzes. Are you adequately informed about diving emergencies? More importantly, are your skills up to date?

You can improve diving's safety record by helping to prevent accidents and by saving the lives of people who get injured while diving. Please take the time to obtain the recommended emergency training, then take the time to compile a local emergency action plan that includes emergency contact information for all appropriate emergency response organizations. If an accident ever occurs, you'll be glad you used your time to get ready to deal with the situation. On the other hand, you might feel badly if you are unprepared to manage a situation. Feel good, not bad. Be prepared.

ACCIDENT MANAGEMENT

 Q:

Safe diving is no accident, but accidents can and do happen from time to time. It is possible that you may have to provide first aid to a diver. You should be trained in first aid and CPR, but is that all you need to know? Find out what else you should know about accident management by answering the questions below.

1. Dive boats and scuba instructors are <u>required</u> to have oxygen present for all paid diving activities.
❏ A. True
❏ B. False

2. A typical scuba regulator may be used safely with a standard oxygen cylinder.
❏ A. True
❏ B. False

3. The modified Trendelenberg position must be maintained during CPR for air embolism casualties.
❏ A. True
❏ B. False

4. For correct positioning of a diving accident casualty, the end of a seven foot backboard should be raised ___ inches.
❏ A. 18
❏ B. 24
❏ C. 36
❏ D. 0

5. If you use the modified Trendelenberg position, you must maintain the position until you obtain professional medical care for the casualty.
❏ A. True
❏ B. False

6. Only certified medical personnel may legally provide oxygen in most states.
❏ A. True
❏ B. False

7. When a litter or basket is being lowered from a helicopter to a boat for the transfer of a victim, you should:
❏ A. Secure all items that can be blown away
❏ B. Clear area of all unnecessary personnel
❏ C. Grab the litter ASAP to prevent damage to the vessel
❏ D. A and B, but not C.

8. Attach a trail line to the litter or basket to stabilize it when a victim is being transferred to a helicopter.
❏ A. True
❏ B. False

9. You cannot provide oxygen to a non-breathing victim unless you use a resuscitator.
❏ A. True
❏ B. False

10. Only EMT's and certified medical personnel may use positive-pressure resuscitators.
❏ A. True
❏ B. False

11. Constant flow oxygen is of little or no value to a diving accident casualty.
❏ A. True
❏ B. False

12. The ideal oxygen first aid method for non-EMT-qualified rescuers is:
❏ A. Constant flow
❏ B. Demand valve
❏ C. Nasal cannula
❏ D. Positive pressure

13. Oxygen units should be factory serviced every:
❏ A. Year
❏ B. Two to three years
❏ C. Three to four years
❏ D. Five years

14. Constant flow oxygen units can deliver oxygen concentrations up to ___%.
❏ A. 16
❏ B. 25
❏ C. 60
❏ D. 100

15. At a flow rate of 10 litres per minute, an "E" oxygen cylinder will last approximately:
❏ A. 15 minutes
❏ B. 35 minutes
❏ C. 60 minutes
❏ D. 5 hours

ACCIDENT MANAGEMENT

Were you surprised by some of the answers in this quiz? Do you feel like to need to know more about handling diving emergencies? Rescue courses, oxygen first aid courses, and EMT training are all valuable and should be considered. Oxygen is invaluable for diving emergencies. You should have a proper, well-serviced unit available at the dive site and know how to use it. Hopefully you will never have an opportunity to manage a diving accident because diving can be an accident-free activity when people abide by the recommended safety practices.

1. A. True. It is now the standard of care for diving professionals to have oxygen available at dive sites, but do not rely on oxygen availability just because you dive with a commercial operation. Ask before you pay.

2. B. False. Not only is the yoke connection for an oxygen valve different than that of a scuba regulator, but special cleaning, O-rings etc. are required because of the extreme fire hazard associated with oxygen. Do not use oxygen equipment in the presence of oils, greases, flammables. Smoking must not be allowed.

3. B. False. CPR cannot be provided effectively unless the casualty is horizontal. It may help to have the casualty's legs elevated, and this can be done while CPR is being administered. First aid is often a matter of priorities, and the requirement for CPR is far more important than any other concern.

4. D. 0 inches. The Trendelenberg position was only a theory and has never been proven to be of value for diving casualties. It can, however, pose many problems. Avoid use of the Trendelenberg position. Place injured divers flat on their back or side.

5. B. False. Maintaining the position for a prolonged period can cause cerebral edema and respiratory discomfort. If you use the T-position at all, the current recommendation is to place a diving accident victim in a supine position after 10 minutes of the Trendelenberg position. Victims of air embolism should never be allowed to sit up, no matter how well they feel.

6. B. False. A recent survey sent to the health and safety officers of all states concludes that there are no regulations pertaining to the oxygen first aid in most states.

7. D. A and B, but not C. Secure all items that can be affected by prop wash. Keep personnel to a minimum. Do not touch anything lowered from a helicopter until it touches the ground or the deck to discharge any static electricity that may have resulted from the flight.

8. B. False. Do not secure a line to the litter because the line could be blown into one of the rotors and cause the helicopter to crash. Learn more about helicoper evacuations. Do you know whether a boat should be underway or at anchor during a transfer?

9. B. False. Not many divers are familiar with the procedure of the rescuer breathing oxygen and exhaling into a casualty, but it is a more effective procedure than standard mouth-to-mouth artificial respiration.

10. A. True. The use of positive-pressure resuscitators requires specialized training and should not be attempted by anyone not qualified to operate a resuscitator. Demand valve units or constant flow units are the types preferred for recreational diving.

11. B. False. Any concentration of oxygen greater than normal atmospheric concentrations is helpful. The higher the concentration, the better. Demand valve units are superior, but constant flow units are less expensive, more commonly available, and certainly better than no oxygen unit at all.

12. B. Demand valve. A demand valve oxygen unit can deliver 100 percent oxygen to a casualty, while free flow units are capable of only a little more than half that concentration. While more expensive, but also more effective and efficient, demand valve units are preferred and recommended.

13. B. Two to three years. Oxygen units should be tested every two months to ensure proper functioning and should receive factory-type service every two to three years. Oxygen units are seldom used, and many owners may not remember how to operate them when the need arises. Familiarize yourself with your emergency equipment on a regular basis.

14. C. 60%. Constant flow units can deliver from 25 to 60 percent oxygen depending on the flow rate and the type of mask being used. A flow rate of 15 liters per minute using a non-rebreather type mask is recommended when this type of unit is used.

15. C. 60 minutes. An "E" cylinder contains 626 litres of oxygen. At a rate of 10 litres per minute, the contents will be expended in 62.6 minutes. Small "C" and "D" cylinders, commonly used, last only 20 minutes and 35 minutes respectively, but a large "M" cylinder contains a five hour supply at the 10 litre per minute rate. An optimum cylinder for dive emergencies is a "Jumbo D", which will provide 45 minutes of oxygen at a flow rate of 15 lpm.

AIR EVACUATIONS

Q:

Hopefully, you never will be involved in the evacuation of an injured diver but, if you are, there are some things you need to know. What should be done? When should it be done? How should it be done? See if you are prepared.

1. Air evacuation services usually are available from:
- ❑ A. The U. S. Coast Guard
- ❑ B. The Sheriff's Search and Rescue Department
- ❑ C. Private carriers
- ❑ D. All of the above

2. When diving from a boat, air evacuation should be arranged for patients with which of the following injuries?
- ❑ A. Pain-only decompression sickness (DCS)
- ❑ B. DCS with neurological symptoms
- ❑ C. Cardiac arrest
- ❑ D. All of the above

3. When diving from a boat, the best way to arrange an air evacuation is to:
- ❑ A. Go as rapidly as possible to the nearest harbor and call 911
- ❑ B. Go as rapidly as possible to the nearest commercial vessel and have the vessel contact the marine operator
- ❑ C. Contact the marine operator and call 911
- ❑ D. Contact the Coast Guard on channel 16

4. Three rules to keep in mind when calling for assistance are:
- A. _____
- B. _____
- C. _____

5. When diving from a boat where an air evacuation has been summoned, three preparatory actions that should be taken include:
- A. _____
- B. _____
- C. _____

6. The best configuration for the dive boat to be in for a helicopter evacuation is:
- ❑ A. At anchor
- ❑ B. Drifting
- ❑ C. Underway with the wind 45 degrees off the bow
- ❑ D. Underway directly into the wind

7. A helicopter will lower a lead line ahead of the litter. The line should be:
- ❑ A. Secured to the vessel
- ❑ B. Allowed to touch the ground or water before being touched
- ❑ C. Disconnected from the litter
- ❑ D. Coiled and placed inside the litter

8. The velocity of helicopter rotor down draft during an air evacuation is approximately:
- ❑ A. 40 mph (64 km/hr)
- ❑ B. 50 mph (80 km/hr)
- ❑ C. 60 mph (97 km/hr)
- ❑ D. 80 mph (129 km/hr)

9. When a litter reaches the deck of a boat for an air lift evacuation, the litter should be immediately:
- ❑ A. Loaded with the patient
- ❑ B. Disconnected from the lift line
- ❑ C. Positioned with the head toward the bow of the boat
- ❑ D. Electrically grounded

10. Select the incorrect statement concerning a litter used for air evacuations over water.
- ❑ A. The patient must be strapped into the litter
- ❑ B. The lead line may be used to help stabilize the litter during the lift
- ❑ C. A second person riding the lift to administer CPR must wear a life jacket
- ❑ D. The patient must wear a life jacket

11. List three actions you can take to assist a helicopter in landing on shore for an evacuation:
- A. _____
- B. _____
- C. _____

12. List three rules for approaching a helicopter that has landed on the ground:
- A. _____
- B. _____
- C. _____

13. Three items to send with a patient being evacuated from the scene of an accident are:
- A. _____
- B. _____
- C. _____

14. A medical emergency air evacuation by private carrier is paid for by:
- ❑ A. Most health insurance coverage
- ❑ B. The patient
- ❑ C. DAN accident insurance
- ❑ D. Both B and C are correct

15. The primary advantage of an emergency air evacuation is:
- ❑ A. Bringing emergency medical care to the patient
- ❑ B. Expediting transport of the patient to emergency medical care
- ❑ C. Minimizing medical transfers of the patient
- ❑ D. All of the above

AIR EVACUATIONS

If you had to coordinate an air evacuation, would you know what to do? Did you score well or did you learn from the quiz? If the quiz was primarily a learning experience instead of a review, consider completion of a diver rescue course so you will be prepared to deal with an emergency. Although safe diving is no accident, accidents can happen.

1. D. All of the above. The U. S. Coast Guard will provide air evacuations for life-threatening situations. If the local Sheriff's Department has a helicopter, it may be used if the Coast Guard helicopter is not available. Private air ambulances are also available but are expensive.

2. B. DCS with neurological symptoms. Air evacuation is not appropriate for all emergencies. Pain only bends are not life-threatening. A victim in cardiac arrest should not be evacuated by air if an air lift is involved or if the helicopter or its personnel will not allow CPR to be continued during flight.

3. D. Contact the Coast Guard on channel 16. People diving from a boat are encouraged to have, as a minimum, a handheld VHF radio for summoning assistance in an emergency. The cost of an adequate radio is not great and it can be invaluable.

4. Rules to keep in mind when calling for assistance are to **state your name or the name of your vessel, your phone number or call sign, your position, that you have a medical emergency involving a scuba diver, to stay on the line or on the air until the party you call terminates the call and to stand by the phone or radio in case the party you contacted calls for additional information.**

5. Preparatory air lift actions when diving from a boat include **clearing the deck, securing all loose gear and preparing the patient.** You should have the patient ready to go and the hovering area prepared when the helicopter arrives.

6. C. Underway with the wind 45 degrees off the bow. A hovering pick-up is more difficult than one where the helicopter is moving. With the wind across the bow, the pilot of the helicopter can position the craft for better visibility of the evacuation area.

7. B. Allowed to touch the ground or water before being touched. The rotor of a helicopter generates static electricity, which must be discharged through the line. If you touch the line before it pro-

vides an electrical ground for the helicopter you will be shocked. The jolt is not lethal but it is unpleasant.

8. D. 80 mph(129 km/hr). The down draft of a helicopter is a gale force wind. Objects must be stowed or secured or they will be blown away. Even worse, objects blown to the side can be drawn up and into the air intake of the aircraft and could cause an accident.

9. B. Disconnected from the lift line. It is hazardous for the helicopter, for people around the litter and for the patient to have the litter connected to the helicopter while the patient is being placed into it.

10. C. A second person riding the lift to administer CPR must wear a lifejacket. A second person may not ride a lift. CPR cannot be administered during a lift, which is why a person in cardiac arrest should not be airlifted. The patient must wear a lifejacket and must be strapped into the litter.

11. Actions you can take to assist a helicopter landing on shore for an evacuation include **identifying and marking a landing area, keeping the landing area clear, directing the pilot to the landing area and indicating the wind direction.**

12. Rules for approaching a helicopter that has landed on the ground are **waiting for a signal from the pilot before approaching the aircraft, approaching from the front or side only and crouching during approach. You should not approach if the helicopter dispatches personnel.**

13. Items to send with a patient being evacuated from the scene of an accident are the **patient's medical history or medical alert information and dive profile information.** Secure the information to the patient in a conspicuous location.

14. D. Both B and C are correct. Air evacuations are costly. Most health insurance policies will not pay for this service. DAN accident insurance does cover emergency air evacuation anywhere in the world. If you do not have this coverage and must

use a private carrier, you will have to pay for the service.

15. B. Expediting transport of the patient to emergency medical care. The crew of a helicopter may not have personnel with medical emergency qualifications. Some helicopters are too small to allow medical treatment during flight. Search and rescue aircraft usually are not air ambulances.

AQUATIC RESCUE BREATHING

Q:

All divers should be able to do aquatic rescue breathing (ARB). There are seldom lifeguards at dive sites and the time required to remove a non-breathing diver from the water is too long to delay artificial respiration until you get a casualty on shore or aboard a boat. What are the various ARB methods? What are the correct procedures for ARB? What is the most effective ARB technique? Answer the following questions to determine what you know about the important skill of ARB.

Note: There are five answers for each True-False (T/F) question.

1. Check a casualty's pulse in the water to determine if the casualty requires CPR. T/F.
- A. Check the pulse for one full minute before beginning ARB. T/F
- B. Check the pulse after the first two breaths of ARB. T/F
- C. Remove the casualty from the water before attempting to detect a pulse. T/F
- D. It is difficult or impossible to detect the pulse of a near-drowned person. T/F

2. The jaw of a near-drowned diver may be locked shut. T/F.
- A. Anoxic seizures cause muscle contractions that may include the jaw muscles. T/F
- B. Although the jaw may be clenched, a trained rescuer can force the mouth open using a jaw thrust maneuver. T/F
- C. A rescuer cannot forcibly open a seized jaw but can ventilate a casualty using mouth-to-nose ARB. T/F
- D. A clenched jaw prevents a rescuer from opening a casualty's airway until the seizure subsides. T/F

3. The triple-airway maneuver requires a rescuer to tilt a casualty's head back:
- ❏ A. Lift the chin, and pinch the nose
- ❏ B. Lift the chin, and open the mouth
- ❏ C. Open the mouth, and pinch the nose
- ❏ D. Thrust the jaw, and lift the chin

4. The ventilation rate for ARB with a scuba diving casualty 100 yards from an exit point should be:
- ❏ A. One breath every three seconds
- ❏ B. One breath every five seconds
- ❏ C. Two breaths every ten seconds
- ❏ D. Two breaths every fifteen seconds

5. ARB from the side of a casualty is easier when you turn a casualty's head toward you during ventilations. T/F.
- A. You should kick up and seal on the casualty before turning the head toward you. T/F
- B. You may keep the casualty's head turned toward you at all times. T/F
- C. You may pivot the casualty's body toward you, but do not turn the head. T/F
- D. Only turn the casualty's head to clear vomitus. T/F

6. Arrange in order from least effective to most effective the following ARB methods during a rough water rescue (surface chop).
- A. Mouth-to-mouth
- B. Mouth-to-nose
- C. Mouth-to-snorkel
- D. Mouth-to-rescue breathing mask

7. Arrange in order from the worst airway to the best airway the following ARB techniques.
- A. Mouth-to-mouth using the "do-se-do" position
- B. Buoyant chin-lift mouth-to-mouth (rescuer on a float)
- C. Mouth-to-snorkel
- D. Mouth-to-rescue breathing mask using the do-se-do position
- E. Mouth-to-rescue breathing mask using a two-handed tow

8. Select the most effective ARB method for any diver rescue situation.
- ❏ A. Mouth-to-mouth
- ❏ B. Mouth-to-nose
- ❏ C. Mouth-to-snorkel
- ❏ D. Mouth-to-rescue breathing mask

9. A rescuer should use the do-se-do ARB technique:
- ❏ A. For all aquatic emergencies requiring in-water artificial respiration
- ❏ B. For rough water aquatic emergencies requiring artificial respiration
- ❏ C. For struggling casualties
- ❏ D. When the casualty lacks buoyancy

10. Arrange the following ARB procedures in order, omitting any that are unnecessary.
- A. Call for help
- B. Check for breathing
- C. Open the casualty's airway
- D. Ventilate the casualty
- E. Check the mouth and throat using a finger sweep
- F. Drain water from the casualty's mouth and throat

11. When you ventilate a casualty during ARB, you should exhale:
- ❏ A. Hard and as much as possible
- ❏ B. Gently and as much as possible
- ❏ C. Hard until the casualty's chest begins to rise
- ❏ D. Slowly until the casualty's chest begins to rise

12. Arrange in order the equipment removal sequence for the rescue of a non-breathing diver in calm water 100 yards from a sloping beach. Assume a single rescuer.
- A. Masks
- B. Rescuer's fins
- C. Casualty's fins
- D. Rescuer's weight belt
- E. Casualty's weight belt
- F. Rescuer's scuba unit
- G. Casualty's scuba unit

13. If you suspect that a non-breathing diver in the water requires CPR, you should:
- ❏ A. Attempt aquatic CPR
- ❏ B. Discontinue ARB, get the casualty out of the water as rapidly as possible, and initiate CPR
- ❏ C. Continue ARB, get the casualty out of the water as rapidly as possible, and initiate CPR
- ❏ D. None of the above

AQUATIC RESCUE BREATHING

 A:

There are 35 points possible (five for each double true-false question and one for each of the remaining questions). If you scored less than 26 points, you need to learn more about ARB. If you are a rescue diver and did not score well, don't be overly concerned. The quiz contains the latest ARB recommendations, which may not yet be implemented in the field. You need to update your rescue knowledge and skills and practice rescue techniques frequently to be an effective rescuer. There are annual diving rescue workshops in many areas of the country. Attend these workshops to acquire new knowledge and polish your rescue skills.

1. False. The pulse of a near-drowned person may occur only once per minute! If you do detect a pulse in the water, it is likely to be yours. **A. False.** A non-breathing casualty needs air! Don't delay ARB for any reason. **B. False.** Do begin ARB, but don't attempt to locate a pulse until you get the casualty out of the water. **C. True. D. True.** The pulse may be weak and extremely slow. Your circulation probably will be strong and rapid. Skin color may a better indicator of circulation than the casualty's pulse.

2. True. Anoxic seizures can cause the jaw muscles to contract. I have personal experience with a casualty whose jaw locked. **A. True. B. False.** You cannot force open the mouth of a casualty when the jaw muscles are in seizure. **C. True.** Use mouth-to-nose rescue breathing until the casualty's jaw relaxes. **D. True.** A seizure will subside and the muscles will relax.

3. B. Lift the chin, and open the mouth. You do need to pinch the nose to ventilate a casualty, but nose pinching is not part of opening the airway. Note that you need to tilt the head and lift the chin for an optimum airway. Head tilting alone allows air to go into a casualty's stomach. Chin lifting helps lessens the likelihood of air going to the stomach.

4. C. Two breaths every ten seconds. When you have to remove equipment or transport a non-breathing casualty, two breaths every ten seconds is superior to one breath every five seconds. You can keep a casualty drier, expedite the rescue, and ventilate the injured diver more effectively with two breaths every ten seconds.

5. False. Turning a casualty's head may cause airway restriction. **A. False.** You should kick up to seal on a casualty, but should not turn the casualty's head. **B. False.** Do not turn the head. **C. True.** Pivoting a casualty's body reduces ARB effort and does not cause airway restriction. **D. True.** Only turn a casualty's head to clear vomitus from the airway.

6. A, B, C, D or A, B, D, C. It is difficult or impossible to keep water out of a casualty with mouth-to-mouth ARB in rough water. Mouth-to-nose is better than mouth-to-mouth for a mild chop. For heavy chop you must seal a casualty's nose and mouth using mouth-to-snorkel or mouth-to-rescue breathing mask ARB. Mouth-to-snorkel ARB is the more difficult of the two techniques, requiring greater skill.

7. A, D, C, B, E. Mouth-to-mouth or mouth-to-mask in the do-se-do position do not provide chin lift. Mouth-to-snorkel provides some chin lift. Buoyant chin lift mouth-to-mouth allows a good airway when a rescuer has a float. Rescue mask ARB with a two-handed tow provides the most effective triple-airway maneuver of any ARB method.

8. D. Mouth-to-rescue breathing mask. Advantages of this technique include ventilation through both mouth and nose, no direct contact with a casualty, an excellent airway, keeping a casualty's airway dry, and allowing a rescuer to swim efficiently while performing ARB. Mouth-to-rescue mask ARB is superior to all other techniques.

9. B. For rough water aquatic emergencies requiring artificial respiration. When the water is so rough that you cannot control a casualty when you hold the person by the head, you must use the do-se-do technique to maintain control of the injured diver. There is no single ARB procedure that is effective for every situation. ARB techniques vary with the circumstances.

10. C, B, A, F, D. To initiate rescue breathing, open the <u>A</u>irway, check for <u>B</u>reathing, <u>C</u>all for help while you <u>C</u>lear the casualty's mouth and throat, <u>D</u>rain water from the non-breathing diver's mouth and throat, and <u>E</u>xhale into the casualty two times. Give several breaths once every five seconds, then continue with ventilations twice every ten seconds. You must seal a casualty's nose for mouth-to-mouth or mouth-to-snorkel ARB. Remember the <u>ABCDE</u> of rescue breathing.

11. D. Slowly until the casualty's chest begins to rise. Hard, prolonged breaths will force air into a casualty's stomach. Exhale gently to moderately for one and a half to two seconds. Cease exhalation into the casualty when you see the person's chest begin to rise. Rescuers tend to provide quick, forceful ventilations, which are undesirable. Practice ARB until you can give gentle ventilations for 1.5 to 2.0 seconds.

12. E, D, A, F, G, B, C. There are a few exceptions for unusual circumstances, but in most instances the optimum equipment removal sequence is to discard the weights, remove the masks, remove the rescuer's scuba unit, and remove the casualty's scuba unit. You then transport the casualty to the exit point where you remove your fins. You may remove the casualty's fins during first aid after you get the casualty out of the water.

13. C. Continue ARB, get the casualty out of the water as rapidly as possible, and initiate CPR. You cannot detect a pulse in the water, so you cannot determine if an aquatic casualty requires CPR. The injured diver's pulse may be extremely slow and weak. Ventilate the casualty while you expedite transport and exit. Providing two breaths every ten seconds will save time. You must get the casualty on a firm, level surface for effective CPR.

EMERGENCY COMMUNICATIONS

Divers frequent remote locations and should know how to obtain assistance in the event of an emergency. Help can be summoned in many ways. Are you familiar with them? Here's an opportunity for you to find out how well you can communicate. Select the most correct answer for each question.

1. If you can telephone for help for a diving accident, your first choice should be the 911 emergency number.
❏ A. True
❏ B. False

2. Which of the following is the telephone number of the Divers Alert Network?
❏ A. (919) 684-8111
❏ B. (919) 681-6841
❏ C. (919) 583-7171
❏ D. None of the above

3. The emergency channel for VHF is:
❏ A. Channel 12
❏ B. Channel 16
❏ C. Channel 22
❏ D. None of the above

4. Other emergency radio frequencies are:
❏ A. 2182 khz and 156.8 MHz
❏ B. 121.5 MHz and 243.0 MHz
❏ C. 1218 khz and 218.2 MHz
❏ D. A and B, but not C

5. Arrange in sequence the following procedures for an emergency radio transmission:
  A. State "Mayday" and identify your craft
  B. State "Mayday" and your identity three times
  C. Transmit alarm signal for 30-60 seconds
  D. State nature of distress
  E. State your location

6. Which of the following flag signals is not officially recognized as an international distress signal?
❏ A. National flag flown upside down
❏ B. An orange flag with a black square and ball
❏ C. Code flags NC
❏ D. A square flag flown above or below a ball

7. Which of the following statements regarding use of flares for emergency signaling is incorrect:
❏ A. Three red flares are recommended
❏ B. The flares may be hand-held, parachute or meteor type
❏ C. Flares aboard boats must carry certification numbers
❏ D. Flare guns are not classified as handguns
❏ E. All of the statements are correct

8. Which of the following is not included in the official international distress signals?
❏ A. Flames aboard a vessel
❏ B. Orange smoke
❏ C. Repeatedly raising and lowering outstretched arms
❏ D. A dye marker in the water
❏ E. Continuous sounding of a fog horn

9. Transmissions from Emergency Position Indicating Radio Beacons (EPIRBs) are monitored by:
❏ A. All aircraft flying over water
❏ B. U. S. and Soviet satellites
❏ C. U. S. Military
❏ D. VHF receivers
❏ E. Any of the above depending on the type of EPIRB

10. The international SOS distress signal consists of transmissions (light, sound, etc.) of:
❏ A. Three shorts, three longs, three shorts
❏ B. Three longs, three shorts, three longs
❏ C. Four shorts, three longs, four shorts
❏ D. None of the above

11. The emergency signal when using a whistle is:
❏ A. SOS blasts
❏ B. Repetitions of four or five short blasts
❏ C. Continuous sounding
❏ D. None of the above

12. Which of the following signaling equipment is least desirable for a diver in the water?
❏ A. Whistle and mirror
❏ B. Flares
❏ C. Smoke bomb and dye marker
❏ D. Flashing strobe light

13. Select the <u>incorrect</u> statement:
❏ A. Some areas have diving emergency phone numbers where all emergency arrangements can be made with one call
❏ B. Information on the nearest operational recompression chamber can be obtained by calling the Experimental Diving Unit (EDU) in Washington, D.C.
❏ C. The U. S. Coast Guard can be contacted for emergency transportation of diving victims
❏ D. All of the above are incorrect.

EMERGENCY COMMUNICATIONS

Did you know all the distress signals? If not, are you now more familiar with them? Be sure when you go diving that you have all required signaling equipment and that it is in good working order. Store the equipment in a dry place and inspect it at least once a year. I hope you never experience a diving emergency situation, but if you do, I hope you will be able to expedite assistance by sending signals correctly.

A:

1. A. True. Emergency medical personnel should evaluate a dive accident victim first—they are trained to initiate treatment based on the victim's condition. These people should contact DAN for dive medical or chamber information if necessary.

2. A. (919) 684-8111. The Divers Alert Network (DAN) provides information for early medical care and the nearest support personnel and facilities. When you call DAN in an emergency, you will receive emergency medical advice and this service is available 24 hours a day. All divers should support DAN by being a member of the network.

3. B. Channel 16. This is the primary VHF channel and is designated for use in distress. Channel 16 is not to be used for non-emergency transmissions except initial contact between vessels. It should be monitored when the radio is not being used for other purposes. Channel 6 is another channel with restricted use. It is designated for intership safety communications only.

4. D. A and B, but not C. 2182 khz is the emergency frequency for single sideband radios, which allow communications beyond VHF range. 156.6 MHz is the operating frequency of Channel 16 of a VHF radio. Some radios may be tuned to specific frequencies rather than just channels. Be sure you are familiar with the radio aboard a vessel and can use it for emergencies. The 121.5 and 243.0 MHz frequencies will be addressed in another answer.

5. C, B, A, D, E. Some radios are equipped with a radio telephone alarm signal button. This signal should be sent first because it attracts the attention of people on watch and, at some stations, even activates automatic alarm devices. Sample verbal emergency transmission: "Mayday, Mayday, Mayday. This is yacht Fundiver, yacht Fundiver, yacht Fundiver, WXY 1234, Mayday, yacht Fundiver, WXY 1234. (Nature of distress, exact location)."

6. A. National flag flown upside down. All of the other flags listed in the possible answers are officially recognized as distress signals. The upside down national flag is recognized unofficially, however, and could be used if no other means of signaling were available.

7. D. Flare guns are not classified as handguns. The laws of some states classify flare guns as weapons. Check local handgun regulations. Both day and night requirements for flares can be met by having three red flares aboard your boat. The flares may be hand-held, parachute, or meteor types.

8. D. A dye marker in the water. Dye markers are not easily seen and their duration is not very great. A dye marker is not without merit, however, because it is a widely recognized distress signal, even though unofficial. Flames, such as a fire of oily rags in a bucket, gain attention quickly on the water; but there is danger associated with a fire signal.

9. E. Any of the above depending on the type of EPIRB. There are three types of EPIRBs: Class A and B for use well offshore, and Class C for use near shore. Some EPIRBs are water activated and some must be switched on manually. Some transmit a signal on 121.5 MHz, the aeronautical emergency frequency. Others transmit on 243.0 MHz, a military search and rescue frequency. Type C transmits on Channel 16 of VHF.

10. A. Three shorts, three longs, three shorts. Everyone should know Morse code for the letters SOS. This distress signal can be transmitted both audibly and visually in a variety of ways.

11. B. Repetitions of four or five short blasts. Whistles—the police whistle type—are very good for use on the water. The sound carries very well over the water and little energy is required to produce a lot of noise. Practice the emergency signal when there is no one around so you can develop the ability to add a sense of urgency to your blasts.

12. C. Smoke bomb and dye marker. The drawbacks of dye markers have already been mentioned and smoke flares can be dangerous. I know a diver who had one attached to his knife sheath, which was strapped to his leg. The flare went off and the diver invented a new dance!

13. B. Information on the nearest operational recompression chamber can be obtained by calling the EDU in Washington, D. C. The EDU used to provide this service, but has discontinued it.

MARINE LIFE INJURIES

There are many creatures in the seas that are capable of inflicting great harm to divers. Fortunately, serious injuries from marine life are uncommon. Accidents do happen, however, and divers should know how to respond if injured by an aquatic animal.

Q:

1. A bite from a sea snake:
- ❏ A. Is extremely painful
- ❏ B. Is nearly always fatal
- ❏ C. Produces symptoms following nearly every bite
- ❏ D. None of the above

2. Neutralize stinging cells of jellyfish by rinsing the wounded area with:
- ❏ A. Alcohol or spirits
- ❏ B. Ammonia or meat tenderizer
- ❏ C. Freshwater
- ❏ D. Gasoline or kerosene
- ❏ E. None of the above

3. Treat stings from sea nettles or sea bladders:
- ❏ A. The same as jellyfish stings
- ❏ B. With vinegar
- ❏ C. With baking soda
- ❏ D. With hot compresses

4. Use of a wound suction is appropriate for:
- ❏ A. Sea snake bites
- ❏ B. Stingray lacerations
- ❏ C. Cone shell wounds
- ❏ D. Freshwater snake bites

5. Select all correct answers: Hot water soaking or compresses are recommended for:
- ❏ A. Venomous fish wounds
- ❏ B. Starfish wounds
- ❏ C. Sea urchin wound
- ❏ D. Stingray wounds

6. Select all correct answers: Skin irritation can occur from handling:
- ❏ A. Starfish
- ❏ B. Seaweed
- ❏ C. Sea cucumbers
- ❏ D. Fish and shellfish

7. Select all correct answers: Applying ice to the wound is the recommended first aid for:
- ❏ A. Stingray lacerations
- ❏ B. Bristle worm stings
- ❏ C. Fire coral stings
- ❏ D. Jellyfish stings
- ❏ E. Sponge stings
- ❏ F. None of the above

8. First aid for urchin spines in the flesh includes all the following except:
- ❏ A. Hot water soaking
- ❏ B. Removal of spines
- ❏ C. Crushing of embedded spines
- ❏ D. Scrubbing the wound

9. Select the incorrect statement:
- ❏ A. Detached parts of a jellyfish can inflict stings
- ❏ B. Adhesive tape is useful for treating some venomous wounds
- ❏ C. Immediate rubbing with sand reduces the effect of a fire coral sting
- ❏ D. The most dangerous stinging-cell-equipped animal is the box jelly fish

10. Select all correct answers: Antivenin is available for:
- ❏ A. Sea wasp stings
- ❏ B. Sea snake bites
- ❏ C. Scorpion fish punctures
- ❏ D. Stingray lacerations

11. Your first action following any venomous wound should be to:
- ❏ A. Exit the water as quickly as possible
- ❏ B. Stop all activity
- ❏ C. Apply direct pressure to the wound
- ❏ D. Obtain assistance

12. Select the incorrect statement:
- ❏ A. If an animal will allow you to touch it, don't
- ❏ B. Venomous marine life is found only in warm, tropical waters
- ❏ C. There are six known species of venomous cone shells
- ❏ D. There are more than 200 species of venomous fish

13. Select all correct answers: A casualty of a serious marine venom injury should be:
- ❏ A. Constantly observed
- ❏ B. Treated for shock
- ❏ C. Transported to a medical facility
- ❏ D. Kept quiet

14. The best way to learn first aid for marine life injuries is:
- ❏ A. A first aid course
- ❏ B. A continuing education course for divers
- ❏ C. Field experience
- ❏ D. From books

15. Prevention of marine life injuries is best accomplished by:
- ❏ A. Being able to identify hazardous animals
- ❏ B. Avoiding contact with any animals not known to be safe to touch
- ❏ C. Wearing protective clothing
- ❏ D. Getting an orientation to hazardous marine life in any new area

MARINE LIFE INJURIES

The purpose of this quiz is to impress readers that although serious injuries are uncommon, there are many animals that are hazardous. We must be familiar with dangerous animals that we may encounter where we dive, must know the first aid procedures for possible injuries, and must know proper first aid in the event of an injury. The requirements mandate training and a commitment to action. Never stop learning, planning, and preparing as a diver.

1. D. None of the above. Sea snake bites are not painful and are not fatal in the majority of instances. Symptoms develop in only about 25 percent of the cases. The venom of sea snakes, however, is 2-10 times as toxic as that of a cobra and a sea snake bite can cause death. These animals should be respected, avoided and not handled.

2. E. None of the above. In spite of a great deal of information—written and passed by word of mouth—the substances listed in the answer can actually aggravate the stinging cells instead of neutralizing them. The correct solution is vinegar (five percent acetic acid), which is also useful for many other marine life injuries.

3. C. With baking soda. Jellyfish stings should be treated with an acid, but sea nettle and sea bladder stings need to be treated with a base. It is important to be able to identify marine animals and parts of them so first aid actions will be effective.

4. D. Freshwater snake bites. Current recommendations discourage the use of tourniquets, incisions, and suction for all marine life injuries. Bites by freshwater snakes, however, should receive suction. The use of pressure immobilization to impede lymphatic and superficial venous blood return may be helpful for the first hour of first aid.

5. A, B, C, D. Marine venom is a protein toxin that can be rendered ineffective by "cooking." Heat also relieves pain. Soaking in very hot, but non-scalding, water (110-115 degrees F or 43-45 degrees C) for 60-90 minutes is preferred, but hot compresses may be used for areas that cannot be soaked. The treatment may be repeated if pain recurs.

6. A, B, C, D. Dermatitis or skin irritation can result from contact with the venomous slime of some starfish, with certain types of seaweed and sponges, with various fish and shellfish and even from handling some sea cucumbers. The importance of protective clothing and avoiding contact assume more importance with the realization that there are many sources of irritation in the underwater world.

7. F. None of the above. Ice should not be applied to any of the injuries listed. In fact, the application of ice would only aggravate the wounds by stimulating stinging cells or driving spicula (microscopic barbs) farther into the wound. Ice and cold packs are good first aid items to have, but not for envenomation injuries.

8. C. Crushing imbedded spines. The idea that urchin spines will dissolve and be absorbed by the body is incorrect. Extremely small fragments may dissolve, but the difficulty of removing larger pieces—which will not dissolve—is increased and may be made impossible by crushing. Urchin spines should be removed, surgically if necessary. Have spines removed as soon as possible because scar tissue will form around spines, making removal more difficult.

9. C. Immediate rubbing with sand reduces the effect of a fire coral sting. This is incorrect. While the rubbing may reduce the immediate discomfort, it stimulates the firing of stinging cells and causes them to inject more venom. The best action is to properly neutralize the stinging cells as soon as possible.

10. A, B and C. Antivenin is available to physicians in some countries for the treatment of several very serious marine life injuries. Lack of widespread availability and the remoteness of diving should limit false hopes about antivenins, however.

11. D. Obtain assistance. Activity increases circulation, which spreads venom. You need to get out of the water quickly, but someone else should assist you and do as much of the work as possible. The quieter you can remain, the better the wound can be controlled. Get help if you get hurt.

12. B. Venomous marine life is found only in warm, tropical waters. Not so! Venomous animals are found in waters around the world—temperate and cold as well as in the tropics. You need to be aware of hazardous animals no matter where you plan to dive. You also should be prepared with first aid measures to handle marine life injuries.

13. A, B and D. Treat casualties for shock, kept them quiet and observe them constantly. Many serious injuries can arrest respiration and even circulation. Transporting a casualty is not recommended, however, because the activity worsens the person's condition. Contact medical personnel and have them come to the casualty.

14. B. A continuing education course for divers. All divers should complete a general first aid course, but marine life injuries are specialized and are not adequately addressed during standard first aid training. You can learn first aid for marine life injuries in an advanced course or a specialty course about the environment.

15. B. Avoiding contact with any animals not known to be safe to touch. All the answers contain good advice that can increase your safety. Literally all marine life injuries require contact, however, and almost always the injury stems from a defensive action by an animal, not an offensive one. Therefore, no contact means no injury.

NEAR-DROWNING

Q:

Drowning is terminal, but near-drowning is not. Many divers have inspired water, been rescued, and have survived. There is always a chance of drowning while diving, so you should know how people behave when they nearly drown, some near-drowning physiology, how to rescue a nearly-drowned diver, and the first aid for a near-drowned casualty.

1. Divers who nearly drown at the surface usually:
- ❏ A. "Go down for the third time"
- ❏ B. Call or signal for help before incapacitation
- ❏ C. Have an injury or a serious equipment problem
- ❏ D. Fail to exercise several self-rescue alternatives

2. When rescuing an unconscious, non-breathing, submerged diver, it is most important to:
- ❏ A. Keep the airway open to prevent lung overexpansion
- ❏ B. Get the diver to the surface as quickly as possible
- ❏ C. Have the diver's regulator in his or her mouth
- ❏ D. Control the diver's ascent so he or she will not get bent

3. The first step in initiating in-water artificial respiration for a person suspected of near-drowning is:
- ❏ A. Calling for help
- ❏ B. Opening the airway
- ❏ C. Administering the Heimlich maneuver
- ❏ D. Looking, listening, and feeling for breathing

4. Which of the following procedures is not recommended when initiating in-water artificial respiration to a near-drowned casualty.
- ❏ A. Open the airway and look, listen, and feel for breathing
- ❏ B. Drain water from the mouth and throat
- ❏ C. Give two full breaths
- ❏ D. Check the casualty's pulse

5. When providing artificial respiration to a near-drowning patient, you should exhale:
- ❏ A. Gently into the casualty because his or her lungs are damaged
- ❏ B. Firmly, but not forcefully into the casualty
- ❏ C. Forcefully into the casualty to re-expand collapsed air sacs in the lungs
- ❏ D. Quickly and forcefully into the casualty

6. The optimum rate for single-rescuer, in-water artificial respiration is:
- ❏ A. One breath every five seconds
- ❏ B. Two breaths every ten seconds
- ❏ C. Three breaths every fifteen seconds
- ❏ D. No respiration until you remove the casualty from the water

7. Concerning water in the lungs and stomach of the diver who has nearly drowned, you should:
- ❏ A. Invert the diver, if possible, and drain as much water as possible.
- ❏ B. Bring the diver to the surface feet first to drain as much water as possible.
- ❏ C. Ignore the water if ventilation is good during artificial respiration.
- ❏ D. Ignore the water unless it comes out during artificial respiration. If it does, drain the casualty.

8. The signs, symptoms, and first aid for a person who has nearly drowned in saltwater differ from those of a person who has nearly drowned in freshwater.
- ❏ A. True
- ❏ B. False

9. The best possible first aid for a non-breathing, pulseless, near-drowned scuba diver is:
- ❏ A. Artificial respiration
- ❏ B. CPR
- ❏ C. CPR with supplemental oxygen
- ❏ D. CPR, automatic external defibrillation, and positive-pressure oxygen

10. A hypothermic diver who nearly drowns has a greater chance of recovery than a near-drowned diver with normal body core temperature.
- ❏ A. True
- ❏ B. False

11. The "mammalian reflex" significantly increases the chances of recovery for divers who nearly drown.
- ❏ A. True
- ❏ B. False

12. If a near-drowned casualty remains cold, unresponsive, and pulseless after 30 minutes of CPR, you should:
- ❏ A. Continue CPR, if able to do so
- ❏ B. Discontinue resuscitation efforts
- ❏ C. Notify the family of the victim
- ❏ D. Both B and C are correct

13. If a near-drowned casualty revives and feels OK, he or she should:
- ❏ A. Be allowed to go home
- ❏ B. Be taken to a hospital
- ❏ C. Be monitored continuously
- ❏ D. Both B and C are correct

NEAR-DROWNING

There are many myths and misconceptions concerning scuba diving near drownings. Prevention is most important. Accidents are prevented by adequate training, maintenance of fitness for diving, proper equipment maintenance, adherence to diving safety practices, and the exercising of good judgment. If an accident cannot be prevented, a prompt, effective rescue is essential. Buddies must be trained and prepared to rescue one another and must maintain contact so they will be aware of an emergency situation.

1. D. Fail to exercise several self-rescue alternatives. Divers who nearly drown do not "go down for the third time." They typically lack positive buoyancy, aspirate water, cough and lose more buoyancy, inspire more water, and lose consciousness. They tend to go through the process quietly and usually do not take any appropriate actions to save themselves or signal for assistance.

2. B. Get the diver to the surface as quickly as possible. It is difficult to get air into an unconscious person, but air will come out freely—regardless of head position. Do not attempt to manage the airway of an unconscious diver underwater, and do not waste time with the diver's regulator. Get the person up. Do not be concerned with the diver getting bent. He or she can be treated for decompression sickness, but drowning is terminal.

3. B. Opening the airway. Often all that needs to be done for an unconscious person is to tilt the head back to open the airway so the casualty can breathe. If breathing starts spontaneously, as it frequently does, the person may soon revive. Diving experts agree the Heimlich maneuver should be used only if the casualty has an obstructed airway. Those who nearly drown swallow large quantities of water. The Heimlich maneuver can cause regurgitation of stomach contents. The aspiration of acid from the stomach will seriously damage the injured person's lungs.

4. D. Check the casualty's pulse. Experts agree a rescuer cannot detect the pulse of a near-drowned person in the water. The pulse of an unconscious person in the water is weak, could occur only once per minute, and is difficult to detect due to peripheral vasoconstriction and low cardiac output. Cold water reduces your sense of touch. The exertion required by the rescuer may cause the rescuer to mistake his or her pulse for that of the casualty. Use skin color and eye dilation as indicators of the casualty's condition until you remove the person from the water.

5. B. Firmly, but not forcefully into the casualty. If you blow fast and forcefully into a person, you are likely to force air down the esophagus into the stomach. Air in the stomach is undesirable because it can cause regurgitation or vomiting. Some firmness of exhalation is required due to the condition of a person's lungs when water is present in them. Inflate the person at a moderate rate of speed and with moderate firmness. Watch the chest and the stomach, and make sure it is the chest that rises.

6. B. Two breaths every ten seconds. Don't be surprised if you missed this question because the procedure is fairly new. One breath every five seconds is the rate on land, but that rate is inefficient in the water. Faster progress can be made and the patient can be kept drier when you give two ventilations every ten seconds. Two breaths every ten seconds is the most current recommendation of rescue experts and diving physicians.

7. C. Ignore the water if ventilation is good during artificial respiration. Those who nearly drown do not inspire large quantities of water into the lungs. The circulation quickly absorbs inspired water. Only the mouth and airway of a near-drowned casualty should be drained. Inversion is likely to cause regurgitation of stomach contents. Concern yourself with getting air and/or oxygen into a patient, not with water coming out.

8. B. False. It was believed for years that the effects of near-drowning in freshwater were markedly different than those resulting if a person nearly-drown in saltwater. This is true if a person takes in large quantities of water and drowns, but is not true for a near-drowning situation. Although the causes vary, the effect is the same—insufficient oxygen to body tissues. The person looks and feels the same regardless of the type of water. The first aid is identical.

9. C. CPR with supplemental oxygen. If a person is not breathing, administer artificial respiration. If he or she has no pulse, administer cardio-pulmonary resuscitation. If oxygen is available, a non-breathing person cannot breathe it. If a rescue breathing mask can be placed over the face of the victim and oxygen can be fed into the mask, a higher concentration of oxygen can be administered during mouth-to-mask artificial respiration. When the person begins breathing independently, have him or her breathe oxygen in the highest concentration possible. A defibrillator will not be effective without the administration of ph-altering drugs or if the person is cold.

10. B. False. The recovery of cold-water drowning victims is limited almost exclusively to children who were quickly submerged into very cold water. A diver is insulated from the cold, and usually goes through a slow cooling process, which is undesirable physiologically. Also, the water temperatures typically encountered in diving are not low enough to be helpful.

11. B. False. Sorry, but the mammalian reflex, often called the "diving reflex," is not in effect in a near-drowned victim. The effects of the reflex are generally over rated. You should assume you have approximately four to five minutes in which to rescue a person who has lost consciousness underwater. Act quickly, and do not rely on unusual physiology to increase a diver's chances for survival.

12. A. Continue CPR, if able to do so. Physicians have a saying that people are not dead until they are warm and dead. Although a casualty may appear lifeless, his or her metabolism may be so slow you are unable to detect life. Continue resuscitative efforts as long as physically able to do so. Miraculous recoveries of near-drowned divers have occurred and are possible.

13. D. Both B and C are correct. If a diver who was unconscious in the water revives, you must assume he or she may have inspired water. The water can cause complications and even lead to death. This consequence is known as "delayed drowning," and must be prevented by medical examination and possible treatment. Monitor the person continuously, and make certain he or she receives professional medical care.

OXYGEN FIRST AID—PART ONE

Q:

Divers know that oxygen is the best first aid for diving injuries, but do you know why oxygen is so valuable? Do you know the first aid procedures for oxygen? Are you familiar with oxygen equipment and how to use and maintain it? What is the best method to provide oxygen to a non-breathing diver? To a breathing, injured diver? There are several question formats, so read the questions carefully. Note: Questions 3, 4, and 5 are double true-false. Answer the stem of the question true or false, then answer each related response true or false.

1. Select all correct answers. Qualified divers should provide oxygen for which of the following diving injuries?
- A. Cerebral arterial gas embolism
- B. Decompression sickness, Type I
- C. Decompression sickness, Type II
- D. Near drowning
- E. Carbon monoxide toxicity

2. Select all correct answers. An injured scuba diver could expect which of the following benefits of oxygen breathing?
- A. Size reduction of bubbles in the body
- B. Increased elimination of nitrogen
- C. Increased oxygenation of deprived tissues
- D. Reduced tissue swelling
- E. Reduced effects of shock

3. In the event of a diving accident, an injured diver should receive the highest possible oxygen concentration of oxygen at the earliest possible moment. True or False?
- A. The concentration of oxygen is more important than the duration of oxygen first aid. T/F
- B. Since an unconscious person can not give you permission, you may not provide oxygen to an unconscious diver. T/F
- C. You must wait until an injured diver's symptoms stabilize because oxygen breathing may mask the diver's symptoms. T/F
- D. You should provide the lowest possible oxygen concentration that gives an injured diver relief. T/F

4. With few exceptions, oxygen first aid for a diving injury should continue uninterrupted until an injured diver receives professional medical care. True or False?
- A. You should adjust oxygen flow so a casualty receives oxygen for the entire time required to obtain medical assistance. T/F
- B. You should provide oxygen until you exhaust your supply or qualified medical personnel order you to discontinue. T/F
- C. After an injured diver breathes oxygen for five hours, interrupt oxygen breathing for one hour of air breathing. T/F
- D. You may discontinue oxygen first aid when an injured diver's symptoms disappear and the diver's condition improves dramatically. T/F

5. The minimum recommended oxygen supply is one Jumbo "D" cylinder or two standard "D" cylinders. True or False ?
- A. The type of delivery system affects the size and number of cylinders required. T/F
- B. The supply depends on the time and distance required to obtain professional medical care for an injured diver. T/F
- C. You should have enough oxygen to ensure that an injured diver can breathe a high concentration for at least one hour. T/F
- D. One "E" cylinder is the minimum acceptable supply of oxygen. T/F

6. Select the most correct answer. The oxygen delivery system preferred for recreational diving oxygen first aid is the:
- A. Fixed-rate constant flow system
- B. Variable-rate constant flow system
- C. Demand inhalator system
- D. Demand valve resuscitation system

7. Select the most correct answer. The minimum recommended flow rate for oxygen first aid with a constant-flow system and a non-rebreather mask is:
- A. 10 liters per minute (lpm)
- B. 12 lpm
- C. 15 lpm
- D. 25 lpm

8. Select the most correct answer. The least desirable oxygen first aid breathing adjunct for diving accident casualties is the:
- A. Pocket Mask™
- B. True-Fit™ mask
- C. Non-rebreather mask
- D. Nasal cannula (tubing with nostril prongs)

9. Match a non-breathing casualty's inspired oxygen concentration with the means of artificial respiration (some numbered answers may be used more than once; some may not be used at all). All numbers are technique-dependent.

A. Mouth-to-Mouth (M-M)/ rescuer breathing air	1. 25%	
B. M-M with rescuer breathing oxygen via nasal cannula	2. 16%	
C. M-M with rescuer breathing oxygen via demand valve	3. 50%	
D. Mouth-to-Pocket Mask™ with 15 lpm constant flow into the mask	4. 90%	

OXYGEN FIRST AID—PART ONE

 A:

Let's review the quiz objectives. Do you know why oxygen is so valuable for diving injuries? Do you know oxygen first aid procedures? Are you familiar with oxygen equipment and how to use and maintain it? Do you know the best method to provide oxygen to a non-breathing diver? To a breathing, injured diver? If you scored well on the quiz, you probably have completed the DAN Oxygen Provider course. If you guessed at the answers and did not score well, you should understand the need to complete the DAN course, which takes only four hours. If you would like to attend an Oxygen First Aid course in your area, call DAN at (919) 684-2948.

1. All answers are correct. All the listed illnesses deprive tissues of oxygen. A high oxygen concentration helps prevent tissue damage caused by hypoxia (low oxygen level in tissues). A qualified rescuer should provide oxygen to an injured diver. If you suspect that you might have symptoms of a diving malady, breathe the highest possible oxygen concentration at the earliest opportunity and seek medical assistance.

2. All answers are correct. Breathing 100 percent oxygen causes a pressure differential on nitrogen in bubbles and may cause the bubbles to shrink in size. Injured tissues swell as they accumulate fluid. Oxygen helps minimize tissue swelling (edema). Traumatic shock affects the circulation of an injured person and may starve some areas of the body for oxygen. To reduce and eliminate body tissue damage, it is important to have oxygen first aid capability for diving emergencies.

3. True. A. True. B. False. You may assume an unconscious person grants permission. Do ask a conscious person for permission, however. **C. False**. Delaying oxygen first aid allows symptoms to worsen, but oxygen breathing can stop and even reverse symptoms of diving illnesses. **D. False**. Provide the highest oxygen concentration possible.

4. True. A. False. Don't reduce oxygen concentration to increase duration. **B. True**. Provide all the oxygen you can for as long as you can or until someone more qualified than you orders you to discontinue oxygen first aid. **C**. It is not likely that you will be able to supply oxygen for more than five hours, but if you can, you should be in contact with a medical facility while transporting a casualty there. Follow the advice of the medical personnel. **D. False**. Do not stop oxygen first aid because a person's condition improves.

5. False. A, B, and C. True. D. False. An "E" cylinder provides a good supply of oxygen, but is not the minimum acceptable supply. You need to consider several factors, which the question statements identify, to determine the amount of oxygen you need. It is a good idea to have more oxygen than you think you might need. A second cylinder can be invaluable when you discover a primary cylinder is empty when you need it.

6. C. Demand inhalator system. Any oxygen delivery system is better than none, but the demand valve is the preferred system because it allows a person to breathe 100 percent oxygen. A demand valve resuscitation (positive pressure) system can provide 100 percent oxygen, but you must have a high level of emergency first aid training to qualify to use such a system. Recreational diver oxygen providers are <u>not</u> qualified to use a resuscitator that inflates an injured person's lungs when you depress a button or lever. You can injure someone if you do not have proper training and credentials for positive-pressure resuscitation.

7. C. 15 lpm. Flow rates for constant-flow systems range from 0-25 liters per minute. Ten to 12 lpm may be adequate for some illnesses that are not related to diving, but the minimum dive accident free-flow rate considered to provide adequate oxygen concentration is 15 lpm. If a casualty breathes hard, you may need a system that can provide 25 lpm.

8. D. Nasal cannula. The correct flow rate for a nasal cannula is four to six liters per minute. Faster rates waste oxygen and irritate the nasal passages. The low rate provides a wearer with a <u>maximum</u> oxygen concentration of only 35 percent. Since the goal of oxygen first aid is the highest possible concentration of oxygen, a nasal cannula is not a desirable breathing adjunct, although it is better than air breathing.

9. A = 2. B = 1. C = 4. D = 3. You use four to five per cent of the oxygen you breathe. You exhale about 16-17 percent oxygen when you breathe air; about 25 percent oxygen with a nasal cannula; and 95 percent oxygen when you breathe from a demand valve. Oxygen flowing into a pocket mask at a rate of 15 lpm during artificial respiration can elevate to oxygen concentration from 16-17 percent for expired air to 50% or higher. While JAMA does not recommend expired-oxygen artificial respiration (AR), the technique is better than expired-air AR.

OXYGEN FIRST AID—PART TWO

1. Match a breathing casualty's inhaled oxygen concentration with optimum use of the oxygen breathing adjunct (some numbered answers may be used more than once; some may not be used at all.). All numbers are technique dependent.

A. Pocket mask™ with oxygen inlet valve	1. 100%
B. Nasal cannula with 4-6 lpm	2. 90%
C. Tru-Fit™ mask with demand valve	3. 50%
D. Pocket mask™ with demand valve	4. 30%
E. Non-rebreather mask and 15 lpm flow	5. 20%

2. Match an injured diver's condition with the correct oxygen first aid response (some numbered answers may be used more than once; some may not be used at all.):

A. Casualty has a seizure	1. Discontinue oxygen
B. Casualty vomits	2. Continue oxygen
C. Casualty revives and feels well	3. Temporarily discontinue oxygen
D. Casualty coughs, wheezes, and is short of breath	

3. Designate each statement True or False:

A. Store oxygen units disassembled until needed.

B. Store oxygen units assembled with the valve open.

C. You must discard used oxygen masks.

D. Have an oxygen unit professionally serviced every five years.

4. Designate each statement True or False:

A. Oxygen cylinders require visual inspections and hydrostatic testing.

B. For oxygen delivery systems, use only cylinders and regulators designated for oxygen use.

C. Petroleum products may ignite spontaneously in the presence of high pressure oxygen.

D. Do not fill the reservoir bag of a non-rebreather face mask before putting the mask on an injured diver.

5. Select the most correct answer. Oxygen training and first aid is regulated by:

❏ A. The National Safety Council

❏ B. The Divers Alert Network

❏ C. The American Red Cross

❏ D. None of the above

6. Select the most correct answer. The preferred source of oxygen provider training for recreational divers is the:

❏ A. American Red Cross Professional Rescuer Course

❏ B. Divers Alert Network Oxygen First Aid in Dive Accidents Course

❏ C. National Safety Council First Responder Program

❏ D. The EMT or Paramedic course approved by your state

OXYGEN FIRST AID—PART TWO

A:

1. A = 3, B = 4, C = 1, D = 1, E = 2. The preferred oxygen first aid configuration is a demand valve regulator and a Pocket or Tru-Fit mask. Both masks allow a casualty to receive 100 percent oxygen. For oxygen first aid with a constant flow system, use a non-rebreather mask at 15 lpm. A Pocket Mask with an oxygen inlet valve allows a person to breathe 25-35 percent oxygen with a 15 lpm flow rate but wastes oxygen. A nasal cannula with oxygen at four to six liters per minute also allows a breathing person to receive 25-35 percent oxygen.

2. A = 3, B = 3, C = 2, D = 3. If a casualty has a seizure, discontinue oxygen until the seizure subsides. When you provide first aid and a casualty vomits, remove the oxygen mask, turn the person onto one side, drain and clear the airway, and resume oxygen first aid. If a casualty breathes oxygen at a concentration greater than 0.6 ATA for many hours, pulmonary (lung) problems may cause coughing, wheezing, and shortness of breath. For pulmonary problems, discontinue oxygen breathing for one hour and follow the advice of professional medical personnel.

3. All the statements are False. Keep an oxygen unit assembled for use, but be sure the on-off valve is closed and the regulator is de-pressurized. You may reuse most oxygen masks provided you disinfect them with a 10 percent bleach solution and rinse them with freshwater. Replace non-rebreather masks. Have oxygen delivery systems professionally serviced every _two_ years.

4. A. False. Oxygen cylinders require hydrostatic testing, but not visual inspections. **B. True.** Cylinders and regulators must be specially cleaned for use with 100 pecent oxygen and must have oxygen-safe components. Never attempt to use standard scuba equipment for oxygen storage and first aid. **C. True.** Petroleum products can cause flash fires in the presence of high concentrations of oxygen. **D. False.** _Do_ fill the reservoir bag of a non-rebreather mask before placing the mask on a casualty.

5. D. None of the above. Oxygen first aid is not "regulated" by any agency but must be consistent with your level of training. If you provide oxygen first aid, be trained in correct procedures. Legal problems for oxygen first aid are no greater than those for any first aid as long as your actions are consistent with your training. There are no clear-cut legal guidelines for oxygen first aid, but the legal ramifications of denying oxygen to an injured scuba diver are much greater than those of providing oxygen.

6. B. Divers Alert Network Oxygen First Aid in Dive Accidents Course. You need to promptly recognize diving-related emergencies. You need to provide _diving_ first aid that differs in some respects from standard first aid. You must provide higher concentrations of oxygen than would normally be given to an injured person. You need to coordinate the management of a diving accident. You learn the foregoing in the DAN oxygen course, which offers excellent entry-level oxygen first aid training for divers.

RESCUE TECHNIQUES

While diving is a statistically safe activity, there is some risk involved, and accidents do sometimes occur. Since diving often takes place in remote locations, you need to know what action to take in the event you are called upon to perform a rescue. It's time to find out what you know.

1. The greatest hazard for a submerged, unconscious diver being brought to the surface is:
- ❏ A. An air embolism
- ❏ B. Decompression sickness
- ❏ C. Hypoxia
- ❏ D. Vomiting

2. Arrange in correct sequence: During a complete rescue of a submerged, unconscious, non-breathing scuba diver by a dive buddy, the recommended order of equipment removal is:
- ❏ A. Casualty's weight belt
- ❏ B. Casualty's mask
- ❏ C. Rescuer's mask
- ❏ D. Rescuer's weight belt
- ❏ E. Rescuer's scuba system
- ❏ F. Casualty's scuba system

3. The best all-around method of in-water artificial respiration is mouth-to-____ ventilation.
- ❏ A. Mouth
- ❏ B. Nose
- ❏ C. Pocket Mask
- ❏ D. Snorkel

4. The initial ventilations for artificial respiration should be:
- ❏ A. Two full breaths
- ❏ B. Four quick breaths
- ❏ C. One complete breath
- ❏ D. Two full breaths followed by two more full breaths

5. If the jaw of an unconscious, non-breathing diver is clenched shut, you should:
- ❏ A. Squeeze the sides of the casualty's mouth to force it open
- ❏ B. Pry the casualty's mouth open
- ❏ C. Perform mouth-to-nose ventilations until the jaw muscles relax
- ❏ D. None of the above

6. The basic principle involved with the effective removal of an unconscious diver from the water for most situations is:
- ❏ A. Physical strength
- ❏ B. Leverage
- ❏ C. Buoyancy
- ❏ D. Buddy system

7. During in-water artificial respiration, ideally the rescuer should be ____ the casualty.
- ❏ A. Higher than
- ❏ B. Lower than
- ❏ C. At the same level as
- ❏ D. Horizontally perpendicular to

8. Three assignments that should be made by a rescuer when going to the rescue of a distressed diver from boat or shore are:
- A. _____
- B. _____
- C. _____

9. A rescue diver should never make contact with a struggling, exhausted diver.
- ❏ A. True
- ❏ B. False

10. List three general methods of establishing buoyancy for a distressed diver and arrange the methods into order of preference:
- A. _____
- B. _____
- C. _____

11. List the first four actions to be taken upon establishing contact with an unconscious, non-breathing diver at the surface (assume casualty is face-up and buoyant).
- A. _____
- B. _____
- C. _____
- D. _____

12. Which of the following is the most commonly observed sign of diver distress at the surface:
- ❏ A. Failure to return signals
- ❏ B. Short whistle blasts
- ❏ C. Low position in the water without a mouthpiece
- ❏ D. Waving arm

13. The most important consideration during the removal of an unconscious, non-breathing diver from the water is:
- ❏ A. Expediency
- ❏ B. Artificial respiration
- ❏ C. Equipment removal
- ❏ D. Checking vital signs

14. The most common difficulty associated with in-water artificial respiration by trained rescuers is:
- ❏ A. Establishing an airway
- ❏ B. Maintaining an open airway
- ❏ C. Keeping water from entering the casualty
- ❏ D. Rescuer exhaustion

15. If a diver has been submerged more than 15 minutes without breathing, don't bother with artificial respiration after recovering the casualty.
- ❏ A. True
- ❏ B. False

RESCUE TECHNIQUES

There is no single diver rescue procedure that works for all situations. The best you can hope for is proficiency with a variety of techniques that are effective, and selecting the ones that are most appropriate. The more methods you have available to you, the better your chances of performing a successful rescue. Learn as many techniques as possible by completing a diver rescue techniques specialty course. You owe it to your buddies to be able to rescue them if they should ever require your assistance.

1. C. Hypoxia. The greatest danger to a submerged, unconscious, non-breathing diver is lack of oxygen in body tissues. Expediency in getting the person to the surface is the paramount action. Unconscious divers will not embolize, so do not attempt airway maneuvers or try to force air from the casualty. Drowning is much more serious than the bends, so don't concern yourself with the diver's rate of ascent. Get him or her up!

2. A, B, C, D, E, F. The removal of equipment is listed in the preferred order, however, the rescuer's weight belt may be removed at various points in a rescue. Masks should be removed for artificial respiration. The rescuer's scuba unit should be removed before the casualty's because the rescuer's unit makes artificial respiration more difficult. Training and practice are needed to remove gear without interrupting ventilations.

3. C. Pocket Mask. The mask covers both the nose and mouth, keeps the subject drier than other methods of artificial respiration, is more sanitary, and is simple to learn to use. The mask fits easily into a BC pocket, is unaffected by salt water or pressure, fits everyone, and is readily available. The next best alternative is mouth-to-mouth. Mouth-to-nose is better than mouth-to-mouth for choppy surface conditions, and mouth-to-snorkel works well for rough water conditions if the rescuer has skill proficiency.

4. A. Two full breaths. The technique of "air packing" four quick breaths into a non-breathing person to initiate artificial respiration has been revised by the Red Cross. The current procedure recommends two full breaths followed by a breath every five seconds. Actually, the more air you can give a person at the outset of artificial respiration, the better, but don't wear yourself out too quickly.

5. C. Perform mouth-to-nose ventilations until the jaw muscles relax. As the oxygen level in the system of a person drops, a stage is reached where muscle spasms occur. When the oxygen level drops even more, the spasms pass. Do not be surprised if you are unable to open the mouth of a non-breathing diver right away.

6. B. Leverage. One of the most difficult aspects of dive rescue techniques is removing a non-breathing diver from the water without interrupting ventilations. There are various methods needed because of different diving situations. Learn methods which prevent back injuries for rescuers and which have minimal interruption of artificial respiration.

7. A. Higher than. A rescuer needs to raise himself or herself in the water to ventilate a non-breathing casualty. In less than two minutes most rescuers push the casualty down because the rescuer becomes exhausted. Flotation can help a rescuer remain higher than the casualty. During Dive Rescue Techniques courses you learn various tips and techniques that make rescues easier and more effective.

8. Assignments that should be made when going to the rescue of a diver from shore or boat include assigning:
   A. **"Spotters" to point to and accurately mark the location of the distressed diver.**
   B. **Someone to standby to call for emergency assistance.**
   C. **A team of divers to don scuba equipment and follow ASAP in case the distressed diver loses consciousness and sinks.**
   D. **Someone to locate and prepare the emergency equipment.**

9. B. False. Diving equipment reduces the mobility of a person in distress, but assists a rescuer. A struggling diver must not be allowed to lose consciousness and sink. Contact should be made with exhausted divers who are not buoyant. Even if the distressed diver clings to the rescuer or climbs onto him or her, the rescuer can establish buoyancy until the diver regains composure.

10. Three general methods of establishing buoyancy in order of preference are:
   A. **Extend flotation to a distressed diver.**
   B. **Establish buoyancy using the distressed diver's equipment.**
   C. **Establish buoyancy using the rescuer's equipment.**

11. After making contact with an unconscious, non-breathing diver at the surface, a rescuer should **open the airway and check for breathing, remove the casualty's mask, drain (pull down one corner of mouth) and check for clear airway and begin artificial respiration.** Don't bother trying to find a pulse or removing equipment other than the weight belt. You can't detect a pulse in the water, and the person needs air more than anything else.

12. C. Low position in the water without a mouthpiece. Divers in distress rarely signal for assistance. A lone diver at the surface without buoyancy and with no snorkel or regulator in the mouth should cause concern from observers. Mask removal and "fried egg" eyes are other common signs of distress. Failure to return a signal is a common error that does not necessarily mean that someone needs to be rescued.

13. B. Artificial respiration. Unless a person requires CPR—and it is nearly impossible to determine that until the casualty is out of the water—the most important consideration is ventilating the non-breathing person. Do artificial respiration even if you suspect that CPR will be required.

14. B. Maintaining an open airway. During evaluations of rescue trainees and instructor candidates, the most common discrepancy is failure to keep the head back (chin up) to maintain an open airway. Keep this in mind when learning and practicing in-water artificial respiration. Use leverage to keep the airway open by lifting up on the casualty's torso while pushing down on his or her forehead.

15. B. False. Depending on the activity level of the diver before losing consciousness, the reason for the loss of consciousness, the water temperature, the age and physical condition of the casualty and other factors, it may be possible for someone to recover after being underwater without air for more than five minutes. Always try to restore life.

SIGNS AND SYMPTOMS

Q:

Provided you are in good health and abide by the established safety practices, it is unlikely you will experience an accident while diving. If you dive while unhealthy or ignore the safety rules, you may be injured. You should know the signs and symptoms of various diving illnesses and how to prevent the maladies.

1. A sign of an injury is best defined as:
- ❏ A. Any objective evidence of a disease, i.e., evidence that is perceptible to an examiner
- ❏ B. Any subjective evidence of a disease, i.e., evidence as perceived by a patient
- ❏ C. Something indicating the presence of a thing; a token
- ❏ D. None of the above

2. A symptom of an injury is best defined as:
- ❏ A. Any objective evidence of a disease, i.e., evidence that is perceptible to an examiner
- ❏ B. Any subjective evidence of a disease, i.e., evidence as perceived by a patient
- ❏ C. Any change in the body or its functions
- ❏ D. None of the above

3. A diver with occasional, brief right ear fullness and vertigo during ascent most likely experiences:
- ❏ A. A reverse ear block
- ❏ B. Alternobaric vertigo
- ❏ C. Inner ear decompression sickness
- ❏ D. Motion sickness

4. The symptoms that precede a sudden death syndrome include:
- ❏ A. Chest pain
- ❏ B. Breathing difficulty
- ❏ C. Exhaustion
- ❏ D. None of the above

5. The symptoms that precede a shallow water blackout include:
- ❏ A. Dizziness
- ❏ B. Tunnel vision
- ❏ C. Tingling
- ❏ D. None of the above

6. The two most common symptoms of decompression sickness are:
- ❏ A. Pain and numbness
- ❏ B. Pain and itching
- ❏ C. Numbness and dizziness
- ❏ D. Numbness and weakness

7. A pale, sweaty diver with nausea; cool, clammy skin; and a rapid, weak pulse is most likely the victim of:
- ❏ A. Heat stroke
- ❏ B. Hypothermia
- ❏ C. Heat exhaustion
- ❏ D. Ciguatera poisoning

8. A submerged diver experiencing restlessness, tingling sensations, tunnel vision, twitching of the face, nausea, and dizziness is on the verge of suffering:
- ❏ A. Motion sickness
- ❏ B. Decompression sickness
- ❏ C. Carbon monoxide toxicity
- ❏ D. Oxygen toxicity

9. Pain, irritation, itching, and burning of the ear canal are symptoms of:
- ❏ A. An internal ear infection
- ❏ B. An external ear infection
- ❏ C. A ruptured ear drum
- ❏ D. An external ear squeeze

10. Select __all__ correct answers. Which of the following signs and symptoms suggest a cerebral arterial gas embolism?
- ❏ A. Chest pain, cough or shortness of breath, blurred vision
- ❏ B. Blindness, numbness and tingling, weakness or paralysis
- ❏ C. Loss of sensation over part of body, dizziness, confusion
- ❏ D. Sudden unconsciousness and cessation of breathing

11. A diver with a feeling of fullness in the neck area, a crackling sensation when you move the skin, and a change in the sound of the voice has probably suffered:
- ❏ A. Mediastinal emphysema
- ❏ B. Subcutaneous emphysema
- ❏ C. Pneumothorax
- ❏ D. Decompression sickness Type I

12. Select __all__ correct answers. A scuba diver losing consciousness during a normal ascent has probably suffered:
- ❏ A. Shallow water blackout
- ❏ B. Carbon monoxide toxicity
- ❏ C. Cerebral arterial gas embolism
- ❏ D. Pneumothorax

13. Sudden onset of a cough, shortness of breath, sharp pain in the chest, swelling of neck veins, and cyanosis (skin blueness) are signs of:
- ❏ A. Mediastinal emphysema
- ❏ B. Subcutaneous emphysema
- ❏ C. Pneumothorax
- ❏ D. Cerebral arterial gas embolism

14. Following a dive in temperate water a diver is mildly confused, has slurred speech, is uncoordinated, and has a stumbling gait. You should suspect:
- ❏ A. Use of drugs
- ❏ B. Hypothermia
- ❏ C. Decompression sickness
- ❏ D. Either B or C

SIGNS AND SYMPTOMS

A:

Did you score well? Would you be able to recognize the signs and symptoms of a diving injury if an accident occurred? Fortunately, the first aid for all serious diving injuries is the same: sustain life, treat for shock, administer oxygen, and seek prompt medical treatment. Do not ignore any physical discomfort you experience after diving. Delayed treatment can cause permanent injury. If you would like to know more about diving physiology, there are several excellent new books that address the subject.

1. A. Any objective evidence of a disease, i.e., evidence that is perceptible to an examiner. A sign is deviation from the normal displayed by a victim and observed by another person, e.g., skin color. When you can detect that something is wrong with someone, you observe a sign of an illness.

2. B. Any subjective evidence of a disease, i.e., evidence as perceived by a patient. A symptom is a deviation from the normal a patient detects in himself or herself, e.g., dizziness. The patient must be conscious. When a patient tells you how he feels, he or she is giving you symptoms of an illness.

3. B. Alternobaric vertigo. The term means dizziness caused by changing pressure. A sudden change of pressure in one ear causes vertigo during descent or ascent, but usually the problem occurs during ascent. Typically the problem occurs to experienced divers who have pressure equalization difficulties in one ear. Do not dive if a Valsalva maneuver at the surface causes vertigo or if you have a difficult time clearing one ear during descent. Severe vertigo while submerged can be extremely hazardous.

4. D. None of the above. As the population of divers grows older and as more and more of the general public are attracted to diving, more sudden deaths are occurring. The cases usually involve middle-aged males who experience mild physical and psychological stress at the end of dives. The victims appear normal one second and are unconscious the next. Middle-aged divers must have a healthy heart and should avoid cold and stress while diving.

5. D. None of the above. A breath-holding diver ascending after a dive preceded by excessive voluntary hyperventilation may lose consciousness without warning owing to a sudden drop in the partial pressure of oxygen during the ascent. A low level of carbon dioxide, caused by the hyperventilation, is insufficient to stimulate the diver to breathe before the oxygen level falls below that needed to sustain consciousness. Avoid excessive hyperventilation before breath-hold dives.

6. A. Pain and numbness. According to the Divers Alert Network annual report on diving accidents, the descending order of symptoms of decompression sickness is: pain, numbness, dizziness, weakness, headache, nausea, extreme fatigue, unconsciousness, difficulty breathing, visual disturbance, rash, personality change, bowel problems, paralysis, restlessness, speech disturbance, convulsions, hearing loss, difficulty walking, bladder problems, and ringing ears.

7. C. Heat exhaustion. If you work hard in a hot, humid environment, your body may not be able to meet the circulatory demands of the skin in addition to those of your brain and muscles. The symptoms of heat exhaustion are similar to those of shock, but shock occurs as a result of trauma. Rest periodically, drink fluids, and keep yourself cool to prevent heat exhaustion before or between dives.

8. D. Oxygen toxicity. Unless you have your tank filled with mixed gas or oxygen or try to use a rebreather, it is not likely that you will experience oxygen toxicity while scuba diving. Nitrox diving is increasing in popularity, so today's divers should be aware of the signs and symptoms of oxygen toxicity—a deadly diving disease you must avoid.

9. B. An external ear infection. When your ear canals remain moist, the skin of the canals softens and may become infected. The infection can completely obstruct an ear canal, abscess, and spread infection into surrounding tissues. Avoid ear infections by drying your ears, using ear solutions, and having an infection treated at the first sign of difficulty.

10. A, B, C, and D. You should suspect a cerebral arterial gas embolism (CAGE) any time a scuba diver suddenly loses consciousness shortly after surfacing from a dive. The signs of CAGE are similar to those of a stroke and may affect only one side of the body. The first aid is lie the patient down and administer the highest possible concentration of oxygen. The only treatment is prompt recompression.

Avoid breath-holding when breathing compressed air.

11. B. Subcutaneous emphysema. The term means air in the tissues under the skin. A breath-holding ascent while breathing compressed air can cause the disease. The conditions of mediastinal emphysema and subcutaneous emphysema may occur simultaneously. The signs and symptoms of the two conditions may overlap. Give patients with the malady the first aid for CAGE and obtain medical treatment.

12. B and C. A diver breathing carbon monoxide at depth may remain conscious owing to a high partial pressure of oxygen. As the partial pressure of oxygen falls during ascent, the diver loses consciousness. A severe CAGE also may cause unconsciousness during ascent. Prevent carbon monoxide toxicity by obtaining air from a reputable source. Prevent lung overexpansion injuries by breathing continuously.

13. A. Mediastinal emphysema. The term means air in the tissues in the middle of the chest. The disease is one of the four lung overexpansion injuries possible when an ascending scuba diver holds his or her breath. The illness indicates lung overpressurization, so you should examine the patient for signs and symptoms of CAGE. Administer the first aid for CAGE and obtain medical treatment.

14. B. Hypothermia. The term means lower than normal body core temperature. When a diver experiences moderate hypothermia, he or she may not complain of the cold and may even undress paradoxically. He or she may experience amnesia. If the diver is numb, confused, has slurred speech, and is uncoordinated, rewarm the diver immediately. Avoid hypothermia by wearing adequate insulation for diving.

SUDDEN, UNEXPLAINED FATALITIES

Q:

From time to time a diver suddenly, unexplainably, and without warning, loses consciousness and cannot be revived. What causes this phenomenon, and what, if anything, can be done to prevent it? Are you familiar with the factors that contribute to these sudden fatalities? While not a pleasant topic, it is important to have knowledge regarding it. Test what you know by answering the questions, then studying the answers.

1. Sudden, unexplained fatalities usually occur in which of the following age groups:
❒ A. 25-45
❒ B. 35-55
❒ C. 45-65
❒ D. 55-75

2. Sudden, unexplained fatalities are most likely to occur when the air temperature is ____ and the water temperature is ____.
❒ A. High, high
❒ B. High, low
❒ C. Low, high
❒ D. Low, low

3. Symptoms preceding the sudden fatality syndrome include:
❒ A. Exhaustion
❒ B. Chest pains
❒ C. Breathing difficulty
❒ D. All of the above
❒ E. None of the above

4. Which of the following signs are usually exhibited by victims of sudden fatalities (select all correct):
❒ A. Calmness
❒ B. Fatigue
❒ C. Exhaustion
❒ D. Complaining
❒ E. Irrational

5. Most victims of sudden fatalities were aware of predisposing medical conditions.
❒ A. True
❒ B. False

6. Scientific studies indicate that sudden fatalities are likely to occur from exertion with a healthy heart.
❒ A. True
❒ B. False

7. Sudden fatalities are usually caused by:
❒ A. Heart arhythmias
❒ B. Heart disrhythmias
❒ C. A heart attack
❒ D. Any of the above

8. Usually an autopsy can detect the cause of a sudden fatality.
❒ A. True
❒ B. False

9. The denial of any physical weakness coupled with aggressive behavior is likely to cause:
❒ A. A heart attack
❒ B. Loss of consciousness
❒ C. Extremely high blood pressure
❒ D. Severe vertigo

10. Irregularities in heart beats occur more frequently than normal when diving.
❒ A. True
❒ B. False

11. Which of the following stresses is most likely to cause a sudden fatality?
❒ A. Cold
❒ B. Exercise
❒ C. Stress
❒ D. Equipment
❒ E. Middle age

12. Premature ventricular contractions of the heart occur commonly beginning at about the age of:
❒ A. 30
❒ B. 40
❒ C. 50
❒ D. 60

13. Sudden fatalities amongst women divers:
❒ A. Are the same proportionally as those for men.
❒ B. Tend to lag 10 years behind in risk.
❒ C. Approach those of men for women who smoke.
❒ D. Are nearly non-existent

14. Sudden fatalities in diving usually occur:
❒ A. Underwater at the beginning of a dive
❒ B. Underwater at the end of a dive
❒ C. At the surface at the end of a dive
❒ D. At random times during dives

15. Sudden fatalities would most likely be prevented by:
❒ A. Closer buddy contact
❒ B. Improved emergency response
❒ C. Good medical and physical fitness for diving
❒ D. Establishing an upper age limit for diving
❒ E. All the above

SUDDEN, UNEXPLAINED FATALITIES

A:

Sudden death is a serious subject for a quiz, but the information needs to be known by as many divers as possible owing to the serious consequences involved. We must be medically and physically fit for diving, protect ourselves from cold, avoid overexertion and harmful habits, and dive within our limitations. These recommendations apply to all divers, but their importance increases with age. Diving medical experts recommend annual physical exams for divers over age 40.

1. B. 35-55. It may seem that this is a young age group for sudden fatalities, but it is supported by the accident statistics. The message is that the problem encompasses more divers than most would expect. The problem is the primary reason that a physical exam at least every two years is recommended for divers 40 years of age and older.

2. B. High, low. When the air temperature is high, the physical stress of gearing up for a dive is also high. The high pre-dive work load coupled with the stress of cold water creates the most likely condition for a sudden fatality. Steps should be taken to minimize the physical stress of suiting up and to insulate against heat loss. Older divers should consider using dry suits when diving in water colder than 65 degrees F and should wear some insulation even when diving in warm water.

3. E. None of the above. Feeling tired may be a symptom in some instances, but the symptom is usually ignored. There are numerous instances in which divers have indicated they were fine and then expired shortly afterward. Part of the problem is the absence of warning symptoms.

4. A. Calmness B. Fatigue. In many instances, victims of sudden fatalities exhibit no signs at all. Those who do usually say they are a little tired but are otherwise "OK". They decline assistance. They appear fine and function well at one moment, then lose consciousness at the next. The point is that there is little to suggest a serious problem is imminent.

5. A. True. The tragedy of many sudden fatalities is that the victims were aware of medical problems that placed them at risk, but chose to ignore them. In many instances this is because "macho" middle-aged men do not realize the magnitude of the risk imposed by diving.

6. B. False. There is no evidence to suggest that sudden fatalities result from individuals with a normal, healthy heart. Victims of this phenomena typically have a history of heart disrhythmias or premature ventricular contractions. Healthy individuals should not fear diving because unhealthy people expire while diving when they should not be diving at all.

7. D. Any of the above. "Arhythmia" means the heartbeat is without rhythm. "Disrhythmia" means the heart is having difficulty beating or that the rhythm is irregular. A heart attack can certainly cause a sudden death, but the phenomena is most likely associated with irregularities in heart rhythm. Cells that fire in the heart to cause it to contract get out of sync with the pacemaker signals from the brain. Loss of consciousness occurs in as little as six seconds if the heart stops pumping blood.

8. B. False. One of the reasons some diving fatalities are unexplained is the absence of information from autopsies. Heart arhythmias or disrhythmias are undetectable with an autopsy, and so is a heart attack unless the victim lives for 6 to 12 hours following the attack. Diving medical experts believe that many coroners incorrectly diagnose the cause of death for some divers.

9. B. Loss of consciousness. People who think they can do more than they are truly capable of doing suffer from extreme stress. The end result is a sudden lowering of blood pressure, decreased circulation to the brain, and unconsciousness, which is a dangerous situation when immersed. This malady is known as "vasovagal syncope." The problem stems from an aggressive "mind-over-matter," "macho" male attitude.

10. A. True. Heart irregularities are much more frequent in diving because of the effects of the diving reflex, cold, and other factors. While irregularities are normal and not a problem in and of themselves, they place those with a previous history of seemingly minor heart problems at great risk when diving.

11. A. Cold. All the answers are serious stressors which can contribute to a sudden fatality for divers who are not physically fit, but the greatest stressor of all is the net effect of becoming chilled. Cold water is not a requirement. A reduction in temperature sensitivity and a thinning of the skin and subcutaneous fat occur as a result of aging. Loss of body heat takes place in seemingly warm water when the body is not adequately insulated.

12. B. 40. Premature Ventricular Contractions (PVCs) occur infrequently at age 20, more commonly at age 40, and are characteristic at age 60. There is a relationship between PVCs and heart disrhythmias, which contribute to sudden, unexplained fatalities. The ability to handle cold stress is also reduced at about 40 years of age. Cardiac rhythm in older persons does not adjust to normal under the stress of cold as much as it does for younger people.

13. C. Approach those of men for women who smoke. The risk of a sudden fatality lags about 20 years behind for women, but the age differential narrows significantly for women who smoke. The risk for men increases for those who smoke. People in general should refrain from smoking, but divers absolutely should not smoke. The influence of drugs and alcohol absolutely compounds the problem for both sexes.

14. C. At the surface at the end of a dive. Most sudden deaths reported occurred without warning while the divers were making their way back to the boat while at the surface at the end of dives. The victims simply lose consciousness. They are frequently rescued quickly, yet fail to respond to first aid. Heart irregularities can be attributed solely to fatigue. The older we become, the more muscular work we require to breathe. The pacing of activity is always a good idea when diving, but its importance increases with age.

15. C. Medical and physical fitness for diving. Usually sedentary, aggressive personalities who have minor heart problems, who become chilled while diving, and who overexert are candidates for sudden fatalities. Age alone does not preclude diving activities for those who are fit. Buddy contact and emergency procedures cannot overcome the malady, which must be prevented by ensuring proper fitness to dive.

APPENDIX: *U.S. NAVY DIVE TABLES*

NO-DECOMPRESSION LIMITS AND REPETITIVE GROUP DESIGNATION TABLE FOR NO-DECOMPRESSION AIR DIVES

Depth (feet)	No-decompression limits (min)	A	B	C	D	E	F	G	H	I	J	K	L	M	N	O
10		60	120	210	300											
15		35	70	110	160	225	350									
20		25	50	75	100	135	180	240	325							
25		20	35	55	75	100	125	160	195	245	315					
30		15	30	45	60	75	95	120	145	170	205	250	310			
35	310	5	15	25	40	50	60	80	100	120	140	160	190	220	270	310
40	200	5	15	25	30	40	50	70	80	100	110	130	150	170	200	
50	100			10	15	25	30	40	50	60	70	80	90	100		
60	60				10	15	20	25	30	40	50	55	60			
70	50				5	10	15	20	30	35	40	45	50			
80	40				5	10	15	20	25	30	35	40				
90	30				5	10	12	15	20	25	30					
100	25				5	7	10	15	20	22	25					
110	20					5	10	13	15	20						
120	15					5	10	12	15							
130	10					5	8	10								
140	10					5	7	10								
150	5					5										
160	5						5									
170	5						5									
180	5						5									
190	5						5									

RESIDUAL NITROGEN TIMETABLE FOR REPETITIVE AIR DIVES

Locate the diver's repetitive group designation from his previous dive along the diagonal line above the table. Read horizontally to the interval in which the diver's surface interval lies.

Next read vertically downward to the new repetitive group designation. Continue downward in this same column to the row which represents the depth of the repetitive dive. The time given at the intersection is residual nitrogen time, in minutes, to be applied to the repetitive dive.

* Dives following surface intervals of more than 12 hours are not repetitive dives. Use actual bottom times in the Standard Air Decompression Tables to compute decompression for such dives.

** If no Residual Nitrogen Time is given, then the repetitive group does not change.

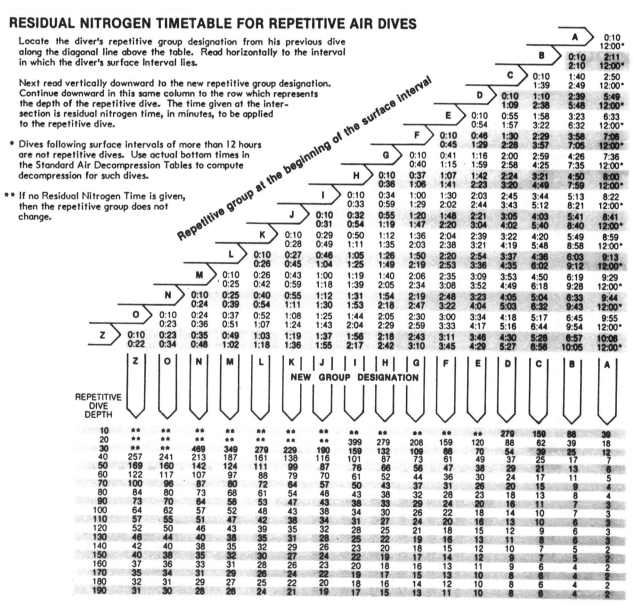

Repetitive group at the beginning of the surface interval

NEW GROUP DESIGNATION

REPETITIVE DIVE DEPTH	Z	O	N	M	L	K	J	I	H	G	F	E	D	C	B	A
10	**	**	**	**	**	**	**	**	**	**	**	**	279	159	88	39
20	**	**	**	**	**	**	**	399	279	208	159	120	88	62	39	18
30	**	**	469	349	279	229	190	159	132	109	88	70	54	39	25	12
40	257	241	213	187	161	138	116	101	87	73	61	49	37	25	17	7
50	169	160	142	124	111	99	87	76	66	56	47	38	29	21	13	6
60	122	117	107	97	88	79	70	61	52	44	36	30	24	17	11	5
70	100	96	87	80	72	64	57	50	43	37	31	26	20	15	9	4
80	84	80	73	68	61	54	48	43	38	32	28	23	18	13	8	4
90	73	70	64	58	53	47	43	38	33	29	24	20	16	11	7	3
100	64	62	57	52	48	43	38	34	30	26	22	18	14	10	7	3
110	57	55	51	47	42	38	34	31	27	24	20	16	13	10	6	3
120	52	50	46	43	39	35	32	28	25	21	18	15	12	9	6	3
130	46	44	40	38	35	31	28	25	22	19	16	13	11	8	6	3
140	42	40	38	35	32	29	26	23	20	18	15	12	10	7	5	2
150	40	38	35	32	30	27	24	22	19	17	14	12	9	7	5	2
160	37	36	33	31	28	26	23	20	18	16	13	11	9	6	4	2
170	35	34	31	29	26	24	22	19	17	15	13	10	8	6	4	2
180	32	31	29	27	25	22	20	18	16	14	12	10	8	6	4	2
190	31	30	28	26	24	21	19	17	15	13	11	10	8	6	4	2

RESIDUAL NITROGEN TIMES (MINUTES)